COMPLETE CURRICULUM
Grade 1

Harcourt
Family Learning™

Copyright © 2006, 2021 by Flash Kids
Adapted from *Steck-Vaughn Core Skills: Reading Comprehension* by Martha K. Resnick, Carolyn J. Hyatt, and Sylvia E. Freiman;
Copyright © 2002 by Harcourt Achieve. • Adapted from *Steck-Vaughn Spelling: Linking Words to Meaning, Level 1*
by John R. Pescosolido; Copyright © 2002 by Harcourt Achieve. • Adapted from *Steck-Vaughn Working with Numbers, Level A*;
Copyright © 2001 by Harcourt Achieve. • Adapted from *Language Arts, Grade 1*; Copyright © 2003 by Harcourt Achieve. •
Adapted from *Experiences with Writing Styles*; Copyright © 1998 by Steck-Vaughn Company and *Writing Skills*;
Copyright © 2003 by Steck-Vaughn Company. • Adapted from *Test Best for Test Prep, Level A*;
Copyright © 1999 by Harcourt Achieve.
Licensed under special arrangement with Harcourt Achieve.

ISBN 978-1-4114-8046-9

Manufactured in China

Lot#:
2 4 6 8 10 9 7 5 3
4/21

FlashKids
New York

Dear Parent,

Beginning a new grade is a milestone for your child, and each new subject is bound to present some challenges that may require some attention out of the classroom. With this comprehensive first-grade workbook at hand, you and your child can work together on any skill that they are finding difficult to master. Here to help are hundreds of fun, colorful pages for learning and practicing reading, spelling, math, language arts, writing, and test preparation.

In the reading section, the wide range of high-interest stories will hold your child's attention and help develop their proficiency in reading. You will also find vocabulary introduced in context and repeated often, comprehension skills applied in context to make the reading more relevant, and multiple-choice exercises that develop test-taking skills. You may wish to have your child read the selections silently or orally, but you will find that sharing the stories and activities with your child will provide additional confidence and support to succeed.

The first two units in the spelling section focus solely on introducing the alphabet and vowel sounds. The next four units present first-grade words in lists grouped by vowel sound. Your child will learn to make the connection between a word's appearance and what it sounds like. To strengthen understanding of the meaning and use of each word, you will also encounter a variety of activities such as alphabetizing, using a dictionary, and writing sentences with spelling words. Each lesson also features a short passage containing spelling and grammar mistakes that your child will proofread and correct.

The math section starts with basics like counting, addition, and subtraction. You'll also find sections on place value and number sense, money, telling time, geometry, and measurement. Throughout each unit, your child will be given ample opportunity to estimate, compare, find patterns, and use logic. Exercises like these help your child develop important thinking and problem-solving skills. They are also the foundation upon which your child will build more complex math skills.

More than 100 lessons in the language arts section provide clear examples of and exercises in language skills such as parts of speech, sentences, mechanics, vocabulary and usage, writing, and research skills. Grammar lessons range from using nouns and verbs to constructing better sentences. Writing exercises include the personal story and the book report. These skills will help your child improve their communication abilities, excel in all academic areas, and increase their scores on standardized tests.

Each of the six units in the writing section will guide your child from recognizing different kinds of words, to identifying and forming sentences, to putting events in sequence, to writing simple paragraphs and letters. Since your first-grader is still developing reading skills, you may wish to read the workbook pages aloud together. In answering the questions, your child will practice writing words and complete sentences. Check that they form uppercase and lowercase letters correctly. Have crayons available, as many inspirational activities ask your child to draw pictures that reflect his or her own sentences.

Lastly, the test prep section employs your child's knowledge in reading, math, and language to the basic standardized test formats that your child will encounter throughout their school career. Each unit in the first half of this section teaches specific test strategies for areas such as word study skills, reading comprehension, mathematics, listening, and language. The second half of the section allows your child to apply these test-taking skills in a realistic testing environment. By simulating the experience of taking standardized tests, these practice tests can lessen feelings of intimidation during school tests.

As standardized testing in the first grade always involves a teacher reading directions, examples, and stories to students, you will need to play the teacher's role. The text you will read aloud is printed in blue. Every test begins with directions to share with your child. Many tests include additional information to be read aloud, such as sentences or paragraphs. From page 694 onward, most of the workbook features separate pages for parents. Read the direc-tions on the left-hand page while your child completes the questions on the right-hand page.

As your child works through the test prep section, help them keep in mind these four important principles of test-taking:

1. Using Time Wisely

All standardized tests are timed, so your child should learn to work rapidly but comfortably. They should not spend too much time on any one question, and mark items to return to if possible. Use any remaining time to review answers. Most importantly, use a watch to keep on track!

2. Avoiding Errors

When choosing the correct answers on standardized tests, your child should pay careful attention to directions, determine what is being asked, and mark answers in the appropriate place. They should then check all answers and not make stray marks on the answer sheet.

3. Reasoning

To think logically toward each answer, your child should read the entire question or passage and all the answer choices before answering a question. It may be helpful to restate questions or answer choices in his or her own words.

4. Guessing

When the correct answer is not clear right away, your child should eliminate answers that they know are incorrect. If that is not possible, skip the question. Then your child should compare the remaining answers, restate the question, and then choose the answer that seems most correct.

An answer key at the back of this workbook allows you and your child to check their work in any of the subject sections. Remember to give praise and support for each effort. Also, learning at home can be accomplished at any moment—you can ask your child to read aloud to you, write grocery lists, keep a journal, or measure the ingredients for a recipe. Use your imagination! With help from you and this workbook, your child is well on the way to completing the first grade with flying colors!

TABLE OF CONTENTS

READING SKILLS

SPELLING SKILLS

MATH SKILLS

Language Arts

Writing Skills

Test Prep

Answer Key

A Guide for Educators

FlashKids Complete Curriculum is a workbook designed to provide students one-stop review and practice for all major curriculum subject areas. Each *FlashKids Complete Curriculum* unit provides direct instruction to review major concepts, often with a guided example, followed by practice items.

These quick, comprehensive activities have applications across learning, from warm-up activities and diagnostic assessment to differentiated instruction and remediation. The single-volume format makes it ideal for a broad range of learning environments, from the classroom to hybrid and blended learning to remote learning or homeschooling.

Contents

Using *FlashKids Complete Curriculum* at Home

- Modeling
- Scaffolded Learning
- Assessment as Learning
- Remediation
- Differentiated Instruction
- Supplementing Classroom, Remote, or Hybrid Learning

Using *FlashKids Complete Curriculum* in the Classroom

- Warm-up Activities
- Diagnostic Assessment
- Supplementing Direct Instruction
- Skills Practice
- Group Work
- Differentiated Instruction
- Formative Assessment and Remediation
- Test Preparation
- Summative Assessment

Using *FlashKids Complete Curriculum* in Remote and Hybrid Learning Environments

Using FlashKids Complete Curriculum at Home

FlashKids Complete Curriculum was designed with home and independent learning in mind. The single-book format, focused review, and extensive practice worksheets offer home instructors convenience and flexibility. As you work with the book, follow these best practices.

Modeling

Modeling is the process of acting out or demonstrating a skill or idea before students try it. It is often a teacher's main tool for instructing students and can be used to introduce a topic, reinforce an idea, troubleshoot a problem, or review what has already been taught.

The instruction, guided practice, and worksheet items in *FlashKids Complete Curriculum* are ideal for modeling.

Effective modeling includes:

- stating what you are going to do before you start, including displaying the items and any materials that will be used.

- working through the item slowly, step-by-step.

- narrating each step, including what you are thinking and your actions.

- highlighting tricky choices or potential mistakes and how to navigate them.

- demonstrating mistakes and how to identify and correct them.

- demonstrating how to check or verify your work.

Younger students may benefit from modeling multiple examples. Model the first as a demonstration, and the following by narrating what a student would do, using second-person or "you." ("Now you will add these two numbers together.") During the second modeling, allow the learner to interrupt, ask questions, or offer suggestions.

Scaffolded Learning

Scaffolded learning is a method of instruction that starts with instructor support and gradually guides learners toward independent work. *The FlashKids Complete Curriculum* book has built in scaffolding by offering direct instruction, concept review, and guided examples before students take on worksheet items.

To enhance scaffolding:

- start with modeling, as described above.

- after modeling, work with your learner to complete an item together, offering assistance whenever asked.

- next, offer the direct instruction text as a "cheat sheet." Have your learner try to work through a problem using the "cheat sheet" as needed. Offer assistance only if your learner gets stuck even after consulting the instruction.

- then, have your learner work through a handful of items independently. Offer reassurance that you will go over mistakes together to figure out the problem. Check your learner's work and review any items that need correction.

- finally, allow your learner to complete a worksheet independently. Offer encouragement and guidance if needed, but only correct or review work once the student is finished.

Scaffolding should guide learners toward independence, but it will not always be a linear process. Offer more or less support depending on your learner's current level of achievement with each skill.

Assessment as Learning

The word **assessment** does not only refer to tests at the end of a lesson that show what learners know. Instructors use assessment before, during, and after learning to continually measure progress and adapt instruction as necessary.

- **Diagnostic assessment** measures where the learner starts. It establishes what learners already know and gives a "baseline" to measure mastery.

- **Formative assessment** is a "snapshot in time" that measures how learners are progressing during learning. It lets you know how well your instruction is working and how quickly your learner is gaining understanding.

- **Summative assessment** is the "end-of-the-lesson" assessment that measures your learner's total progress and identifies which skills have been mastered and which have not.

FlashKids Complete Curriculum review and worksheets can be used for each type of assessment. You can assign guided instruction or partial worksheets as diagnostic assessment, review individual items as formative assessment, and use the Test-Prep sections as summative assessment.

Remediation

Remediation reinforces skills that learners struggle to master. During formative or summative assessment, you may find that your learner struggles with one or more skills, while excelling in others. This is common, and *FlashKids Complete Curriculum* worksheets were written with remediation in mind.

During regular instruction, set aside one or more worksheets in each skill type to use as remediation if you notice that your learner needs more practice. Having learners repeat a worksheet they already completed can often be a low-stakes form of additional practice.

If needed, use modeling or scaffolding when you assign a remediation worksheet, taking time to work through example problems together to reinforce the concepts.

If necessary, allow learners to use the direct-instruction "cheat sheets" or other aids to shore up their learning of a challenging skill.

Differentiated Instruction for At-Home Learning

Differentiated instruction is customized learning to meet individual needs, including enrichment for advanced learners, remediation for struggling learners, and accommodations for special needs. When working in a home environment, you are likely already tailoring your educational materials to suit your learner's individual needs. *FlashKids Complete Curriculum* offers great flexibility for you to differentiate your instruction:

- advanced learners can use the instruction and review to complete the activities fully independently.

- additional worksheets can act as "extra credit."

- guided examples and reviews can offer scaffolding for support and remediation.

- the wide range of skills and large number of activities offered in a single book allow multiple opportunities for additional practice and remediation.

In addition, you can adapt the worksheets to provide additional support for your learner's individual needs:

- partially complete a worksheet by filling in every other item or parts of items, such as one digit in a math expression, to provide guidance.

- provide sentence "frames," which are partially completed sentences that students can adapt by filling in blanks.

- use highlighters or colored pencils to annotate the text and create color-coded "cheat sheets" or guides.

- provide support for phonics and literacy using alphabet cards or high-frequency word cards (for common words such as the or she).

Supplementing Classroom, Remote, or Hybrid Learning

In addition to working in a fully at-home learning environment, *FlashKids Complete Curriculum* can also supplement in-person classes, remote, or hybrid learning. The single-book format makes it easy to find activities that supplement your learner's school assignments.

- Look through school materials such as course overviews, scope and sequences, or tables of contents to identify the skills your child is learning at school, and select the corresponding units within *FlashKids Complete Curriculum*.

- Communicate with your learner and their teacher to identify skills that could benefit from additional practice.

- Use the best practices described above to supplement your learner's school activities.

The Test-Prep section can be particularly useful for learners who face high-stakes testing. Preparing for tests in the low-stakes, supportive home environment can give learners the confidence they need to perform at their best.

- Read through the test-preparation instructions and tips with your learner. Allow them to annotate the text as they wish.

- Work through the guided examples and tips together.

- Allow your learner to complete the practice tests without grading, or allow them to repeat previously completed tests to exercise "test-taking muscles" without the pressure of performing.

- Supplement your learner's test performance with remediation.

Using FlashKids Complete Curriculum in the Classroom

Warm-up Activities

Warm-up activities help familiarize students with lesson content before classroom instruction and activate any prior knowledge they may have about the topic being taught. To warm up or introduce content in a low-stakes environment, work with your students to read the direct instruction. Guide students to identify the most important ideas in each lesson before going into more detail during classroom instruction.

Diagnostic Assessment

Diagnostic assessment helps gauge each student's starting point for understanding or mastery of lesson concepts so that you can accurately monitor progress as you teach.

- For a quick diagnostic assessment, observe students as they read through or work on the guided example or the first page of items.

- For a more thorough assessment of students' skills, have students work on a full worksheet or lesson.

- If assigning a full worksheet, revisit the worksheet later as a formative assessment to gauge student progress.

- The test prep units collate items across multiple skills. Use the test-prep practice items as a course- or unit-wide diagnostic assessment. Omit the test-prep strategies unless you are specifically addressing standardized testing.

Supplementing Direct Instruction

The **direct instruction** at the start of each section is designed to serve as an overview and review. In addition to serving as a potential warm-up, this instruction can be an ideal student reference guide to reinforce classroom direct instruction.

- Provide students with copies of the instructional text pasted on index cards, or provide the copies and create the cards together as a class. Use colored pencils or colored highlighters to color-code information.

- Provide enlarged versions or digital versions that students can annotate, highlight, or cut and paste to create their own guides. Students can do this individually, in pairs, or in groups.

- Hang poster-sized versions around the classroom to serve as quick reminders.

Modeling is a great way to help students apply their learning.

- The guided examples featured throughout the book offer an ideal opportunity for classroom modeling. Display or distribute the example item and walk through the instructions step by step in order to illustrate and reinforce concepts.

- Use the items in the worksheet as model items for direct instruction. Students can follow along individually in their books.

- Verify or work through the worksheets as a whole-class activity, asking individuals to work through problems or narrate as you model.

- Scaffold the items in the worksheet by modeling an item, then having students complete an item with opportunities to ask questions or get help, and finally have them complete items independently.

Skills Practice

FlashKids Complete Curriculum worksheets provide ideal practice during and following direct instruction.

- Use the guided examples or the worksheet items as guided practice or group work as students apply their learning for the first time.

- Use worksheets as in-class practice to reinforce skills.

- Offer worksheets or partial worksheets to review skills or to warm up before moving on to new units.

Group Work

FlashKids Complete Curriculum is easily adapted for group practice and review.

- **Peer teaching:** Pair students to work on problems together. Allow pairs to consult their reference guides to reinforce their progress.

- **Group verification:** After completing the worksheets (either in class, for extra practice, or at home), have student pairs compare answers. They can flag answers that differ or items they are unsure about. Work as a class to identify and work through items that cause confusion.

- **Group writing:** Several sections of the *FlashKids Complete Curriculum* book offer writing or extended response opportunities. Have students complete writing assignments as a group, assigning roles (researcher, drafter, editor) or having students complete sentences independently and combining them.

Differentiated Instruction for In-Classroom Learning

The *FlashKids Complete Curriculum* workbooks are an excellent resource for planning and implementing lessons that feature differentiated instruction.

- Customize the student reference guides to accommodate the learning styles of different students in your class.

- Select worksheets or exercises as differentiated instruction. Offer additional practice for struggling students or opportunities to work ahead for those who work quickly.

- During group work, group students with similar skill levels to support each other through remediation or extra practice.

- Pair students with dissimilar skills, such as a struggling student and a high-achieving student, to offer the opportunity to serve as instructor and learner.

Formative Assessment and Remediation

Track students' progress on *FlashKids Complete Curriculum* worksheets as a form of formative assessment.

Allow students who need remediation to review the direct instruction or reference guides at the start of each section. You may work with struggling students as a group, or assign individual remediation.

Scaffold instruction as needed, modeling items, working one-on-one with struggling students to solve items or complete a worksheet, and then asking students to complete a worksheet individually.

Test Preparation

The *FlashKids Complete Curriculum* book contains a full section on preparing for standardized testing, including:

- an overview of test-taking tips and strategies
- model test items with tips and hints to help scaffold learning
- full subject-matter practice tests

The test-taking tips and strategies can serve as direct instruction for these skills. Allow students to cut out or annotate the tips offered throughout the model test items as additional assistance. Use the gradual introduction of test items and testing stakes as a form of scaffolding.

Summative Assessment

The Test-Prep sections of *FlashKids Complete Curriculum* are designed to model and prepare students for standardized tests, but, like live tests, these practice tests can also serve as final assessments.

The units within the Test-Prep sections are correlated to skill areas, making it easy to identify where students are achieving, and where students need more instruction.

Using FlashKids Complete Curriculum in Remote and Hybrid Learning Environments

The single-book format of *FlashKids Complete Curriculum* lends itself to remote and hybrid learning, as it allows a seamless shift between subjects without the time and disruption associated with switching materials and reduces the amount of materials students need to keep track of.

You may find that much of the classroom instruction detailed above transitions easily to remote or hybrid learning, including:

- using the worksheets for warm-up activities
- using worksheets for diagnostic and formative assessments
- supplementing direct instruction through modeling and scaffolding
- assigning worksheets as skills practice
- using worksheets for group work
- assigning worksheets for differentiated instruction
- independent test preparation
- remediation

Your remote- or hybrid-learning technology will determine how you assign the activities and how your students submit their work.

If students have the ability to annotate the worksheets digitally or to submit pictures of their completed work, *FlashKids Complete Curriculum* worksheets can function as full digital learning activities, allowing you to assign them as homework, practice, assessment, or remediation.

If students will work individually, you can verify their work by going over individual items one on one, in groups, or as a class.

If your remote or hybrid technology allows breakout groups, follow the classroom suggestions for group work, peer teaching, group verification, or group writing.

As you adapt your classroom routines to remote or hybrid learning, use these tips to make the most of the *FlashKids* materials:

- export direct instruction separately to allow students to create their reference guides.
- assign worksheets independently, then connect with each student individually to go over a problem, track their progress, or intervene as necessary.
- for situations in which you are working with a single student, consider playing the role of peer in order to take advantage of some of the paired work suggestions.
- consider working in an online collaborative environment such as Google Docs, so that students can work together and give each other feedback in real time.

Reading Skills

Here Is a Spider

30 (A+)

Here is a spider.
The spider can work.
The spider can make a new house.

See the new home.
The spider says,
"Walk in here, bugs.
Walk in the new house."

The spider can get food.
The spider eats a bug.

Read each question. Write **yes** or **no**.

30

1. Can a house walk?

no

2. Can a spider eat bugs?

yes

3. Can people walk?

yes

4. Can children eat?

yes

5. Can a house work for food?

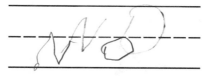
no

6. Can a spider make a new home?

yes

7. Can a spider walk?

yes

Read the words. Match the picture to the right word. One is done for you.

30
10

house

food

people

Mom and Dad Work

Ⓐ

(handwritten: firefighter, mom)

See Jill and Mom.   3 0
Mom works.
Here is what Mom can do.

(handwritten: Firefighter)

(handwritten: mom)

(handwritten: computers)

See Will and Mom.
Mom can work.
See what Mom can do.

Here are Nan and Dad.
See Dad work.
Dad works and works.

(handwritten: Dad)

(handwritten: builder)

(handwritten: Dad)

See Dan and Dad.
Dad is working.
Dad works here.

(handwritten: Docter)

Who? What?   Draw a line under the right one.

1. Who can make a house?

2. What cannot walk?

3. Who can eat?

   home   dad   live

4. What lives here?

   says   see   spider

5. Who can walk?

   food   mom   new

6. Who are people?

   a house   children and dad   walk and walk

7. Who can get a new house?

   mom and dad   live and eat   food and work

8. What cannot eat?

   house   children   people

Read the words. Put an **X** on the people.

Dan	Will	houses	not
walk	Mom	live	Dad
for	home	Nan	is
children	eat	food	get
do	new	Jill	in

Draw a circle around the right words.

1. 10 30

cannot walk

can eat

2.

can make food

is in a house

3.

works in a house

can eat

4.

is not new

is new

The Tree Is a Home

See the tree.
The tree is a home.
What can live in the house?

See what lives here.
It is for a raccoon.
Raccoons can live in trees.

The raccoon can go in.
It can go out to get food.
It gets corn and fish to eat.

Draw a line under the best name for this story.

1. A House for a Fish
2. The Raccoon's Home
3. The Tree's Food

Read each story. Draw a line under
the best name for the story.

Will gets a fish to eat.
The raccoon sees Will.
It walks to Will.
Will says, "No, Raccoon!
The fish is for people."

1. The Raccoon Gets Food
    Will Eats the Raccoon
    Food for People

Dad Raccoon says,
"Walk in! Here is corn.
Eat and eat.
No people are here."

2. The People Eat Food
    The Raccoons Get Food
    The Raccoons Get Fish

Read each sentence. Write **yes** or **no**.

1. A tree can have fish in it.

   _____

2. Raccoons can get
   a new home.

   _____

3. Corn is food for raccoons.

   _____

4. Jill can eat corn and fish.

   _____

5. Trees can eat raccoons.

   _____

6. A fish can eat.

   _____

7. Corn can walk out to a tree.

   _____

Many Bees Live Here

What lives here?
Can children live here?
No. It is a home for bees.
Many bees live here.

Many bees work here.
They go to the flowers.
They take something from the flowers.

Bees take something into the house.
They make food from it.
The food is good to eat.
People will eat what the bees make.
What food do bees make?

Can they get home?
Draw a line to the right home.

1.

2.

3.

4.

5.

Write the best word to finish the sentence.

1. Bees go to the _____.

    from   flowers

    _____
    - - - - - - - - - - -
    _____

2. From flowers bees get _____.

    something   see

    _____
    - - - - - - - - - - -
    _____

3. Bees take something _____.

    home   have

    _____
    - - - - - - - - - - -
    _____

4. Bees make _____.

    flowers   food

    _____
    - - - - - - - - - - -
    _____

5. The food is _____.

    go   good

    _____
    - - - - - - - - - - -
    _____

6. People will eat _____.

    it   is

    _____
    - - - - - - - - - - -
    _____

7. Corn is something to _____.

    it   eat

    _____
    - - - - - - - - - - -
    _____

Who? What?

Draw a line under the right one.

1. Who can take a walk?

2. What can make something?

3. What cannot eat?

raccoons   hills   bees

4. What can people do?

make a new ant

make a new house

make a new raccoon

5. Which are **not** people?

Nan and Dan

bugs and flowers

many children

Read each story. Draw a circle around a good name for it.

Raccoons eat corn and fish.
Ants eat many foods.
Fish eat bugs.

1. Who Can Walk?

2. What Animals Eat

3. What Bugs Eat

The children take a walk.
They go to the flowers.
They get many flowers.
They take the flowers to Mom.

1. The Flowers Walk

2. Mom Takes a Walk

3. Something for Mom

What do you see? Draw a circle around the right ones.
There are two right ones for each picture.

1. Raccoons live in the flowers.

2. Bees take something from flowers.

3. Bees work here.

4. The bees make a home.

1. Dan gets something new.

2. Dan gets something to eat.

3. Dan sees something new here.

4. Dan takes a walk.

The tree is a home.
It is a house.
See what lives here.

Here is the squirrel's home.
One squirrel lives here.
The squirrel climbs the tree.

Two birds live here.
They fly home.

What lives here?
Bugs live here.
Little bugs climb the tree.

What is at home here? Write the words in
the correct spaces. Use the words in the box.

| squirrel | raccoon | children | bird | people |

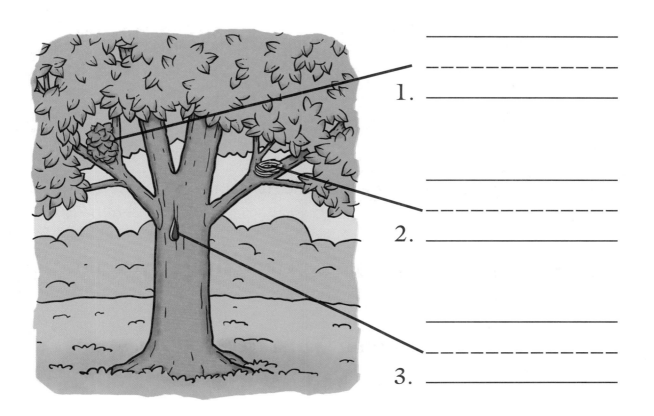

_____

----

1. _____

_____

----

2. _____

_____

----

3. _____

_____

----

4. _____

_____

----

5. _____

 Read each question. Circle **yes** or **no**.

1. Can a squirrel climb?   yes no

2. Can trees fly?   yes no

3. Can two flowers make a house?   yes no

4. Can two little children climb trees?   yes no

5. Can one raccoon live in a tree?   yes no

6. Can one squirrel take a walk?   yes no

7. Can fish live in hills?   yes no

8. Do bugs climb?   yes no

9. Do hills fly?   yes no

10. Is corn something good to eat?   yes no

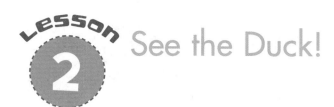

See the Duck!

Here is a pond.
What can be in a pond?
Many animals can live here.

Ducks live here.
The ducks look for food.
They look in the water.

See the duck!
Look at its food.
Fish live in water.
Little fish can be food for ducks.

What can be in the pond?

bugs   flowers   frogs

Read the story on page 25. Then answer the questions below by putting a ✔ by the right answer. One is done for you.

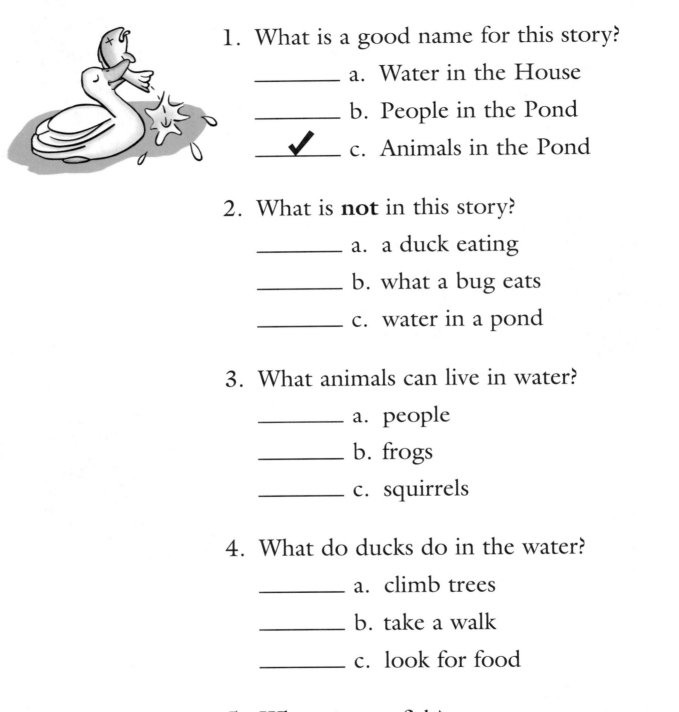

1. What is a good name for this story?

_____ a. Water in the House

_____ b. People in the Pond

___✔___ c. Animals in the Pond

2. What is **not** in this story?

_____ a. a duck eating

_____ b. what a bug eats

_____ c. water in a pond

3. What animals can live in water?

_____ a. people

_____ b. frogs

_____ c. squirrels

4. What do ducks do in the water?

_____ a. climb trees

_____ b. take a walk

_____ c. look for food

5. What can eat fish?

_____ a. people, raccoons, and ducks

_____ b. ducks, ponds, and trees

_____ c. flowers, trees, and houses

Look at the pictures. Read the sentences.
Match each picture to the best sentence.

a.

1. The frog is not in the pond.

b.

2. Two people play in the water.

3. It looks for something to eat.

c.

4. The fish eats the flower.

5. The bug can fly.

d.

Many animals live in ponds.
They have to swim.
See the grass by the pond.
Animals can live in the grass.

Frogs live in the pond.
They go into the grass too.

Ducks can be in the grass.
They can go into the water too.

Many animals play in the water.
Many animals play by the water.
They have fun.

Read each sentence. Draw a line under the correct picture. One is done for you.

1. Mom can swim.

a.    b.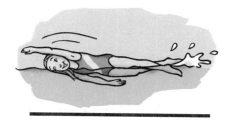

2. I have fun.

a.    b.

3. Children play by a tree.

a.    b.

4. Bees fly home.

a.    b.

5. Fish can live here.

a.    b.

Who?
What?

Draw a circle around the right one.

1. Who lives in a hill?

   are   ant   out

2. Who will eat corn?

   be   by   bird

3. What is something to eat?

   can   corn   climb

4. Who can live in water?

   dad   duck   do

5. Who gets something from flowers?

   bee   be   by

6. Who can have fun?

   play   pond   people

7. Who can have a home?

   are   ant   out

I Am Big

The bug says, "Look! I am big."
The bird says, "No! **I** am big.
You are little."

The bird says, "I am little."
The fox says, "Yes, you are little.
I am big."

Dad says, "Look here, Fox.
I am big.
You are the little one."
The fox says, "I can look.
I can see you.
You are the big one."

Draw a line from each sentence to the correct picture.
One is done for you.

a.   1. I am big.

b.   2. I am little.

a.   3. It is something little.

b.   4. It is something big.

a.   5. See the little one.

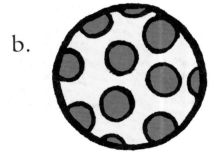

b.   6. See the big one.

Write the best word to finish the sentence.

1. The bird looks for food.

   _____

   - - - - - - - - - - - - - -

   It will eat _____.   children   bugs

2. Here is something good to eat.

   _____

   - - - - - - - - - - - - - -   fish   fly

   People will eat _____.

3. A fox will climb.

   _____

   - - - - - - - - - - - - -   hill   pond

   It can climb a _____.

4. Animals can have fun.

   _____

   - - - - - - - - - - - - -   play   pond

   They will _____.

5. The frogs have fun in the water.

   _____

   - - - - - - - - - - - - - -   swim   fly

   They will _____.

Reading Roundup

Write the name of each thing in the picture. Use these words.

grass   fish   duck   raccoon   flower   frog

1. _____   2. _____   3. _____

4. _____   5. _____   6. _____

Read each story. Draw a circle around a good name for it.

The fox and the frog play.
They play by the water.
They play in the grass.
They have fun.

1. The Fox Eats

2. The Animals Have Food

3. The Animals Have Fun

The fox says, "I will get something good to eat."
The frog says, "You will not get a frog to eat."
The frog gets into the water.
A little frog can swim.
A fox cannot swim.

1. The Fox Will Not Eat a Frog
2. The Fox Eats a Frog
3. The Fox Gets a Duck

Write the best word to finish the sentence.

1. Mom will go out to play. Mom will have _____.

fly   fun

2. Jill has something to eat. Jill has _____.

corn   climb

3. The flower is little. A flower cannot _____.

something   swim

4. Dad has something new. Dad says, "It is for _____."

you   out

5. The spider has a web. The spider will get _____.

hills   bugs

The Home Is in the Ground

Chipmunk says, "I have a good house.
It is in the ground by the rocks."
A big fox says, "I want to see
where Chipmunk lives."

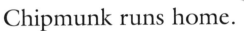

Chipmunk runs home.
The home is in the ground.

The fox says,
"I see where
Chipmunk lives.
I want to eat. I will
get into Chipmunk's house."
The fox is not happy.
She says, "I am too big.
I cannot get into the little home."

Make a circle around the best ending for each sentence.

1. The fox wants to get into the chipmunk's house.
   She wants to

   a. play with the chipmunk.

   b. swim with the chipmunk.

   c. get food.

2. The fox cannot get into the chipmunk's home.
   The fox says,

   a. "I will not eat a duck."

   b. "I will not eat a chipmunk."

   c. "I will eat good rocks."

Write the word to finish the sentence.
Use the words in the box.

fox	lives	run	ground

1. A chipmunk's house is in the _____.

2. The chipmunk can _____.

3. Here is where the animal _____.

Underline the words that match the picture.

1.

not on the ground

on the ground

2.

happy people

happy ducks

3.

the rock

two rocks

4.

a frog by a bug

a frog by a flower

5.

on the grass

on the water

6.

is a bird

is not a bird

Here Comes a Snake

Chipmunk says, "I am happy.
The fox cannot get me."

Here comes a snake.
She says, "I am not too big.
I will get into Chipmunk's house.
I like to eat little animals."
Chipmunk sees the snake.
She runs back into her house fast.

The snake is fast too.
She is in Chipmunk's house.

Chipmunk says, "The snake cannot get me.
I have a back door to my house!
The back door is by the rocks."

Read the story on page 39.
<u>Underline</u> the best name for the story.

1. Food for a Chipmunk

2. A Snake in the House

3. Food for a Fox

Write the word to finish the sentence.
Use the words in the box.

fast	me	rocks	door

1. A chipmunk runs _____.

2. She runs out the _____.

3. The back door is by the _____.

What came first in the story? Write **1** in the box next to it.
What came next? Write **2**. What came last? Write **3**.

☐ Chipmunk runs out the back door.

☐ Chipmunk runs into the house.

☐ Snake gets into Chipmunk's house.

What will come next? Put a ✔ by it.
One is done for you.

1. The snakes have no food.

   _____ a. They are happy.

   __✔__ b. They look for something to eat.

   _____ c. They go to live with a spider.

2. The frogs are in the pond.

   _____ a. They will run.

   _____ b. They will walk.

   _____ c. They will swim.

3. The bugs have a home in the tree.

   _____ a. They have to climb.

   _____ b. They have to swim.

   _____ c. They can get a fish.

4. The spider works to make a new house.

   _____ a. She will get bugs to eat.

   _____ b. She will get a bird.

   _____ c. She will live in the ant hill.

5. The snake gets into Chipmunk's house.

   _____ a. The snake works with Chipmunk.

   _____ b. The chipmunk and snake play.

   _____ c. The chipmunk runs out the back door.

The duck says, "It is cold.
You will not see me, dog.
I will go away. Good-bye."

The dog says, "Where will you go?"
The duck says, "Where it is not cold."

The frog says, "Good-bye, dog.
I will go away too. It is too cold."
The dog says, "Where will you go, frog?"

Frog says, "I go under the water here.
I get into the mud.
I will sleep in the mud."

The dog sees the duck fly away.
He sees the frog swim away.

The dog says, "It is cold.
I will go into my house."

Draw a circle around the answer to each question.

1. What is this story about?

    a. Dogs sleep under the water.

    b. A cat is under the flowers.

    c. Animals want to go away.

2. What is not in the story?

    a. The dog says, "It is cold."

    b. A cat sleeps in the mud.

    c. A duck can fly away.

Where is the bird? Draw a line from
the words to the correct picture.

1.    under a flower   2.

on the corn

3.    on a squirrel   4.

on the hill

5.    on a raccoon   6.

in a spider's home

Make a circle around the answer to each question.

1. What cannot fly away?

2. What do raccoons eat?

3. Where is something under a tree?

4. What can you climb?

Reading Roundup

Underline the sentence that answers the question.
One is done for you.

1. What makes Dan happy?

   a. He has new flowers.

   b. He has a new animal.

2. Where is the bird?

   a. It plays by the tree.

   b. It is in its home.

3. Where is the bee?

   a. It is under the flower.

   b. It is on the flower.

4. Who can sleep?

   a. A door can sleep.

   b. A dog can sleep.

Read the story. Underline the best name for the story.

The children want
something to eat.
They get food they like.
They play and run fast.
They have fun.

1. The Happy People

2. The Happy Rocks

3. By the Door

Write the best word to answer the question.

1. Where do frogs sleep?

_____

\- \- \- \- \- \- \- \- \- \- \- \-

_____

mom   mud   many

2. What can go fast?

_____

\- \- \- \- \- \- \- \- \- \- \- \-

_____

a rock   a snake   ground

3. Where can ducks fly?

_____

\- \- \- \- \- \- \- \- \- \- \- \-

_____

away   and   are

4. What cannot be happy?

_____

\- \- \- \- \- \- \- \- \- \- \- \-

_____

a door   birds   children

5. What do spiders want to eat?

_____

\- \- \- \- \- \- \- \- \- \- \- \-

_____

people   rocks   bugs

6. Where do ants want to live?

_____

\- \- \- \- \- \- \- \- \- \- \- \-

_____

a door   a hill   a pond

Underline the best answer.

1.   The bird wants to eat ants.

   a. So the ants have to run fast.

   b. So the ants play with the bird.

   c. So the ants eat the bird.

2. We like to fish.

   a. So we fly into the tree.

   b. So we live by the water.

   c. So we look for fish in the ground.

Write the word to finish the sentence. Use the words in the box.

ground	want	happy	fast

1. People have fun. They are _____.

2. She can run _____.

3. What do you _____?

Read the story. What came first? Write **1** in the box next to it.
What came next? Write **2**. What came last? Write **3**.

Dan says, "I do not want a big rock here. I will take it out."
He gets the rock out. Dan sees a big snake on the ground.
He turns and runs home.

☐ He runs home fast.

☐ He sees a big snake.

☐ Dan wants the rock out.

What Animal Is This?

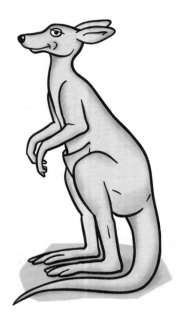

This animal has a big tail.
It has big back paws.
It jumps on its back feet.
Its front paws are like hands.

Look at your little finger.
This animal's new baby is that little.
The baby has no fur. It cannot see.
It lives in the mother's pouch.
It lives there a long time.
It gets big in the pouch.
What animal is this?

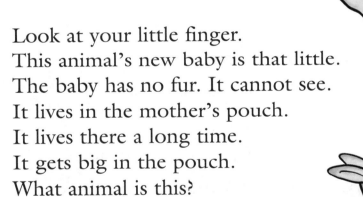

It is a kangaroo.

Which one is right? Put a ✔ by it. One is done for you.

1. What has a pouch?
   _____ a. a new baby
   _____ b. your hand
   ___✔___ c. the mother animal

2. What animal is this?
   _____ a. kangaroo
   _____ b. rabbit
   _____ c. lion

3. Where must a new baby kangaroo live?
   _____ a. in an egg
   _____ b. in the mother's pouch
   _____ c. in a nest

4. How do these animals walk?
   _____ a. on four paws
   _____ b. on three paws
   _____ c. on two paws

5. What is a good name for this story?
   _____ a. A Little Finger
   _____ b. A Funny Animal
   _____ c. A Little Bunny

6. What do you know about the new baby?
   _____ a. It has brown fur.
   _____ b. It has no back paws.
   _____ c. It cannot see.

Draw lines to match the words.
One is done for you.

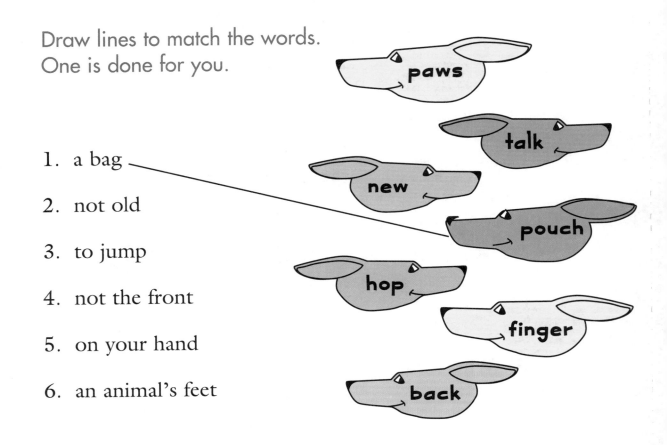

1. a bag

2. not old

3. to jump

4. not the front

5. on your hand

6. an animal's feet

Write the words in the right place.
One is done for you.

paw   pouch   fur

tail   hop   back   front

1. _fur_

2. _____

3. _____

4. _____

5. _____

6. _____

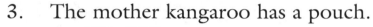

Who? What? Circle the right words. One is done for you.

1. Kangaroos are funny animals.

    | She |
    | ~~They~~ (circled) |

    jump far.

2. The new baby cannot see.

    | It |
    | They |

    cannot jump.

3. The mother kangaroo has a pouch.

    | He |
    | She |

    has a baby in the pouch.

4. The kangaroo's tail is big.

    | She |
    | It |

    is not little.

5. Father kangaroo lives far away.

    | He |
    | She |

    can hop fast.

6. Baby kangaroos have no fur.

    | It |
    | They |

    will get fur soon.

7. The pouch is on the kangaroo.

    | It |
    | They |

    has a baby in it.

The Ducks Have Food

One day Mother Duck walked.
She walked on the grass.

She said, "Let's swim in the water.
You will do something new.
Do what I do.
It will be fun."

The ducks have food.
They got it in the pond.
The little ducks did something new.

Which one is right? Put a ✔ by it. One is done for you.

1. When did this story happen?
    ___✔___ a. day
    _____ b. night
    _____ c. at the pond

2. Where did Mother Duck take the baby ducks?
    _____ a. to the farm
    _____ b. to the water
    _____ c. to school

3. What new thing did the baby ducks do?
    _____ a. get food
    _____ b. go to sleep
    _____ c. play a game

4. How do baby ducks learn?
    _____ a. by reading a book
    _____ b. by eating fish
    _____ c. by looking at big ducks

5. What is the best name for this story?
    _____ a. Baby Ducks Can Fly
    _____ b. Baby Ducks Run Away
    _____ c. Baby Ducks Do Something New

Draw lines to match the words.
One is done for you.

1. not old

2. something to eat

3. to go fast in the water

4. some water

5. a good time

6. something feet can do

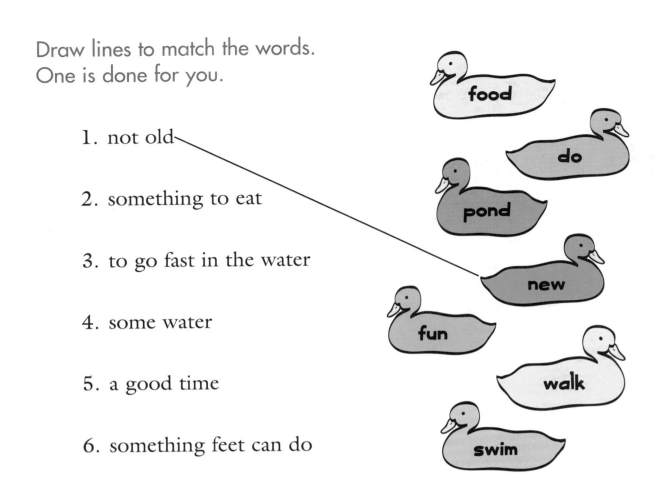

Each picture goes with a sentence.
Draw lines to match them.

1.

2.

3.

Flowers are in the pond.

A duck is flying.

Ducks swim.

The duck walks with Mother Duck.

A duck is eating.

Who? What? Circle the right word. One is done for you.

1. The ducks are on the grass.

She
(They)
   are walking.

2. The flower was in the pond.

It
He
   was white.

3. Fish can swim.

We
They
   can go fast.

4. Ann is by the water.

He
She
   looks at the fish.

5. Tim can swim.

He
They
   can have fun.

Can you tell the story? Some things are not in the right place. Put **1**, **2**, and **3** in the boxes. One is done for you.

[ ] The ducks went into the water.

[ ] They got food.

[**1**] The ducks walked on the grass.

One morning the robins were working.
They were making a nest.
The nest was in an old oak tree.
Mr. Robin found some grass for the nest.
Mrs. Robin got mud for the nest.
The nest was made of mud and grass.
Soon Mrs. Robin will lay eggs in the nest.
The eggs will be blue.
What will come out of the robins' eggs?

Which one is right? Put a ✔ by it.

1. When were the robins working?

_____ a. at night

_____ b. at noon

_____ c. in the morning

2. What were the robins making?

_____ a. a school

_____ b. a home

_____ c. an oak tree

3. Where was the nest?

   _____ a. in an apple tree

   _____ b. in the brown sand

   _____ c. in an oak tree

4. What was used to make the nest?

   _____ a. grass and mud

   _____ b. sand and mud

   _____ c. grass and sand

5. What will Mrs. Robin do?

   _____ a. dig a hole

   _____ b. lay eggs in the nest

   _____ c. play and run

6. What color is a robin's egg?

   _____ a. white   _____ b. brown   _____ c. blue

7. What will come out of robins' eggs?

   _____ a. baby chickens

   _____ b. baby birds

   _____ c. baby turtles

8. What is the best name for the story?

   _____ a. A Nest in the Sand

   _____ b. A Nest in a Tree

   _____ c. A Nest in the Grass

Draw lines to match these. One is done for you.

1. green plants

2. time of the day

3. kind of bird

4. what a woman is called

5. a tree

6. color of a robin's egg

7. what a man is called

8. home for birds

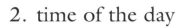
robin

morning

oak

Mrs.

grass

Mr.

nest

blue

make

Each picture goes with a sentence.
Draw lines to match them.

1.

2.

3.

The robin finds some grass.

Three eggs are in the nest.

The robins make a nest.

The oak tree is big.

Two eggs are in the nest.

Who? What? Circle the right word for each story.

1. The eggs are blue.

   What will come out of | them / it | ?

2. Mr. Robin and Mrs. Robin made a nest.

   | They / She | got grass for the nest.

3. Mrs. Robin saw a man.

   Mrs. Robin went away from | them / him | .

4. The birds live in the tree.

   They have a nest in | it / them | .

5. Mrs. Robin will lay eggs soon.

   | Our / Her | eggs will be blue.

Can you tell the story? Some things are not in the right place. Put **1**, **2**, and **3** in the boxes. One is done for you.

☐ Mrs. Robin will lay eggs in the nest.

☐ They made a nest in the oak tree.

1 Mr. and Mrs. Robin got grass and mud.

Ann and Andy Went to the Store

One afternoon Mom wanted some food. Ann and Andy went to the store for her. They walked a long way down Duck Street. Then they went around a corner. They walked by the park. Then they got to the store.

Ann and Andy found eggs, bread, fish, and milk. A woman put the food into a bag for them. They gave the woman some money. Then Ann and Andy walked home.

When Mom looked inside the bag, she said, "You forgot the lettuce!"

Ann and Andy had to go all the way back to the store. Then they had to walk home again.

Which one is right? Put a ✔ by it.

1. Who went to the store?

_____ a. two children

_____ b. Mom

_____ c. two boys

2. When did they go to the store?

_____ a. at night

_____ b. in the morning

_____ c. in the afternoon

3. Where did the woman put the food?

_____ a. in a bag

_____ b. in a box

_____ c. in the park

4. What did Ann and Andy give the woman?

_____ a. food _____ b. lettuce _____ c. money

5. Why did Ann and Andy go back to the store?

_____ a. to get money

_____ b. to get lettuce

_____ c. to see Mom there

6. What do we know about the store?

_____ a. It was a long way from home.

_____ b. It was next to Ann and Andy's house.

_____ c. It was on Old Street.

7. What is the best name for this story?

_____ a. The Lost Lettuce

_____ b. Fun at the Store

_____ c. Two Long Walks

Draw lines to match these. One is done for you.

1. a place to play

2. did not think about

3. a green food

4. a white drink

5. used to pay for things

6. boys and girls

7. a time of day

8. where two streets
come together

lettuce

milk

park

forgot

corner

duck

afternoon

children

money

Pick out the right word from the bag.
Write the word. One is done for you.

walk   black   milk
day   house   girl

1. lettuce, bread, eggs,

milk

2. school, store, home,
_____
- - - - - - - - - -
_____

3. run, skip, jump,
_____
- - - - - - - - - -
_____

4. Mom, woman, sister,
_____
- - - - - - - - - -
_____

5. green, blue, brown,
_____
- - - - - - - - - -
_____

Who? What?

Circle the right word for each story.

1. The lettuce was green.

   | It
   | They | was in a brown bag.

2. Ann got some eggs.

   She wanted to eat | it
   | them | .

3. The children went down Duck Street.

   | She
   | They | went around the corner.

4. Andy had some money.

   | He
   | She | gave it to a woman.

5. Ann walked with Andy.

   Ann was next to | her
   | him | .

Can you tell the story? Some things are not in the right place. Put **1**, **2**, and **3** in the boxes.

[ ] Ann and Andy forgot to get the lettuce.

[ ] Mother wanted some food from the store.

[**3**] Ann and Andy had to go back to the store.

Reading Roundup

Read the question. Write the answer next to each one.
How many paws do they have? Write the words.

zero   one   four

1. _____

2. _____

3. _____

4. _____

5. _____

6. _____

7. _____

8. _____

Who?
What?   Circle the right word for each story.

1. Dad got some eggs at the store.

   | He |
   | She | took the eggs home.

2. Ann and Andy ran around the corner.

   | They |
   | She | ran fast.

3. Mom forgot to take the bags.

   She had to go home to get | it |
   | them | .

Draw lines to match these.

1. a kind of bag

2. something to eat

3. time after morning

4. one more time

5. place to play

6. time for bed

7. not the back

Read each sentence. Finish it. Circle the right picture.

1. Mrs. Robin will lay a blue _____ in the nest.

a.   b.   c.

2. The kangaroo has a big _____.

a.   b.   c.

3. The little ducks eat _____.

a.   b.   c.

Circle the right word.

1. We saw the kangaroo [hot / hop] in the tall grass.

2. Robins make a nest of [grass / green] and [mad / mud].

3. The dog had a bath in a [but / tub].

4. Ann and Andy [forgot / four] the lettuce.

5. They had to go [black / back] to the store.

6. Mother gave them [money / many] to get food.

7. Mother Duck walked on the [goats / grass].

Can you tell about the story on page **60**? Some things are not in the right place. Put **1**, **2**, and **3** in the boxes.

☐ A woman put the food into a bag.

☐ Mom said, "You forgot the lettuce!"

☐ Ann and Andy walked to the store.

Each picture goes with a sentence. Draw lines to match them.

1.

      a. The baby gets big in the pouch.

2.

      b. People can get a bath in this tub.

3.

      c. The robins look for food.

4.

      d. The children got them at the store.

5.

      e. The robins made a nest of grass and mud.

The Toy Shelf

Mom and Dad wanted the children to take care of their toys. Every night the children put all the big toys in their rooms. Then they put all the little toys on a toy shelf. Each child had a shelf.

Bob was ten. He had the top shelf. Bev was eight. She had the middle shelf. Bill was seven. He had the bottom shelf.

On Sunday evening, Dad and Mom found lots of toys on the rug. They went to look at the toy shelf. They saw no toys on the middle shelf.

Mom said, "Now I know who did not put the toys away."

Dad said, "I can guess who it is too."

Can you guess who forgot to put away toys?

Which one is right? Put a ✓ by it.

1. What was the story about?

    _____ a. getting a new rug

    _____ b. getting a toy shelf

    _____ c. a child who forgot to do something

2. What did Mom and Dad want the children to do?

    ————   a. go to the store

    ————   b. put away the toys

    ————   c. make a new shelf

3. Where did the children put their big toys?

    ————   a. on a shelf

    ————   b. under a bed

    ————   c. in their rooms

4. Where did Dad and Mom find some toys?

    ————   a. on the chair

    ————   b. on the rug

    ————   c. at the store

5. When did Dad and Mom find toys on the rug?

    ————   a. Tuesday evening

    ————   b. Sunday evening

    ————   c. Sunday afternoon

6. Who forgot to put the toys away?

    ————   a. Bev

    ————   b. Bill

    ————   c. Bob

7. How did Mom know who did not put away toys?

    ————   a. She saw toys on every shelf.

    ————   b. She saw no toys on one shelf.

    ————   c. She asked the children.

Draw lines to match these.

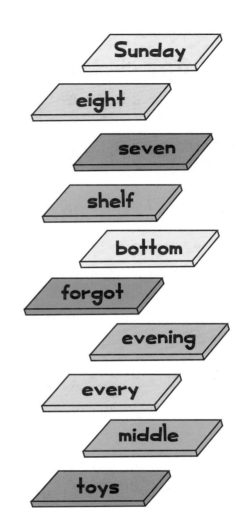

1. six and one

2. part that is under

3. day of the week

4. late in the day

5. seven and one

6. place to put things on

7. all of them

8. things to play with

9. not the top or
   the bottom

Put some things on the big shelf.

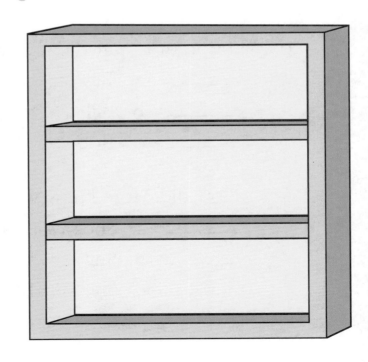

1. Put a blue ✖ on
   the middle shelf.

2. Put a brown ✔ on
   the bottom shelf.

3. Put a blue egg on
   the middle shelf.

4. Put a black box on
   the top shelf.

5. Put a red ▲ on
   every shelf.

Circle one word that fits both sentences.

1. A bird sat on _____ of the tree.

   too   top

2. Bill played with his toy _____.

3. Mom and Dad went to see a _____.

   play   day

4. Children like to run and _____.

5. The children must take _____ of the toys.

   can   care

6. Bob did not _____ when Bev took his toy.

Look back at the story on page 68.
Put the right child's name on each line.

1. _____ was seven years old.

2. _____ was eight.

3. _____ was ten years old.

4. _____ had the top toy shelf.

5. _____ had the middle shelf.

6. _____ forgot to put away the toys.

Ducks in the Water

Ducks like to be in water. They can swim fast. They play games in the water. They find food there too. Ducks eat little bugs and fish. They pull plants out of the water to eat.

Ducks have big orange feet. The feet are good for pushing the water. Their feet make ducks good swimmers. Ducks' feet are not so good for walking and running. Their feet are not good for climbing.

Sometimes ducks must come out of the water. They cannot walk as well as they can swim. Ducks must take care on land. If ducks are not careful on land, a fox may catch them.

Why do you think a fox likes to catch a duck?

Which one is right? Put a ✔ by it.

1.   Why do foxes like to catch ducks?

_____ a. to make friends

_____ b. to play games

_____ c. for food

2. What do ducks like to eat?

   _____ a. birds

   _____ b. foxes

   _____ c. bugs and plants

3. What can ducks use their feet to do?

   _____ a. climb trees

   _____ b. push water

   _____ c. talk fast

4. Why don't foxes catch ducks in the water?

   _____ a. Foxes don't swim well.

   _____ b. Water is too cold.

   _____ c. Ducks catch foxes.

5. Which animal is most like a duck?

   _____ a. robin

   _____ b. bee

   _____ c. fox

6. What will you never see a duck do?

   _____ a. climb a big tree

   _____ b. eat in the water

   _____ c. swim very fast

7. What is the best name for this story?

   _____ a. How Ducks Climb

   _____ b. How Ducks Catch Bugs

   _____ c. Why Ducks Like Water

What do you know about ducks? Circle the right ones.

1. Which is the duck's foot?

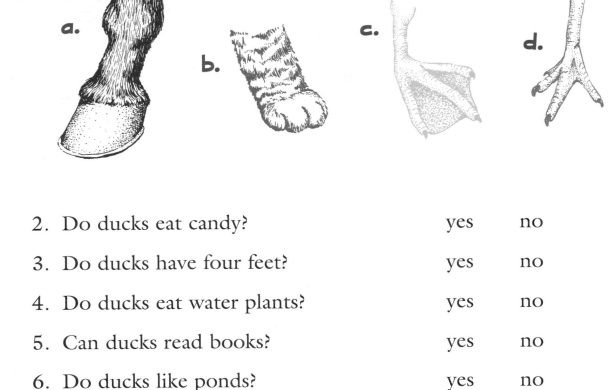

2. Do ducks eat candy?   yes   no

3. Do ducks have four feet?   yes   no

4. Do ducks eat water plants?   yes   no

5. Can ducks read books?   yes   no

6. Do ducks like ponds?   yes   no

7. Do ducks swim on land?   yes   no

8. Do ducks catch bugs?   yes   no

9. Can a fox catch a duck on land?   yes   no

Can you guess the riddles? Circle the right word.

1. I am little.
   I have many feet.
   Ducks eat me.
   Children do not eat me.
   What am I?

   bag   bug   bird

2. I am an animal.
   I have four feet.
   Ducks must watch
   out for me.
   What am I?

   bug   fox   bird

Draw lines to match the opposites.
One is done for you.

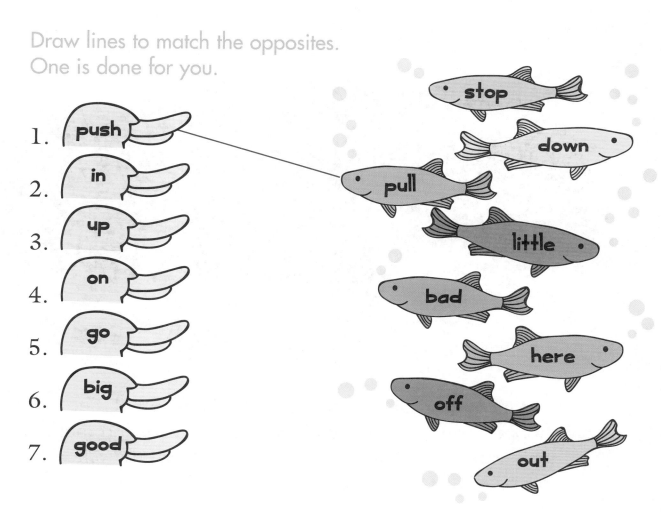

1. push
2. in
3. up
4. on
5. go
6. big
7. good

stop
down
pull
little
bad
here
off
out

Look at a book's Table of Contents page. You can see
the number of the page where each story starts.
Can you answer these?

Stories

1. On which page can you
   find **Fish's Home**? _____

2. What story starts on page 8?
   _____
   _____
   _____

3. Is there a story about a turtle
   in this book?
   _____
   _____
   _____

A Little Yellow Bird

One night a little yellow bird hopped around. She hopped around in the grass. She looked here and there. She was looking for something to eat. Soon the yellow bird saw a fat worm in the grass. She went to pick up the fat worm.

Just then, a tiger went by. The tiger hid in the tall grass. He looked at the little bird. When the bird pulled at the worm, the tiger jumped! He jumped at the yellow bird! He wanted to eat the bird.

Birds are quick. The little yellow bird got away! She flew far away. The tiger was left with the fat worm.

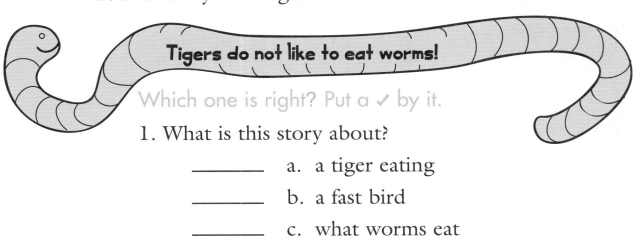

Tigers do not like to eat worms!

Which one is right? Put a ✔ by it.

1. What is this story about?

_____ a. a tiger eating

_____ b. a fast bird

_____ c. what worms eat

2. What was the bird doing?

_____ a. looking for food

_____ b. sitting in a tree

_____ c. looking for a tiger

3. What was the tiger doing?

_____ a. eating worms

_____ b. flying away

_____ c. looking for food

4. Where was the bird?

_____ a. in a tree

_____ b. in a nest

_____ c. in the grass

5. When was the bird looking for food?

_____ a. in the morning

_____ b. in the afternoon

_____ c. at night

6. Who got some food in the story?

_____ a. no one

_____ b. the tiger

_____ c. the bird

7. What color was the bird?

_____ a. brown

_____ b. yellow

_____ c. blue

8. What do you think the worm did?

_____ a. ate the bird

_____ b. got away

_____ c. looked for a tiger

9. A **quick** tiger is a _____ tiger.

_____ a. pretty

_____ b. little

_____ c. fast

10. What is the best name for this story?

_____ a. The Tiger's Dinner

_____ b. How Worms Get Birds

_____ c. The Bird That Got Away

Read the words on the worms. Then read what to do.
Can you mark the right words?

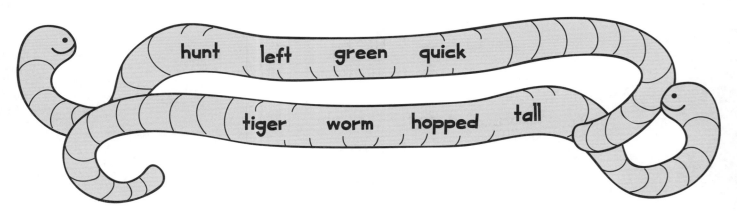

hunt   left   green   quick

tiger   worm   hopped   tall

1. Make a ✔ on the word that means **jumped.**
2. Circle the name of the animal with four feet.
3. Put a box around the color of grass.
4. Put an **X** on the word that means **went away.**
5. Circle the word that means **big.**
6. Put a △ on the word that means **to look for.**
7. Put a line under the word that means **fast.**

Put a ✔ by each one that is right about the story on page 76.

_____ 1. The tiger found some grass to eat.

_____ 2. The worm wanted to eat a fat tiger.

_____ 3. Tigers like to eat worms.

_____ 4. The bird pulled at the worm.

_____ 5. Birds like to eat worms.

_____ 6. The bird got away fast.

_____ 7. The bird picked up the tiger.

_____ 8. The worm was fat.

_____ 9. The tiger hid in the tall grass.

What are Betty Bird and Will Worm doing? Put a ✔
by each sentence that tells what they are doing.

1. _____ a. Betty hunts for food.

   _____ b. Betty hops into the water.

   _____ c. Betty plays with a tiger.

2. _____ a. Will hid in a box.

   _____ b. Will hid in the grass.

   _____ c. Will hid in an apple.

3. _____ a. Betty Bird pulls on a worm.

   _____ b. Will Worm pulls on a bird.

   _____ c. The bird and worm play.

One! Two! Three! Go!

Last Monday, ten children had a race. The race was on the school playground.

Mr. Pack started the race. He told the children to stand side by side.

"Get ready. One! Two! Three! Go!" called Mr. Pack.

Away went the children. They ran faster and faster. Other children saw them run by.

"Hurry! Hurry! Run faster!" the other children called out.

Lupe fell down. Then he could not run again. Pam's shoe came off. She had to stop too! Mr. Pack called, "May wins the race!"

Jeff came in second, with Rita after him. Ted was last in the race.

How did they do in the race? Look at the story again. Write the names on the lines.

first

1. _____

second

2. _____

next

3. _____

last

4. _____

1. What is this story about?

_____ a. Mr. Pack's playground

_____ b. a boat race

_____ c. children in a race

2. When was the race?

_____ a. last Monday

_____ b. last night

_____ c. last Sunday

3. Who watched the race?

_____ a. children

_____ b. fathers

_____ c. mothers

4. Why did Pam stop running?

_____ a. She fell.

_____ b. She saw her friend.

_____ c. Her shoe came off.

5. Who stopped running before the race was over?

_____ a. two girls

_____ b. a boy and a girl

_____ c. two boys

6. How many children ran to the end of the race?

_____ a. ten

_____ b. nine

_____ c. eight

7. Who came in before Rita?

_____ a. Jeff   _____ b. Ted   _____ c. Bob

8. Who won the race?

_____ a. Rita   _____ b. Jeff   _____ c. May

9. If you **hurry**, you are _____.

_____ a. sad   _____ b. quick   _____ c. happy

Draw lines to match these.

1. to go very fast

2. goes on a foot

3. a place to learn

4. after the first

5. looked at

6. made it begin

7. name of a day

8. set to go

9. at the end

10. a place to play

11. a game to see who can go fast

second

hurry

school   side

Monday

shoe   race

started   last

watched   ready

playground

Read each action word. When you put **er** on the action word, you name a person who does the action.

help $\longrightarrow$ helper   start $\longrightarrow$ starter
run $\longrightarrow$ runner   play $\longrightarrow$ player
win $\longrightarrow$ winner   jump $\longrightarrow$ jumper

Circle the right word for each sentence.

1. Mr. Pack will _____ the race.

   start   starter

2. May was the _____ of the race.

   win   winner

3. There were ten _____ in the race.

   run   runners

4. Lupe fell and could not _____ again.

   run   runner

Fun time! Can you do this?

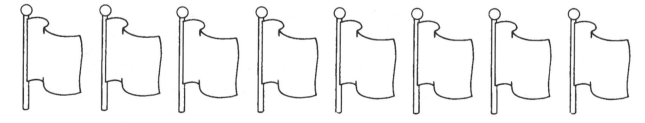

1. How many flags do you see? _____
2. Color the first one blue.
3. Color the last one yellow.
4. Color the second one green.
5. Circle the next to the last one.
6. Color the next to the last one brown.
7. Color four others red.

The Snow Is Too Deep

It snowed all day on Monday. On Tuesday Pat and Bill played in the white snow. They jumped and fell in it.

Bill lost one mitten and some money. Pat lost her ring in the deep, deep snow.

"I want my ring," said Pat. "Please help me find it, Mom!"

Mom said, "No, Pat. The snow is too deep."

"Where is my money?" asked Bill. "No one will help me find it."

Then Dad said, "Soon something big and yellow will help you find the lost things."

On Wednesday, the Sun was in the sky. There was less snow.

On Thursday there was just a little snow. On Friday, the snow was gone. In the mud was a wet mitten! By the fence was a little ring. Bill's money was there too.

What was the children's helper?

Which one is right? Put a ✔ by it.

1. When did the snow start to fall?

    _____ a. Monday

    _____ b. Wednesday

    _____ c. Thursday

2. How do you think Bill's money got lost?

_____ a. Pat hid it in the snow.

_____ b. When Bill fell, the money dropped out.

_____ c. Someone took it out of his mitten.

3. Why didn't Pat find her ring?

_____ a. The trees hid it.

_____ b. Pat left it in her room.

_____ c. The snow was too deep.

4. Where was the ring?

_____ a. under the tree

_____ b. by the fence

_____ c. under the flowers

5. What came first in the story?

_____ a. A mitten was found.

_____ b. Pat asked Mom for help.

_____ c. They played in the snow.

6. What was the children's helper?

_____ a. a truck

_____ b. a moon

_____ c. the Sun

7. What is the best name for this story?

_____ a. Fun in the Mud

_____ b. The Sun and the Snow

_____ c. The Lost Fence

Draw lines to match these.

1. not as many

2. something for hands

3. cannot be found

4. falls from the sky

5. the color of snow

6. day after Wednesday

7. a penny

Which one is right? Put a ✓ by it.

1. Three of us came into the room. I came in first.
   Bill came in last. Pat was _____.

   _____ a. the last one

   _____ b. the first one

   _____ c. the middle one

2. Pat and Bill wanted to go to the zoo on Monday.
   Mom and Dad had to work on Monday. Dad said
   they would all go to the zoo the next day. When
   will they go to the zoo?

   _____ a. on Monday

   _____ b. on Tuesday

   _____ c. on Sunday

Write the days in order.

Friday   Wednesday   Tuesday   Monday   Thursday

1. Sunday   2. _____

3. _____   4. _____

5. _____   6. _____

7. Saturday

Read each story. Circle the words that tell about the story.

1. The Sun is hot. It helps the trees get big. It melts the snow.

   This story is about the _____.

    a. trees   b. Sun   c. flowers

2. On Monday, there was a lot of snow. The Sun came out on Tuesday. On Wednesday, there was less snow. On Thursday, the snow was gone.

   This story is about _____.

    a. how the snow hid the cars

    b. how deep the snow was

    c. how the snow melted

3. Bill's cat was by the fence. The snow fell. The cat ran into the house. Pat had to dry the cat's feet.

   This story is about _____.

    a. wet mittens   b. wet feet   c. wet money

Reading Roundup

Read this story.

All the children are going to a show.
Bev is going to the show on Monday.
Lupe is going the day before Bev.
Jeff is going the day after Bev.
Rita is going the day before Sunday.
Pat is going the day after Tuesday.

When are they going to the show?
Draw lines to match each child to the right day.

1. Pat

2. Rita

3. Bev

4. Lupe

5. Jeff

a. Sunday

b. Monday

c. Tuesday

d. Wednesday

e. Thursday

f. Friday

g. Saturday

Each shelf must have three words.
Put the words below on the right shelves.

Colors

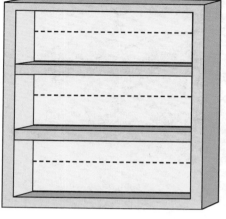

1. tiger
4. worm
7. duck
10. again

Numbers

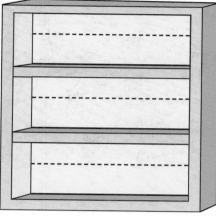

2. yellow
5. seven
8. green

Animals

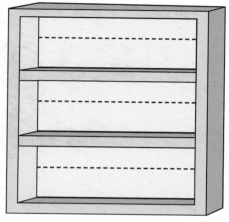

3. eight
6. white
9. nine

Draw lines to match these.

1. not as much

2. to look for

3. after the first

4. went away

5. late in the day

6. at the end

7. fast

8. all of them

snow
left
less
evening
hunt
second
every
quick
last

Can you guess the riddles? Circle the right word.

1. I go up, up, up.
   I have grass on me.
   You can run up
   and down on me.
   What am I?

   hill   fox   water

2. I am white.
   I fall from the sky.
   I fall on cold days.
   Children play with me.
   What am I?

   Sun   rain   snow

3. I am wet.
   Fish live in me.
   Children swim in me.
   Ducks sit on me.
   What am I?

   water   hill   box

4. I am a swimmer.
   I like the water.
   I have no feet.
   You like to catch me.
   What am I?

   fox   fish   duck

5. I am little.
   Birds try to get me.
   I have no feet.
   I stay in the grass.
   What am I?

   worm   fox   cat

6. I can run fast.
   I run after birds.
   I have four legs.
   I do not eat worms.
   What am I?

   bug   duck   tiger

Can you do this?

1. Put an **X** on the middle book.

2. Color the top book green.

3. Color the bottom book orange.

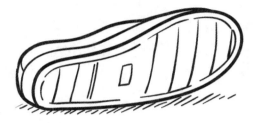

4. Make a hole in the bottom.

5. Color the hole brown.

6. Color the shoe yellow.

Circle the one word that fits both sentences.

1. Turn _____ at the corner.

2. The bird _____ in a hurry.

last   left

3. I was _____ in line.

4. The race will _____ a long time.

last   left

Stories

Jeff's Ring 3

A Lost Puppy 6

The Ice Melts 8

Can you do this?

1. Put an **X** on the page where **Jeff's Ring** starts.

2. Put a line under the story found on page 8.

3. On what page is **A Lost Puppy**? Write it here. _____

The Purple Flower

In the spring, Fay planted seeds in a window box. Pete helped her plant the seeds. They liked the color red. They planted all red flowers.

Little green plants came up first. Then red flowers came out of the green plants. The window box looked very pretty.

Two birds came to the window box. The birds had some seeds in their beaks. One bird dropped a seed. The seed fell into the window box. Fay and Pete did not see the birds.

One day, the children looked at their pretty red flowers. They saw a big purple flower with all the red flowers! What a surprise!

"How did the purple flower get there?" asked Pete.

"I do not know," said Fay. "We planted all red flowers."

They never found out how the purple flower got there. Do you know?

Which one is right? Put a ✔ by it.

1. When did Fay plant seeds in the window box?

_____ a. fall

_____ b. winter

_____ c. spring

2. What is this story about?

_____ a. a big red flower

_____ b. what birds eat

_____ c. a purple surprise

3. What came out of the seeds first?

_____ a. red flowers

_____ b. green plants

_____ c. brown birds

4. Why did the birds have seeds?

_____ a. to plant them

_____ b. to eat them

_____ c. for gifts to the children

5. How did the purple flower get into the box?

_____ a. Pete planted it there.

_____ b. Fay put it there as a surprise.

_____ c. A bird dropped a seed.

6. What is the best name for this story?

_____ a. A Big Surprise

_____ b. Pretty Colors

_____ c. A Nest in the Window Box

Draw lines to match these.

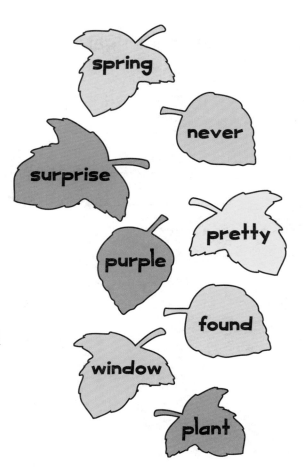

1. time of year

2. made of glass

3. at no time

4. saw where it was

5. a color

6. put seeds in the ground

7. something we did not
   know about

Circle the right word.

1. Little plants came

| us |
| up |

.

2. Two birds

| can |
| came |

to the window.

3. I saw a seed

| drop |
| chop |

into the box.

4. How did the seed get

| there |
| they |

?

5. They

| every |
| never |

did find out.

Read these sentences.

1. How did the purple flower get here?
2. I did not plant purple flowers.

> The first sentence **asks** something.
> Use a **?** at the end.
> The second sentence **tells** something.
> Use a **.** at the end.

Put **?** or **.** at the end of each sentence.

1. Fay planted some seeds
2. Did Pete help plant seeds
3. Will little green plants come up first
4. Then flowers come out of the plants
5. A seed fell into the window box
6. Did a bird drop the seed

Find the sentence that means the same as the first one. Put a ✔ by it.

1. They planted all red flowers.

   _____ Every flower they planted was red.

   _____ They planted one red flower.

2. Little green plants came up first.

   _____ Little green plants came up after the flowers.

   _____ Little green plants came up before the flowers.

3. The purple flower was a surprise.

   _____ They planted the purple flower.

   _____ They did not know the purple flower was there.

The Day Ray Lost Some of His Things

Mr. and Mrs. Hill had three children. Jay was ten years old. Kay was eight. Ray was six years old.

One afternoon, Ray came home from school. He had lost some of his things. He had lost his new book bag! He had lost his lunch box! And he had even lost all the buttons from his coat!

Mrs. Hill said, "Let's help Ray find his things."

The family hunted and looked. Jay found two buttons around the corner. Kay found one button in the doghouse. Mrs. Hill found one button by the flowers. Mr. Hill saw the book bag under a tree. But they did not find the lunchbox.

The next day, Ray went to school again. There was his lunchbox by a window. Ray had left it there.

Which one is right? Put a ✔ by it.

1. How old was Ray?

_____ a. seven

_____ b. four

_____ c. six

2. What is this story about?

_____ a. a lost girl

_____ b. two boys who lost things

_____ c. how the family helped Ray

3. How many buttons were on Ray's coat?

_____ a. four

_____ b. three

_____ c. two

4. Who found the lunchbox?

_____ a. Kay _____ b. Ray _____ c. Jay

5. Who found two buttons?

_____ a. Kay _____ b. Ray _____ c. Jay

6. Who found the book bag?

_____ a. Mrs. Hill

_____ b. Mr. Hill

_____ c. Kay Hill

7. How did the book bag get under the tree?

_____ a. Kay put it there.

_____ b. Ray put it there and forgot it.

_____ c. The book bag walked there.

8. What must Ray learn to do?

_____ a. stay at home

_____ b. get a new coat

_____ c. take care of his things

Read the story on page 96. Where was each thing found? Draw lines to match them.

THINGS

PLACES

1. around the corner

a.

2. under a tree

b.

3. by the flowers

c.

4. in a hole

d.

5. in a doghouse

6. at school

e.

Find the sentence that means the same as the first one. Put a ✔ by it.

1. Mr. and Mrs. Hill had three children.

_____ They had three girls and one boy.

_____ They had one girl and two boys.

2. Ray left the school at noon.

_____ He went into the school at noon.

_____ He came out of the school at noon.

3. They lost the book again.

_____ They lost the book one more time.

_____ They never lost the book.

Draw lines to match these.

1. two and one
2. a man
3. did not find
4. let us
5. noon meal
6. on a coat

let's
Mr.
button
Mrs.
lost
three
lunch

Put the words that tell **where** in the **WHERE?** box.
Put the words that tell **when** in the **WHEN?** box.
Draw lines to the right box. The first one is done for you.

1. the next day

2. under a tree

WHERE?

3. on the window

4. at night

5. one day

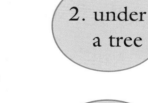

WHEN?

6. by the flowers

7. in the house

8. after lunch

Where Was Baby Seal's Mother?

Baby Seal was asleep on a big rock. Mother Seal was gone. She went to look for food in the water.

Baby Seal got up and looked around. He saw many big mother seals. But he did not see his mother.

A mother seal came up out of the water. Baby Seal barked, "Mother!" He went over to her. The mother seal looked at him.

"You are not my little pup!" she barked. Then Baby Seal began to cry. He looked far out at the sea. Where was his mother?

Two more seals came out of the sea. Baby Seal barked a happy seal bark. He could smell his mother. His mother could smell him.

Baby seals know their mothers. Mother seals know their babies. Now Baby Seal had found his mother.

Which one is right? Put a ✔ by it.

1. This story is about a seal

_____ a. looking for its home.

_____ b. looking for its mother.

_____ c. looking for a hunter.

2. What are baby seals called?

_____ a. pups

_____ b. kids

_____ c. kittens

3. What noise do seals make?

_____ a. mew   _____ b. bark   _____ c. moo

4. Which one came first?

_____ a. Baby Seal found his mother.

_____ b. A seal said, "You are not my pup."

_____ c. Baby Seal began to cry.

5. Why did Baby Seal cry?

_____ a. He wanted to go to sleep.

_____ b. He fell into the cold water.

_____ c. He wanted to be with his mother.

6. How do mother seals know their babies?

_____ a. by their smell

_____ b. by their look

_____ c. by their cry

Draw lines to match these.

1. baby seal or dog

2. takes care of her children

3. something seals sit on

4. not here

5. a very little child

6. made a dog noise

7. move in the water

8. tell with your nose

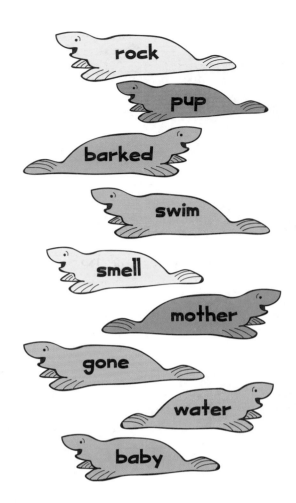

rock

pup

barked

swim

smell

mother

gone

water

baby

Every sentence has a mark at the end that says "Stop!"
A sentence that **asks** you something has **?** at the end.
A sentence that **tells** you something has **.** at the end.
Put **?** or **.** at the end of each sentence.

1. What did the seals find in the sea

2. Is the water cold

3. The seals barked

4. Is the rock too big to pick up

5. Seals can smell each other

6. Could they see any seals

7. Who began to cry

8. Did they eat many fish

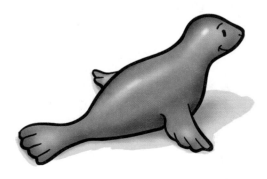

a. **Zoo Animals**

b. **Plants to Grow**

c. **Work We Do**

Look at the three books. Which book would you use to find out about each thing? Write a letter in each box. The first one is done for you.

b	1. flowers that grow fast
	2. how to put out fires
	3. animals that live in water
	4. tigers and monkeys
	5. little trees
	6. cleaning the streets
	7. building a house
	8. seeds of many kinds
	9. working on cars
	10. animals that can fly

Found at the Pond

One afternoon Roy and Rosa were at the pond. Rosa saw something on a water plant. She said, "Here is something funny. What can it be, Roy?"

The thing looked like jelly. It had little black spots in it.

The children put the thing into a big jar with water. They took it home. They watched it every day.

After six days, tadpoles came out of the eggs. They had long tails.

Soon back legs began to come out. The tails got shorter.

Then front legs began to come out. The tails got even shorter.

All four legs got big. The tails were gone!

Rosa said, "Now I know. I found frog eggs. Tadpoles came out of the eggs. Tadpoles are baby frogs!"

Which one is right? Put a ✔ by it.

1. Who found something?

_____ a. a girl   _____ b. a boy   _____ c. a frog

2. Where did they see something funny?

_____ a. in the water

_____ b. in the sand

_____ c. on a shelf

3. What is a tadpole?

_____ a. a baby fish

_____ b. a little duck

_____ c. a little frog

4. What looked like jelly?

_____ a. tadpoles _____ b. frogs _____ c. eggs

5. What came out first?

_____ a. front legs

_____ b. back legs

_____ c. boots

6. What happened to the tadpole?

_____ a. Its tail got very big.

_____ b. It became an egg.

_____ c. It became a frog.

7. What is the best name for this story?

_____ a. What the Frog Found

_____ b. What Rosa Found

_____ c. A Bad Frog

Draw lines to match these.

1. something to hold water

2. the opposite of back

3. used to walk

4. something on
the back of animals

5. not as long

6. something to eat on bread

When?
Where? Go for a hop with the frog. Put a ✓ on the ones
that tell **when**. Put an **X** on the ones that tell **where**.

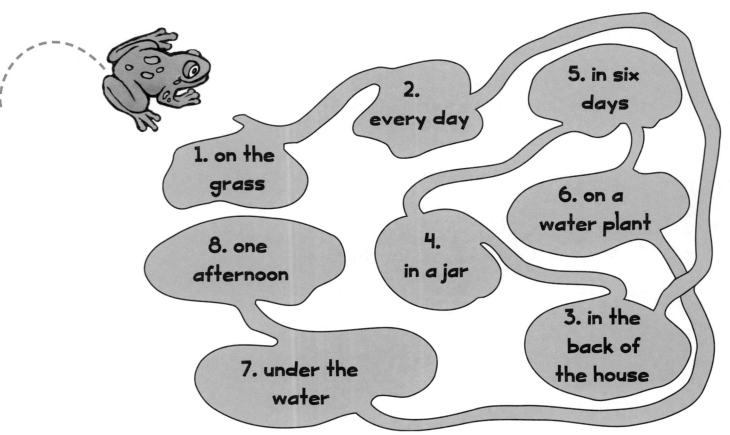

Fun time! Read the sentence. Finish it. Circle the right picture.

1. Roy put the funny thing in a _____.

a.

b.

c.

2. They found eggs in the _____.

a.

b.

c.

3. A front door is found on a _____.

a.

b.

c.

4. Roy and Rosa found something that looks like _____.

a.

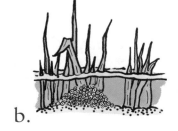
b.

c.

Foxes Looking for Food

One afternoon, a mother fox was out looking for food. Her two little foxes were with her. They saw some ducks in the pond.

Fred Fox said, "I like to eat duck. I wish we could catch one."

Mother Fox said, "We can't catch ducks in the water. They can swim too fast."

The foxes hid in the tall grass. They watched the ducks playing in the pond. At last, eight ducks came out on the land.

Mother Fox said, "Now we can catch a duck. Ducks don't walk fast."

"I'll grab that first duck," said Fran Fox.

"I'll grab that last duck," said Fred Fox.

Mother Fox said, "Wait until they get near us. Ready? Go!" The foxes jumped out of the grass.

As quick as can be, the ducks got away. Did they run away? No! Did they swim away? No! The ducks flew away!

Mother Fox said, "I forgot that ducks have wings. Now we have nothing to eat!"

Which one is right? Put a ✓ by it.

1. Which one happened first?

_____ a. The foxes jumped at the ducks.

_____ b. The ducks came out of the water.

_____ c. The ducks got away.

2. Where did the ducks play?

_____ a. in the pond

_____ b. in the barn

_____ c. in the yard

3. Why did the foxes wait before jumping?

_____ a. They wanted to surprise the ducks.

_____ b. They wanted some help.

_____ c. They wanted Mother Fox to rest.

4. How did the ducks get away?

_____ a. by walking fast

_____ b. by jumping in the pond

_____ c. by flying away

5. What helps a duck fly?

_____ a. feet

_____ b. water

_____ c. wings

6. What is the best name for this story?

_____ a. A Good Dinner for the Foxes

_____ b. No Dinner for the Foxes

_____ c. Fred Fox Gets a Duck

Draw lines to match these.

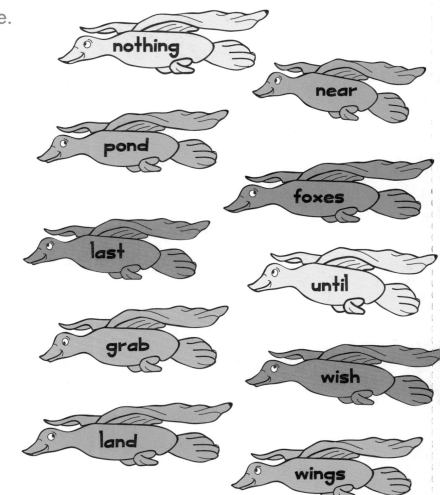

1. not far

2. take away fast

3. not anything

4. water to swim in

5. animals

6. to want

7. up to the time of

8. help birds fly

9. ground

A sentence that tells something ends with **.**
A sentence that asks something ends with **?**.
Put **.** or **?** at the end of each sentence.

1. Are you ready to catch a duck

2. The foxes hid in the grass

3. The ducks played in the pond

4. Can foxes catch ducks in the water

5. Did the ducks run away

6. The ducks did not swim away

7. Do ducks have wings

8. Why did the ducks fly away

9. How many ducks did the foxes grab

Find the sentence that means the
same as the first one. Put a ✔ by it.

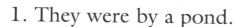

1. They were by a pond.

_____ a. They were near a fence.

_____ b. They were near the water.

_____ c. They were near the tall grass.

2. Fran walked last.

_____ a. Fran was in the middle.

_____ b. Fran was in back.

_____ c. Fran was first.

Find the sentence that goes with each picture.
Put the right letter under the picture.

1. _____ 2. _____ 3. _____

a. A duck's feet can push the water.
b. Birds use them to fly.
c. This animal likes to eat ducks.
d. The ducks fly over the pond.

The Best Food

One afternoon Mrs. Giraffe went to the water hole. She went to get a drink. Baby Giraffe did not want to go with her mother.

Mrs. Giraffe said, "Stay here, Baby Pat, and do not go away."

Soon Pat wanted something good to eat. She forgot what her mom told her.

She walked into the tall grass. She saw a fat worm.

Pat wanted to eat the worm. But Pat was too tall. The worm crawled away.

Next Pat saw a little bird on a nest.

"That looks good to eat," said Pat as she bent her long neck to reach the tiny animal.

Surprise! Little birds have wings. The bird flew away. Baby Pat said, "Birds are too fast for me."

She lifted her long neck. Pretty green leaves were right by her mouth. Her mouth opened, and Pat ate the leaves.

Dad Giraffe came by. "Good for you!" he said. "You have found the best food for giraffes. You found it by yourself."

Which one is right? Put a ✔ by it.

1. Which one happened first?

    _____ a. The worm crawled away.

    _____ b. The giraffe saw a worm.

    _____ c. The giraffe ate some leaves.

2. Where did Mom Giraffe go?

    _____ a. to the water hole

    _____ b. to the big tree

    _____ c. to see the bird in the nest

3. Why are leaves the best food for giraffes to eat?

    _____ a. The leaves are pretty and are by the water hole.

    _____ b. Long necks help giraffes reach leaves on tall trees.

    _____ c. Giraffes can reach down to little animals under the grass.

4. What words tell about giraffes?

    _____ a. long necks, long legs, wings

    _____ b. short back legs, short tail, long fat neck

    _____ c. long legs, long neck, spots on fur

5. What is the best name for this story?

    _____ a. Dad at the Water Hole

    _____ b. A Giraffe Helps Herself

    _____ c. Mom Giraffe Finds a Drink

Draw lines to match these.

1. to get up to something

2. very little

3. where to put food

4. to take away fast

5. to move on hands and feet

6. picked up

7. look at something
   for a long time

8. the thing under your head

9. what we do with milk

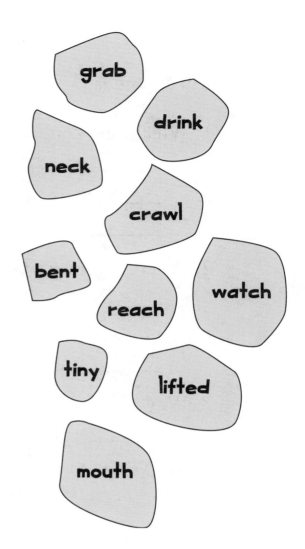

grab

drink

neck

crawl

bent

watch

reach

tiny

lifted

mouth

Do the animals eat plants or meat? If they eat other animals, they are meat eaters. Write **plants** next to the plant eaters. Write **meat** next to the meat eaters.

1. _____

2. _____

3.  _____

4.  _____

Find the sentence that means the same as the first one. Put a ✔ by it.

1. Ray can reach the shelf.

_____ a. He can play with it.

_____ b. He can get to it.

_____ c. He cannot get to it.

2. Baby Giraffe walked in front of the others.

_____ a. She was in the middle.

_____ b. She was the first.

_____ c. She was in back.

3. They lifted a frog.

_____ a. They saw an animal.

_____ b. They picked up an animal.

_____ c. They put down an animal.

Put a ✔ by the words that tell **where**.
Put an **X** by the words that tell **when**.

1. _____ that evening

2. _____ into her pouch

3. _____ before dinner

4. _____ on the leaves

5. _____ on the grass

6. _____ after school

7. _____ all day

8. _____ under the nest

A Bird That Lives on Ice

Look at this animal.
Its feathers look like
a black-and-white suit.
It walks on two feet.
It has a bill.
It cannot fly, but it swims.
Its flippers help it swim.
It is a penguin, a bird
that lives on ice.

It was a dark, cold winter day. Many penguins left the water and met on the ice. The penguins made a lot of noise. They called to each other.

Mr. Penguin called to Mrs. Penguin. Mrs. Penguin heard his voice. They met and walked.

After several days, Mrs. Penguin laid one egg on the ice. It was time to make a nest for the baby penguin egg.

Mr. Penguin rolled the egg onto his two feet. His stomach feathers covered the egg and kept it warm.

Soon Mrs. Penguin called, "Good-bye!" She and the other mother penguins went into the sea. They went to eat fish.

The dads stayed on the ice to care for the eggs. They kept the eggs warm for many weeks. They ate nothing. They got very skinny.

One day, the father penguins were talking.

"Where are the mothers?" one penguin asked. "It's time for the eggs to open."

Another penguin said, "I hope they are safe."

Surprise! The next day, the eggs started to open. The little baby penguins began to make noise. The dads were happy.

But where were the mother penguins?

Which one is right? Put a ✓ by it.

1. Where did Mr. Penguin keep his egg?

_____ a. in the mud

_____ b. on his feet

_____ c. on his bill

2. When did the mother penguins go away?

_____ a. after the babies came

out of the eggs

_____ b. before they laid the eggs

_____ c. after they laid the eggs

3. While the father penguins held their eggs, when did they eat?

_____ a. when it was dark

_____ b. never

_____ c. when they had an egg sitter

4. Where were the mother penguins?

_____ a. getting food from the sea

_____ b. getting skinny

_____ c. at the store getting food

5. What is a good name for this story?

_____ a. A Funny Nest

_____ b. A Nest in a Tree

_____ c. Mother Penguin

Sits on the Eggs

6. When did the penguins meet on the ice?

    _____ a. in the winter

    _____ b. never

    _____ c. when it was warm

7. What is something penguins never do?

    _____ a. swim

    _____ b. make noises

    _____ c. fly

8. What animals eat penguins?

    _____ a. horses

    _____ b. sharks

    _____ c. cows

Draw lines to match these. One is done for you.

1. what your ears did

2. something to put on

3. something very cold

4. very thin

5. what you hear when
   someone talks

6. what covers all birds

7. more than two

8. where food goes when you eat

ice

stomach

feathers

voice

heard

each

suit

skinny

several

What happened first? Next? Last? Put **1**, **2**, and **3** in the boxes.

□   Mr. Penguin kept the egg warm.

□   The egg began to open.

□   Mrs. Penguin laid an egg.

Circle the right word. One is done for you.

1. The two penguins | men / (met) | there.

2. I heard her | very / voice | .

3. Penguins' feathers look like a | seven / suit | .

4. One egg was laid by | each / reach | bird.

5. The eggs must be | worm / warm | .

6. All birds have feathers and | bills / pills | .

Surprise!

Surprise! The baby penguins came out of the eggs. Another surprise! The same day, the mother penguins came back from the sea. They were fat from eating many fish. They came back to care for the baby penguins.

Mrs. Penguin saw all the dads and baby penguins. They were all making noise. But Mrs. Penguin knew Mr. Penguin's voice. She walked right to him.

Mr. Penguin said, "Meet our new little girl, Penny."

"Oh," said Mrs. Penguin. "What a pretty little baby she is!"

Baby Penny was hungry. Hungry penguin babies peck on their parents' bills. Then the parents put food in the babies' mouths. Mrs. Penguin fed Baby Penny.

"I'm very hungry too," said Mr. Penguin. "Now it's my turn to eat."

"We are too," said all the father penguins. They waved their skinny flippers and said, "Good-bye." They all went into the water to find food.

For two weeks, Mr. Penguin and all the father penguins ate fish. They ate fish night and day. They ate fish heads, fish tails, fish fins, and fish gills. They got round and fat. Their stomachs were full.

Then the fathers were ready to swim home. They were ready to help care for the baby penguins.

A shark saw fat Mr. Penguin swimming home. The shark followed Mr. Penguin.

Mr. Penguin moved down, down into the deep water. The shark went swimming after him.

Quick as a flash, Mr. Penguin zoomed up, up. His flippers moved as fast as the wind.

He rolled onto his stomach. He slid through the water right up to the icy shore.

The hungry shark's mouth opened. He reached for Mr. Penguin's tail feathers. The shark was unlucky. Mr. Penguin, quick as a flash, slid out of the water. He zoomed over the ice on his stomach.

He heard Mrs. Penguin's voice. He heard Baby Penny's voice. He slid right over to them.

Which one is right? Put a ✔ by it.

1. How was Mrs. Penguin different when she came back?

_____ a. She was round and fat.

_____ b. She was very skinny.

_____ c. She was hungry.

2. When did Mr. Penguin go to eat?

_____ a. the week before the egg opened

_____ b. when the egg was on his feet

_____ c. after the egg opened

3. Why did Mr. Penguin go away from Mrs. Penguin?

_____ a. He wanted to play.

_____ b. He needed a new suit.

_____ c. He needed food.

4. Why do you think Mr. Penguin slid on his stomach?

_____ a. His feet hurt.

_____ b. It was quicker than walking on ice.

_____ c. It was the only way he could move.

5. What is the best name for this story?

_____ a. Penny Gets Away from a Shark

_____ b. The Baby Penguin Turns Around

_____ c. Mr. and Mrs. Penguin Take Turns

Write the word to complete the sentence.
Use the words in the box.

| flippers | parents | waved |
| followed | another | |

1. The baby _____ his parents.

2. Penguins swim with their _____ .

3. The moms _____ good-bye.

4. Your mom and dad are your _____ .

Read the sentences. Put an **X** next to ones that are **not** right. Put a ✓ next to the ones that are right.

_____ 1.　　Penguins have warm fur.

_____ 2.　　Mother penguins keep the eggs on their feet.

_____ 3.　　The parents take turns helping the baby.

_____ 4.　　Penguins fly quickly.

_____ 5.　　Penguins' feathers are black-and-white.

_____ 6.　　The penguin slid on his stomach
　　　　　　　　quick as a flash.

Here is a penguin. Draw a line from each word to its picture.

1. bill

3. stomach

5. feet

2. head

4. flipper

6. tail

Circle the right word.

1. The penguins waved their ⬚ flippers / followed .

2. Mrs. Penguin did not come back the ⬚ some / same day.

3. Penguins swim quick as a ⬚ feather / flash .

4. Fish have ⬚ gills / bills .

Reading Roundup

Four leaves are on each tree. Put the number of each word on the right tree. The first one is done for you.

ANIMALS   PLACES   NUMBERS

1. sea   2. kangaroo   3. pond
4. giraffe   5. five   6. eight
7. six   8. seal   9. school
10. ten   11. bird   12. doghouse

Draw lines to match these.

1. to pick up

2. to get to it

3. not as long

4. one who works with you

5. up to the time of

6. made a dog noise

7. a baby frog

until

reach

crawl

helper   barked

lift

shorter

tadpole

What do you know about foxes and seals?

1. Circle the fox's nose.
2. Put a ✔ on the seal's nose.

Circle **yes** or **no**.

1. Does a kangaroo have two ears?	**yes**	**no**
2. Can a tadpole push a car?	**yes**	**no**
3. Will a fox eat a bird?	**yes**	**no**
4. Do giraffes have wings?	**yes**	**no**
5. Do giraffes have long necks?	**yes**	**no**
6. Will a seal eat a fish?	**yes**	**no**
7. Can a seal fly?	**yes**	**no**
8. Do tadpoles have tails?	**yes**	**no**
9. Can a seal swim?	**yes**	**no**
10. Do seals read fast?	**yes**	**no**

Put **?** or **.** at the end of each sentence.

1. How did the purple flower get there
2. What hopped on two big back feet
3. Are the front legs shorter
4. Ray found his lunchbox at school
5. Did the seals eat many fish
6. Baby Seal could smell his mother
7. The giraffe reaches leaves with its long neck

Can you do this?

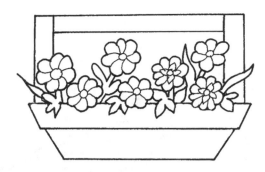

1. Color six flowers purple. Color the other one red.

2. Sara and Dad worked until five o'clock. Show this time on the clock.

3. Here is Ray's coat. Put four green buttons on it.

4. Mother Fox and her little foxes are looking for food. Color the two little foxes brown. Color Mother Fox red.

Put the words that tell **when** in the **WHEN?** box. Put the words that tell **where** in the **WHERE?** box. Draw lines to the right box.

1. at school

2. in the pond

3. long ago

4. in the winter

5. now

6. on the sofa

7. one day

8. next to me

9. after lunch

10. by the sea

WHERE?

WHEN?

Find the sentence that means the same as the first one. Put a ✔ by it.

1. We hunted for the toy.

    _____ a. We played with the toy.

    _____ b. We looked for the toy.

2. Rosa is shorter than Roy.

    _____ a. Rosa is not as tall as Roy.

    _____ b. Rosa is bigger than Roy.

3. The worm crawled to the rock.

    _____ a. The worm reached the rock.

    _____ b. The worm dropped the rock.

Circle the right word.

1. Mother Seal went back to the rock.
   She wanted to _____ for her baby.

   car   care   can

2. Mother frogs lay eggs. Then they go away.
   They _____ see the tadpoles come out.

   ever   every   never

3. Mother came in and found a _____.
   Black spots were on the sofa. Mother saw
   the cat's feet. She knew where the spots came from.

              surprise   nothing   something

Spelling
Skills

spelling strategies

What can you do when you aren't sure how to spell a word?

Say the word aloud. Make sure you say it correctly. Listen to the sounds in the word. Think about letters for the sounds.

Guess the spelling of the word and check it in a dictionary.

Write the word in different ways. Choose the spelling that looks correct.

rad   rid   (red)

Draw the shape of the word to help you remember its spelling.

c o l d

Choose a rhyming helper and use it. A rhyming helper is a word that rhymes with the word and is spelled like it.

cat—mat

Create a memory clue to help you remember the spelling.

The tree is by the street.

STUDY STEPS TO LEARN A WORD

Use the steps on this page to study words that are hard for you.

1 **Say** the word.
What sounds do you hear?

2 **Look** at the letters in the word.
Think about how each sound is spelled.
Close your eyes.
Picture the word in your mind.

3 **Spell** the word aloud.

4 **Write** the word.
Say each letter as you write it.

5 **Check** the spelling.
If you did not spell the word correctly,
use the study steps again.

m, d, f, g

Mouse begins with the m sound.
Write m if the picture name begins
with the m sound.

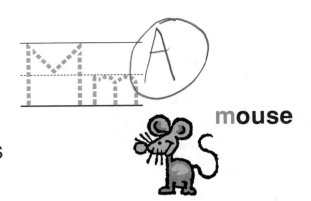

mouse

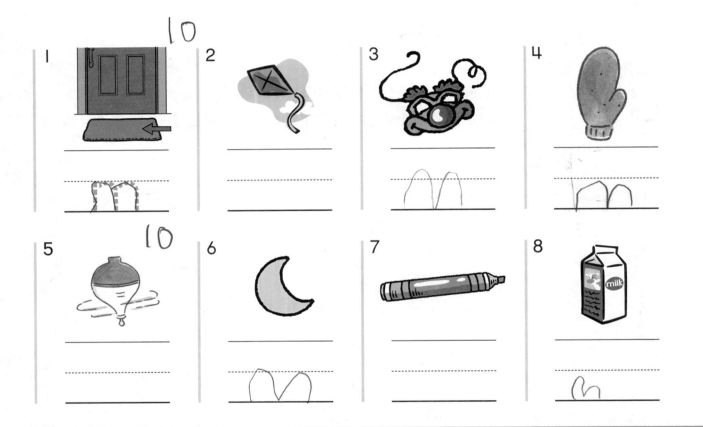

1. 10

2.

3.

4.

5. 10

6.

7.

8.

Possum ends with the m sound. Write m if
the picture name ends with the m sound.

possum

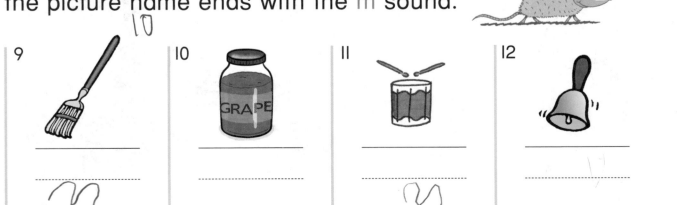

9. 10

10.

11.

12.

Dog begins with the d sound.
Write d if the picture name
begins with the d sound.

dog

1. dad
2. duck
3. _ig
4. doll

5. desk
6. door
7. dig
8. _un

Bed ends with the d sound. Write d if the
picture name ends with the d sound.

bed

9. lid
10. sad
11. ca_
12. food

Fan begins with the f sound.
Write f if the picture name
begins with the f sound.

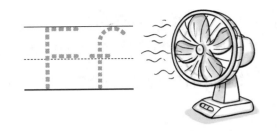

fan

1 *10*

f

2

f

3

4

f

5 *10*

6

f

7

f

8

Leaf ends with the f sound. Write f if the
picture name ends with the f sound.

leaf

9 *10*

10

f

11

f

12

f

Gum begins with the g sound.
Write g if the picture name
begins with the g sound.

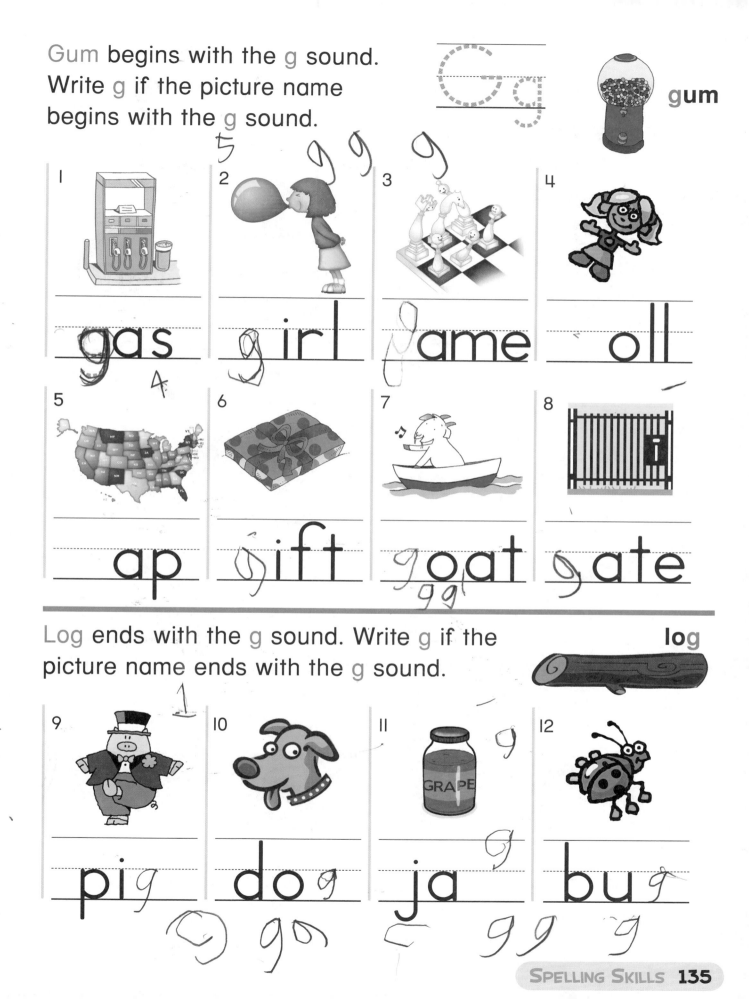

gum

1. gas
2. girl
3. game
4. oll
5. ap
6. gift
7. goat
8. gate

Log ends with the g sound. Write g if the picture name ends with the g sound.

log

9. pig
10. dog
11. jag
12. bug

b, t, s, w

Bell begins with the b sound.
Write b if the picture name begins
with the b sound.

bell

1

_b_

2

3

4

5

6

7

8

Tub ends with the b sound. Write b if the
picture name ends with the b sound.

tub

9

10

11

12

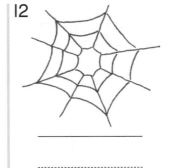

Ten begins with the t sound.
Write t if the picture name
begins with the t sound.

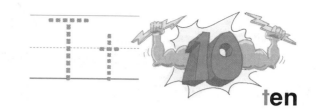

ten

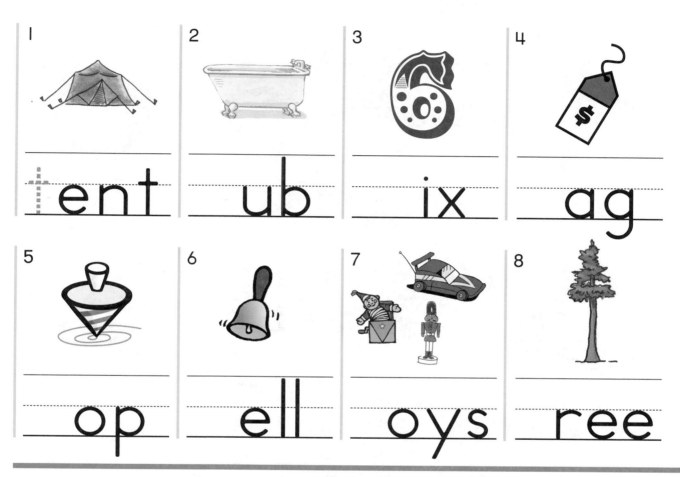

1	2	3	4
__t__ent	___ub	___ix	___ag

5	6	7	8
___op	___ell	___oys	___ree

Net ends with the t sound. Write t if the
picture name ends with the t sound.

net

9	10	11	12
ra___	nu___	do___	ba___

Sun begins with the s sound.
Write s if the picture name
begins with the s sound.

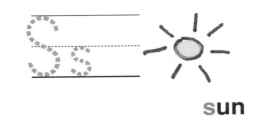

sun

1

_____
s

2

_____

3

_____

4

_____

5

_____

6

_____

7

_____

8

_____

Bus ends with the s sound. Write s if the
picture name ends with the s sound.

bus

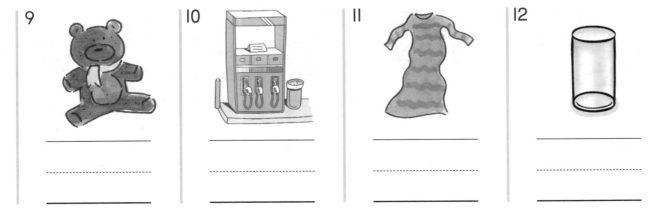

9

_____

10

_____

11

_____

12

_____

Wig begins with the w sound.
Write w if the picture name
begins with the w sound.

wig

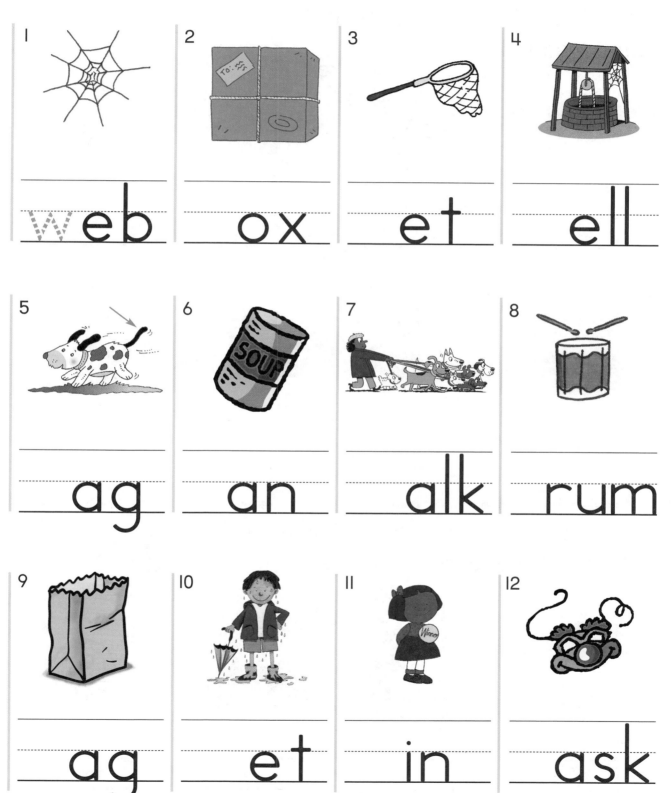

1	2	3	4
__w__eb	___ox	___et	___ell

5	6	7	8
___ag	___an	___alk	___rum

9	10	11	12
___ag	___et	___in	___ask

k, j, p, n

Key begins with the k sound.
Write k if the picture name begins
with the k sound.

key

1

k

2

k

3
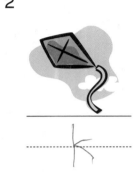

4

k

5

k

6

7

8
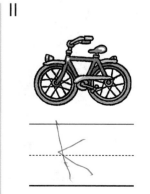

k

Book ends with the k sound. Write k if the
picture name ends with the k sound.

 **book**

9
k

10
k

11
k

12

Jam begins with the j sound.
Write j if the picture name
begins with the j sound.

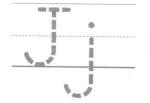  **j**am

1	2	3	4
jar	**M**ap	**J**une	**B**ird

5	6	7	8
Box	**M**ug	**S**ip	**j**ump

9	10	11	12
jog	**N**et	**j**eep	**B**at

Pan begins with the p sound.
Write p if the picture name
begins with the p sound.

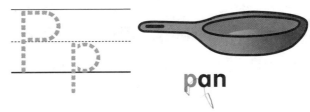

pan

1. p

2. P

3. S

4. P

5. P

6. G

7. P

8. P

Cup ends with the p sound. Write p if the
picture name ends with the p sound.

cup

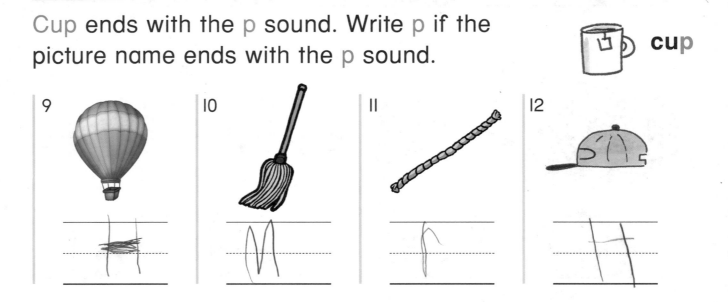

9.

10. M

11.

12.

Nut begins with the n sound.
Write n if the picture name
begins with the n sound.

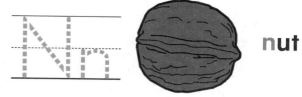

nut

1	2	3	4

net · nap · nail · nub

cat · note · nest · nose

Can ends with the n sound. Write n if the
picture name ends with the n sound.

can

9	10	11	12

fan · run · sun · cat

c, h, l, r

Cat begins with the c sound.
Write c if the picture name begins
with the c sound.

cat

1	2	3	4
c	B	C	C

5	6	7	8
C	C	S	C

9	10	11	12
B	C	C	J

Hat begins with the h sound.
Write h if the picture name
begins with the h sound.

hat

1	2	3	4

Home Hen Shoe Hand

5	6	7	8

Hurt Mole Hop Hook

9	10	11	12

___it ___ill ___orn ___ish

Lamp begins with the l sound.
Write l if the picture name begins
with the l sound. (A+)

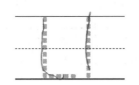

lamp

1	2	3	4

5	6	7	8

Snail ends with the l sound. Write l if
the picture name ends with the l sound.

10

snail

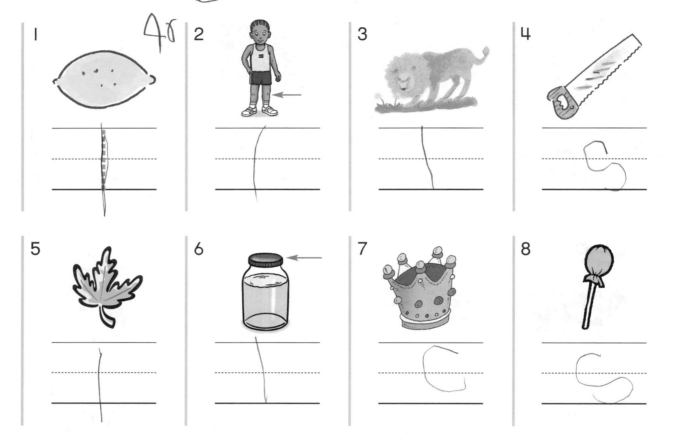

9	10	11	12

Rug begins with the r sound.
Write r if the picture name
begins with the r sound.

rug

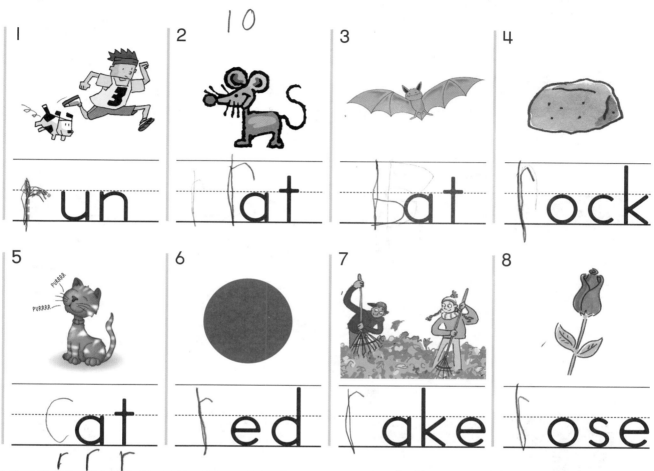

1	2 *10*	3	4
r̲un	̲at	̲bat	̲ock
5	6	7	8
̲Cat	̲red	̲ake	̲ose

Car ends with the r sound. Write r if the
picture name ends with the r sound.

car

9	10	11	12
ja̲	drum̲	sta̲r	fou̲

v, y, z, qu, x

Vest begins with the v sound.
Write v if the picture name begins
with the v sound.

vest

1
_____
~~v~~

2
_____
_____

3
_____
_____

4
_____
_____

5
_____
_____

6
_____
_____

7
_____
_____

8
_____
_____

9
_____
_____

10
_____
_____

11
_____
_____

12
_____
_____

Yam begins with the y sound.
Write y if the picture name
begins with the y sound.

yam

1	2	3	4
yo-yo	at	arn	alt

5	6	7	8
ard	ag	olk	ig

9	10	11	12
og	awn	ift	ellow

Zip begins with the z sound. Write
z if the picture name
begins with the z sound.

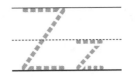

zip

1

2

3

4

5

6

7

8

Flash Kids
120 Fifth Ave.
New York, NY 10011

9

10

11

12

Quilt begins with the qu sound.
Write qu if the picture name
begins with the qu sound.

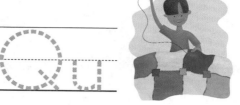

quilt

1	2	3

qu een   ___ og   ___ art

4	5	6

___ est   ___ ack   ___ ail

Six ends with the x sound. Write x if
the picture name ends with the x sound.

 six

7	8	9	10

bu ___   bo ___   mi ___   a ___

Write the letter that stands for the first sound in each picture name.

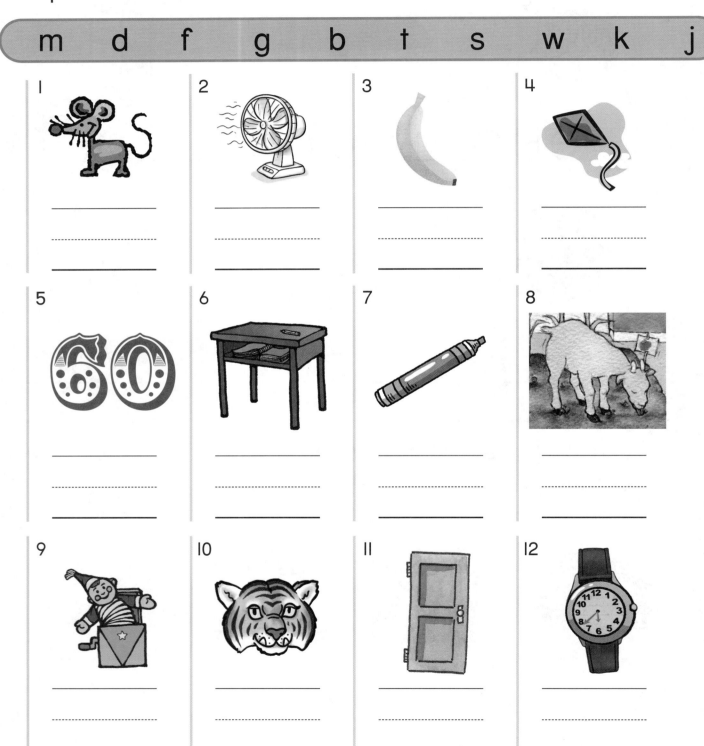

m d f g b t s w k j

1

2

3

4

5

6

7

8

9

10

11

12

Write the missing letter or letters to complete each word.

m d h s w qu t n
v g p r x y z c

1 
ca

2 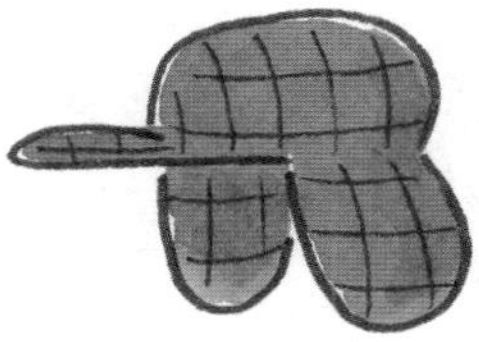
at

3 
up

4 
ba

5 
ig

6 
bo

7 
an

8 
ba

9 
un

10 
ie

11 
arn

12 
te

13 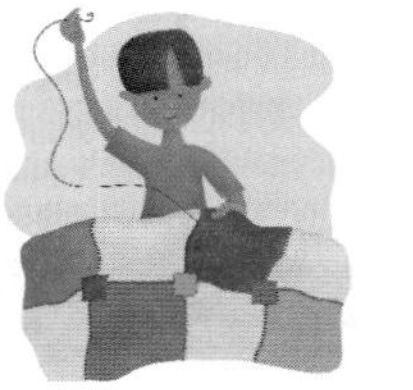
ilt

14 
ero

15 
ing

16 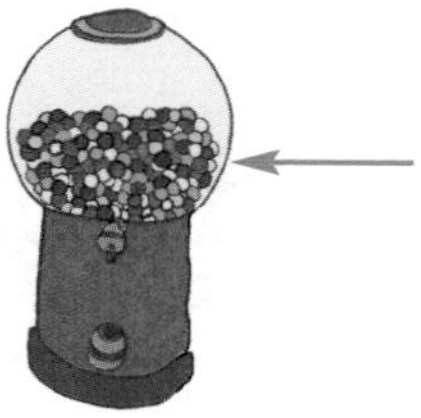
gu

Short a

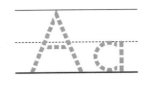

cat

Cat has the short a sound.
Say each picture name.
Write a if you hear the short a sound.

1 _____
   a

2 _____
   _____

3 _____
   _____

4 _____
   _____

5 _____
   _____

6 _____
   _____

7 _____
   _____

8 _____
   _____

9 _____
   _____

10 _____
   _____

11 _____
   _____

12 _____
   _____

Say each picture name.
Write a if you hear the short a sound.
Color each short a picture.

1 h a m

2 p _ n

3 c _ p

4 m _ p

5 b _ x

6 b _ g

7 p _ g

8 h _ t

9 m _ t

Say the word that names the first picture.
Circle the pictures whose names rhyme with the word.

1   **pan**

2   **bag**

3   **cat**

4   **cap**

5   **sad**

Say each picture name. Trace the first letter.
Then write an to make the word.

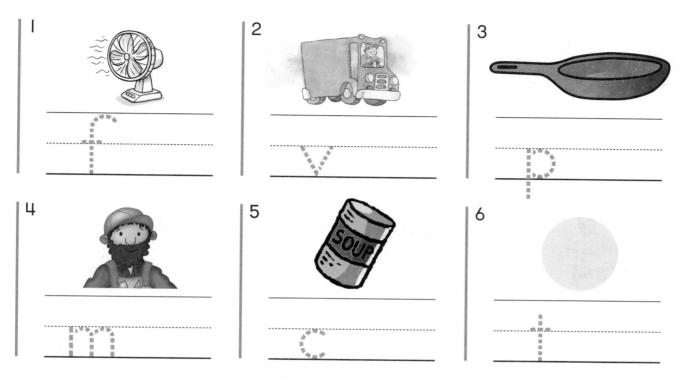

1. f ___
2. v ___
3. p ___
4. m ___
5. c ___
6. t ___

Say each picture name. Trace the first letter.
Then write at to make the word.

7. b ___
8. c ___
9. h ___
10. m ___
11. r ___

Short e

Bed has the short e sound.
Say each picture name.
Write e if you hear the short e sound.

bed

1

_____

_ _ _e_ _ _

2

_____

_____

3

_____

_____

4

_____

_____

5

_____

_____

6

_____

_____

7

_____

_____

8

_____

_____

9

_____

_____

10

_____

_____

11

_____

_____

12

_____

_____

Say each picture name.
Write e if you hear the short e sound.
Color each short e picture.

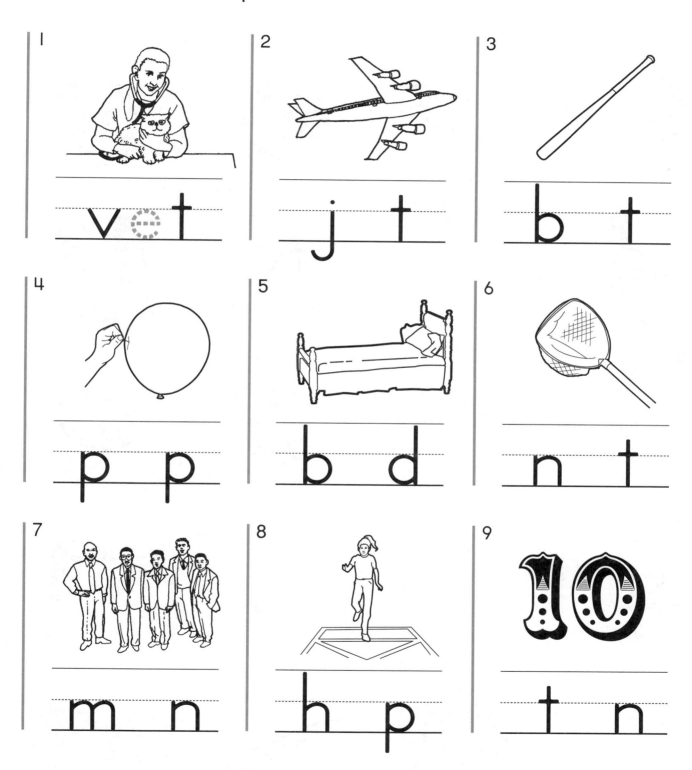

1. v e t

2. j _ t

3. b _ t

4. p _ p

5. b _ d

6. n _ t

7. m _ n

8. h _ p

9. t _ n

word that names the first picture.

the pictures whose names rhyme with the word.

1 **bed**

2 **bell**

3 **leg**

4 **vet**

5 **hen**

Say each picture name. Trace the first letter or letters.
Then write ell to make the word.

1

b_____

2

s_____

3

sh_____

4

w_____

5

sm_____

Say each picture name. Trace the first letter.
Then write en to make the word.

6

h_____

7

m_____

8

t_____

Short i

Pig has the short i sound.
Say each picture name.
Write i if you hear the short i sound.

pig

1

2

3

4

5

6

7

8

9

10

11

12

Say each picture name.
Write i if you hear the short i sound.
Color each short i picture.

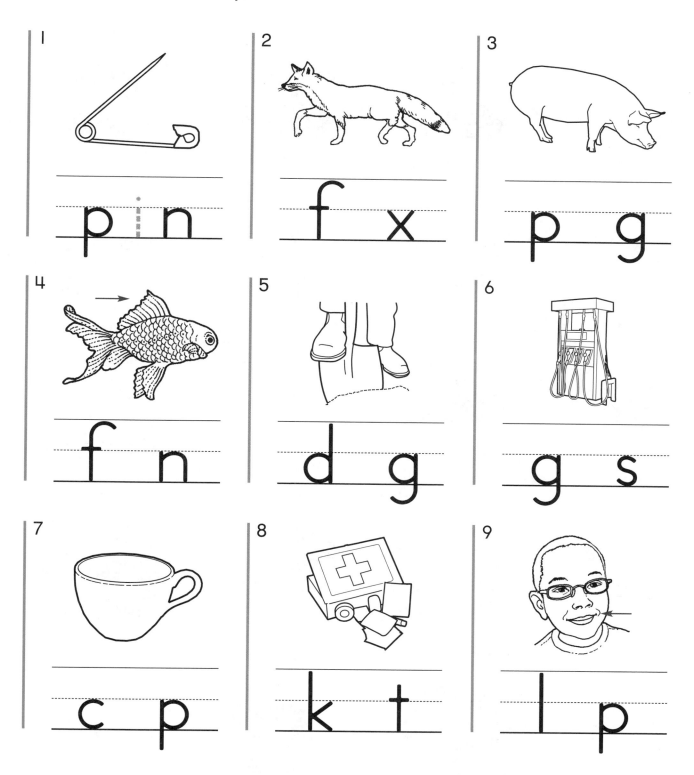

1   p i n

2   f _ x

3   p _ g

4   f _ n

5   d _ g

6   g _ s

7   c _ p

8   k _ t

9   l _ p

Say the word that names the first picture.
Circle the pictures whose names rhyme with the word.

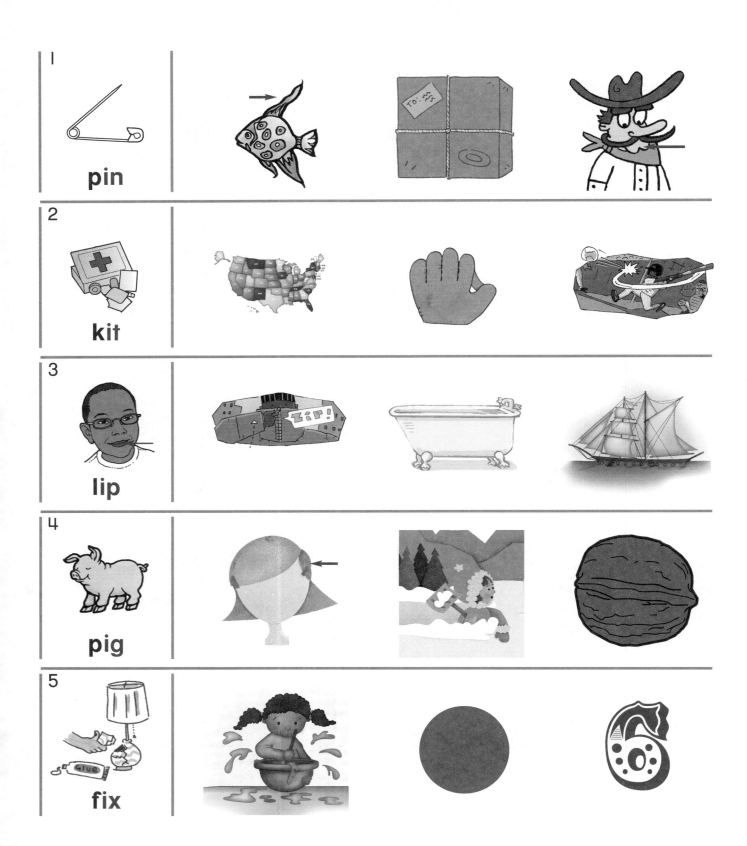

1 pin

2 kit

3 lip

4 pig

5 fix

Say each picture name. Trace the first letter.
Then write it to make the word.

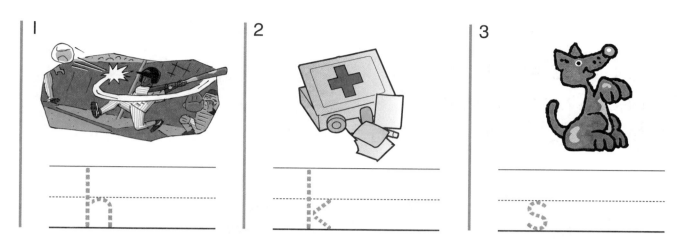

1
h _ _

2
k _ _

3
s _ _

Say each picture name. Trace the first letter.
Then write ig to make the word.

4
d _ _

5
p _ _

6
w _ _

7
b _ _

Short o

Pop has the short o sound.
Say each picture name.
Write o if you hear the short o sound.

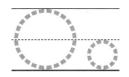

pop

1

_____
- - - - - - - - -

2

_____
- - - - - - - - -

3

_____
- - - - - - - - -

4

_____
- - - - - - - - -

5

_____
- - - - - - - - -

6

_____
- - - - - - - - -

7

_____
- - - - - - - - -

8

_____
- - - - - - - - -

9

_____
- - - - - - - - -

10

_____
- - - - - - - - -

11

_____
- - - - - - - - -

12

_____
- - - - - - - - -

Say each picture name.
Write o if you hear the short o sound.
Color each short o picture.

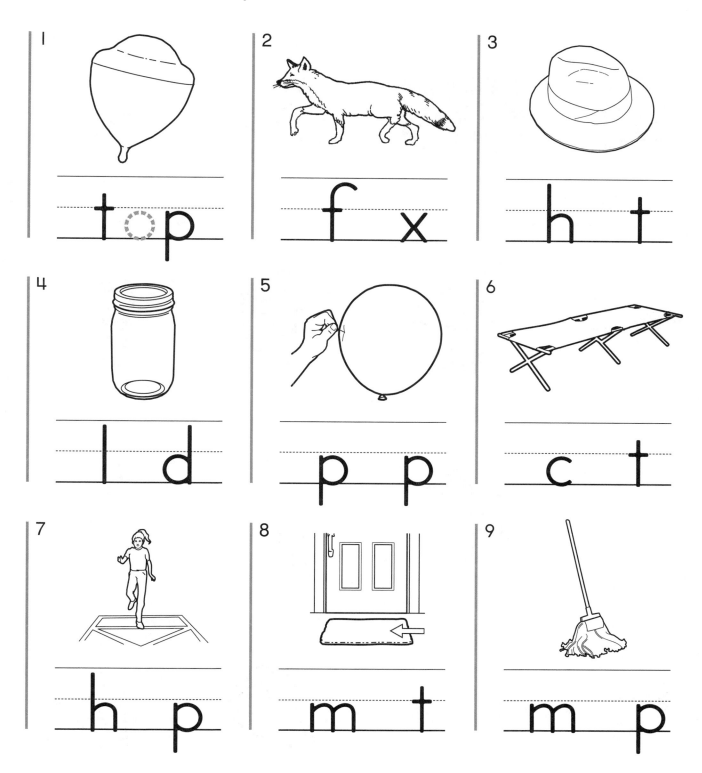

1   t __ p

2   f __ x

3   h __ t

4   l __ d

5   p __ p

6   c __ t

7   h __ p

8   m __ t

9   m __ p

Say the word that names the first picture.
Circle the pictures whose names rhyme with the word.

1 hot

2 fox

3 pop

4 sock

Say each picture name. Trace the first letter.
Then write op to make the word.

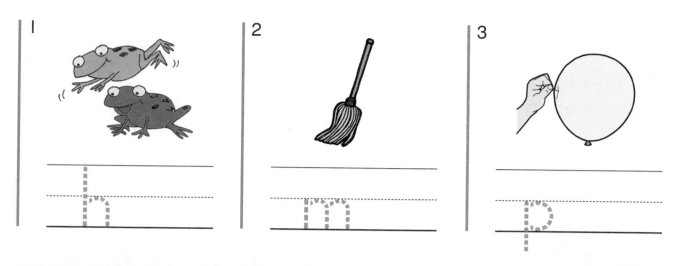

1

h

2

m

3

p

Say each picture name. Trace the first letter or letters.
Then write ot to make the word.

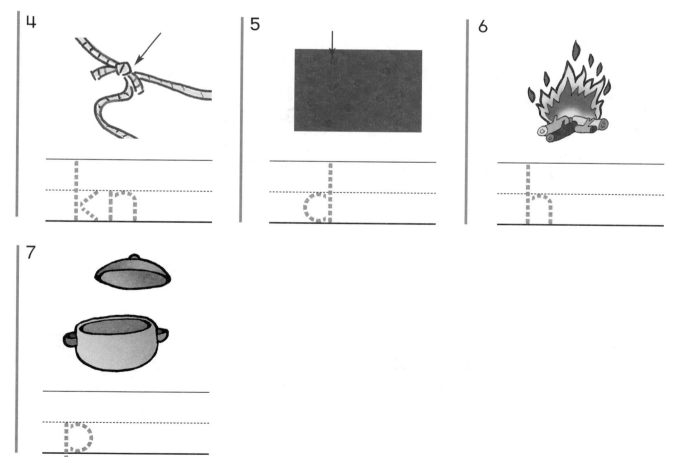

4

kn

5

d

6

h

7

p

Short u

cup

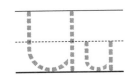

Cup has the short u sound.
Say each picture name.
Write u if you hear the short u sound.

1	2	3	4
___ u	___ ___	___ ___	___ ___

5	6	7	8
___ ___	___ ___	___ ___	___ ___

9	10	11	12
___ ___	___ ___	___ ___	___ ___

Say each picture name.
Write u if you hear the short u sound.
Color each short u picture.

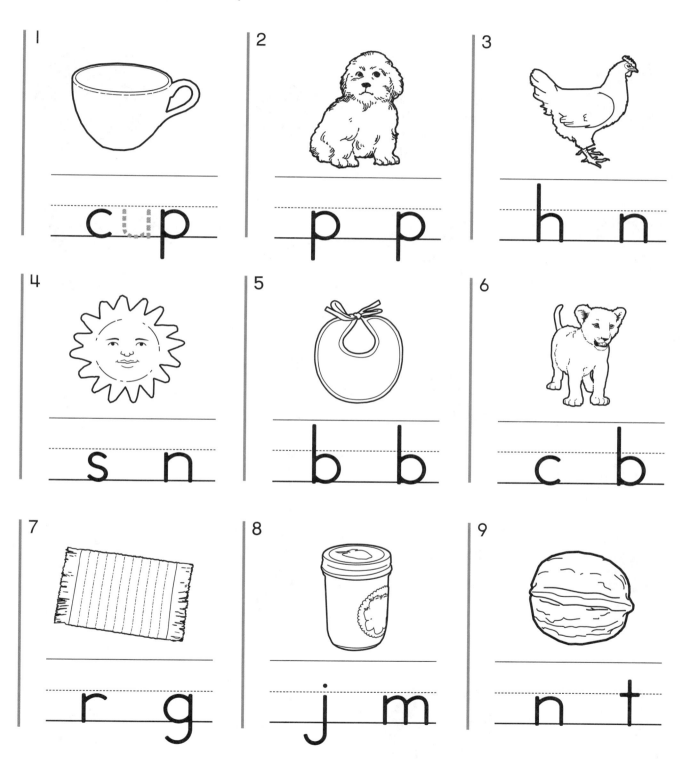

1 c u p

2 p __ p

3 h __ n

4 s __ n

5 b __ b

6 c __ b

7 r __ g

8 j __ m

9 n __ t

Say the word that names the first picture.
Circle the pictures whose names rhyme with the word.

1 hut

2 sun

3 tub

4 gum

5 mug

Say each picture name.
Trace the first letter.
Then write ug to make the word.

1	2	3
m ___	h ___	j ___

4	5	6
b ___	t ___	r ___

Say each picture name. Trace the first letter.
Then write ut to make the word.

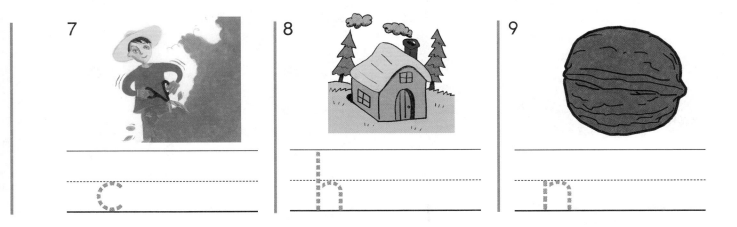

7	8	9
c ___	h ___	n ___

unit 2 review
Lessons 6-10

Say each picture name. Circle the letter for the vowel sound. Then write the letter.

cat   bed   pig   pop   cup

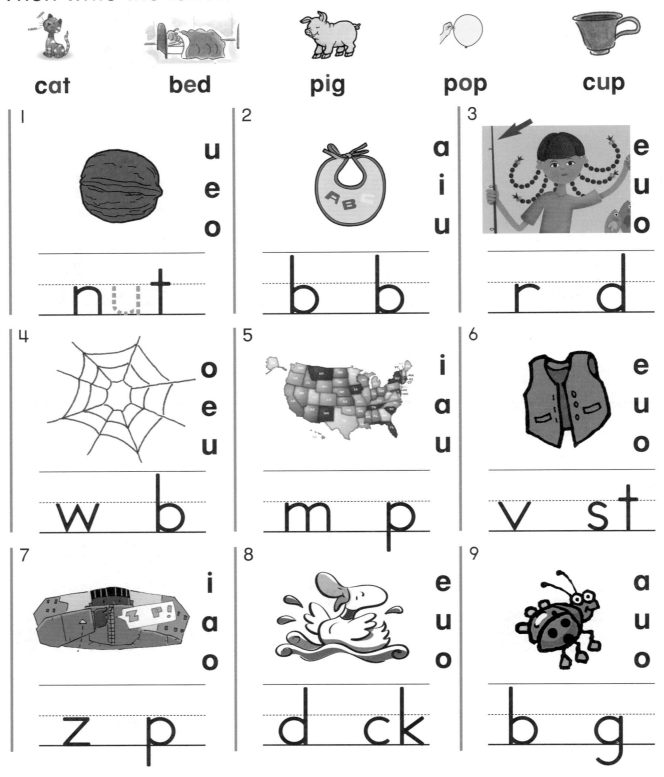

1.
u
e
o

n u t

2.
a
i
u

b   b

3.
e
u
o

r   d

4.
o
e
u

w   b

5.
i
a
u

m   p

6.
e
u
o

v   st

7.
i
a
o

z   p

8.
e
u
o

d   ck

9.
a
u
o

b   g

Say each picture name. Trace the first letter.
Then write the letters from the box that complete the name.

an	en	in	op	ut

1 
m _____

2 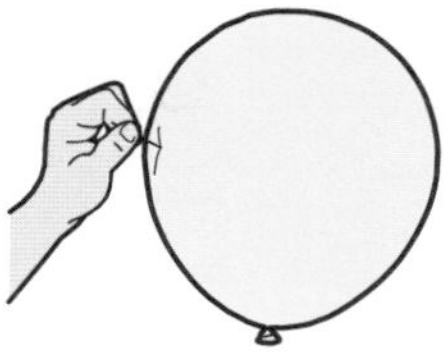
p _____

3 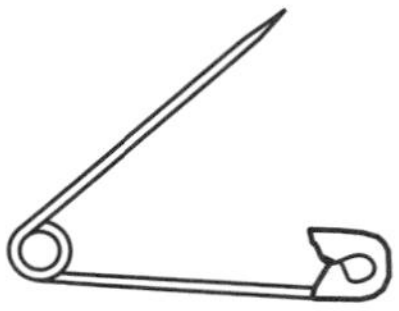
p _____

4 
m _____

5 
m _____

6 
f _____

7 
f _____

8 
p _____

9 
h _____

10 
n _____

11 
h _____

12 
c _____

Words with Short a

Say and Write

1.  am

2.  at

3.  can

4.  ran

5.  fast

6.  last

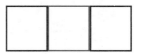

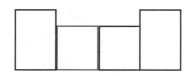

The short a sound can be spelled a, like ran and fast.

Spell and Write

Write the spelling word that completes each sentence.

am	ran
at	fast
can	last

1.

_____

I _____ Pam.

2.

_____

A duck _____ swim.

3.

_____

The dog is _____ the park.

4.

_____

The pig _____ to him.

5.

_____

My dog can run _____ .

6.

_____

The frog is _____ .

Read and Write

Write the spelling words to complete the story.

_____

Randy Rabbit _____ on a path. The path

_____

was _____ the park. Randy ran well. He ran

_____   _____

_____. That was _____ week.

_____

Now he will run again. "I _____ ready," Randy

_____

says. "I _____ do it!"

Proofreading

Circle each word that is spelled wrong.
Write the word correctly.

Dad,

Lunch is et 11:00.

We cin meet then.

I im in Room 102.

Sam

1. _____

2. _____

3. _____

Language Skills

A sentence that tells something ends with a period.

Write each sentence correctly.

Lad is my dog.

4. Lad is fast

_____

_____

5. We ran to Dad

_____

_____

6. I was the last one

_____

_____

More Words with Short a

Say and Write

1. sat

2. van

3. has

4. hand

5. that

6. have

The short a sound can be spelled a, like van and hand.

 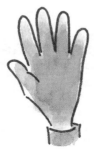

Spell and Write

Write the spelling word that completes each sentence.

sat	hand
van	that
has	have

1. Mack has a _____.

2. Will you get _____ for me?

3. Dan can draw his _____.

4. Jan _____ by her pal.

5. Hal and Jack _____ big bags.

6. My cat _____ a bell.

Read and Write

Write the spelling words to complete the selection.

sat
van
has
hand
that
have

_____

Nan _____ with her dad. They sat in their

_____   _____

_____ . Nan had a book in her _____.

She got it from the library in her town. The library

_____

_____ many good books to read. Nan likes

_____   _____

_____ library. Do you _____ a library

where you live?

Proofreading

Circle each word that is spelled wrong.
Write the word correctly.

Jack's List

1. Help wash the vaan.

2. Find out who hes my cap.

3. Get thut book for Gran.

1. _____

2. _____

3. _____

Language Skills

A sentence begins with a capital letter.

Stan has a van.

Write each sentence correctly.

4. we have a van.

_____

_____

5. i sat in back.

_____

_____

6. mom held my hand.

_____

_____

Words with Short e

Say and Write

1. end

2. ten

3. red

4. wet

5. tell

6. seven

The short e sound can be spelled e, like end and tell.

Spell and Write

Write the spelling word that completes each sentence.

end	wet
ten	tell
red	seven

1. The dog is _____ .

2. Ben's hat is _____ .

3. Five plus five is _____ .

4. I am at the _____ of the line.

5. Three plus four is _____ .

6. Mr. Silva will _____ a story.

Read and Write
Write the spelling words to complete the story.

end
ten
red
wet
tell
seven

_____

_____

Rex washes his socks. Some are _____.

_____

_____

Some are white. The socks are dripping _____.

Rex puts them on the line. He has five pairs. There are

_____

_____ socks on the line. Three socks on the

_____   _____

_____ fall. Now only _____ socks

_____

_____

are on the line. Who will _____ Rex?

Proofreading

Circle each word that is spelled wrong.
Write the word correctly.

There were tun pets in bed.

Then sevin fell out.

How does this story ind?

1. _____

2. _____

3. _____

Dictionary Skills

Look at a dictionary. The words are in ABC order. Words that begin with a come first.

4. Write the first word in your dictionary.

_____

5. Write the last word in your dictionary.

_____

6. Write a dictionary word that begins with c.

_____

7. Write a dictionary word that begins with m.

_____

More Words with Short e

Say and Write

1. get

2. pet

3. help

4. went

5. best

6. when

The short e sound can be spelled e, like pet and help.

Spell and Write

Write the spelling word that completes each sentence.

get	went
pet	best
help	when

1. Brett's _____ is a dog.

2. My cat naps _____ I nap.

3. This dog is the _____!

4. Dad _____ to the store.

5. Ted and Ned _____ the plants.

6. Ken can _____ his mom.

Read and Write

Write the spelling words to
complete the selection.

get
pet
help
went
best
when

A puppy is a good _____. Would you like

to _____ a puppy? You can _____

take care of it. You can feed your puppy _____

it is hungry. You can play with it. You will wonder where

the time _____. Do you think a puppy is the

_____ pet?

Proofreading

Circle each word that is spelled wrong.
Write the word correctly.

Help Wanted

I need help with my pett.

You must feed it whin I am gone.

I need the bist.

1. _____

2. _____

3. _____

Writing

Write a sentence about a pet. Use a spelling word.

_____

_____

_____

Words with Short i

Say and Write

1. in

2. is

3. it

4. with

5. sick

6. quit

The short i sound can be spelled i, like in and sick.

Spell and Write

Write the spelling word that completes each sentence.

in	with
is	sick
it	quit

1. Nick feels _____.

2. I have milk _____ my fish.

3. He _____ happy.

4. Kim plays _____ the yard.

5. Jim wants the rain to _____.

6. The flower has a bee on _____.

Read and Write

Write the spelling words to complete
the selection.

in
is
it
with
sick
quit

Sometimes people get _____. Then they

must stay _____ bed. It _____ not

much fun. You can make a picture for a sick friend. Get

some paper. Draw on _____. Paint on it

_____ bright colors. Don't _____ until

it looks great. Give it to your friend. Say, "Get well quick!"

Proofreading
Circle each word that is spelled wrong.
Write the word correctly.

Will,

Are you seck?

Hot tea iz good.

Stay en bed and rest.

Jim

1. _____

2. _____

3. _____

Dictionary Skills
Write the spelling words in ABC order.

| quit | with | it | sick |

4. _____

5. _____

6. _____

7. _____

Word Math

Add letters and take away letters.
Write the spelling word.

am   can   fast

1. ham – h = _____

2. fan – n + st = _____

3. cap – p + n = _____

Proofreading

Circle the word that is spelled wrong. Write it correctly.

has   that   have

4. Dad and I hav hats. _____

5. The dog haas a hat? _____

6. Is thet my hat? _____

Missing Words

Write the word that completes each sentence.

get   help   when

_____

1. Ben will _____ a puppy.

_____

2. Beth likes to _____ Dad cook.

_____

3. We will go _____ it gets dark.

What's the Right Word?

The word in dark type does not make sense in the sentence.
Write the spelling word that makes sense.

in   sick   with

_____

4. Rex is white **quit** brown spots. _____

_____

5. Do you feel **pig**? _____

_____

6. The cans are **it** the bag. _____

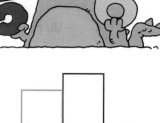

More Words with Short i

Say and Write

1. if

2. six

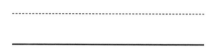

3. sit

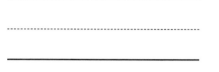

4. big

5. did

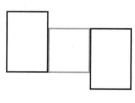

6. this

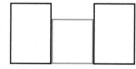

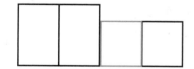

The short i sound can be spelled i, like six and big.

Spell and Write

Write the spelling word that completes each sentence.

if	big
six	did
sit	this

1. Milly has _____ puppies.

2. We will get wet _____ it rains.

3. We _____ together.

4. The red box is the _____ one.

5. Dad and I _____ the shopping.

6. I drew _____.

Read and Write

Write the spelling words to complete
the story.

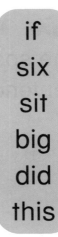

if
six
sit
big
did
this

_____

I have _____ little kittens. My kittens will

_____

not always be little. Soon they will be _____.

_____

The kittens _____ on me. They go to sleep

_____

in my lap. They wake up _____ I move. Then

_____

_____ is what they do. They cry, "Mew! Mew!"

_____

They _____ it just now!

Proofreading

Circle each word that is spelled wrong.
Write the word correctly.

Sis,

You left a bigg mess!

I diid not like it.

Please pick up thes mess now!

Sid

1. _____

2. _____

3. _____

Dictionary Skills

Circle the first letter of each word.
Write each group of words in ABC order.

4. big   am   can

_____

_____

_____

_____

5. six   if   has

_____

_____

_____

_____

6. this   sit   ran

_____

_____

_____

_____

Words with Short o

Say and Write

1. on

2. top

3. not

4. hop

5. hot

6. stop

The short o sound can be
spelled o, like hop and stop.

Spell and Write
Write the spelling word that completes each sentence.

on	hop
top	hot
not	stop

1. A frog can _____ .

2. We must _____ and wait.

3. The lamp is _____ the table.

4. Dot is _____ .

5. Roxie will _____ come.

6. The little box is on _____ .

Read and Write

Write the spelling words to complete
the story.

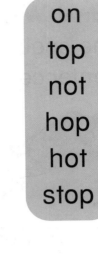

on
top
not
hop
hot
stop

Bonnie likes to _____. She hops and hops.

Bonnie hops _____ the path. She hops on the

grass. She does _____ fall. Then she hops

to the _____ of the hill. When will Bonnie

_____? She will have to stop when she gets

too _____!

Proofreading

Circle each word that is spelled wrong.
Write the word correctly.

Rules for Safe Biking

Put your helmet un.

Do nott ride too fast.

Stap at red lights.

1. _____

2. _____

3. _____

Language Skills

A sentence that asks a question ends with a question mark.

Where is Mopsy?

Write each sentence correctly.

4. Is Mopsy at the top

_____

_____

5. Is Mopsy hot

_____

_____

6. Will he hop down

_____

_____

More Words with Short o

Say and Write

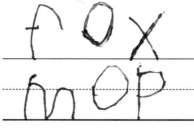

1. fox   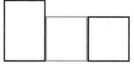

2. mop   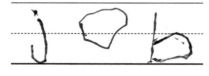   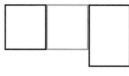

3. job      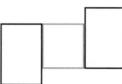

4. box   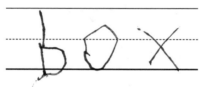   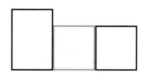

5. lock   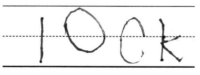   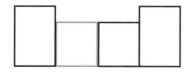

6. sock   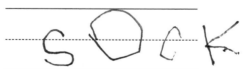   

The short o sound can be spelled o, like fox and socks.

Spell and Write

Write the spelling word that completes each sentence.

fox	box
mop	lock
job	sock

1. _____
   _____
   Ron lost a _____.

2. _____
   _____
   Dot can _____ up the mess.

3. _____
   _____
   Mom has a _____ at school.

4. _____
   _____
   A _____ lives in the woods.

5. _____
   _____
   Tom put a key in the _____.

6. _____
   _____
   The toys go in a _____.

Read and Write

Write the spelling words to
complete the story.

fox
mop
job
box
lock
sock

Bob the ox had a _____ to do. He had to

_____. A _____ came in. He had

a _____. The fox took out a brush. "Put this

on your _____," he said.

Bob did it. Then he put a brush on his other sock.

He started to mop. "This is fast!" Bob said. "Soon I can

_____ up and go have fun!"

Proofreading

Circle each word that is spelled wrong.
Write the word correctly.

I have a jub to do.

I put the toys in the bax.

Then Mom can moop my room.

1. _____

2. _____

3. _____

Writing

Write a sentence about a job you do.
Use a spelling word.

_____

_____

_____

Words with Short u

Say and Write

1. us

2. run

3. fun

4. jump

5. much

6. duck

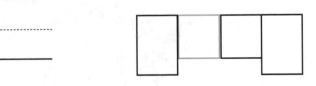

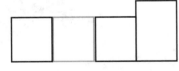

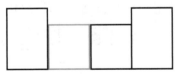

The short u sound can be spelled u, like run and duck.

Spell and Write

Write the spelling word that completes each sentence.

1. Bud walks with _____.

2. They can _____ fast.

3. Meg and Gus _____ rope.

4. She feeds the _____.

5. Josh and Mack had _____.

6. How _____ will Gran read?

Read and Write

Write the spelling words to complete the selection.

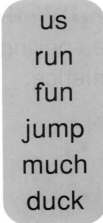

us
run
fun
jump
much
duck

A baby _____ is called a duckling. A

duckling cannot _____ fast. A duckling can have

_____. It can _____ into the water.

It can swim, too. The mother duck quacks if a duckling

swims too far away. She is saying, "You have gone

_____ too far. Come back to _____!"

Proofreading

Circle each word that is spelled wrong.
Write the word correctly.

Dusty,

Thanks for coming to see os.

I had fon with you.

I like you very mach.

Sunny

1. _____

2. _____

3. _____

Writing

Write a sentence about someone you like.
Use a spelling word.

_____

_____

_____

More Words with Short u

Say and Write

1. up

2. cut

3. bus

4. but

5. must

6. just

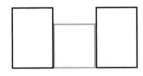
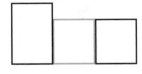

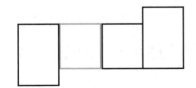

The short u sound can be spelled u, like up and bus.

Spell and Write

Write the spelling word that completes each sentence.

up	but
cut	must
bus	just

1. She will ride the _____ _____ .

2. Russ _____ _____ pick up the toys.

3. Sunny will _____ _____ the string.

4. The girls look _____ _____ alike.

5. It is cold, _____ _____ there is no snow.

6. The ball goes _____ _____ and down.

Read and Write
Write the spelling words to complete the selection.

up
cut
bus
but
must
just

Do you know what to do on a _____?

You _____ sit down when the bus is moving.

You cannot stand _____. You can play a game.

You can sing a song, too. You can draw, _____

do not use scissors. You might _____ yourself.

You can read, or you can _____ sit and rest.

Proofreading

Circle each word that is spelled wrong.
Write the word correctly.

I jist saw Chuck.

He was on the bos.

We mest get him on our team.

1. _____

2. _____

3. _____

Language Skills

Use is to write about one thing.
Use are to write about more than one thing.

Write the sentences. Use is and are correctly.

4. The cut _____ on my hand.

_____

_____

5. My house _____ up the street.

_____

_____

6. We _____ going home now.

_____

_____

unit 4 review
LESSONS 16-20

Missing Letters
Write the missing letter. Then write the word.

big   did   this

1. d _____ d   _____

2. th _____ s   _____

3. b _____ g   _____

Proofreading
Circle the word that is spelled wrong.
Write it correctly.

on   not   stop

4. The rain will stap soon.   _____

5. I will play un the sidewalk.   _____

6. I do nat like to stay inside.   _____

Label the Picture

The words in the box go in this picture.
Write each word on the correct line.

job   box   sock

Words with Long a

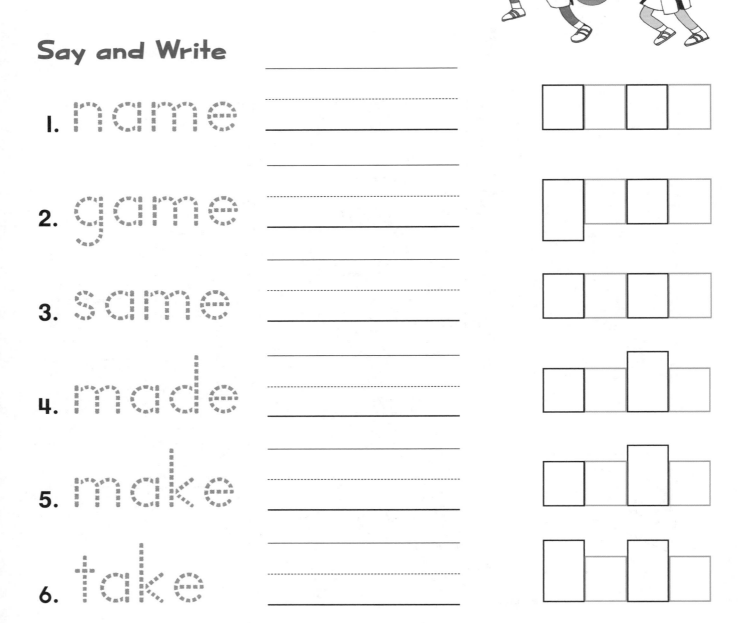

Say and Write _____

1. name _____

2. game _____

3. same _____

4. made _____

5. make _____

6. take _____

The long a sound can be spelled a_e, like game and take.

Spell and Write

Write the spelling word that completes each sentence.

name	made
game	make
same	take

1. They will _____ a snack.

2. Jake and Kate play a _____ .

3. The cat's _____ is Gabe.

4. Are the socks the _____ ?

5. Jade will _____ her lunch.

6. Tate _____ a plane.

Read and Write

Write the spelling words to complete
the selection.

name
game
same
made
make
take

Polly plays the piano with her pet parrot.

_____   _____

What is your _____? Play a _____

_____

with your name. To begin, _____ the first letter of

your name, such as **P**. Think of words that begin with the

_____   _____

_____ letter. Next, _____ a sentence

with the words. Then, add more words to the sentence you

_____

_____.

Proofreading

Circle each word that is spelled wrong.
Write the word correctly.

Mom let me tak a dog home.

I have to give him a naam.

We will play a geme.

1. _____

2. _____

3. _____

Writing

Write a sentence about a game you like.
Use a spelling word.

_____

_____

_____

More Words with Long a

Say and Write

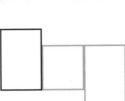

1. day

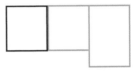

2. may

3. say

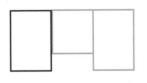

4. pay

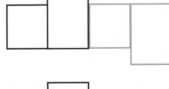

5. stay

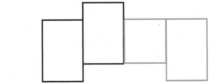

6. play

The long a sound can be spelled ay, like pay and play.

Spell and Write

Write the spelling word that completes each sentence.

1. Jay will _____ for the book.

2. It is a nice _____.

3. Fay must _____ in bed.

4. It _____ rain today.

5. The kitten likes to _____.

6. What will Mom _____?

Read and Write

Write the spelling words to complete the selection.

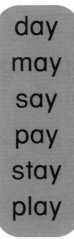

day

may

say

pay

stay

play

_____

Some work places have a special _____.

_____

Children _____ go to work with an adult. They

_____

can _____ all day. They learn about jobs. They

_____

have fun, but it is not a time to _____. The

_____

children _____ they learn a lot. They see how

_____

adults work for their _____.

Proofreading

Circle each word that is spelled wrong.
Write the word correctly.

Wayne,

Will you come stae with me?

We could pla a lot.

Please sey you will.

Jake

1. _____

2. _____

3. _____

Language Skills

Sentences begin with a capital letter.
Names of people begin with a capital letter, too.

We play with Jay.

Write each sentence correctly.

4. we may play with jay all day.

_____

_____

5. he will pay kay today.

_____

_____

Words with Long e

Say and Write

1. me

2. we

3. he

4. be

5. she

6. eat

The long e sound can be spelled e or ea, like we and eat.

Spell and Write

Write the spelling word that completes each sentence.

1. _____

"Are _____ late?" Lee asked.

2. _____

It is time to _____.

3. _____

Is _____ calling Mom?

4. _____

"Will you help _____?" he asked.

5. _____

She will _____ awake soon.

6. _____

Will _____ come and play?

Read and Write

Write the spelling words to complete the story.

me
we
he
be
she
eat

My family sleeps a lot in winter. We need food before

_____   _____

_____ sleep. We _____ a lot!

_____

Today Mom showed _____ how to catch fish.

_____

Then _____ showed my brother. I know

_____

_____ likes fish. Soon we will find a cave.

_____

A cave is a good place to _____ in winter.

Proofreading

Circle each word that is spelled wrong.
Write the word correctly.

Neal,

Can you bea home by 3:00?

Then wi will go to the game.

Dad said hee will take us.

Jean

1. _____

2. _____

3. _____

Language Skills

Unscramble each sentence and write it.
Use capital letters and periods correctly.

4. my went me with sister

_____

5. likes be me she to with

_____

6. eat to we pizza went

_____

Lesson 24

More Words with Long e

Say and Write

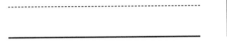

1. see
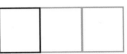

2. feet

3. keep
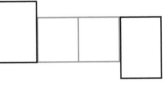

4. tree
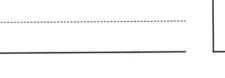

5. street
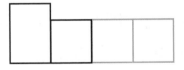

6. three

The long e sound can be spelled ee, like in tree or see.

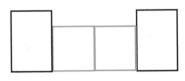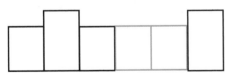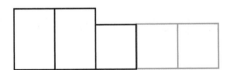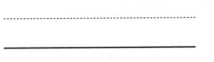

Spell and Write
Write the spelling word that
completes each sentence.

see	tree
feet	street
keep	three

1. A leaf fell from the _____.

2. They walk across the _____.

3. This thing has many _____.

4. What does she _____?

5. Pete can _____ things in the box.

6. The _____ kittens play all day.

Read and Write

Write the spelling words to complete the story.

see
feet
keep
tree
street
three

Dee's dad took her on a hike with _____ of

_____

her friends. They all live on the same _____.

"Please _____ walking on the trail," Dad said.

Something went splash! "What is on the other side of that

_____

_____?" Dad asked.

"I _____ a creek!" Lee said. "Some kids are

_____

in the water. May we get our _____ wet, too?"

Proofreading

Circle each word that is spelled wrong.
Write the word correctly.

We planted a trea.

It will kep growing.

It will be 12 fete tall.

1. _____

2. _____

3. _____

Dictionary Skills

Look up each word in a dictionary.
Copy the sentence that helps you
know what the word means.

4. see

_____

_____

5. street

_____

_____

6. three

_____

_____

Words with Long i

Say and Write

1. ride

2. nine

3. five

4. hide

5. mine

6. time

The long i sound can be spelled i_e, like five and ride.

Spell and Write

Write the spelling word that
completes each sentence.

ride	hide
nine	mine
five	time

1. Where did the mouse _____?

2. I will share _____ with Mike.

3. What _____ is it?

4. The dog will _____ in the wagon.

5. There are _____ eggs left.

$8 + 1 =$ ____

6. Eight and one make _____.

Read and Write

Write the spelling words to complete the selection.

A bike contest can test how well you _____.

Don't run and _____. Set up _____

big cones. Ride around them one at a _____.

Ride slowly for four or _____ minutes. Now you

are ready for the contest. You might get to say, "The prize

is _____!"

Proofreading

Circle each word that is spelled wrong.
Write the word correctly.

I like to ridee *my* bike.

I'm on it all the tim.

I got it when I was fiv.

1. _____

2. _____

3. _____

Writing

Write two sentences about a bike.
Use two spelling words.

_____

_____

_____

_____

_____

Word Puzzle

Write the spelling word for each clue.

game   made   take

1. It means "did make."

2. It means "to get."

3. People play this.

Proofreading

Circle the word that is spelled wrong.
Write it correctly.

day   say   play

4. Clay wants to pla a game. _____

5. What did you sae? _____

6. What a great daay it is! _____

Dictionary Skills
Write the words in ABC order.

> we   she   eat

1. _____

2. _____

3. _____

Missing Words
Write the word that completes each sentence.

> keep   three   see

4. I went to _____ a play.

5. One plus two is _____.

6. May I _____ this puppy?

More Words with Long i

Say and Write

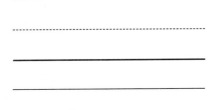

1. my

2. by

3. fly

4. why

5. try

6. cry

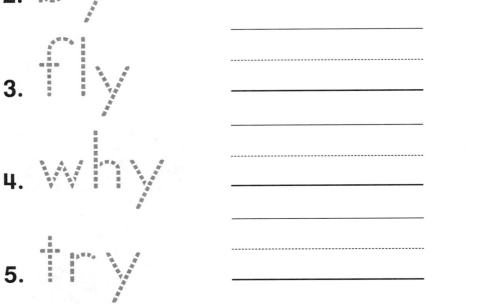

The long i sound can be spelled y, like my and fly.

Spell and Write

Write the spelling word that completes
each sentence.

my	why
by	try
fly	cry

1. The baby began to _____.

2. That little bird wants to _____!

3. The cat knows _____ the vase fell.

4. I put on _____ coat.

5. She will _____ to skate.

6. The bag is _____ the door.

Read and Write

Write the spelling words to complete
the story.

my
by
fly
why
try
cry

I made a kite. I made _____ kite from a

_____

bag. I wanted it to _____ up high. People

stood _____ me. They asked _____

I used a bag. I wanted to _____ it. That's why.

The bag did not fly very high, but I did not _____.

I just made another kite.

Proofreading

Circle each word that is spelled wrong.
Write the word correctly.

This is *miy* bird.

He likes to *flye*.

He likes to sit *bi* me.

1. _____

2. _____

3. _____

Writing

Write two sentences about a bird.
Use two spelling words.

_____

_____

_____

_____

_____

Words with Long o

Say and Write

1. so

2. go

3. old

4. told

5. cold

6. over

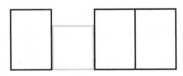

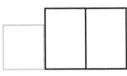

The long o sound can be spelled o, like go and cold.

Spell and Write

Write the spelling word that completes each sentence.

so	told
go	cold
old	over

1. The shop was closed, _____ we left.

2. Jo _____ Bo a joke.

3. Mom held the paper _____ her head.

4. The ball will _____ far.

5. The little dog was _____.

6. The big tree was very _____.

Read and Write

Write the spelling words to complete the story.

JoJo wanted to _____ to a special place.

She wanted to go _____ the rainbow. JoJo

packed an _____ bag. She got her coat in case

it was _____. JoJo _____ Gran

about her plan. Gran wanted to go, too, _____

they went together. Good luck, JoJo and Gran!

Proofreading

Circle each word that is spelled wrong.
Write the word correctly.

Mom,

May I ask Lin to come ovr?

She is soo much fun.

Then can we goe for pizza?

Joey

1. _____

2. _____

3. _____

Language Skills

Use was to write about one thing.
Use were to write about more than one thing.

Write the sentences. Use was and were correctly.

4. We _____ in an old store.

_____

_____

5. Mom _____ by the milk.

_____

_____

6. I told Mom I _____ cold.

_____

_____

More Words with Long o

Say and Write

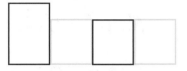

1. home

2. hope

3. note

4. nose

5. road

6. coat

The long o sound can be spelled o_e or oa, like home and road.

Spell and Write

Write the spelling word that completes each sentence.

1. _____
   _____
   I ride down the _____.

2. _____
   _____
   We _____ it rains today.

3. _____
   _____
   My _____ is green.

4. _____
   _____
   He has a big red _____.

5. _____
   _____
   Mr. Lo's _____ is in a big city.

6. _____
   _____
   Joan wrote me a _____.

Read and Write
Write the spelling words to complete the story.

home
hope
note
nose
road
coat

One day Mole wanted to take a walk. Dad was not at

_____   _____

_____. Mole wrote Dad a _____.

_____

Then she walked down the _____. She walked

_____

a long way. A cold wind came. Mole's _____

_____

was blue. She wanted her warm _____.

_____

"I _____ I am not lost!" she said. Then Mole

saw her house. She smiled and went inside.

Proofreading

Circle each word that is spelled wrong.
Write the word correctly.

Mom,

I lost my cote.

I hoap you are not mad.

I will stay hoam to look for it.

Joan

1. _____

2. _____

3. _____

Dictionary Skills

Circle the first letter of each word.
Then write the words in ABC order.

4. road   home   note

_____

_____

_____

5. told   nose   go

_____

_____

_____

Words with the Vowel Sound in food

Say and Write

1. zoo

2. food

3. room

4. moon

5. soon

6. school

The vowel sound in food can be spelled oo, like zoo and school.

Spell and Write

Write the spelling word that
completes each sentence.

zoo	moon
food	soon
room	school

1. What jumped over the _____?

2. Where do you go to _____?

3. Will cleaned his _____.

4. It will be dark _____.

5. We had fun at the _____.

6. Dad and Joel shop for _____.

Read and Write

Write the spelling words to complete the selection.

zoo
food
room
moon
soon
school

Would you like to camp at a _____? At one

zoo, you can sleep in a _____ with beds. You

can sleep under the _____ and stars, too. You

can give _____ to the animals. Your class from

_____ might want to go zoo camping. Find out

about zoo camping _____!

Proofreading

Circle each word that is spelled wrong.
Write the word correctly.

I went on a schul trip.

We went to the zo.

We gave foode to the seals.

1. _____

2. _____

3. _____

Writing

Write two sentences about a zoo.
Use two spelling words.

_____

_____

_____

_____

_____

_____

_____

More Words with the Vowel Sound in food

Say and Write

1. too

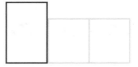

2. who

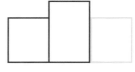

3. two

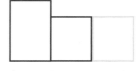

4. do

5. shoe

6. you

The vowel sound in food can be spelled oo, o, oe, or ou, like too, two, shoe, and you.

Spell and Write

Write the spelling word that completes each sentence.

too	do
who	shoe
two	you

1. It's time to _____ our work.

2. The hat is _____ big.

3. Stu, where are _____ ?

4. Lou said, "I know _____ you are."

5. The bike has _____ wheels now.

6. Boo has my _____ .

Read and Write

Write the spelling words to complete the selection.

too
who
two
do
shoe
you

_____

Look at your _____ feet. Is there a

_____

_____ on each foot? Shoes keep your feet safe.

_____

Shoes should not be _____ big or too small.

_____

No one knows _____ made the first

shoes. Early people made them from animal skins. Now

_____

_____ can buy shoes in a store. What kind of

_____

shoes _____ you like to wear?

Proofreading

Circle each word that is spelled wrong.
Write the word correctly.

Sue,

How much doo you like the circus?

I have tou tickets.

Will yoe come with me?

Dooley

1. _____

2. _____

3. _____

Language Skills

Use to to mean into. Use too to mean more than enough.
Use two to mean the number after one.

Write the sentences. Use to, two, and too correctly.

4. Who are those _____ girls?

_____

_____

5. That shoe is _____ big.

_____

_____

6. Did they go _____ the store?

_____

_____

unit 6 review
LESSONS 26-30

Missing Letter
Write y in each box. Then write the word.

my   why   try

1. tr [ ] = _____   **2.** wh [ ] = _____

3. m [ ] = _____

Proofreading
Circle the word that is spelled wrong.
Write it correctly.

go   told   over

4. I can fly ovr a house.   _____

5. I can goa to the top of a tree.   _____

6. I toald my dad to look at me.   _____

Rhyming Words

Help Toad find her way home. For each word
on the trail, write the rhyming word from the box.

hope   road   coat

1. _____

2. _____

3. _____

commonly misspelled words

about	girl	one	too
am	have	or	two
and	her	our	very
are	him	outside	want
because	his	people	was
came	house	play	went
can	in	said	were
color	into	school	when
every	know	some	with
family	like	teacher	would
friend	little	their	your
friends	me	there	
get	my	they	

sight words

the	to	very
and	all	your
a	for	good
you	said	take
of	they	how
he	so	about
it	in	know
I	with	any
had	there	their
we	can	here
was	them	after
at	like	before
she	would	old
but	come	been
on	long	who
	will	again

Math
Skills

A+

Counting to 5

Draw a line from each number to the matching group of objects.

50

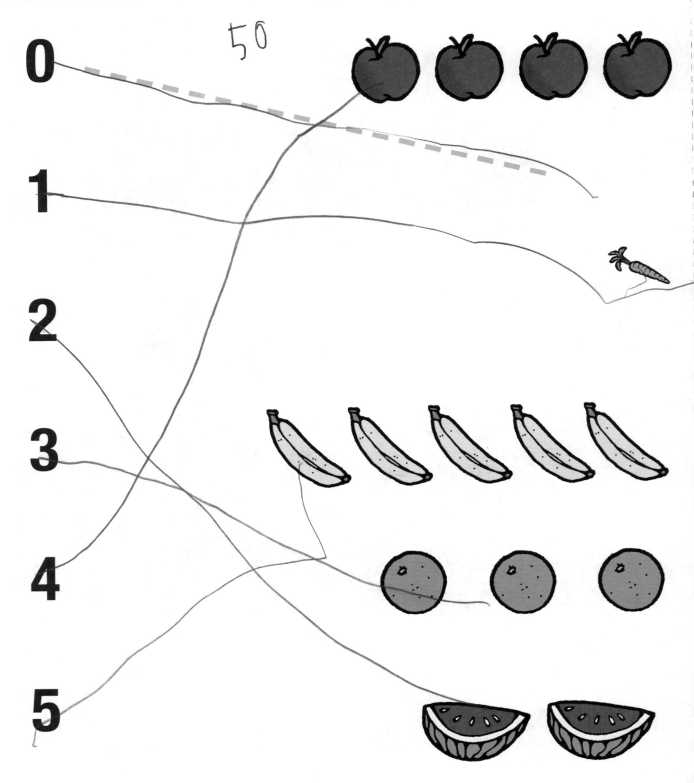

0

1

2

3

4

5

Counting to 5

Color a group of apples to match each number.

2

5

0

3

1

4

Counting and Numbering to 5

Count the number of candies in each group. Write the number.

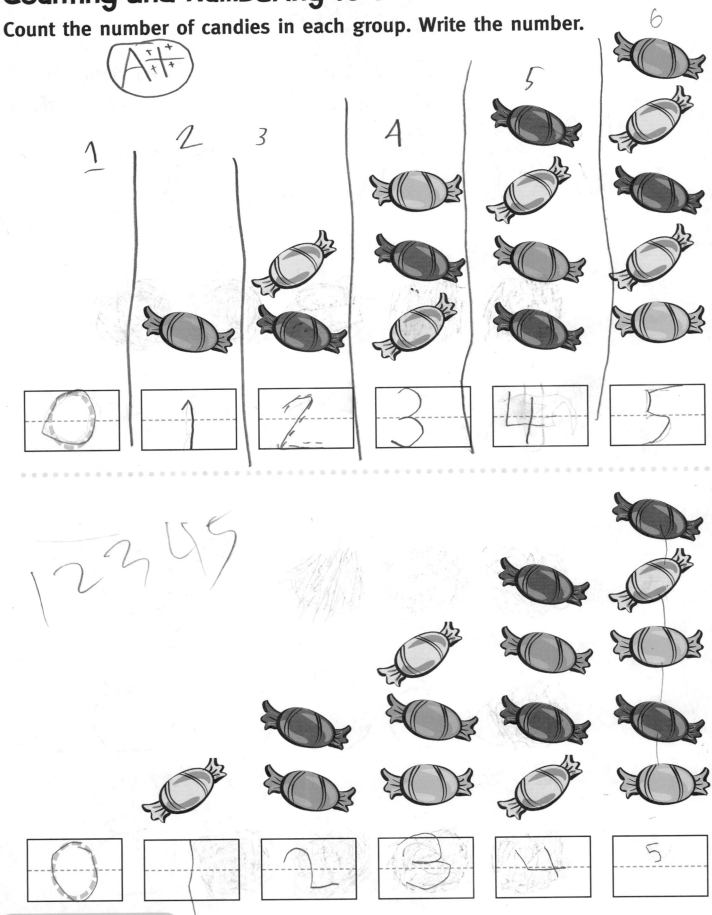

Counting and Numbering to 5

Count the number of candies in each group. Write the number.

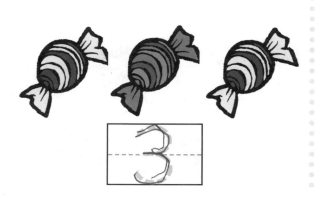

3

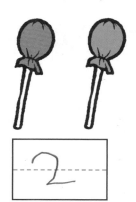

2

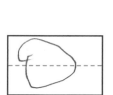

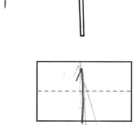

1

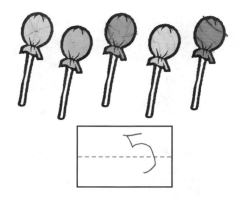

5

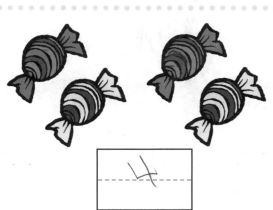

4

Counting and Numbering to 10

Count the cubes in each group. Write the number.

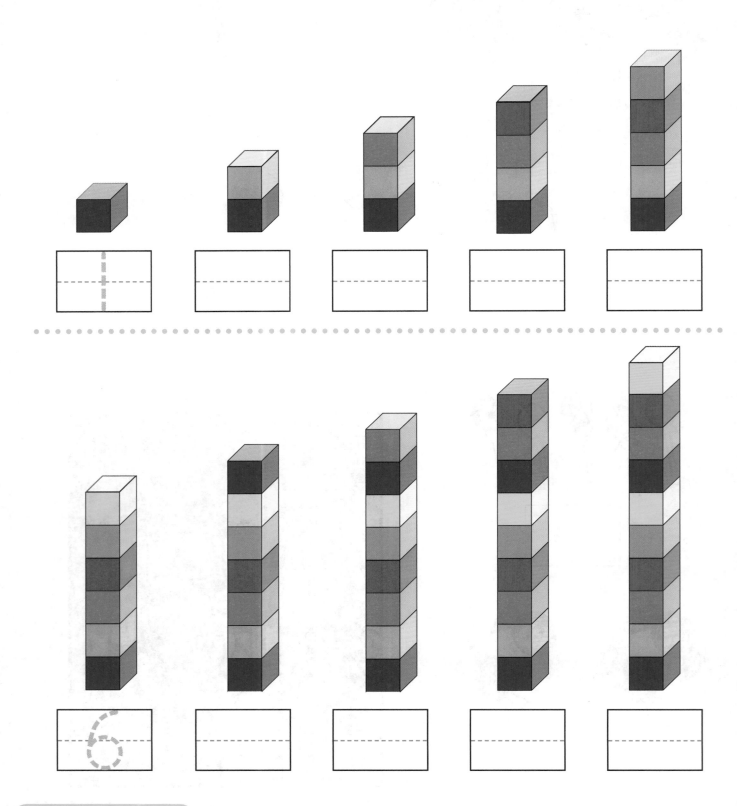

Counting and Numbering to 10
Count the cubes in each group. Write the number.

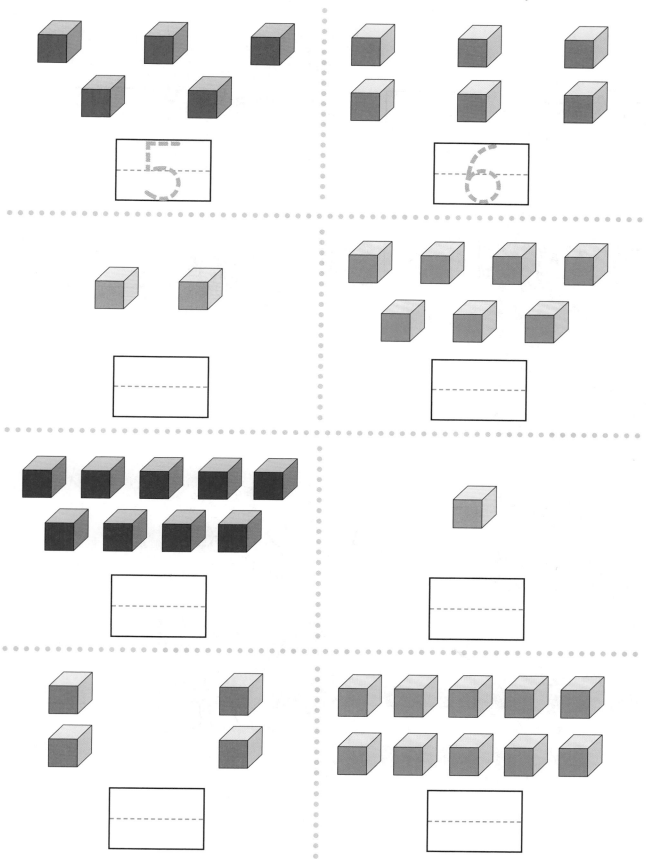

Counting and Numbering to 10

Count the objects on each flag. Write the number.

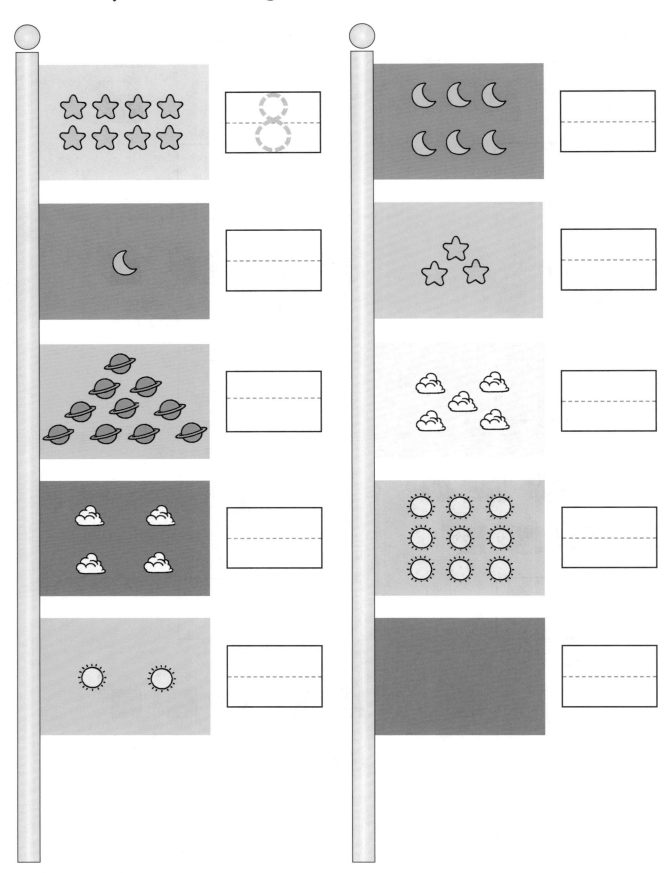

Counting and Numbering to 10

Write the numbers 1 to 10 in order.
Draw a line from each number to the matching group of objects.

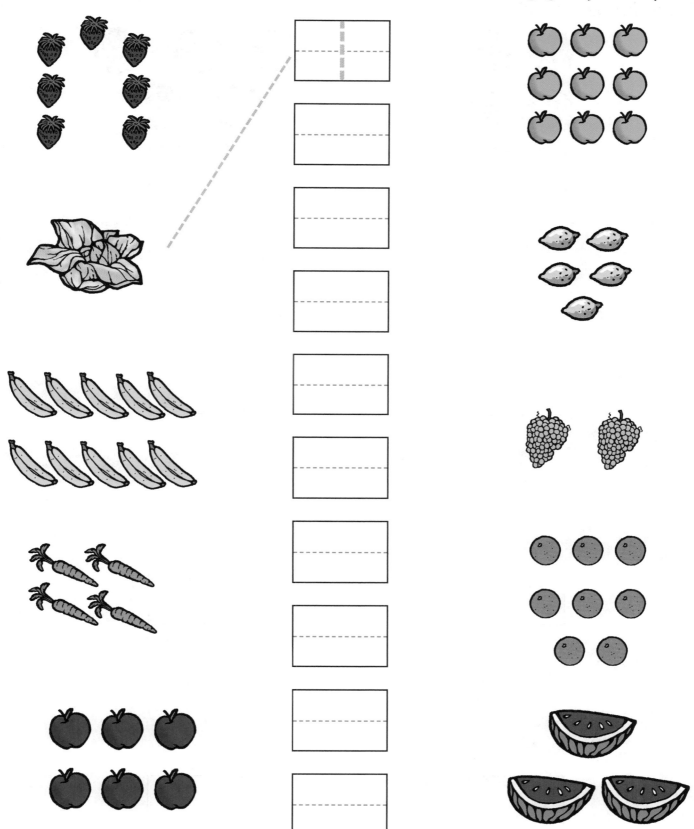

One More

Count each group of circles. Write the number.
Next to each group, draw a group with one more circle.
Write the new number.

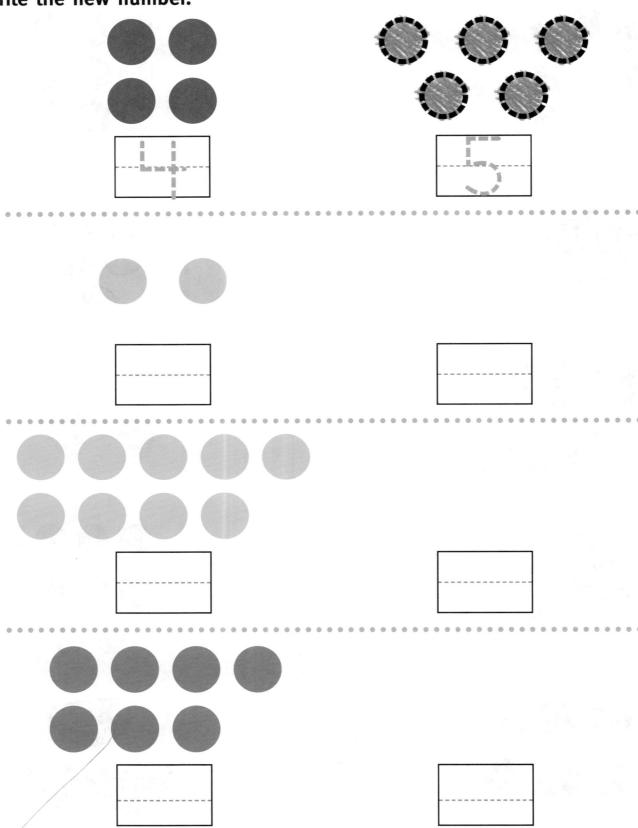

One Fewer

Count each group of circles. Write the number.
Next to each group, draw a group with one fewer circle.
Write the new number.

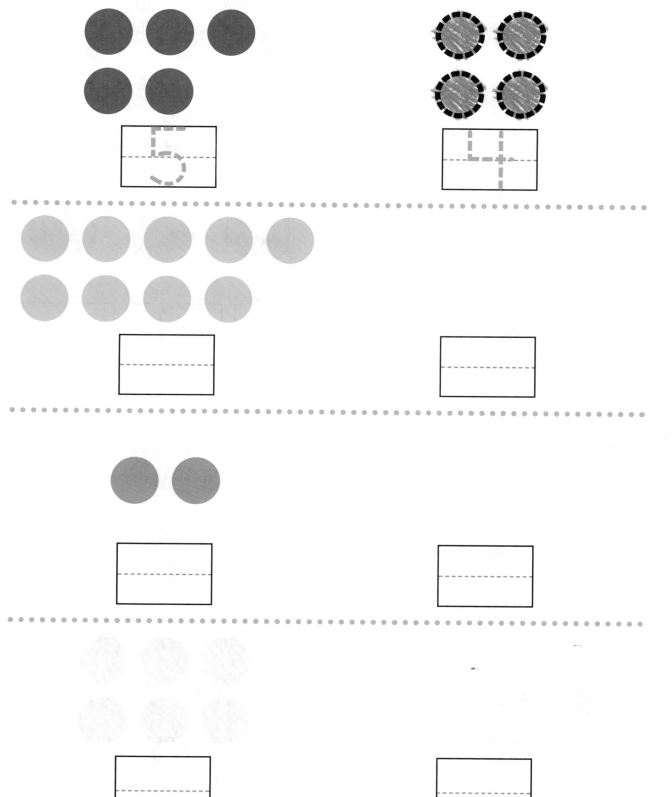

Before and After

Write the numbers that come before and after the ones shown.

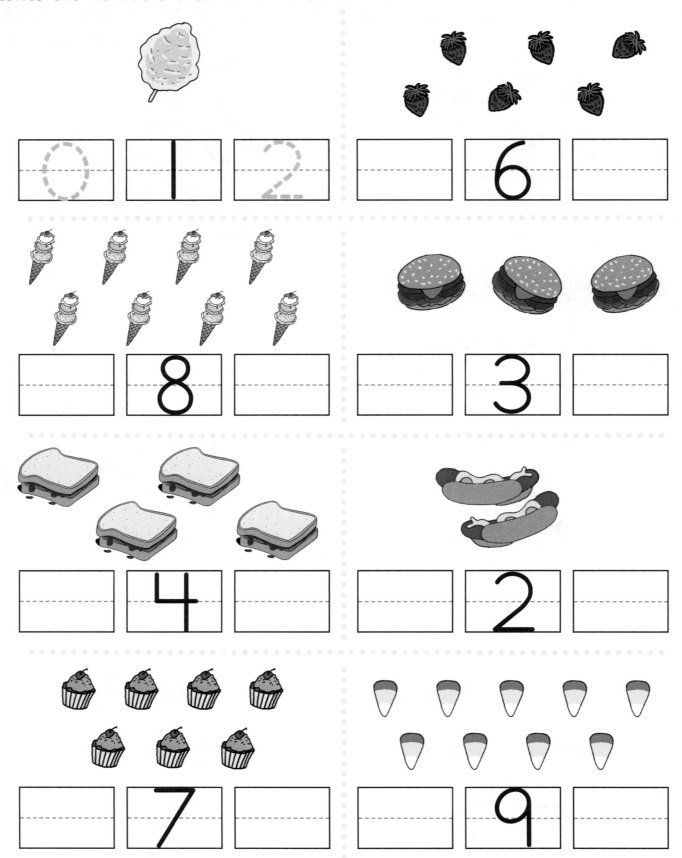

Missing Numbers

Count the windows in order. Write the missing numbers.

Missing Numbers

Write the missing numbers in the train cars.

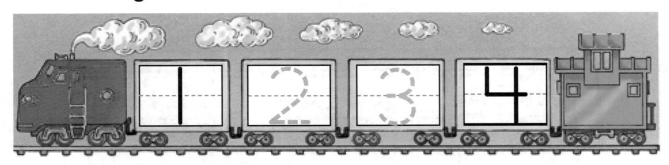

Practice Counting

Write the numbers to practice counting.

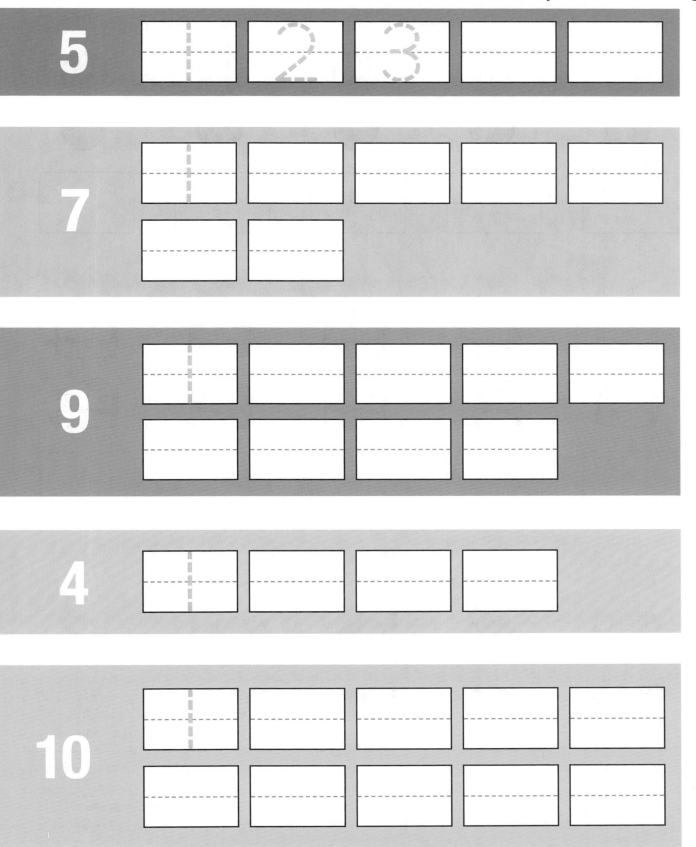

Skip Counting

Skip count by twos. Write the numbers to show how many in all.

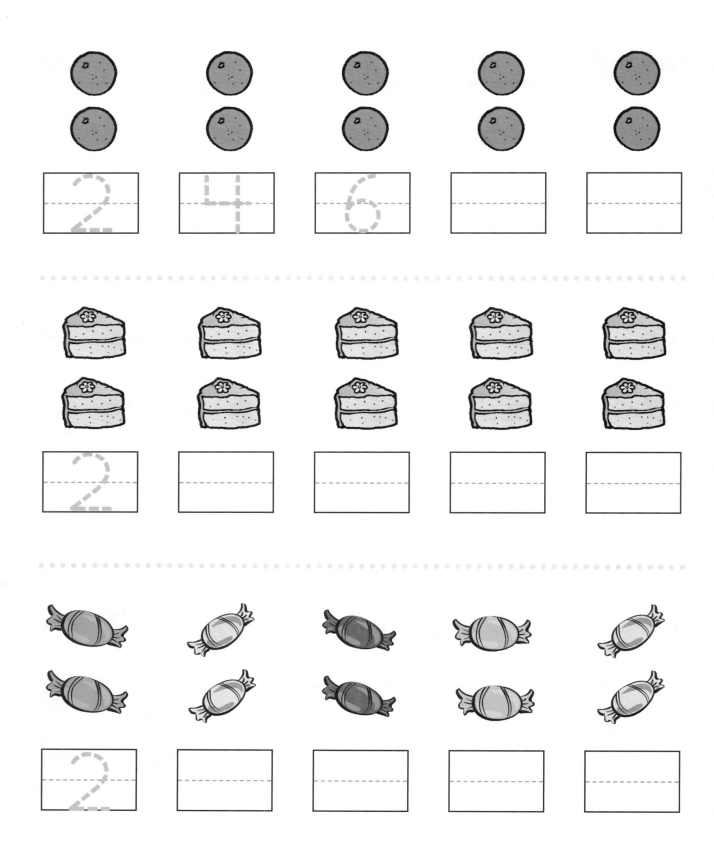

Skip Counting

Skip count by twos. Write the numbers to show how many in all.

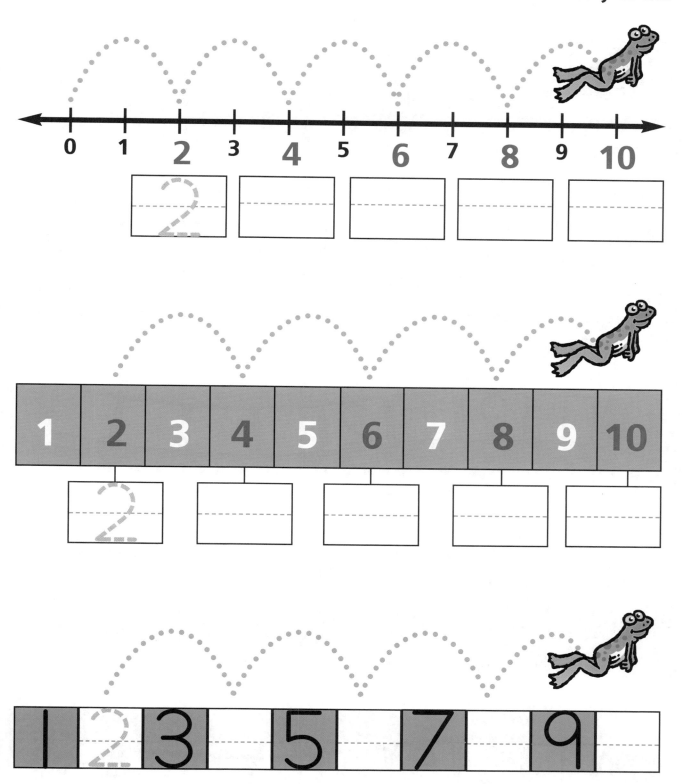

Find a Pattern

Write the missing number in each number pattern.

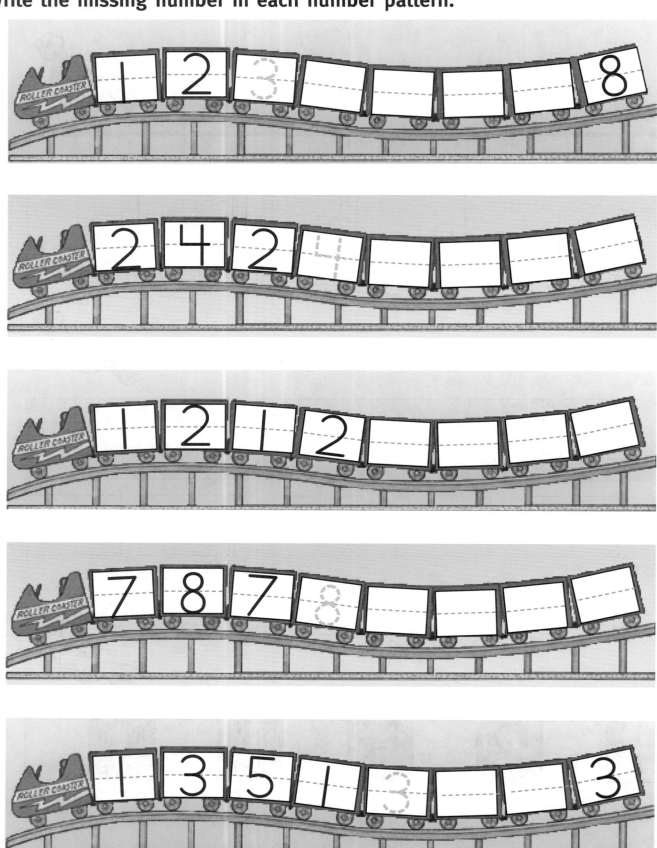

Find a Pattern

Draw and color the next shape in each pattern.

Unit 1 Review

Write the missing numbers.

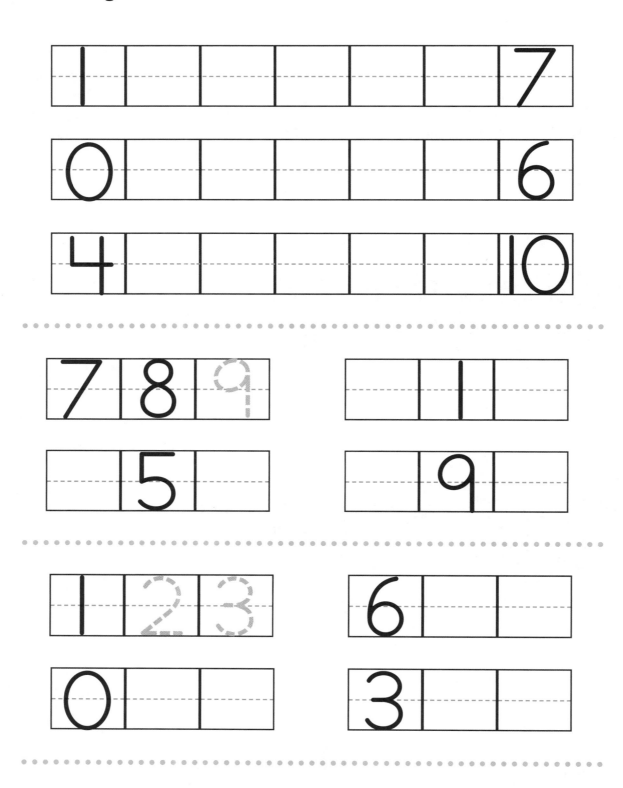

Count the objects. Write the numbers that tell how many of each.

. . . .

Draw and color the next shape in the pattern.

UNIT 2
Addition

Sums to 6

Add the objects in each row. Write the numbers that tell how many in all.

2   +   1   =   

1   +   4   =   

3   +   1   =

1   +   1   =   

1   +   5   =

288 MATH SKILLS

Sums to 6

Add the objects in each row. Write the numbers that tell how many in all.

3   +   2   =

1   +   3   =

2   +   4   = _____

2   +   2   =

Sums of 5

Draw and color circles to show each number sentence.

1   +   4   =   5

....

2   +   3   =   5

....

3   +   2   =   5

....

4   +   1   =   5

....

5   +   0   =   5

Draw and color circles to show each number sentence.

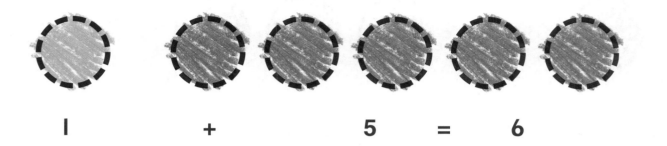

1 + 5 = 6

· ·

2 + 4 = 6

· ·

3 + 3 = 6

· ·

5 + 1 = 6

· ·

6 + 0 = 6

Number Sentences

Write the number sentences.

$$\underline{\quad 1 \quad} + \underline{\quad 3 \quad} = \underline{\quad 4 \quad}$$

$$\underline{\qquad} + \underline{\qquad} = \underline{\qquad}$$

$$\underline{\qquad} + \underline{\qquad} = \underline{\qquad}$$

$$\underline{\qquad} + \underline{\qquad} = \underline{\qquad}$$

$$\underline{\qquad} + \underline{\qquad} = \underline{\qquad}$$

Number Sentences

Write the number sentences.

2   **+**   **3**   **=**   _5_

_____   +   _____   =   _____

_____   +   _____   =   _____

_____   +   _____   =   _____

_____   +   _____   =   _____

Using a Graph

Find the number of each object on the graph. Then write the sums.

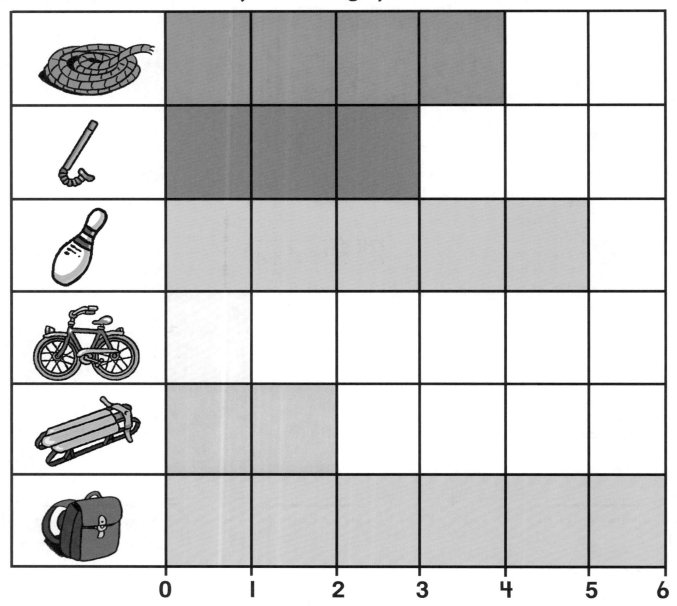

 _3_ + 2 = _5_   ___ + | = ___

 ___ + 0 = ___   ___ + | = ___

___ + 5 = ___   ___ + 3 = ___

Using a Graph

Find the number of each object on the graph.
Then write the number that is added to equal each sum.

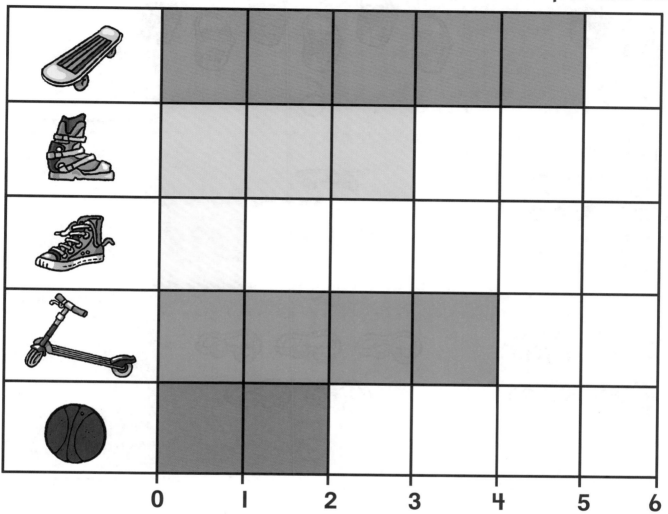

0   1   2   3   4   5   6

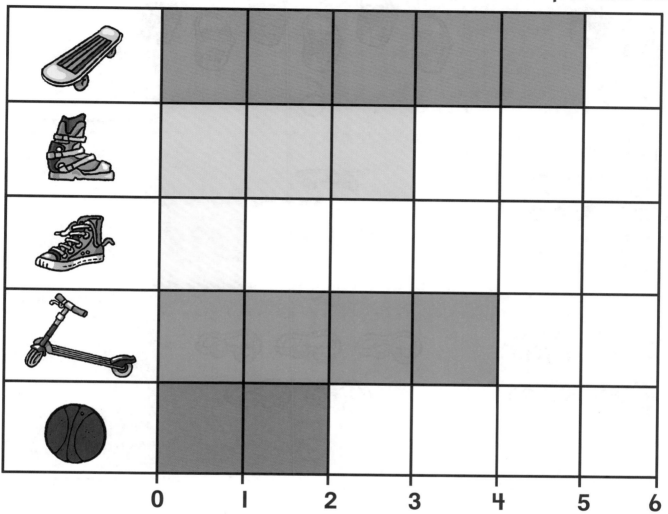 __2__ + __4__ = 6   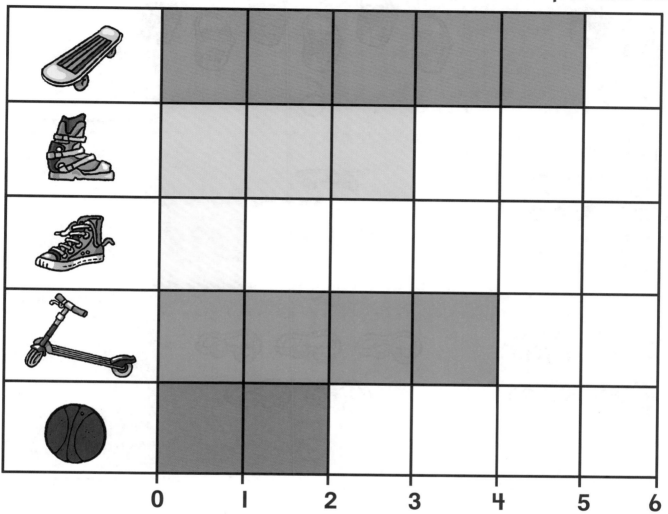 ____ + ____ = 4

 ____ + ____ = 2   ____ + ____ = 6

 ____ + ____ = 5   ____ + ____ = 3

Sums to 10

Add the objects in each row. Write the numbers that tell how many in all.

2   +   6   =   8

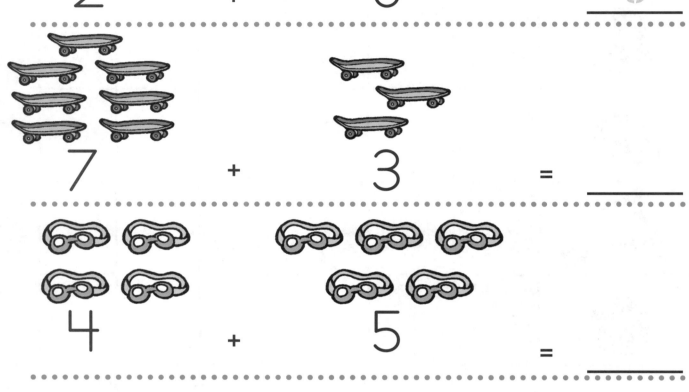

7   +   3   = _____

4   +   5   = _____

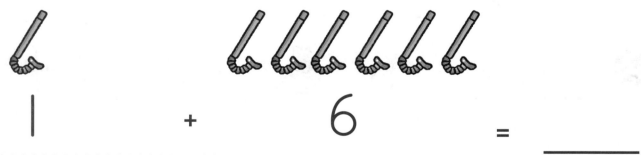

1   +   6   = _____

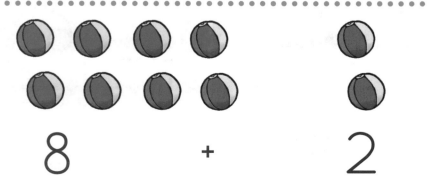

8   +   2   = _____

Write the number sentences that match the objects on the flags.

 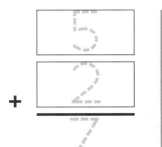

$5 + 2 = 7$

___ + ___ = ___

 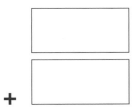 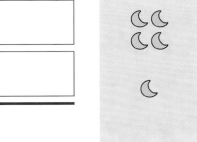

___ + ___ = ___

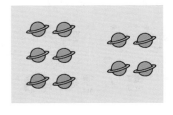  

___ + ___ = ___

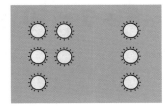 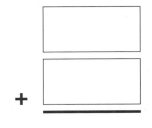 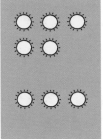

___ + ___ = ___

Sums of 10

Color the circles to show each number sentence.

●●●●●●●●●● **1 + 9 = 10**

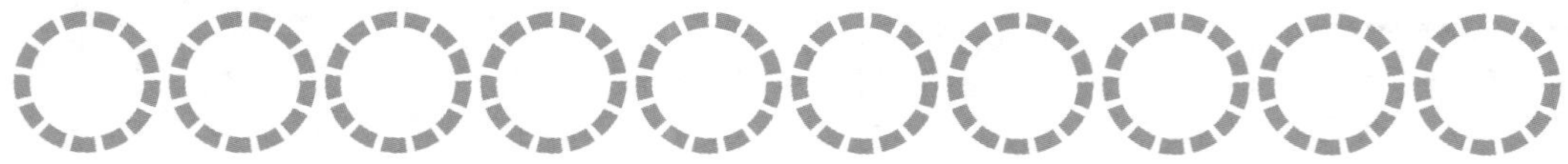

○○○○○○○○○○ **6 + 4 = 10**

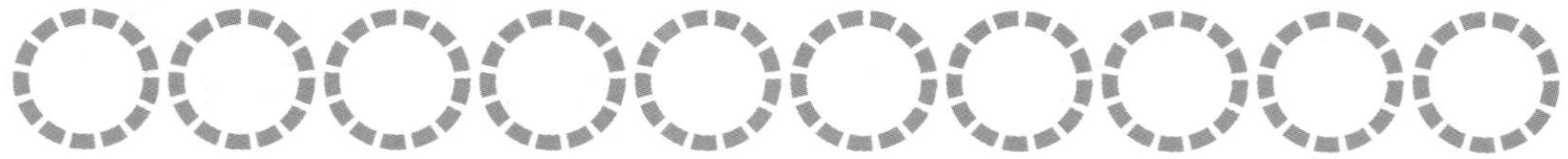

○○○○○○○○○○ **4 + 6 = 10**

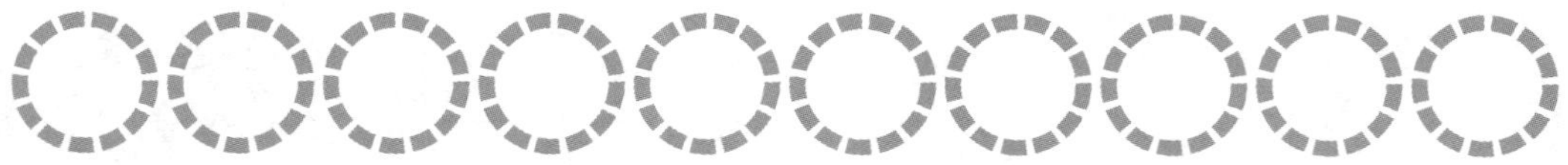

○○○○○○○○○○ **3 + 7 = 10**

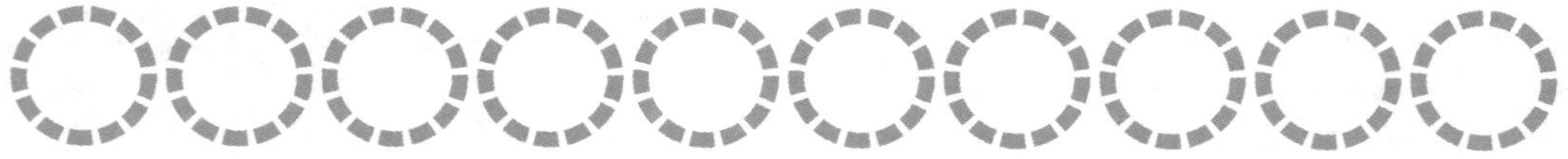

○○○○○○○○○○ **10 + 0 = 10**

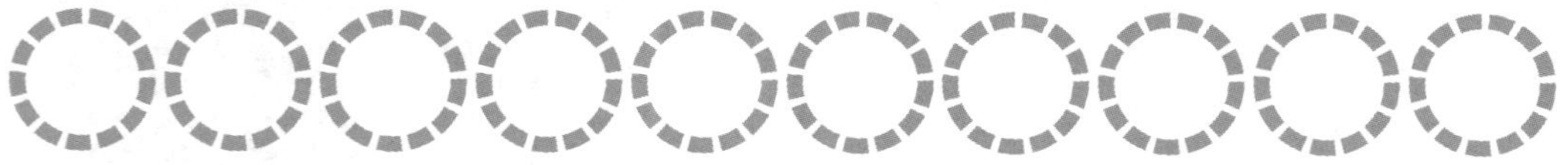

○○○○○○○○○○ **8 + 2 = 10**

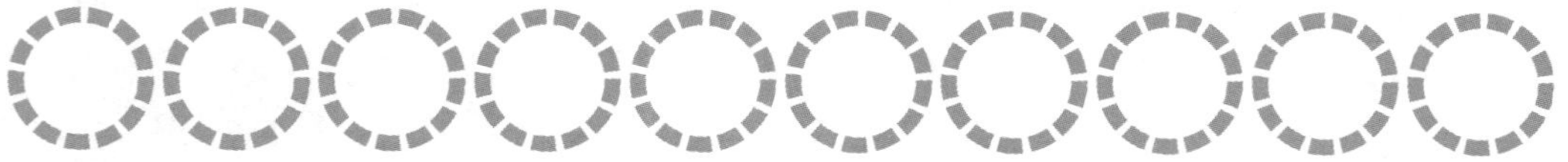

○○○○○○○○○○ **5 + 5 = 10**

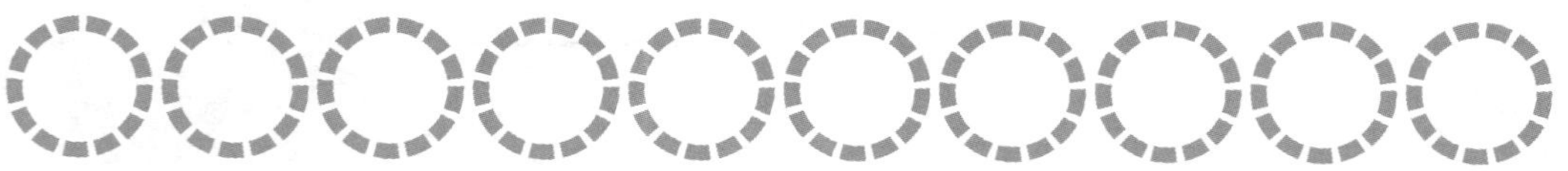

○○○○○○○○○○ **9 + 1 = 10**

Write the numbers that match the pictures. Then write the sums.

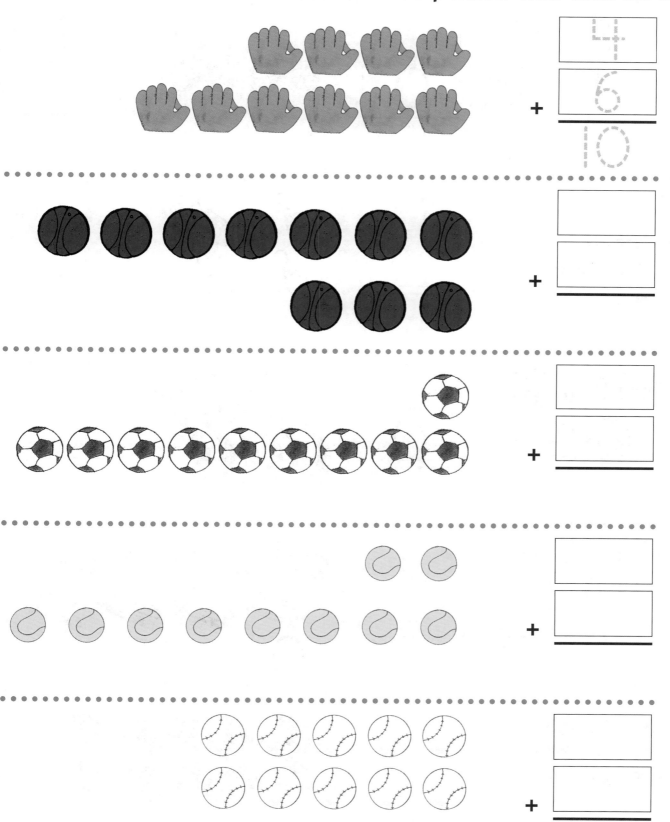

```
  4
+ 6
———
 10
```

```
  
+ 
———
 
```

```
  
+ 
———
 
```

```
  
+ 
———
 
```

```
  
+ 
———
 
```

Adding Zero

Write the number sentences that match the pictures.

⬚
+ ⬚ 0
___

⬚ 0
+ ⬚
___

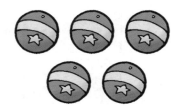
⬚ 0
+ ⬚
___

⬚
+ ⬚ 0
___

⬚
+ ⬚ 0
___

⬚ 0
+ ⬚
___

___ 7 + 0 = ___ 7

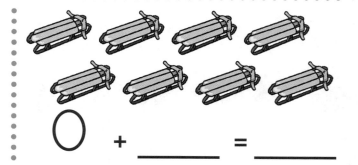
0 + ___ = ___

___ + 0 = ___

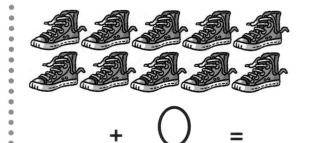
___ + 0 = ___

Doubles

Write the number sentences that match the objects on the flags.

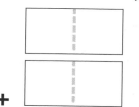

$\underline{\hspace{1cm}1} + \underline{\hspace{1cm}1} = \underline{\hspace{1cm}2}$

$+ \hspace{1cm} \underline{\hspace{2cm}}$
$\underline{\hspace{2cm}} \; 2$

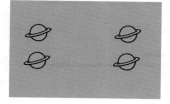

$\underline{\hspace{1cm}} + \underline{\hspace{1cm}} = \underline{\hspace{1cm}}$

$+ \hspace{1cm} \underline{\hspace{2cm}}$
$\underline{\hspace{2cm}}$

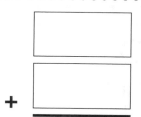 

$\underline{\hspace{1cm}} + \underline{\hspace{1cm}} = \underline{\hspace{1cm}}$

$+ \hspace{1cm} \underline{\hspace{2cm}}$
$\underline{\hspace{2cm}}$

$\underline{\hspace{1cm}} + \underline{\hspace{1cm}} = \underline{\hspace{1cm}}$

$+ \hspace{1cm} \underline{\hspace{2cm}}$
$\underline{\hspace{2cm}}$

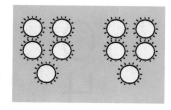

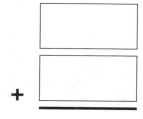 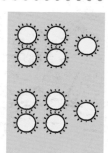

$\underline{\hspace{1cm}} + \underline{\hspace{1cm}} = \underline{\hspace{1cm}}$

$+ \hspace{1cm} \underline{\hspace{2cm}}$
$\underline{\hspace{2cm}}$

Unit 2 Review

Write the sums.

$7 + 3 =$ _____ $2 + 4 =$ _____

$1 + 1 =$ _____ $5 + 0 =$ _____

$3 + 6 =$ _____ $4 + 4 =$ _____

$1 + 9 =$ _____ $2 + 3 =$ _____

$0 + 7 =$ _____ $8 + 2 =$ _____

$$\begin{array}{r} 5 \\ + 4 \\ \hline \end{array}$$
$$\begin{array}{r} 3 \\ + 5 \\ \hline \end{array}$$
$$\begin{array}{r} 6 \\ + 1 \\ \hline \end{array}$$

$$\begin{array}{r} 4 \\ + 3 \\ \hline \end{array}$$

$$\begin{array}{r} 0 \\ + 4 \\ \hline \end{array}$$

Unit 2 Review

Find the number of each object on the graph. Complete the number sentences. Then draw a line from each number sentence to its model.

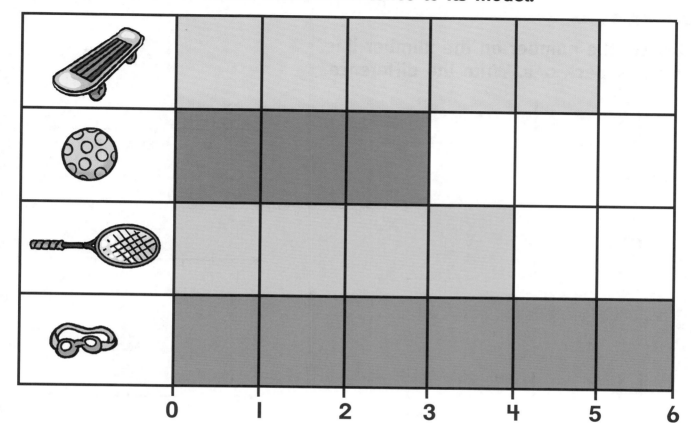

| 0 | 1 | 2 | 3 | 4 | 5 | 6 |

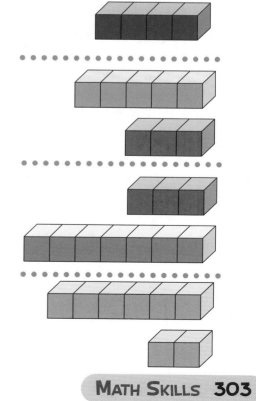

_____ + 3 = _____

_____ + _____ = 8

_____ + 0 = _____

_____ + _____ = 10

Subtract 1

First circle the number on the number line.
Then count back one. Write the difference.

6 − 1 = 5

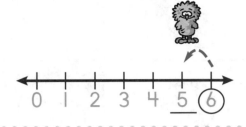

5 − 1 = ___

4 − 1 = ___

3 − 1 = ___

2 − 1 = ___

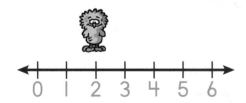

1 − 1 = ___

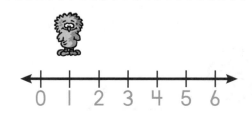

Subtract 2

First circle the number on the number line.
Then count back two. Write the difference.

8 − 2 = 6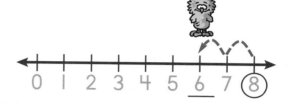

0 1 2 3 4 5 6 7 (8)

7 − 2 = ___

0 1 2 3 4 5 6 7 8

6 − 2 = ___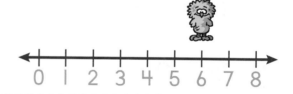

0 1 2 3 4 5 6 7 8

5 − 2 = ___

0 1 2 3 4 5 6 7 8

4 − 2 = ___

0 1 2 3 4 5 6 7 8

3 − 2 = ___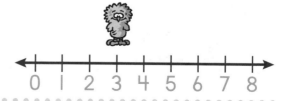

0 1 2 3 4 5 6 7 8

2 − 2 = ___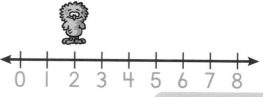

0 1 2 3 4 5 6 7 8

Subtract 3

Cross out the animals to subtract. Write the differences.

   9 - 3 = 6

   8 - 3 = ___

7 - 3 = ___

6 - 3 = ___

   5 - 3 = ___

4 - 3 = ___

3 - 3 = ___

Subtract 0

Write how many of each animal. Then write the difference.

 $\underline{3} - O = \underline{3}$

 $\underline{} - O = \underline{}$

 $\underline{} - O = \underline{}$

$\underline{} - O = \underline{}$

$\underline{} - O = \underline{}$

 $\underline{} - O = \underline{}$

$\underline{} - O = \underline{}$

Differences from 5

Cross out the dogs to subtract. Write the differences.

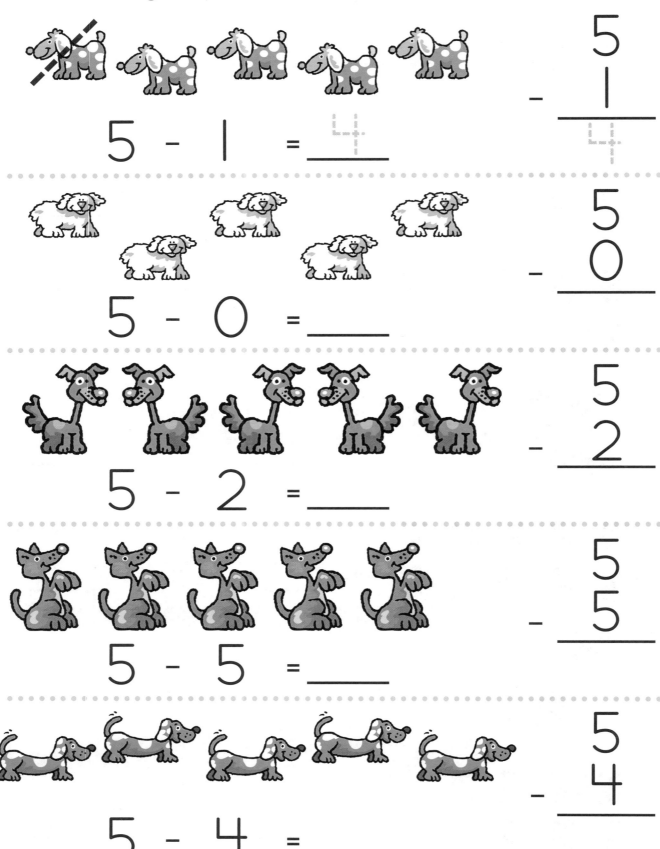

5 - 1 = ___

$$\begin{array}{r} 5 \\ -\ 1 \\ \hline \end{array}$$

5 - 0 = ___

$$\begin{array}{r} 5 \\ -\ 0 \\ \hline \end{array}$$

5 - 2 = ___

$$\begin{array}{r} 5 \\ -\ 2 \\ \hline \end{array}$$

5 - 5 = ___

$$\begin{array}{r} 5 \\ -\ 5 \\ \hline \end{array}$$

5 - 4 = ___

$$\begin{array}{r} 5 \\ -\ 4 \\ \hline \end{array}$$

Differences from 6

Cross out the cats to subtract. Write the differences.

$$6 - 5 = \underline{\quad}$$

$$\begin{array}{r} 6 \\ -\ 5 \\ \hline \end{array}$$

$$6 - 3 = \underline{\quad}$$

$$\begin{array}{r} 6 \\ -\ 3 \\ \hline \end{array}$$

$$6 - 6 = \underline{\quad}$$

$$\begin{array}{r} 6 \\ -\ 6 \\ \hline \end{array}$$

$$6 - 0 = \underline{\quad}$$

$$\begin{array}{r} 6 \\ -\ 0 \\ \hline \end{array}$$

$$6 - 2 = \underline{\quad}$$

$$\begin{array}{r} 6 \\ -\ 2 \\ \hline \end{array}$$

Differences from 7

Write the differences. Draw a line from each subtraction problem to its model.

$$\begin{array}{r} 7 \\ -\ 0 \\ \hline \end{array}$$

$$\begin{array}{r} 7 \\ -\ 1 \\ \hline \end{array}$$

$$\begin{array}{r} 7 \\ -\ 2 \\ \hline \end{array}$$

$$\begin{array}{r} 7 \\ -\ 3 \\ \hline \end{array}$$

7 - 4 = ___

7 - 5 = ___

7 - 6 = ___

7 - 7 = ___

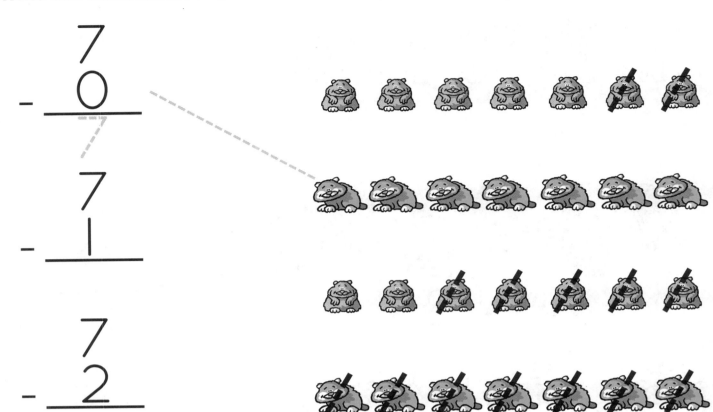

Write the differences. Draw a line from each subtraction problem to its model.

$$\begin{array}{r} 8 \\ -\ 0 \\ \hline 8 \end{array}$$

$$\begin{array}{r} 8 \\ -\ 1 \\ \hline \end{array}$$

$$\begin{array}{r} 8 \\ -\ 2 \\ \hline \end{array}$$

$$\begin{array}{r} 8 \\ -\ 3 \\ \hline \end{array}$$

$8 - 4 = \rule{1cm}{0.4pt}$

$8 - 5 = \rule{1cm}{0.4pt}$

$8 - 6 = \rule{1cm}{0.4pt}$

$8 - 7 = \rule{1cm}{0.4pt}$

$8 - 8 = \rule{1cm}{0.4pt}$

Differences from 9

Cross out the eggs to subtract. Write the differences.

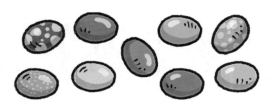

$$9 - 0 = \underline{}$$

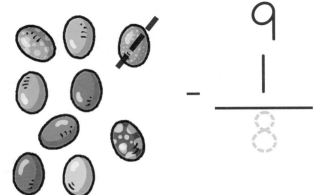

$$\begin{array}{r} 9 \\ -\ 1 \\ \hline \end{array}$$

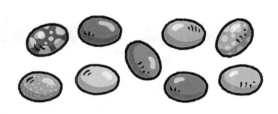

$$9 - 6 = \underline{}$$

$$\begin{array}{r} 9 \\ -\ 5 \\ \hline \end{array}$$

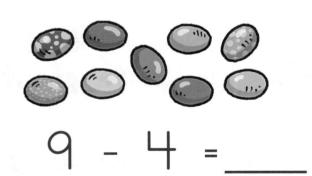

$$9 - 4 = \underline{}$$

$$\begin{array}{r} 9 \\ -\ 9 \\ \hline \end{array}$$

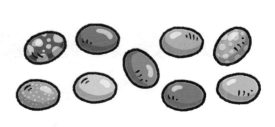

$$9 - 8 = \underline{}$$

$$\begin{array}{r} 9 \\ -\ 3 \\ \hline \end{array}$$

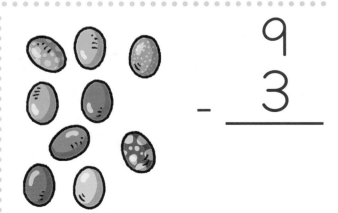

Differences from 10

Draw a line to the matching model on the left.
Write the differences on the right.

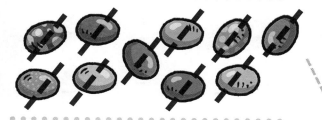

$10 - 6 =$ ___

$10 - 9 =$ ___

$10 - 7 =$ ___

$10 - 4 =$ ___

$10 - 10 =$ ___

$10 - 3 =$ ___

$10 - 8 =$ ___

Fact Families to 5

Write the fact family for each set of numbers.

3

__1__	+	__2__	=	__3__
__2__	+	__1__	=	__3__
__3__	−	__2__	=	__1__
__3__	−	__1__	=	__2__

4

____ + ____ = ____

____ + ____ = ____

____ − ____ = ____

____ − ____ = ____

5

____ + ____ = ____

____ + ____ = ____

____ − ____ = ____

____ − ____ = ____

5

____ + ____ = ____

____ + ____ = ____

____ − ____ = ____

____ − ____ = ____

Write the fact family for each set of numbers.

6

$4 + 2 = 6$

$2 + 4 = 6$

$6 - 4 = 2$

$6 - 2 = 4$

7

___ + ___ = ___

___ + ___ = ___

___ - ___ = ___

___ - ___ = ___

7

___ + ___ = ___

___ + ___ = ___

___ - ___ = ___

___ - ___ = ___

8

___ + ___ = ___

___ + ___ = ___

___ - ___ = ___

___ - ___ = ___

Unit 3 Review

Write the differences.

5 - 2 = ___   7 - 4 = ___

6 - 3 = ___   8 - 0 = ___

9 - 7 = ___   4 - 3 = ___

```
   5          9          6
 - 4        - 5        - 1
 ———        ———        ———


  10          8          4
 - 5        - 1        - 0
 ———        ———        ———
```

Complete the fact families.

5 + 3 = ___   6 + 4 = 10

___ + ___ = ___   ___ + ___ = ___

___ - ___ = ___   ___ - ___ = ___

___ - ___ = ___   ___ - ___ = ___

Unit 3 Review

Choose the operation. Then write the number sentence for each picture.

8

6		2		8		8
+ 2		+ 6		− 6		− 2
8		8		2		6

9

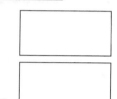

+		+		−		−

5

+		+		−		−

10

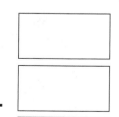

+		+		−		−

Numbers to 19

Count each group of ladybugs. Write the sums.

$10 + 0 = \underline{10}$

$10 + 1 = \underline{11}$

$10 + 2 = \underline{}$

$10 + 3 = \underline{}$

$10 + 4 = \underline{}$

$10 + 5 = \underline{}$

$10 + 6 = \underline{}$

$10 + 7 = \underline{}$

$10 + 8 = \underline{}$

$10 + 9 = \underline{}$

Numbers to 19

Count each group of bees.
Write the numbers that tell how many tens and ones.

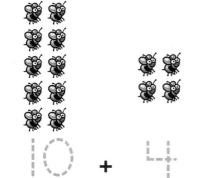

$$\underline{10} + \underline{4} = 14$$

$$\underline{} + \underline{} = 19$$

$$\underline{} + \underline{} = 15$$

$$\underline{} + \underline{} = 11$$

$$\underline{10} + \underline{0} = 10$$

$$\underline{} + \underline{} = 13$$

$$\underline{} + \underline{} = 17$$

$$\underline{} + \underline{} = 18$$

Tens

Count how many tens. Then write the numbers.

1   ten   = _10_

2   tens   = _20_

3   tens   = _____

4   tens   = _____

5   tens   = _____

6   tens   = _____

7   tens   = _____

8   tens   = _____

9   tens   = _____

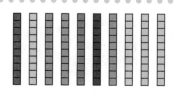

10   tens   = _____

Add the tens. Then write the sums.

50 + 10 = 60

20 + 10 = ___

0 + 10 = ___

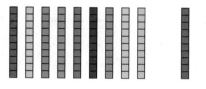

80 + 10 = ___

90 + 10 = ___

10 + 10 = ___

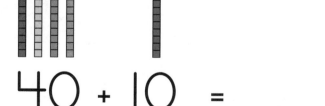

40 + 10 = ___

70 + 10 = ___

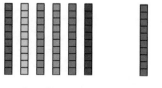

60 + 10 = ___

30 + 10 = ___

MATH SKILLS **321**

Tens and Ones to 20

Write how many tens and ones. Then write the numbers.

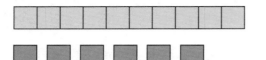

Tens	Ones
1	6

= 16

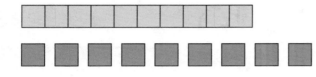

Tens	Ones

= _____

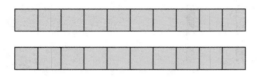

Tens	Ones

= _____

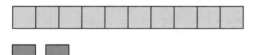

Tens	Ones

= _____

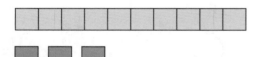

Tens	Ones

= _____

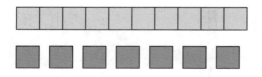

Tens	Ones

= _____

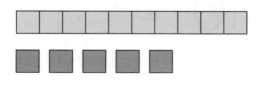

Tens	Ones

= _____

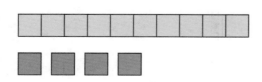

Tens	Ones

= _____

Tens and Ones to 30

Write how many tens and ones. Then write the numbers.

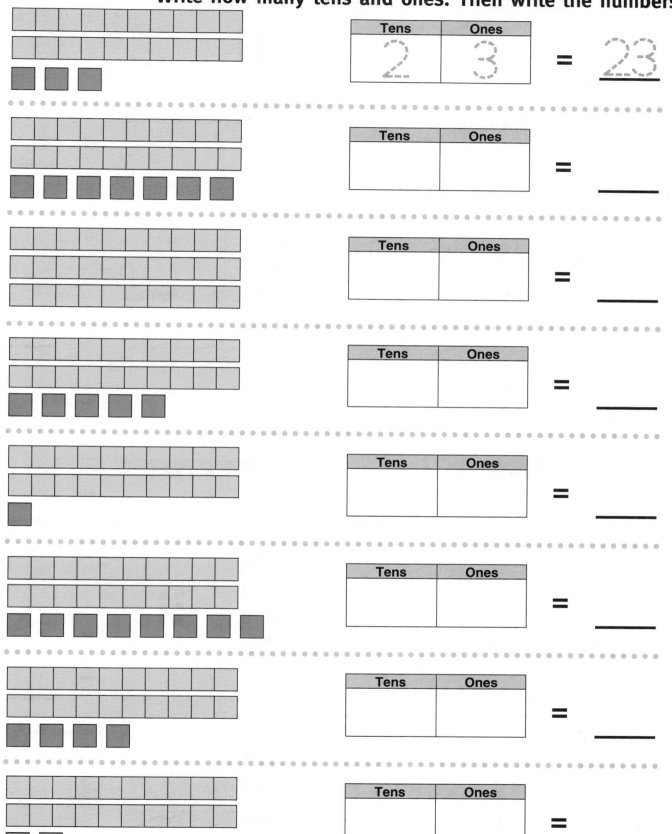

Tens	Ones
2	3

= 23

Tens	Ones

= _____

Tens	Ones

= _____

Tens	Ones

= _____

Tens	Ones

= _____

Tens	Ones

= _____

Tens	Ones

= _____

Tens	Ones

= _____

Tens and Ones to 40

Write how many tens and ones. Then write the numbers.

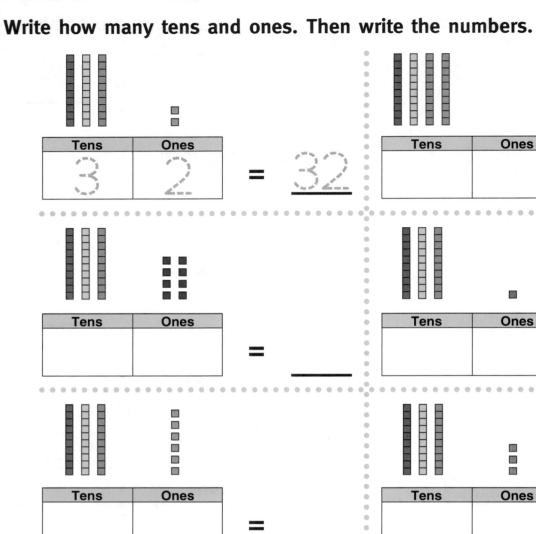

Tens	Ones
3	2

= 32

Tens	Ones

= ___

Tens	Ones

= ___

Tens	Ones

= ___

Tens	Ones

= ___

Tens	Ones

= ___

Tens	Ones

= ___

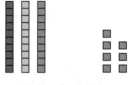

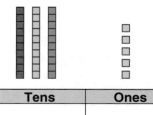

Tens	Ones

= ___

Tens	Ones

= ___

Tens and Ones to 50

Write how many tens and ones. Then write the numbers.

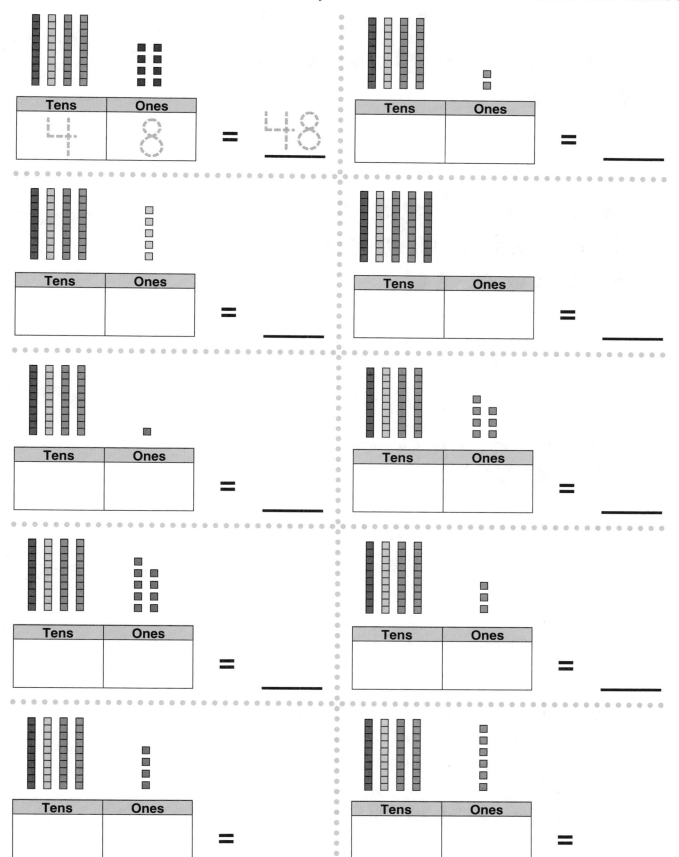

Tens	Ones
4	8

= 48

Tens	Ones

= ___

Tens	Ones

= ___

Tens	Ones

= ___

Tens	Ones

= ___

Tens	Ones

= ___

Tens	Ones

= ___

Tens	Ones

= ___

Tens	Ones

= ___

Tens	Ones

= ___

Groups of Ten

Circle groups of ten.
Then write the numbers that tell how many tens and ones.

Tens	Ones
1	3

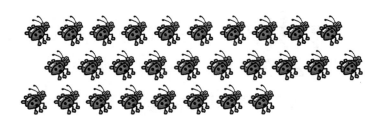

Tens	Ones

Tens	Ones

Tens	Ones

Tens	Ones

Groups of Ten

Circle groups of ten.
Then write the numbers that tell how many tens and ones.

Tens	Ones
1	9

Tens	Ones

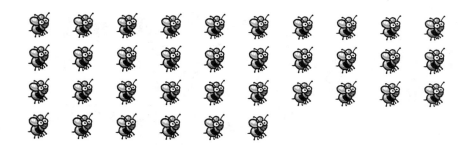

Tens	Ones

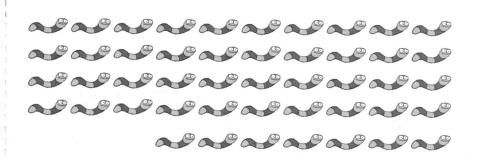

Tens	Ones

Tens	Ones

Guess and Check

Guess the nearest ten. Then count and write how many in each group.

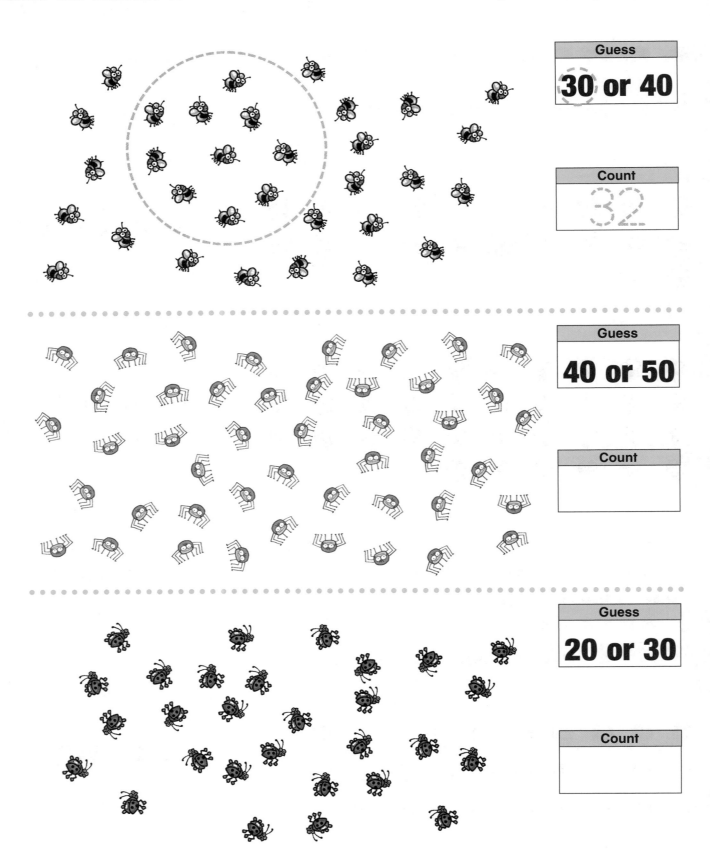

Guess
30 or 40

Count
32

Guess
40 or 50

Count

Guess
20 or 30

Count

Guess and Check

Guess the nearest ten. Then count and write how many in each group.

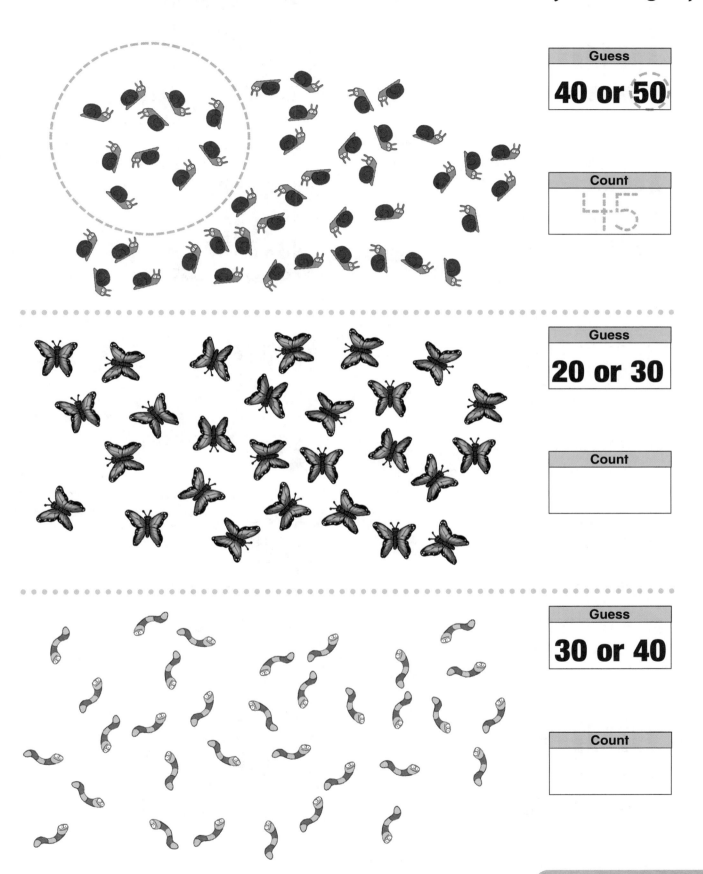

Guess
40 or 50

Count
45

Guess
20 or 30

Count

Guess
30 or 40

Count

Tens and Ones to 100

Write how many tens and ones. Then write the numbers.

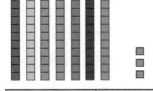

Tens	Ones
7	3

= 73

Tens	Ones
10	0

= 100

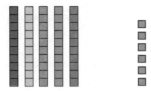

Tens	Ones

= _____

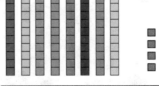

Tens	Ones

= _____

Tens	Ones

= _____

Tens	Ones

= _____

Tens	Ones

= _____

Tens	Ones

= _____

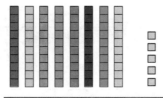

Tens	Ones

= _____

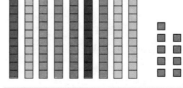

Tens	Ones

= _____

Tens and Ones to 100
Write how many tens and ones. Then write the numbers.

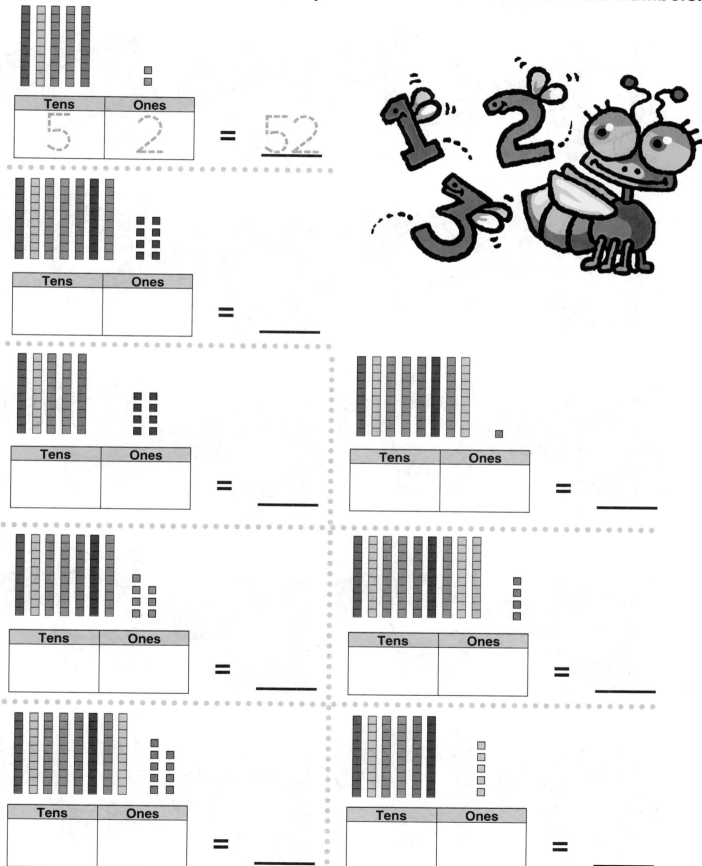

Tens	Ones
5	2

= 52

Tens	Ones

= ____

Tens	Ones

= ____

Tens	Ones

= ____

Tens	Ones

= ____

Tens	Ones

= ____

Tens	Ones

= ____

Tens	Ones

= ____

Missing Numbers

Write the missing numbers.

Before and After

Write the numbers that come just before and just after the ones shown.

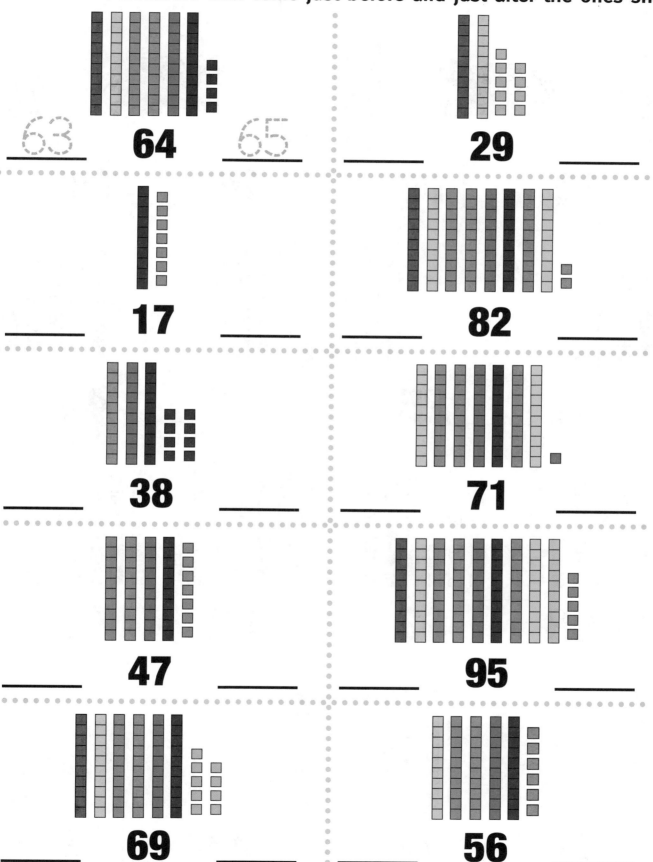

63   **64**   65

_____   **29**   _____

_____   **17**   _____

_____   **82**   _____

_____   **38**   _____

_____   **71**   _____

_____   **47**   _____

_____   **95**   _____

_____   **69**   _____

_____   **56**   _____

Comparing Numbers

Compare the numbers. Then write > or < in each box.

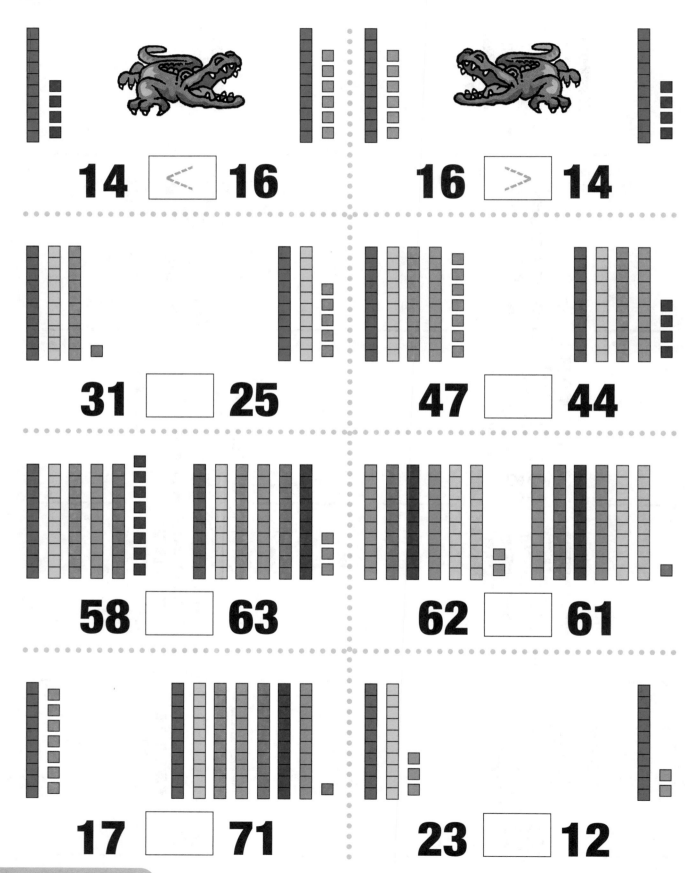

14 $<$ 16

16 $>$ 14

31 [ ] 25

47 [ ] 44

58 [ ] 63

62 [ ] 61

17 [ ] 71

23 [ ] 12

Comparing Numbers

Compare the numbers. Then write >, <, or = in each box.

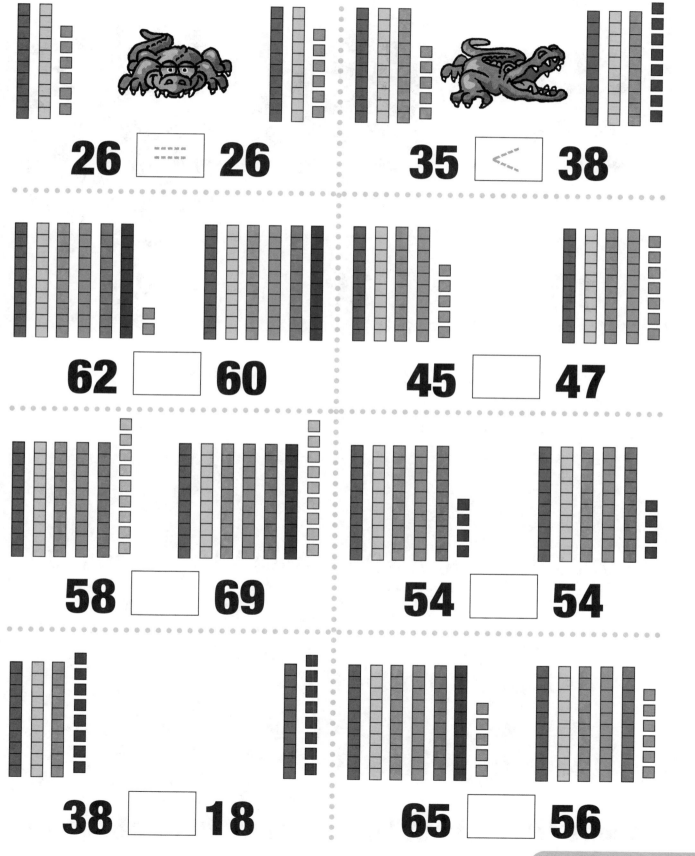

26 $=$ 26

35 $<$ 38

62 ☐ 60

45 ☐ 47

58 ☐ 69

54 ☐ 54

38 ☐ 18

65 ☐ 56

Using Estimation

Write how many tens and ones.
Use the groups at the top of the page to choose the better estimates.

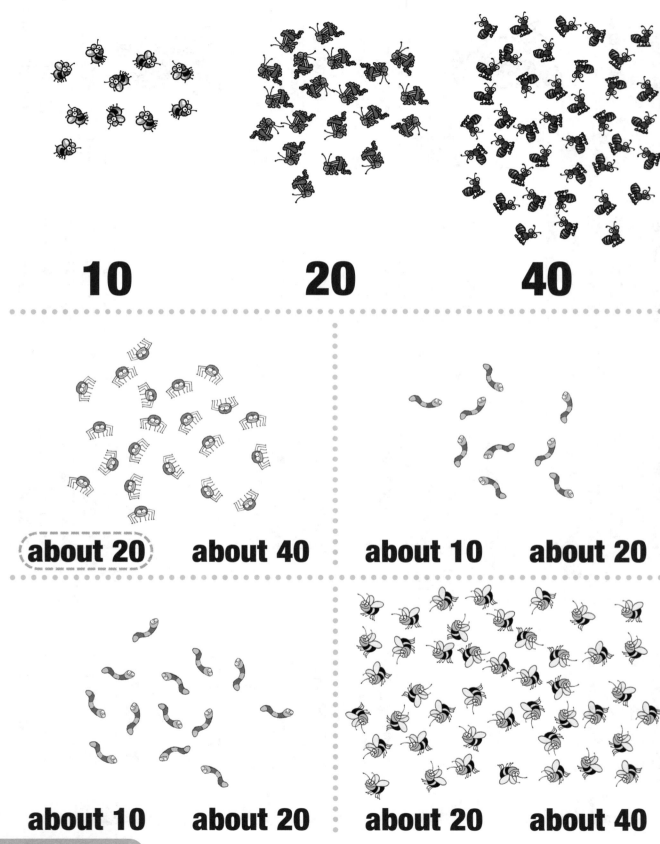

10 **20** **40**

about 20 about 40 about 10 about 20

about 10 about 20 about 20 about 40

Draw a line from each number to its most reasonable estimate.

12

18

63

84

39

97

about 20

about 40

about 80

about 100

about 10

about 60

Write each number.

10 + 3 = _____   10 + ___ = 15

80 + 10 = _____   50 + 10 = _____

4 tens = _____   7 tens = _____

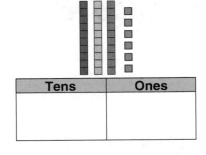

Tens	Ones

= _____

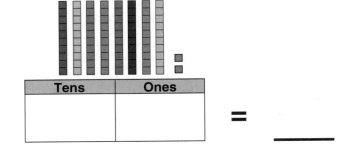

Tens	Ones

= _____

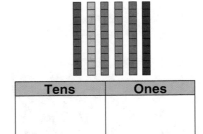

Tens	Ones

= _____

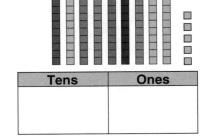

Tens	Ones

= _____

Compare the numbers. Write >, <, or = in each box.

69 ☐ 99   35 ☐ 37

15 ☐ 15   88 ☐ 78

Write the numbers in order.

| 91 | | | 94 | | | | 99 | |

Guess to the nearest ten. Then count and write how many in each group.

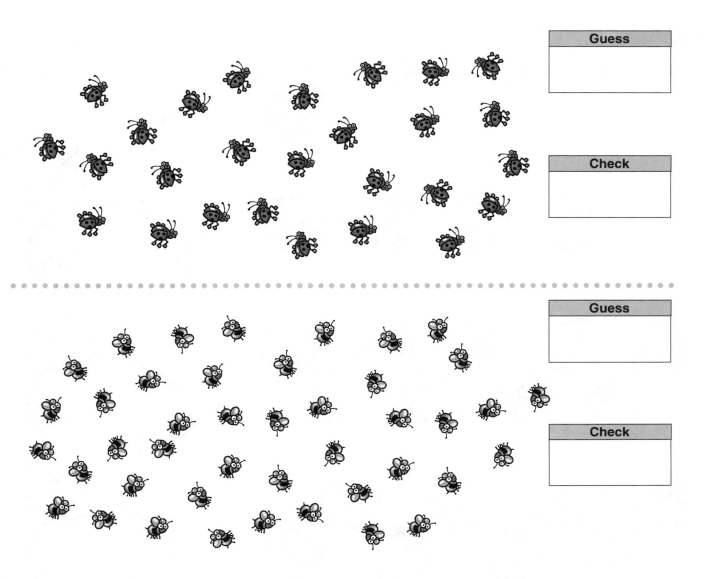

Guess

Check

Guess

Check

Choose the best estimate for the group of grasshoppers.

about 20   about 40

Pennies

Count the pennies. Write the total amount of money on each money bag.

 = 1 cent = 1¢

        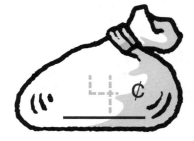
4¢

___¢

___¢

___¢

Pennies

Circle the number of pennies needed to buy each item.

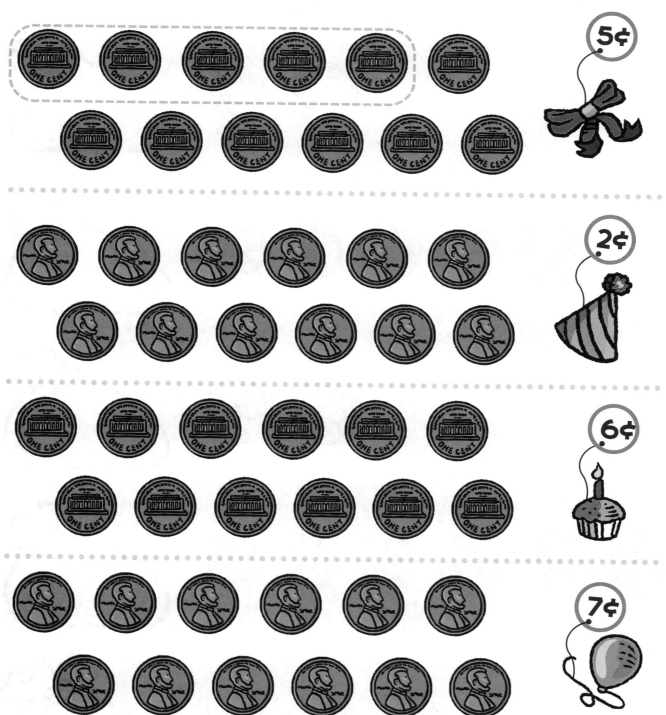

Nickels and Pennies

Count the pennies and nickels.
Write the total amount of money on each money bag.

 = 5 cents = 5¢

   ¢

      ¢

   ¢

      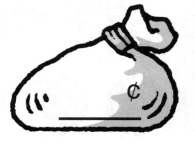 ¢

    ¢

Nickels and Pennies

Draw a line from each item to the coins needed to buy it.

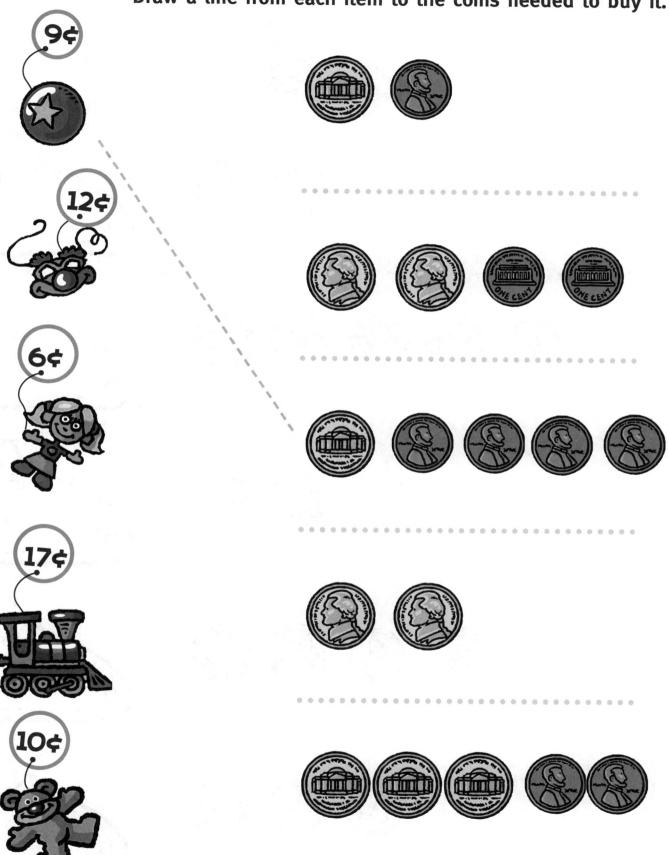

Dimes and Pennies

Count the pennies and dimes.
Write the total amount of money on each money bag.

 = 10 cents = 10¢

Dimes and Pennies

Draw a line from each item to the coins needed to buy it.

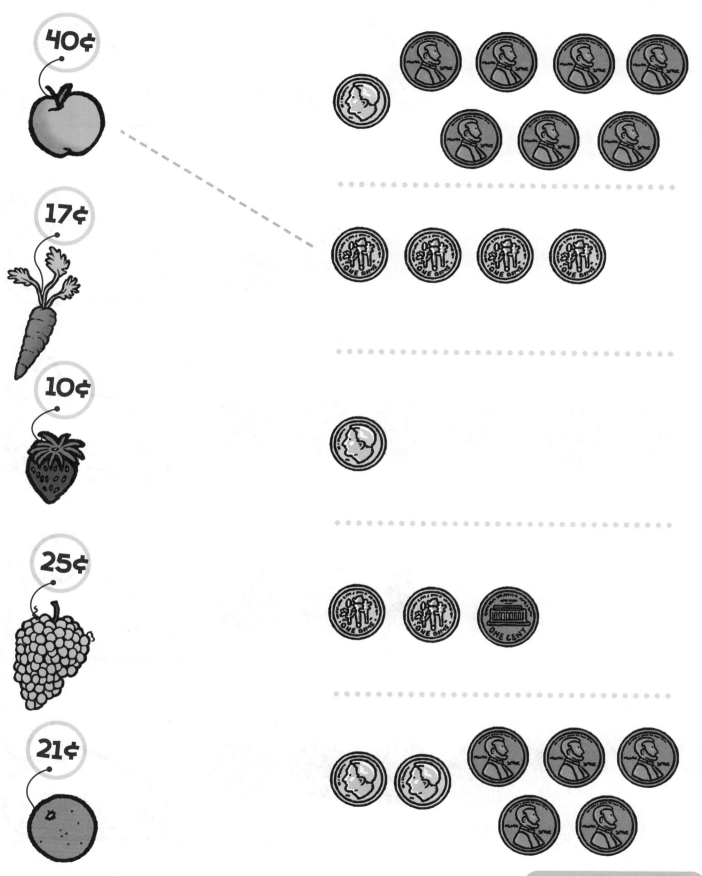

40¢

17¢

10¢

25¢

21¢

Pennies, Nickels, and Dimes

Count the pennies, nickels, and dimes. Write the total amount of money on each money bag.

Pennies, Nickels, and Dimes

Draw a line from each item to the coins needed to buy it.

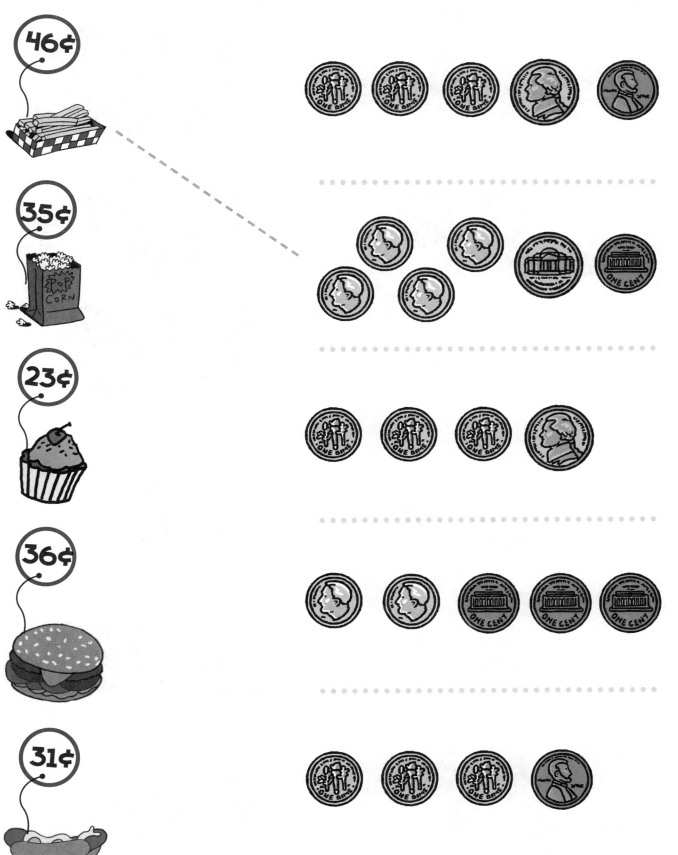

Money Equivalents

Draw lines from the coins on the left to the coins on the right to match equal amounts of money.

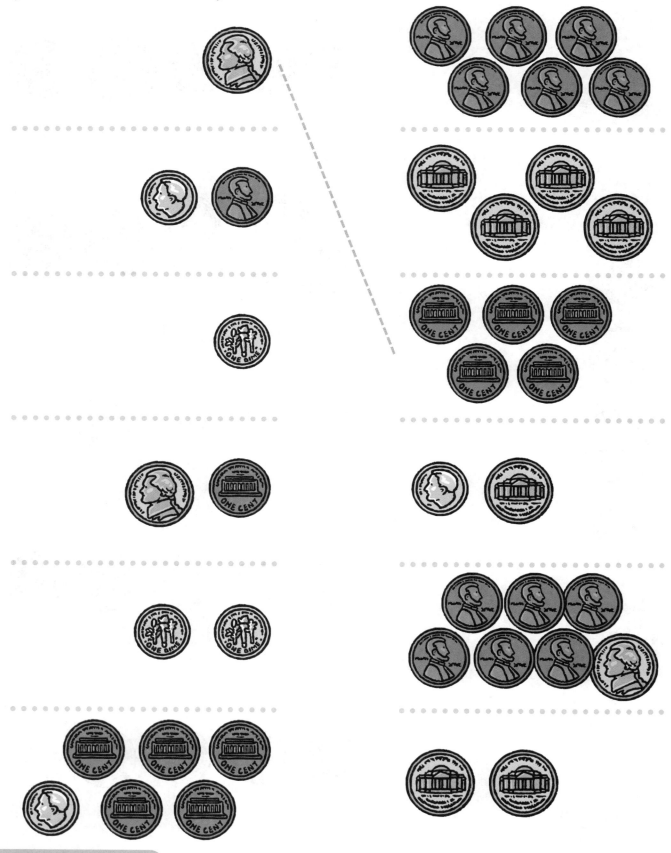

Money Equivalents

Count each group of coins and write the amounts.
Then draw lines to match equal amounts of money.

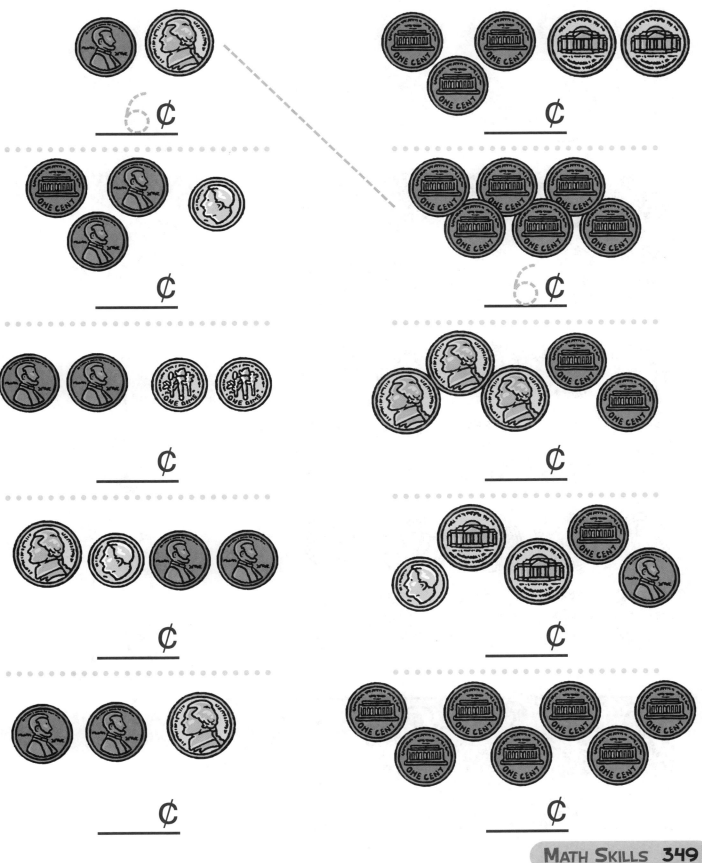

Show How Much

Circle the coins needed to buy each item.

13¢

14¢

20¢

35¢

Show How Much

Circle the coins needed to buy each item.

30¢

31¢

6¢

22¢

40¢

Using Logic

Count how much money is in each group of coins.
Then draw how much more money you need to buy each item.

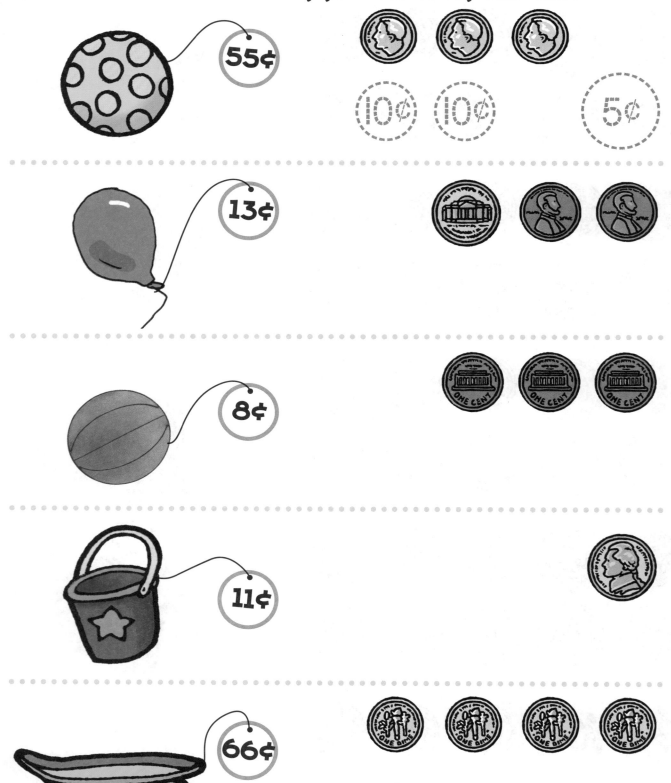

Using Logic

Count how much money is in each group of coins.
Then draw how much more money you need to buy each item.

 **22¢**

 **16¢**

 **25¢**

 **37¢**

 **42¢**

Write the total amount of money for each group of coins.

_____ ¢

_____ ¢

_____ ¢

_____ ¢

Draw lines to match equal amounts of money.

_____ ¢   _____ ¢

_____ ¢   _____ ¢

Unit 5 Review

Draw the coins needed to buy each item.

Draw the coins that are missing.

Parts of a Clock

Color the face yellow, the hour hand pink, and the minute hand blue. Then circle the number where the hour hand points.

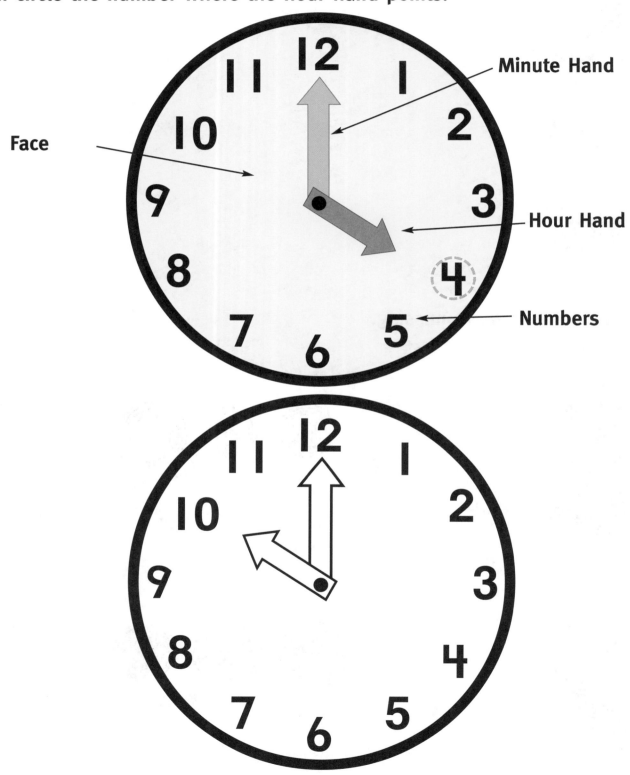

Minute Hand

Face

Hour Hand

Numbers

Hours

Write the numbers where the hour and minute hands point.

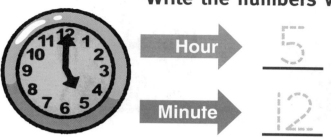

Hour ➤ 5
_____

Minute ➤ 12
_____

5 o'clock or 5:00

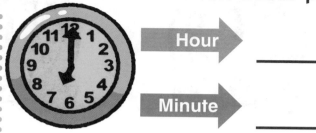

Hour ➤ _____

Minute ➤ _____

7 o'clock or 7:00

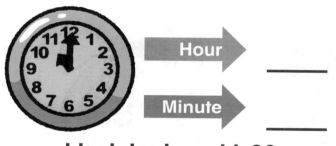

Hour ➤ _____

Minute ➤ _____

11 o'clock or 11:00

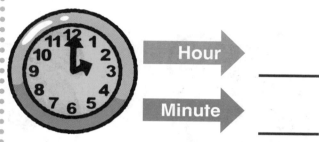

Hour ➤ _____

Minute ➤ _____

2 o'clock or 2:00

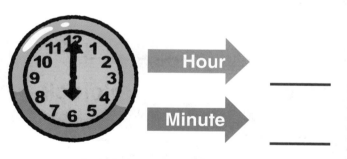

Hour ➤ _____

Minute ➤ _____

6 o'clock or 6:00

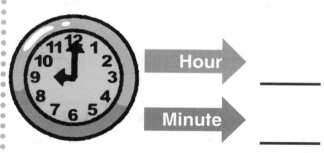

Hour ➤ _____

Minute ➤ _____

9 o'clock or 9:00

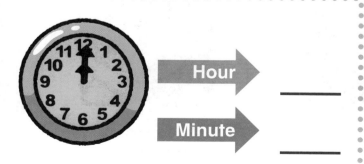

Hour ➤ _____

Minute ➤ _____

12 o'clock or 12:00

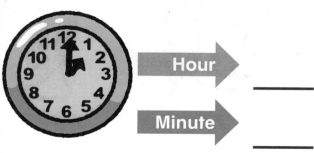

Hour ➤ _____

Minute ➤ _____

1 o'clock or 1:00

Telling Time: Hours

Write the time shown on each clock in two different ways.

1 1 : 0 0

1 1 _____ o'clock

_____ : _____

_____ o'clock

_____ : _____

_____ o'clock

_____ : _____

_____ o'clock

_____ : _____

_____ o'clock

_____ : _____

_____ o'clock

_____ : _____

_____ o'clock

_____ : _____

_____ o'clock

_____ : _____

_____ o'clock

Telling Time: Hours

Write the times on the digital clocks to match the first clock in each pair.

Telling Time: Hours

Draw an hour hand on each clock to show the time.

Complete a Pattern

Draw hands on the clocks to show the next time in each pattern.

Half Hours

Write where the hour and minute hands point.

Hour ➤ between __2__ and __3__

Minute ➤ __6__

30 minutes after 2 o'clock

2:30

Hour ➤ between ____ and ____

Minute ➤ ____

30 minutes after 10 o'clock

10:30

Hour ➤ between ____ and ____

Minute ➤ ____

30 minutes after 8 o'clock

8:30

Hour ➤ between ____ and ____

Minute ➤ ____

30 minutes after 4 o'clock

4:30

Hour ➤ between ____ and ____

Minute ➤ ____

30 minutes after 12 o'clock

12:30

Write where the hour and minute hands point.

Hour → between ___1___ and ___2___

Minute → ___6___

30 minutes after 1 o'clock   **1:30**

Hour → between _____ and _____

Minute → _____

30 minutes after 6 o'clock   **6:30**

Hour → between _____ and _____

Minute → _____

30 minutes after 11 o'clock   **11:30**

Hour → between _____ and _____

Minute → _____

30 minutes after 3 o'clock   **3:30**

Hour → between _____ and _____

Minute → _____

30 minutes after 9 o'clock   **9:30**

Telling Time: Half Hours

Write the times on the digital clocks to match the first clock in each pair.

Telling Time: Half Hours

Draw a line between the clocks that show the same time.

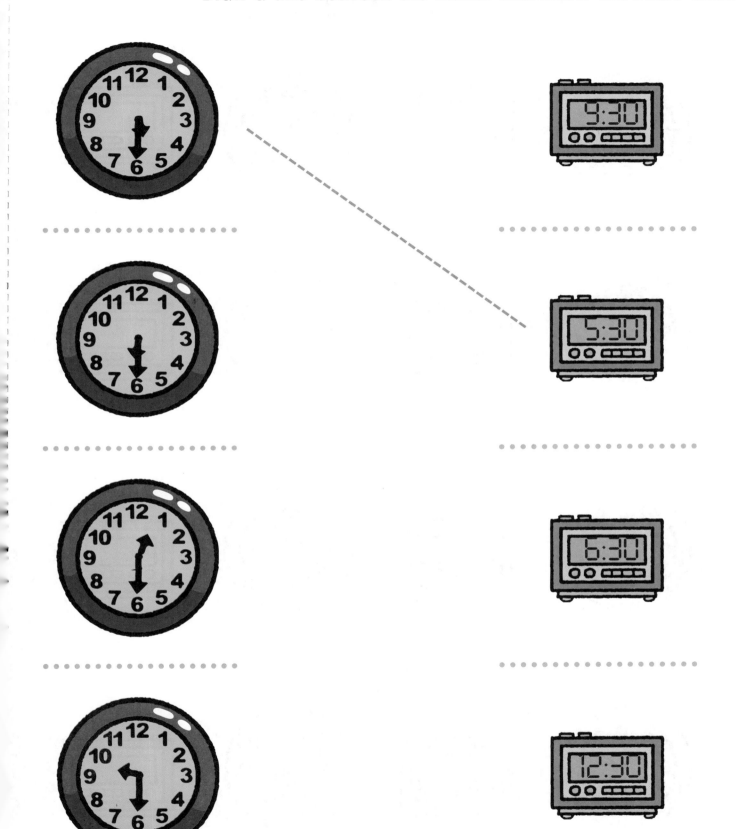

Using Logic

Look at the time shown on the first clock.
Then write the time that shows one hour later on the digital clock.

Using Logic

Look at the time shown on the first clock.
Then write the time that shows one half hour later on the digital clock.

Unit 6 Review

Write the time shown on each clock.

1 : 00

_____ o'clock

___ : ___

_____ o'clock

___ : ___

_____ o'clock

___ : ___

_____ o'clock

___ : ___

_____ o'clock

___ : ___

_____ o'clock

___ : ___

___ : ___

___ : ___

Unit 6 Review

Write the next time to complete each pattern.

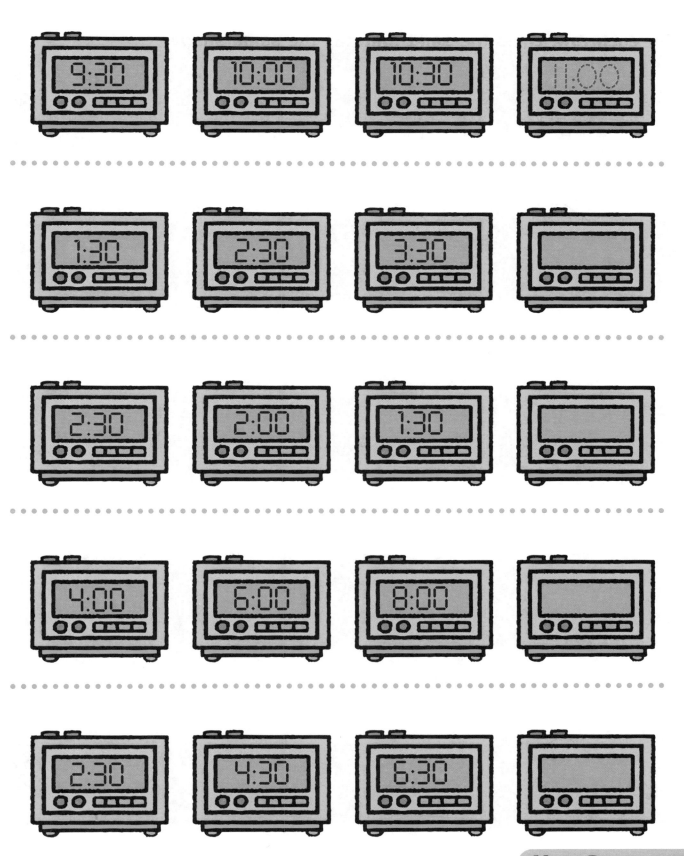

9:30   10:00   10:30   11:00

1:30   2:30   3:30   _____

2:30   2:00   1:30   _____

4:00   6:00   8:00   _____

2:30   4:30   6:30   _____

Solid Figures

For each row, circle the solid that has the same shape.

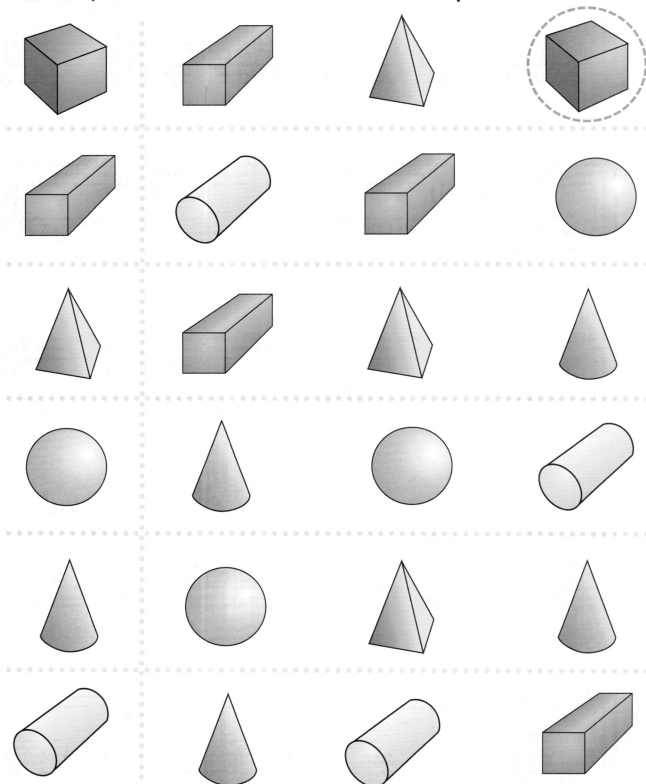

Solid Figures

Draw a line between the solids that have the same shape.

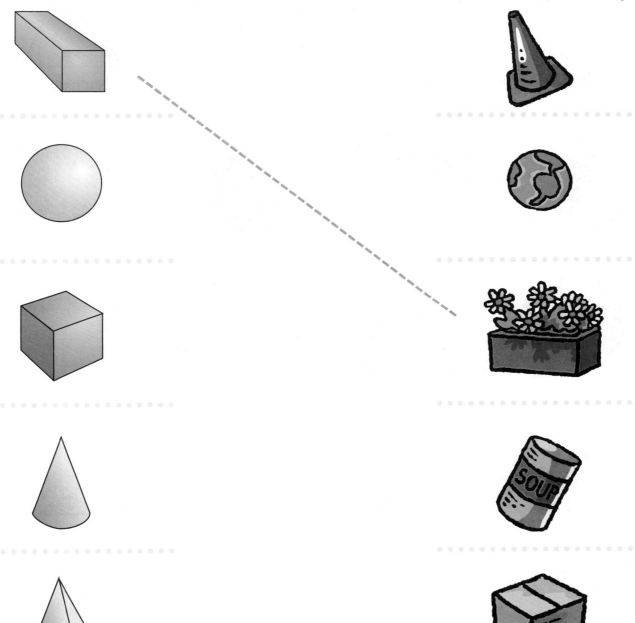

Plane Figures

In each row, mark the figure that is the same shape as the first.

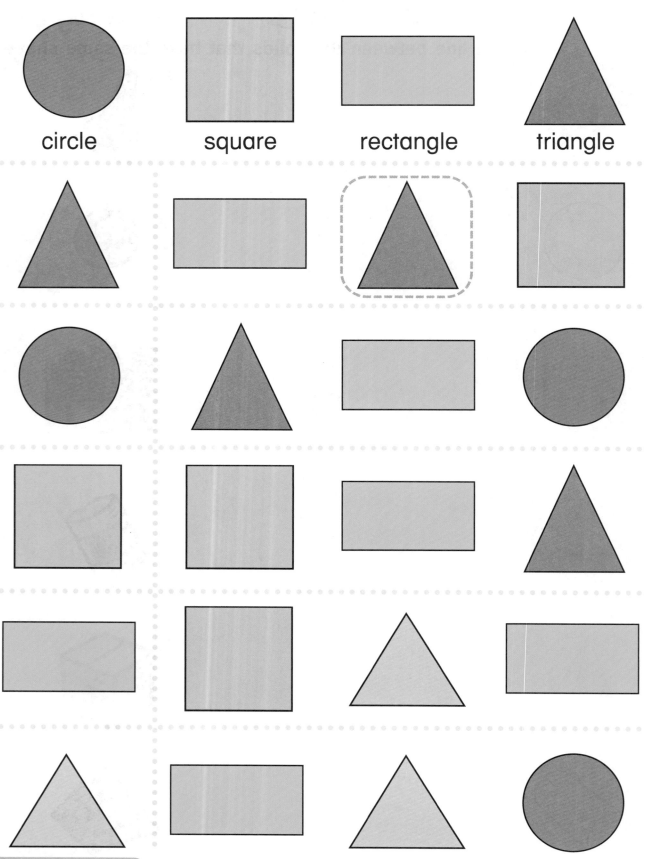

circle   square   rectangle   triangle

Plane Figures

Write the name of the shape for each picture.

rectangle

Congruence

Draw a shape to match each one shown.

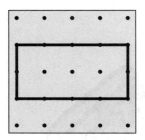 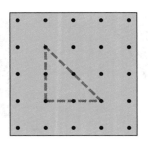 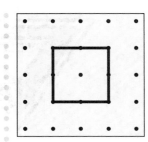 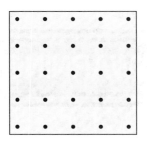

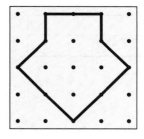 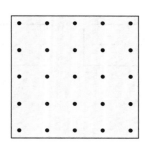 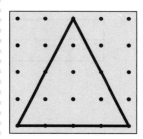 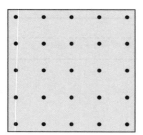

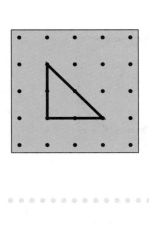 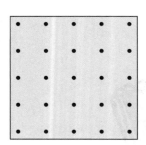 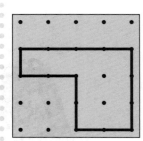 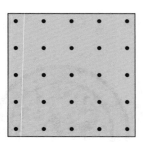

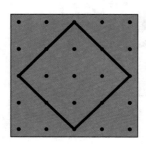 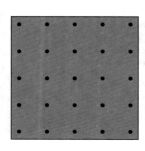 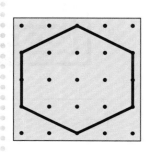 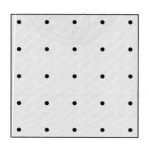

Symmetry

Draw the other half of each shape.

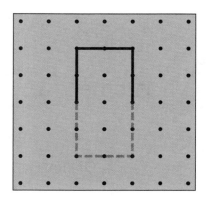

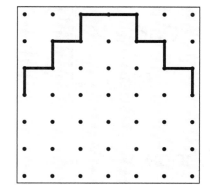

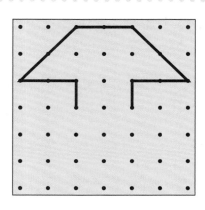

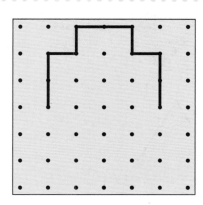

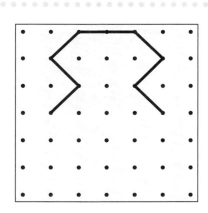

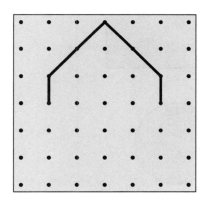

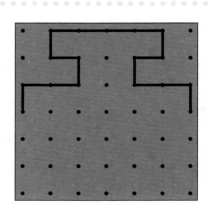

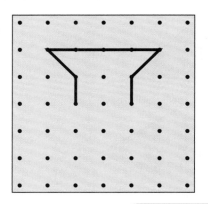

Using a Table

Write how many straight sides and corners each plane figure has.

Shape	Sides	Corners
	4	4

Using a Table

Look at each solid to see if it has corners, faces, or curves.
Write yes or no in each box.

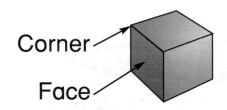

Corner
Face

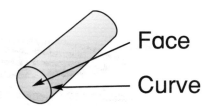

Face
Curve

Shape	Corners	Faces	Curves
	yes	yes	no

Measuring: Nonstandard Units

Write the length of each object.

about _____4_____ units

about _____ units

about _____ units

Measuring: Nonstandard Units

Write the length of each object.

about _____5_____ units

about _____ units

about _____ units

Measuring: Inches

Write the length of each object.

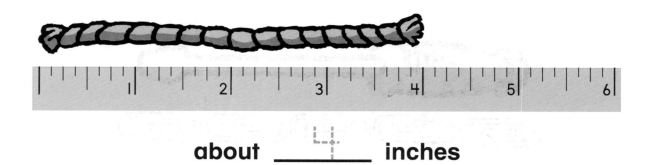

about _____4_____ inches

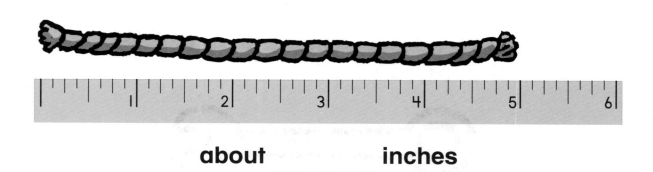

about _____ inches

about _____ inches

about _____ inches

Using an Inch Ruler

Use an inch ruler to measure each object.

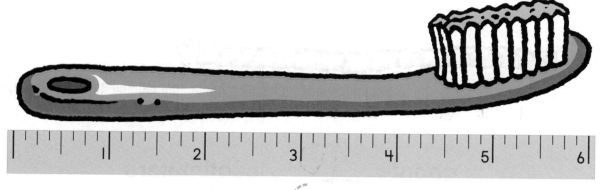

about ____6____ inches

about _____ inches

about _____ inches

about _____ inches

Measuring: Centimeters

Write the length of each object.

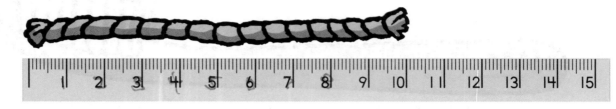

about ___10___ centimeters

about ___13___ centimeters

about ___4___ centimeters

about ___6___ centimeters

Using a Centimeter Ruler

Use a centimeter ruler to measure each object.

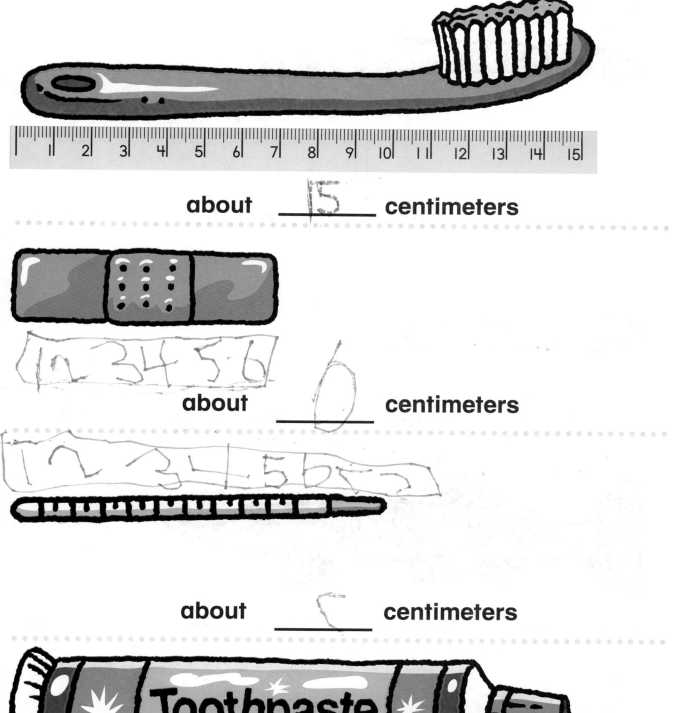

about ___5___ centimeters

about ___0___ centimeters

about ___6___ centimeters

about ___40___ centimeters

Guess and Check

Guess the length of each object.
Then measure with an inch ruler to check.

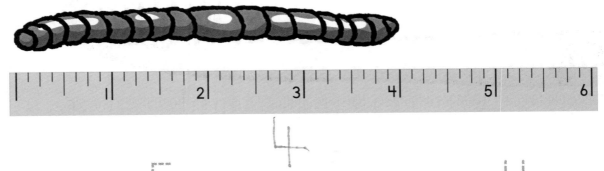

guess: about __5__ inches   check: about __4__ inches

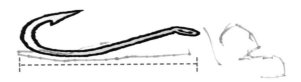

guess: about ___ inches   check: about ___ inches

guess: about ___ inches   check: about ___ inches

guess: about ___ inches   check: about ___ inches

Guess the length of each object.
Then measure with a centimeter ruler to check.

guess: about __11__ centimeters   check: about __10__ centimeters

guess: about ____ centimeters   check: about ____ centimeters

guess: about ____ centimeters   check: about ____ centimeters

guess: about ____ centimeters   check: about ____ centimeters

For each row, circle the shapes that are the same.

 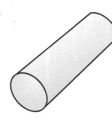 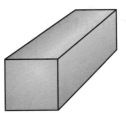 

Measure each object with a ruler.

about _____ centimeters

about _____ inches

Guess how many inches long each object is.
Then measure with an inch ruler to check.

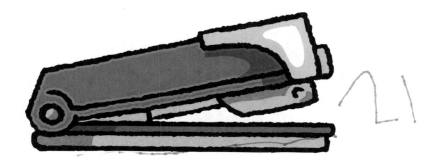

guess: about ___ inches   check: about ___ inches

guess: about ___ inches   check: about ___ inches

guess: about ___ inches   check: about ___ inches

Language Arts

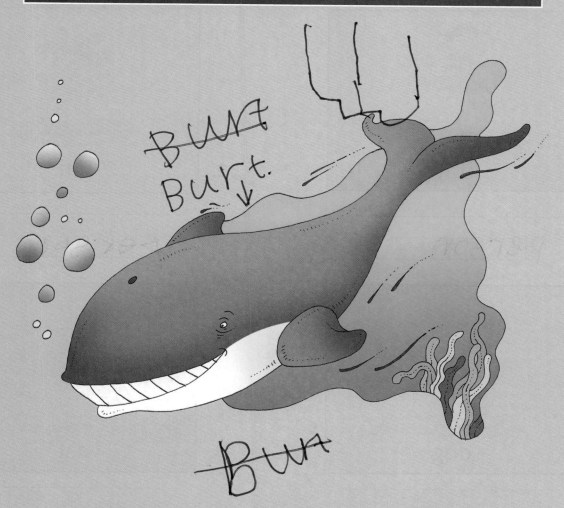

Naming Words

A–

> **Naming words** are called **nouns**.
> Nouns name people, places, and things.
> *Examples:*
>   man   house   boat

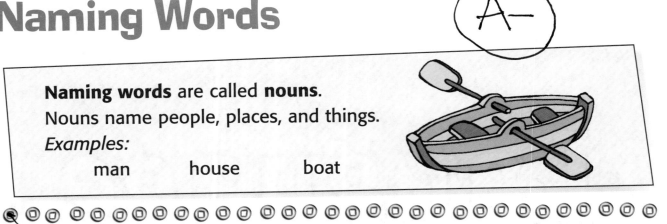

DIRECTIONS Look at each picture. Say the naming word under each picture. Then, write the naming word on the line.

1.
   boy

   person

2.
   girl

   person

3.
   dog

   person

4.
   cat

   person

More Naming Words

Remember, naming words are called nouns. Nouns name people, places, and things.

DIRECTIONS Read the word in each box. Look at each picture. Then, write the naming word for each picture on the line.

1.
man

person

2.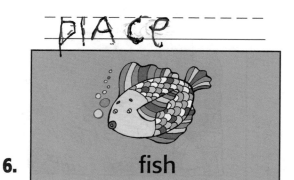
baby

Person

3.
school

PIACe

4.
store

PIACe

5.
car

Thing

6.
fish

Thing

Naming Words for People

Some nouns name people.
Examples:

    sister   teacher   dad

DIRECTIONS   **Read the words in the box. Look at each picture.**
Name each person. Write a word from the box.

farmer	doctor	cook	worker

1. doctor

2. FArmer

3. Worker

4. Cook

Naming Words for Animals

Some nouns name animals.
Examples:
pig
horse
whale

DIRECTIONS Complete each sentence. Write a word from the box.

frog	fish	dog	cat	bird	fox

1. A _____ FISH _____ swims in the sea.

2. A _____ FroG _____ jumps out of a pond.

3. A _____ FOX _____ runs in the woods.

4. A _____ Bird _____ flies in the sky.

5. A _____ DOG _____ barks at strangers.

6. A _____ CAT _____ meows.

Naming Words for Places

Some nouns name places.
Examples:
    city   beach   library

DIRECTIONS → Read the words in the box. Look at each picture. Name the place. Write a word from the box.

house	farm	lake	park

1. _____

2. _____

3. _____

4. _____

Naming Words for Things

Some nouns name things.
Examples:
    toy
    chair
    shoes

⊙ ⊙⊙ ⊙⊙ ⊙⊙⊙ ⊙⊙ ⊙⊙ ⊙⊙⊙ ⊙⊙⊙⊙⊙ ⊙⊙ ⊙⊙⊙⊙ ⊙⊙ ⊙⊙ ⊙⊙ ⊙⊙ ⊙

DIRECTIONS ▷ **Complete each sentence. Write a word from the box.**

cup	hat	bed	apple	crayons	box

1. I drink juice from a _____.

2. I use _____ for coloring.

3. I eat an _____ with lunch.

4. I sleep in a _____.

5. I wear a _____ on my head.

6. I keep my toys in a _____.

Practice with Naming Words

A noun can name a person, place, thing, or animal.
Examples:

mother   grass   duck   pencil

DIRECTIONS **Read the clues. Fill in the puzzle with words from the box.**

car   snake   teacher   tree   house

Down

1. This kind of plant has a trunk.

2. A family can live in this place.

4. You can drive in this thing.

Across

1. This person works in a school.

3. This animal is long and thin.

Two Kinds of Naming Words

Some words name common things. These words are called **common nouns**.

Examples:

child   park   story

Some words name special things. These words are called **proper nouns**. They begin with capital letters.

Examples:

<u>S</u>am   <u>P</u>eace <u>P</u>ark   "<u>T</u>he <u>R</u>ed <u>P</u>ony"

DIRECTIONS Read each sentence. Circle the special name in each sentence. Then, write the special name on the line.

1. That boy is Chris. _____

2. That girl is Lina. _____

3. My friend is Lee Chin. _____

4. I live on Main Street. _____

5. I read "All About Worms." _____

Special Names of People and Places

The special name of a person begins with a capital letter.
The special title of a person begins with a capital letter.
The special name of a place begins with
a capital letter.

Examples:

    Katie

    Dr. Jones

    New York City

DIRECTIONS → **Write each special name or title correctly. Be sure to use capital letters.**

1. This book is for sam. _____

2. mr. Sosa has a new car. _____

3. My friend goes to parker school. _____

4. We live on bakers road. _____

Practice with Proper Names

A special name of a person begins with a capital letter. The special title of a person begins with a capital letter. The special name of a place begins with a capital letter.

Examples:

Ms. Reed

Chicago

Lucy

DIRECTIONS > Answer each question using the special name of a person or a place. Remember to use capital letters.

1. What is your name? _____

2. What is your teacher's name? _____

3. What is the name of your school? _____

4. What is the name of your town or city? _____

5. What is your best friend's name? _____

DIRECTIONS > On another piece of paper, draw a picture of one person or place you wrote about above.

Naming One and More Than One

A naming word can name **one**.
A naming word can name **more than one**.
Many naming words add <u>s</u> to name more than one.
Example:

one **cat**

two **cat<u>s</u>**

◎ ◎ ◎◎ ◎ ◎◎ ◎◎◎ ◎ ◎◎ ◎ ◎◎ ◎ ◎◎ ◎ ◎◎ ◎

DIRECTIONS ▷ **Write the naming word in ( ) to complete each sentence.**

1. I see two _____.
(bird, birds)

2. I see one _____.
(bug, bugs)

3. I see two _____.
(girl, girls)

4. I see one _____.
(dog, dogs)

5. I see three _____.
(frog, frogs)

Practice with Naming More Than One

Many naming words add <u>s</u> to name more than one.
Example:
    one **bird**
    two **bird<u>s</u>**

DIRECTIONS Read the first sentence. Finish the second sentence to show more than one.

1. We planted a new tree.

Now we have six _____ in our yard.

2. Ruby picked one flower.

Ned picked two _____ .

3. Dad had one seed.

Mom had two _____ .

4. We found one nest.

They found three _____ .

I and Me

The words <u>I</u> and <u>me</u> take the place of some naming words.
Use <u>I</u> in the naming part of a sentence. The
word <u>I</u> is always written as a capital letter.
Use <u>me</u> in the telling part of a sentence.
Examples:

I have a new dog.

The dog licks **me**.

DIRECTIONS ▷ Write <u>I</u> or <u>me</u> to complete each sentence.

1. _____ am a big red rooster.

2. Can you find _____?

3. _____ am not in the henhouse.

4. Surprise! _____ am in the garden!

5. Now you can see _____.

Practice with I and Me

Remember, use I in the naming part of a sentence. The word I is always written as a capital letter. Use me in the telling part of a sentence.

Examples:

I like pizza.

Will you make a pizza for **me**?

DIRECTIONS → **Write I or me to complete each sentence.**

1. _____ like to skate.

2. Mom takes _____ to the pond on Saturdays.

3. _____ practice all day.

4. Mom claps for _____ .

5. _____ have a lot of fun.

We and They

The words <u>we</u> and <u>they</u> take the place of some naming words.
Use <u>we</u> and <u>they</u> in the naming part of a sentence.
Examples:

<u>Jim and I</u> will talk.
We will talk.

<u>Kay and Chris</u> will talk.
They will talk.

DIRECTIONS → Rewrite each sentence. Write <u>We</u> or <u>They</u> to take the place of the underlined names.

1. <u>Sam and I</u> are here.

_____

2. <u>Kay and Amy</u> are not here.

_____

3. <u>Kim and I</u> will play ball.

_____

4. <u>Ann, Pat, and Chad</u> found a kitten.

_____

Practice with <u>We</u> and <u>They</u>

Remember, use <u>we</u> and <u>they</u> in the naming part of a sentence.
Examples:

<u>John and I</u> are best friends.
We are best friends.

<u>Olivia and Adam</u> are twins.
They are twins.

◎ ◎

DIRECTIONS ⟩ **Rewrite each sentence. Write <u>We</u> or <u>They</u> to take the place of the underlined names.**

1. <u>Evan and Alan</u> are brothers.

_____

_____

2. <u>Emma and I</u> are sisters.

_____

_____

3. <u>Evan and Emma</u> are in second grade.

_____

_____

4. <u>Alan and I</u> are in first grade.

_____

_____

He, She, and It

The words <u>he</u>, <u>she</u>, and <u>it</u> take the place of some naming words.
Use <u>he</u> for a man or a boy.
Use <u>she</u> for a woman or a girl.
Use <u>it</u> for an animal or a thing.
Examples:

He rows the boat.
She rides in **it**.

DIRECTIONS   Rewrite each sentence. Use <u>He</u>, <u>She</u>, or <u>It</u> in place of the underlined words.

1. <u>Amy</u> likes to write.

2. <u>John</u> likes to read.

3. <u>The book</u> is on the table.

4. <u>Jenna</u> saw the bird.

Practice with He, She, and It

Remember, use <u>he</u> for a man or a boy.
Use <u>she</u> for a woman or a girl.
Use <u>it</u> for an animal or a thing.
Examples:
My dad is nice. **He** is also funny.
My sister is little. **She** is only three years old.
Our house is big. **It** is blue.

DIRECTIONS ➤ Read the first sentence. Then complete the second sentence using <u>He</u>, <u>She</u>, or <u>It</u>.

1. My dad works at a school. _____ is a teacher.

2. The school is big. _____ has many classrooms.

3. My mom works in a hospital. _____ is a doctor.

4. The hospital is on Main Street. _____ has ten floors.

5. Mom lets me visit her at work. _____ shows me her office.

6. Dad takes me to his school. _____ shows me his classroom.

Action Words

An **action word** tells what someone or something does. Action words are called **verbs**.
Examples:
Tom **sleeps**.
Birds **fly**.
Dogs **bark**.

⊚ ⊚⊚ ⊚⊚ ⊚⊚⊚ ⊚⊚ ⊚⊚ ⊚⊚⊚ ⊚⊚⊚ ⊚⊚ ⊚⊚ ⊚⊚ ⊚⊚ ⊚⊚ ⊚⊚ ⊚⊚ ⊚

DIRECTIONS Complete each sentence. Write an action word from the box.

talks	ride	eats	sing	waves

1. The girl _____ the food.

2. Dad _____ good-bye.

3. The boy _____ on the phone.

4. We _____ songs.

5. We _____ our bikes.

Using Clear Action Words

Some action words tell exactly how people and things move.
Examples:

    The dog **races** across the grass.

    The horse **gallops** across the field.

◎ ◎◎ ◎◎ ◎◎◎ ◎ ◎◎ ◎ ◎◎ ◎ ◎◎◎ ◎◎◎ ◎◎◎ ◎◎◎ ◎◎◎ ◎◎◎ ◎◎◎ ◎◎ ◎◎◎ ◎

DIRECTIONS   Complete each sentence. Choose the word in ( ) that tells exactly how each animal moves. Write the new sentence.

1. The fish (swims, stays) in the lake.

_____

- -

_____

2. The rabbit (goes, hops) up and down.

_____

- -

_____

3. The snake (sits, crawls) on the ground.

_____

- -

_____

4. The birds (fly, move) in the sky.

_____

- -

_____

Action Word Web

There are many action words. Sometimes, more than one word can tell about an action.
Examples:

    Cari **goes** to school.
    Cari **walks** to school.
    Cari **runs** to school.
    Cari **skips** to school.

DIRECTIONS Complete the word web. Write action words to replace the word <u>talk</u> in the sentence.

The children <u>talk</u> about the wind.

DIRECTIONS Write a sentence. Use an action word from the web.

Action Words with One or More Than One

Action words can tell what one person or thing does. Action words can also tell what more than one person or thing does.

Add <u>s</u> to an action word that tells about one person or thing.

Example:

The two boys **play** ball.

The one boy **play<u>s</u>** ball.

DIRECTIONS Complete each sentence. Write an action word.

1. The two girls _____ rope.

The one girl _____ rope.

2. The balls _____ slowly.

The ball _____ slowly.

3. The dogs _____.

The dog _____.

Action Words about Now

An action word can tell about now. Action words that tell about
one person, place, or thing end with <u>s</u>. Action words that tell about
more than one person, place, or thing do not end with <u>s</u>.
Examples:

Ray **helps** his dad.

Sam and Sara **throw** the ball.

**DIRECTIONS** Circle the action word in each sentence.

1. The sun shines all day long.

2. The seeds grow in the garden.

3. The frog hops over the log.

DIRECTIONS Complete each sentence. Choose the correct action word
in ( ). Write the word on the line.

4. The flowers _____ water.
(need, needs)

5. The boy _____ some water.
(get, gets)

More Action Words about Now

Remember, action words that tell about one person, place, or thing end with s. Action words that tell about more than one person, place, or thing do not end with s.

Examples:

David **drinks** a glass of milk.

David and his sister **wash** the dishes.

DIRECTIONS Finish the story using words from the box.

| welcomes | smile | puts | walk | thinks | eats | finds |

Today is the first day of school. Madison _____

pancakes. She _____ on her dress and shoes.

She and her sister _____ to school.

Madison _____ her classroom.

The teacher _____ the students.

The children _____ at their new teacher.

Madison _____ it will be a good year.

Action Words about the Past

An action word can tell about the past. Some action words that tell about the past end with <u>ed</u>.
Examples:
A mother duck **walk<u>ed</u>** across the grass.
She **quack<u>ed</u>** for the little ducks.

⊚ ⊚⊚ ⊚⊚ ⊚⊚⊚ ⊚⊚ ⊚⊚ ⊚⊚⊚ ⊚⊚⊚ ⊚⊚⊚ ⊚⊚ ⊚⊚⊚ ⊚⊚ ⊚⊚ ⊚⊚ ⊚⊚ ⊚

DIRECTIONS Complete each sentence. Choose the word in ( ) that tells about the past. Write the new sentence.

1. Two little ducks (plays, played) in the water.

_____

- -

_____

2. The mother duck (look, looked) at them.

_____

- -

_____

3. Two little ducks (jumped, jump) out of the water.

_____

- -

_____

4. They all (walk, walked) away.

_____

- -

_____

Practice with Action Words

Remember, action words can tell about now.
Example:
    I **play** checkers with my brother.
Action words can also tell about the past.
Example:
    Last night I **played** checkers with my sister.

DIRECTIONS   Read each sentence. Choose the correct word in ( ) to complete the sentence.

1. Last summer we _____ in the lake.
                                 (fish, fished)

2. Last night Sara _____ TV.
                                (watch, watched)

3. Now Harry and Sam _____ to music.
                                (listen, listened)

4. Last year Anna _____ a picture.
                                (paint, painted)

5. Mike bought food to _____ for dinner.
                                (cook, cooked)

Using Is and Are

Use is to tell about what one person or thing is doing now. Use are to tell about what more than one person or thing are doing now.
Examples:

Jack **is** sick today.

Jack's friends **are** sick, too.

◎ ◎◎ ◎◎ ◎◎◎ ◎◎ ◎◎ ◎◎◎ ◎◎◎ ◎◎◎ ◎◎ ◎◎◎ ◎◎◎ ◎◎ ◎◎ ◎◎ ◎

DIRECTIONS ⟩ Complete each sentence. Write is or are.

1. He _____ my father.

2. She _____ my mother.

3. They _____ in the garden.

4. Sue and I _____ in the garden, too.

5. The flowers _____ pretty.

6. Our dog _____ black and white.

Practice with Is and Are

Remember, use <u>is</u> to tell about what one person or thing is doing now. Use <u>are</u> to tell about what two or more people or things are doing now.

Examples:

He **is** running very fast.

The other children **are** running, too.

DIRECTIONS Write <u>is</u> or <u>are</u> in each blank to complete the story.

Luke _____ very smart. We _____

best friends. We _____ in first grade. Mr. Jackson

_____ our teacher. We _____

learning about birds. Luke _____ making a birdhouse.

Using <u>Was</u> and <u>Were</u>

Use <u>was</u> to tell about one person or thing in the past.
Use <u>were</u> to tell about more than one person or thing in the past.
Examples:

One cat **was** on the mat.
Two cats **were** on the bench.

◎ ◎◎ ◎◎ ◎◎◎ ◎◎ ◎◎ ◎◎◎ ◎◎◎ ◎◎◎ ◎◎◎

DIRECTIONS **Complete each sentence. Write <u>was</u> or <u>were</u>.**

1. I _____ at the lake.

2. Carl and Bert _____ there, too.

3. We _____ going to sleep.

4. The rain _____ a big surprise.

5. The tent _____ all wet.

6. Dad _____ calling us.

Practice with <u>Was</u> and <u>Were</u>

Remember, use <u>was</u> to tell about what one person or thing did in the past. Use <u>were</u> to tell about what two or more people or things did in the past.
Examples:

Ava **was** in her bedroom.

Tom and Ben **were** in the yard.

DIRECTIONS ▷ Write <u>was</u> or <u>were</u> in each blank to complete the story.

Tyler and Haley _____ moving to a new

house. Mom and Dad _____ filling the truck.

Haley _____ putting her toys in a box.

Tyler _____ cleaning his room. The children

_____ ready to see their

new home. They _____

also sad to leave their old house.

Using See, Come, and Run

Use see, come, and run to tell about something that happens now.
Use saw, came, and ran to tell about something
that happened in the past.
Examples:

    I **see** a red balloon now.

    Dad **came** home yesterday.

 **DIRECTIONS**   Complete each sentence. Circle the correct action word in ( ).

1. Last night Kim (run, ran) to the store.

2. Now I (run, ran) to the store.

3. Last week Bob (see, saw) a new movie.

4. Yesterday Tina (come, came) to my house.

5. Now Tina and Kim (come, came) to my house.

DIRECTIONS   Write sentences. Use the word in ( ) in your sentence.

6. (see)

_____

— —

_____

7. (run)

_____

— —

_____

Practice with See, Come, and Run

Remember, use <u>see</u>, <u>come</u>, and <u>run</u> to tell about something that happens now. Use <u>saw</u>, <u>came</u>, and <u>ran</u> to tell about something that happened in the past.

Examples:

Yesterday I **ran** home.

Today I **run** to school.

DIRECTIONS ▶ Complete each sentence with a word from the box.

| see | saw | come | came | run | ran |

1. My grandparents _____ to visit last week.

2. Can you _____ the rainbow now?

3. Now Lisa and I _____ to the store.

4. Wes _____ in the race yesterday.

5. Last night I _____ a good show.

6. Can Eric _____ to my house right now?

Using <u>Go</u> and <u>Went</u>

The words <u>go</u> and <u>went</u> are action words. Use <u>go</u> to tell about now. Use <u>went</u> to tell about the past.

Examples:

Today we **go** to school.

Last week we **went** to the beach.

DIRECTIONS — Write <u>go</u> or <u>went</u> to complete each sentence.

1. Last Friday we _____ to the park.

2. Yesterday we _____ swimming.

3. Now we _____ home.

4. Last night my cat _____ outside.

5. Now I _____ outside.

6. My cat and I _____ inside now.

Practice with Go and Went

Remember, use go to tell about something happening now.
Use went to tell about something that happened in the past.

Examples:

Last year we **went** to visit my aunt.
Now we **go** to visit my grandmother.

DIRECTIONS Write go or went to complete each sentence.

1. Last year we _____ to New York on a plane.

2. Now we _____ to Texas in a car.

3. Last year I _____ to Turner School.

4. Now I _____ to Park Lane School.

5. Now Kara and Ted _____ to the pool to swim.

6. Last week they _____ to the track to run.

Contractions with <u>Not</u>

A **contraction** is a word made by joining two words.
An **apostrophe (')** shows where a letter or letters are left out.
Many contractions are made with the word <u>not</u>.
Examples:

> do + not = **don't**
> had + not = **hadn't**
> will + not = **won't**

DIRECTIONS — Complete each sentence. Write the words in ( ) as a contraction. Use an apostrophe (') in your contraction.

1. I _____ like snakes.
   (do not)

2. I _____ go near a snake.
   (will not)

3. You _____ make me touch one.
   (can not)

4. Zack _____ here.
   (is not)

5. I _____ seen him all day.
   (have not)

6. You _____ go there.
   (should not)

Practice with Contractions

Remember, a contraction is a word made by joining two words.
An apostrophe shows where a letter or letters are left out.
Examples:

do + not = **don't**

can + not = **can't**

is + not = **isn't**

 **DIRECTIONS** Complete each sentence with a word from the box.

haven't	shouldn't	can't	isn't	don't	won't

1. You _____ swim alone.

2. I _____ been to China.

3. It _____ time to go yet.

4. She _____ tie her shoes.

5. He _____ tell anyone the secret.

6. Please _____ throw that!

Words That Tell Where

Some words tell where.
Example:
   The frog is **on** the log.

DIRECTIONS Complete each sentence. Use a word from the box.

in	under	out	on	up

1. The cat is looking _____ the box.

2. The cat sat _____ the chair.

3. The cat is _____ the chair.

4. The balloon goes _____.

5. A gopher peeks _____ of its hole.

Practice with Words That Tell Where

Some words tell where.
Example:
The bird is **in** the tree.

DIRECTIONS Circle the word in each sentence that tells where.
Draw a picture to go with each sentence.

1. A bug is on the rug.	**2.** The kite goes up.
3. The boy is under the umbrella.	**4.** The flower is in a pot.

Describing Words

Describing words tell about naming words.
Examples:
> **three** birds
> **tall** boy
> **little** bear
> **happy** girl

Circle each describing word. Then, write it on the line.

1. green frog

_____

2. loud noise

_____

3. wet dog

_____

4. two girls

_____

5. blue water

_____

6. funny clown

_____

Describing Words about Feelings

Some describing words tell how people **feel**.
Examples:
Yesterday Sandi was **sad**.
Now Sandi is **happy**.

DIRECTIONS ➤ Complete each sentence. Choose a word from the box. Write it on the line.

hungry	sleepy	glad	sick	angry

1. When Freddy is _____, he takes a nap.

2. When Freddy is _____, he goes to the doctor.

3. When Freddy is _____, he eats.

4. When Freddy sees his friend, he is _____.

5. When Freddy is _____, he is not happy.

Describing Words about Size and Shape

Some describing words tell about **size** and **shape**.
Examples:
  big dog
  square book

◎ ◎◎ ◎◎ ◎◎◎ ◎◎ ◎◎ ◎◎◎ ◎◎◎ ◎◎◎ ◎◎◎ ◎◎ ◎◎◎ ◎◎◎ ◎◎◎ ◎◎◎ ◎◎ ◎◎

DIRECTIONS ▷ **Answer each question. Choose a word in ( ). Write the word on the line.**

1. What size is a whale? _____
   (sad, big)

2. What size is an ant? _____
   (small, sleepy)

3. What size is a tree? _____
   (green, tall)

4. What shape is a ball? _____
   (round, blue)

DIRECTIONS ▷ **Write a sentence. Use a describing word about size or shape.**

5. _____

Describing Words about Color

Some describing words tell about **color**.
Examples:
>**blue** water
>**black** cat
>**gray** whale

 **DIRECTIONS** Complete each sentence. Choose a describing word from the box. Write the word on the line.

| blue | yellow | pink | white | green | red |

1. The grass is _____ .

2. The flowers are _____ .

3. That bird is bright _____ .

4. Watch it fly into the _____ sky.

5. It is flying into a _____ cloud.

6. I am flying a _____ kite.

Describing Words about Numbers

Some describing words tell **how many**.
Examples:

> **one** nose
> **five** toes

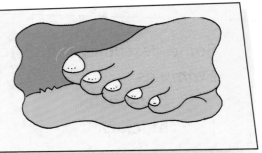

DIRECTIONS
 Complete each sentence. Use a number word from the box. Use the picture to help you.

one	two	three	four	five
six	seven	eight	nine	ten

1. I have _____ carton of milk.

2. I have _____ cookies.

3. I see _____ balloons.

4. The cake has _____ candles.

5. I see _____ pumpkins.

Describing Words about Taste and Smell

Some describing words tell how things **taste**.
Some describing words tell how things **smell**.

Examples:

This is **salty** popcorn.
The flower smells **sweet**.

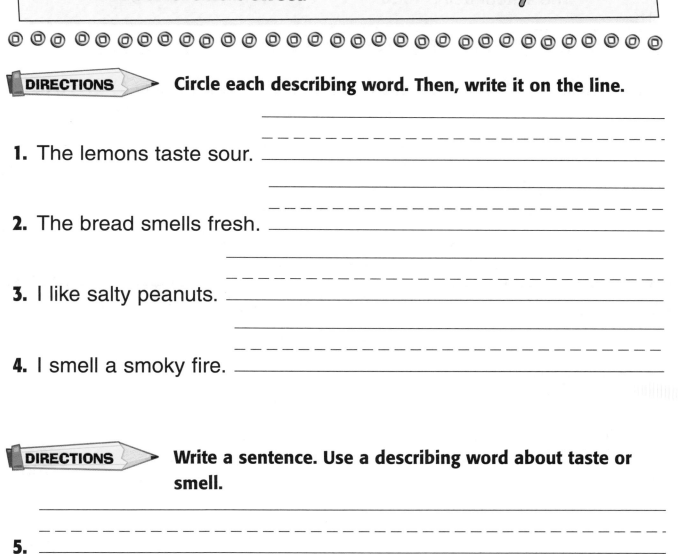

DIRECTIONS ▶ Circle each describing word. Then, write it on the line.

1. The lemons taste sour. _____

2. The bread smells fresh. _____

3. I like salty peanuts. _____

4. I smell a smoky fire. _____

DIRECTIONS ▶ Write a sentence. Use a describing word about taste or smell.

5. _____

Describing Words about Feel and Sound

Some describing words tell how things **feel**.
Some describing words tell how things **sound**.

Examples:

Ice cream feels **cold**.
The school bell is **loud**.

◎ ◎◎ ◎◎ ◎◎◎ ◎◎◎ ◎◎ ◎◎◎ ◎◎◎ ◎◎◎ ◎◎◎ ◎◎◎ ◎◎ ◎◎ ◎◎◎ ◎◎◎ ◎◎ ◎

DIRECTIONS Complete each sentence. Choose a word in ( ) that tells
about feel or sound. Write the word on the line.

1. The kitten is _____.
(soft, small)

2. I like to read in _____ rooms.
(two, quiet)

3. The sunshine is _____.
(long, hot)

4. I put _____ ice in my drink.
(cold, tall)

5. The ticking clock is _____.
(wet, noisy)

Describing Words about the Weather

Some describing words tell about the **weather**.
Example:

We had **stormy** weather yesterday.

○○ ○○ ○○ ○○○○○○○○ ○○ ○○○ ○○○ ○○○○○○○○ ○○○ ○○○○○○ ○○ ○○ ○

DIRECTIONS ▶ Look at each picture. Complete each sentence. Choose a weather word from the box. Write it on the line.

rainy	snowy	sunny	windy	cloudy

1. It is a _____ day.

2. It is a _____ day.

3. It is a _____ day.

4. It is a _____ day.

5. It is a _____ day.

Using Describing Words

DIRECTIONS Write a describing word for each naming word.

1. toad

_____
- - - - - - - - - - - - - - -
_____

2. cow

_____
- - - - - - - - - - - - - - -
_____

3. chick

_____
- - - - - - - - - - - - - - -
_____

4. whale

_____
- - - - - - - - - - - - - - -
_____

5. lion

_____
- - - - - - - - - - - - - - -
_____

6. rabbit

_____
- - - - - - - - - - - - - - -
_____

Practice with Describing Words

Remember, describing words tell about naming words.

DIRECTIONS → Write a sentence for each describing word.

1. red

2. fast

3. funny

4. rainy

5. small

DIRECTIONS → Draw a picture to go with one of the sentences you wrote.

Describing Words That Compare

Some describing words tell how two things are different. Add <u>er</u> to a describing word to tell how two things are different.
Some describing words tell how more than two things are different. Add <u>est</u> to a describing word to tell how more than two things are different.
Examples:

small, smaller, smallest
The cat is **small**.
The mouse is **smaller** than the cat.
The ant is the **smallest** of all.

◎ ◎◎ ◎◎ ◎◎◎ ◎◎ ◎◎ ◎◎◎ ◎◎◎ ◎◎◎ ◎◎◎ ◎◎◎ ◎◎ ◎◎

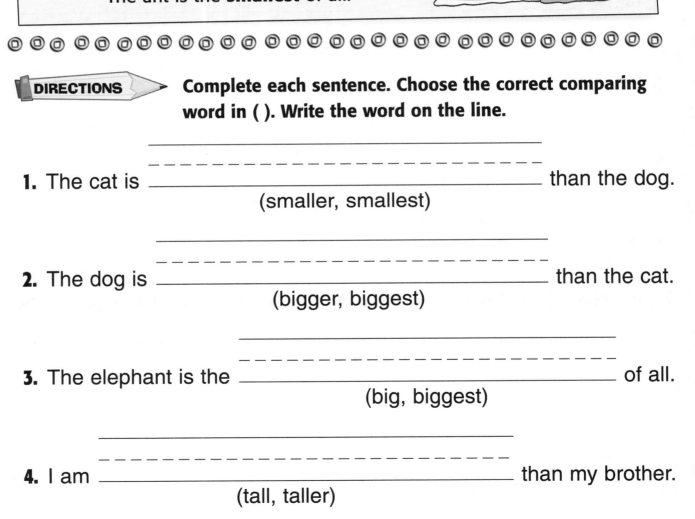

> **DIRECTIONS** → **Complete each sentence. Choose the correct comparing word in ( ). Write the word on the line.**

1. The cat is _____ than the dog.
(smaller, smallest)

2. The dog is _____ than the cat.
(bigger, biggest)

3. The elephant is the _____ of all.
(big, biggest)

4. I am _____ than my brother.
(tall, taller)

More Describing Words That Compare

DIRECTIONS Answer each question. Circle the correct picture.

1. Which goat is <u>bigger</u>?

2. Which bridge is <u>longer</u>?

3. Which is the <u>tallest</u> tree of all?

4. Which is the <u>highest</u> building of all?

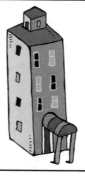

Using A and An

Use <u>a</u> before words that begin with a consonant sound.
Use <u>an</u> before words that begin with a vowel sound.
The vowels are <u>a</u>, <u>e</u>, <u>i</u>, <u>o</u>, and <u>u</u>.
Examples:
    a car, **a** skate
    an ant, **an** egg

DIRECTIONS ➤ Read each word. Write <u>a</u> or <u>an</u> on the line.

1. _____ tent

2. _____ train

3. _____ orange

4. _____ owl

5. _____ book

6. _____ bike

7. _____ apple

8. _____ oak tree

Practice with A and An

Remember, use <u>a</u> before words that begin with a consonant sound. Use <u>an</u> before words that begin with a vowel sound. The vowels are <u>a</u>, <u>e</u>, <u>i</u>, <u>o</u>, and <u>u</u>.
Example:

an apple, **a** cat

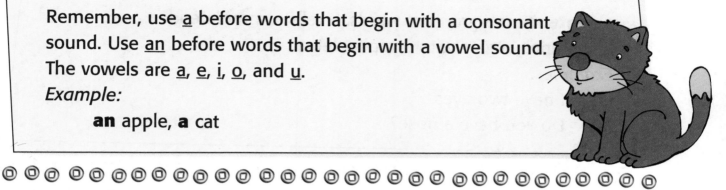

 **DIRECTIONS** Look at each word in the word box. If it begins with a vowel, write it in the <u>an</u> side of the chart. If it begins with a consonant, write it in the <u>a</u> side of the chart.

| uncle | radio | bear | airplane | fish |
| ape | lamp | inch | ocean | queen |

a	**an**

Sentences

A **sentence** is a group of words. It tells a complete idea.
A sentence begins with a capital letter.
Examples:

I have two eyes.
Do you have a nose?

> **DIRECTIONS** Underline the groups of words that are sentences.

1. I see a lion.
see a lion.

2. throws the ball.
Jan throws the ball.

3. I hear a bird.
a bird.

> **DIRECTIONS** Write the sentences correctly.

4. my cat can jump.

_____

- -

_____

5. the dog barks.

_____

- -

_____

Is It a Sentence?

Remember, a sentence tells a complete idea.
A sentence begins with a capital letter.

DIRECTIONS Read each group of words. Write <u>yes</u> if the words are a sentence. Write <u>no</u> if the words are not a sentence.

1. Today is my birthday.

2. have a party.

3. open the presents.

4. We will eat some cake.

5. All my friends are here.

6. play some games.

7. making ice cream.

8. My birthday party is fun.

Sentence Parts

A sentence has two parts. The **naming part** tells who or what the sentence is about.

The **telling part** tells what someone or something does.

A naming part and a telling part make a complete sentence.

Examples:

Naming Part	Telling Part
Sari	plants some seeds.
The girls	sing a song.

 **DIRECTIONS** ➤ Underline the naming part in each sentence.

1. A frog jumped in the grass.

2. A cat saw the frog.

3. A dog ran after the cat.

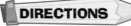 **DIRECTIONS** ➤ Circle the telling part in each sentence.

4. Dogs chew bones.

5. Birds eat worms.

6. Jacy walks to school.

Practice with Sentence Parts

Remember, a naming part and a telling part make a complete sentence.

Example:

Naming Part	**Telling Part**
Andrew	plays drums.

DIRECTIONS ▷ **Draw a line to match each naming part with a telling part.**

1. The fisherman   draws a picture.

2. The dancer   gets a fish.

3. The artist   helps the sick girl.

4. The doctor   spins on stage.

Naming Parts of Sentences

A sentence has a **naming part**. It tells
who or what the sentence is about.
Examples:

The friends play.   **The duck** is brown.

○○○○○○○○○○○○○○○○○○○○○○○○○○○○○○○○○○○○○

DIRECTIONS ▷ Read each sentence. Then, read the question. Write the
answer to the question on the line.

1. Rick went to the zoo.

_____

Who did something? _____

2. His mother went with him.

_____

Who did something? _____

3. The bear ate some food.

_____

What did something? _____

4. The monkey did some tricks.

_____

What did something? _____

5. The tiger slept in its cage.

_____

What did something? _____

6. The turtle swam in the water.

_____

What did something? _____

Naming Parts of Sentences, page 2

Remember, the naming part tells who or what the sentence is about.

◎ ◎

DIRECTIONS ➤ Complete each sentence. Write a naming part. Use the words in the box.

Who	What
My sister	The blue kite
Amy	The wind
	The red kite

1. _____ flies a blue kite.

2. _____ has a red kite.

3. _____ takes the kites up.

4. _____ is hard to see.

5. _____ is easy to see.

Telling Parts of Sentences

A sentence has a **telling part**. It tells
what someone or something does or is.
Examples:

   Pat **plays in the grass**.
   The grass **is green and tall**.

◎◎◎◎◎◎◎◎◎◎◎◎◎◎◎◎◎◎◎◎◎◎◎◎◎◎◎◎◎◎◎◎

DIRECTIONS ➤ Read each sentence. Then, read the question. Write the
answer to the question on the line.

1. Anna found a puppy.

_____

What did Anna do? _____

2. The puppy ate some food.

_____

What did the puppy do? _____

3. The puppy played with Anna.

_____

What did the puppy do? _____

4. Anna named the puppy Skip.

_____

What did Anna do? _____

5. Anna threw the ball.

_____

What did Anna do? _____

6. Skip ran after the ball.

_____

What did Skip do? _____

Telling Parts of Sentences, page 2

Remember, the telling part tells what someone or something does or is.

○○○○○○○○○○○○○○○○○○○○○○○○○○○○○○○○○○○○○

DIRECTIONS Complete each sentence. Write a telling part. Use the words in the box.

Telling Parts
will show you
are fun to grow
gives them light
plant seeds
waters the seeds

1. Flowers _____.

2. I _____.

3. You _____.

4. The rain _____.

5. The sun _____.

Writing Sentences with Naming Parts

Remember, the naming part tells who or what the sentence is about.

⊚⊚⊚⊚⊚⊚⊚⊚⊚⊚⊚⊚⊚⊚⊚⊚⊚⊚⊚⊚⊚⊚⊚⊚⊚⊚⊚⊚

DIRECTIONS ➤ Complete each sentence. Write a naming part.

1. _____ has a bike.

2. _____ is green.

3. _____ is tall.

4. _____ found a pretty rock.

5. _____ reads a book.

6. _____ climbs a tree.

7. _____ barks at a cat.

8. _____ runs to the store.

Writing Sentences with Telling Parts

Remember, the telling part tells what someone or something does or is.

◎ ◎

DIRECTIONS ▷ **Complete each sentence. Write a telling part.**

_____
1. The man _____.

_____
2. The cat _____.

_____
3. The fish _____.

_____
4. The balloon _____.

_____
5. My friend _____.

_____
6. The bird _____.

_____
7. The boy _____.

_____
8. The girl _____.

Word Order in Sentences

Words in a sentence are in order.
The words must be in order to make sense.
Example:

      book a Pablo gets. (makes no sense)

      Pablo gets a book. (makes sense)

DIRECTIONS Write each sentence in correct word order.

1. fast Jim swims

_____

2. can not swim Jane

_____

3. Mike art likes

_____

4. to town Eva walks

_____

5. Kim bird sees a

_____

6. sing The birds to me

_____

Telling Sentences

A **telling sentence** tells about something or someone. It begins with a capital letter. It ends with a **period (.)**.
Examples:

<u>A</u> frog hops away.
<u>We</u> try to get it.

◎◎◎◎◎◎◎◎◎◎◎◎◎◎◎◎◎◎◎◎◎◎◎◎

DIRECTIONS   Write each telling sentence correctly.

1. i have a pig

_____

_ _

_____

2. he and I play

_____

_ _

_____

3. he has a cold nose

_____

_ _

_____

4. my pig is my friend

_____

_ _

_____

5. we have fun

_____

_ _

_____

Telling Sentences, page 2

Remember, a telling sentence tells about something or someone. It begins with a capital letter. It ends with a period (.).

DIRECTIONS → Write a sentence for each picture. Tell about the animals.

1. _____

2. _____

DIRECTIONS → Write a telling sentence about yourself.

3. _____

Asking Sentences

An **asking sentence** asks about something or someone. It begins
with a capital letter. It ends with a **question mark (?)**.
Examples:
    How old are you?
    Do you like pets?

DIRECTIONS ➤ Write each asking sentence correctly.

1. what is your name

_____

_____

2. where do you live

_____

_____

3. when is your birthday

_____

_____

4. do you have a pet

_____

_____

5. who is your best friend

_____

_____

Asking Sentences, page 2

Remember, an asking sentence asks about something or someone.
An asking sentence often begins with a question word.
Examples:

What are you doing?

Where have you been?

 **DIRECTIONS** ⟩ Complete each sentence. Write a question word from the box.

Question Words

Who

What

When

Where

1. _____ did the circus come to town?

2. _____ took you to the circus?

3. _____ did you see first?

4. _____ are the elephants?

5. _____ climbs the rope?

6. _____ did the clowns do?

Telling or Asking?

Remember, a telling sentence tells about something or someone.
An asking sentence asks about something or someone.
Examples:

    I have a new pencil.
    When did you get it?

DIRECTIONS   Read each sentence. Write <u>tell</u> if it is a telling sentence.
Write <u>ask</u> if it is an asking sentence.

1. I saw a fish.

2. Where did you see it?

3. I saw it in the lake.

4. What color was the fish?

5. Who took my lunch?

6. I like to swim.

7. How cold is the water?

Writing Sentences with Describing Words

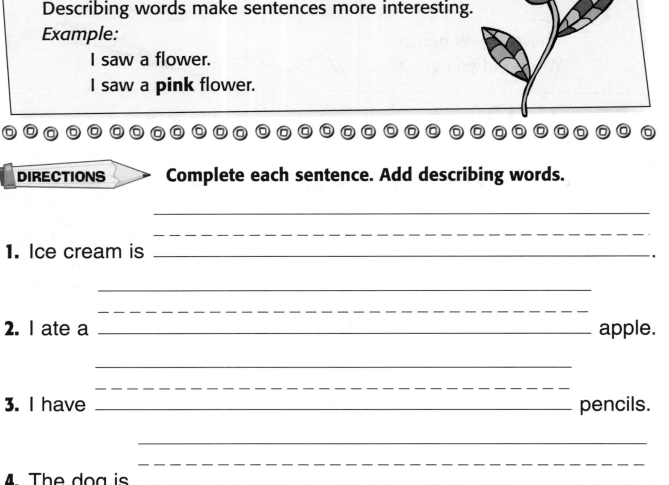

Describing words make sentences more interesting.
Example:
    I saw a flower.
    I saw a **pink** flower.

◎◎◎◎◎◎◎◎◎◎◎◎◎◎◎◎◎◎◎◎◎◎◎◎◎◎◎◎◎◎◎◎

DIRECTIONS   **Complete each sentence. Add describing words.**

1. Ice cream is _____.

2. I ate a _____ apple.

3. I have _____ pencils.

4. The dog is _____.

5. The cat is _____.

6. The rabbit is _____ and
_____.

Joining Naming Parts

A sentence has a naming part. Sometimes the naming parts of two sentences can be joined. Use the word and to join the parts.

Example:

Turtle looked. **Fox** looked.
Turtle **and** **Fox** looked.

ⓞ ⓞ

> **DIRECTIONS** — Join the naming parts of the sentences. Use the word and. Write the new sentences.

1. Turtle hid. Fox hid.

_____

_____

2. Jon played ball. Teri played ball.

_____

_____

3. Brett ate lunch. Max ate lunch.

_____

_____

4. Cat played with Duck. Frog played with Duck.

_____

_____

Joining Telling Parts

A sentence has a telling part. Sometimes the telling parts of two sentences can be joined. Use the word <u>and</u> to join the parts.
Example:
    The birds **fly**. The birds **sing**.
    The birds **fly** <u>and</u> **sing**.

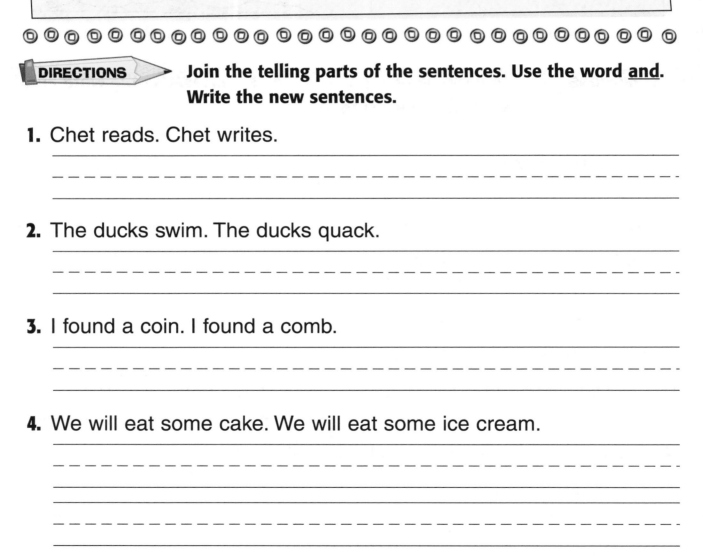

> **DIRECTIONS** ▸ Join the telling parts of the sentences. Use the word <u>and</u>. Write the new sentences.

1. Chet reads. Chet writes.

_____
_____
_____

2. The ducks swim. The ducks quack.

_____
_____
_____

3. I found a coin. I found a comb.

_____
_____
_____

4. We will eat some cake. We will eat some ice cream.

_____
_____
_____
_____

Beginning Sentences with a Capital Letter

A sentence always begins with a capital letter.
Examples:
    The horse ran away.   A dog ran after the horse.
    I ran after the dog.

DIRECTIONS ➤ **Write each sentence correctly. Be sure to begin each sentence with a capital letter.**

1. the sun is hot.

_____

_____

2. we will go home.

_____

_____

3. you can come with us.

_____

_____

4. i will get some water.

_____

_____

5. do you have a cup?

_____

_____

6. where is the door?

_____

_____

The Word I

The word I is always written with a capital letter.
Examples:
  I have a new bike.
  Tomorrow I will ride to school.
  Where can I find a flower?

DIRECTIONS ▶ **Answer the questions. Write sentences. Begin each sentence with I can.**

1. What can you ride?

_____

- -

_____

2. What can you make?

_____

- -

_____

3. How can you help at home?

_____

- -

_____

4. What can you write?

_____

- -

_____

Writing Names of People

The names of people always begin with a capital letter. The first letter in each name is a capital letter.

Examples:

    Carla Cantu

    Yuko Ito

    Aunt Angela

    Uncle Bart

DIRECTIONS Rewrite each name. Begin each name with a capital letter.

1. pat long

2. eva ramos

3. uncle thomas

4. will smith

5. ling chung

6. mori adams

Practice with Names of People

Remember, the names of people always begin with a capital letter. The first letter in each name is a capital letter.

Example:

Laura Lewis

Titles in a name also begin with a capital letter.

Examples:

Mr. Li

Dr. Green

DIRECTIONS ➤ Answer each question with a name. Begin each name with a capital letter.

1. Who is your teacher? _____

2. Who sits next to you at school? _____

3. Who plays with you? _____

4. Who lives with you? _____

5. Who are you? _____

Writing Names of Pets

The names of pets also begin with a capital letter. The first letter in each name is a capital letter.
Examples:

    Winky   Silver   Rin Tin Tin

**DIRECTIONS** ➤ **Name each pet. Use a name from the box. Write each name under the pet. Begin each name with a capital letter.**

chip	muff	king	jet	goldy	speedy

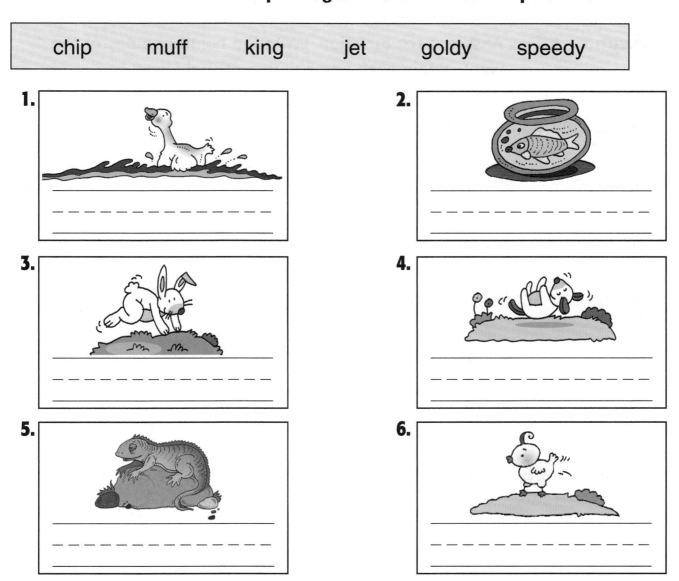

1. _____

2. _____

3. _____

4. _____

5. _____

6. _____

Writing Names of the Days

The names of the days of the week begin with a capital letter.
The first letter in each name is a capital letter.

Examples:

Sunday   Monday

Tuesday   Wednesday

Thursday   Friday

Saturday

August						
Sun	Mon	Tues	Wed	Thur	Fri	Sat
			1	2	3	4
5	6	7	8	9	10	11
12	13	14	15	16	17	18
19	20	21	22	23	24	25
26	27	28	29	30	31	

DIRECTIONS → **Answer each question. Write the name of a day of the week. Begin each name with a capital letter.**

1. What day comes before Tuesday? _____

2. What day comes after Thursday? _____

3. What day comes before Monday? _____

4. What day begins with the letter <u>W</u>? _____

5. What two days start with the letter <u>T</u>?

_____   _____

6. What two days start with the letter <u>S</u>?

_____   _____

Writing Names of the Months

The names of the months of the year begin with a capital letter.
The first letter in each name is a capital letter.
Examples:

    June   August   November

DIRECTIONS Read the name of each month. Then, rewrite each name. Begin each name with a capital letter.

1. january

2. february

3. march

4. april

5. may

6. june

7. july

8. august

9. september

10. october

11. november

12. december

Practice with Names of the Months

Remember, the names of the months of the year begin with a capital letter. The first letter in each name is a capital letter.

Answer each question with the name of a month. Begin each name with a capital letter.

1. What month were you born?

2. What month did school begin?

3. What is the first month in a year?

4. What is the last month in a year?

5. What month do you like best?

Writing Names of Holidays

The names of holidays begin with a capital letter. The first letter in each important part of the name is a capital letter.

Examples:

New Year's Day
Fourth of July
Earth Day

 **DIRECTIONS** Read each sentence. Write the name of each holiday correctly. Begin each important part of the name with a capital letter.

1. I get cards on valentine's day.

_____

- -

_____

2. Let's plant a tree on arbor day.

_____

- -

_____

3. Dad likes independence day.

_____

- -

_____

4. Did you go away on thanksgiving day?

_____

- -

_____

5. I like to dress up on halloween.

_____

- -

_____

Writing Names of Special Places

The names of special places begin with a capital letter. Some special places are streets, cities, and states. The first letter in each part of the name is a capital letter.

Examples:

    First Street   New York City   Florida

DIRECTIONS   **Read each sentence. Underline the names of streets, cities, or states. Then, rewrite each sentence correctly. Use capital letters where they are needed.**

1   Billy lives on jane street.

_____

_____

2.   My uncle lives on river road.

_____

_____

3.   I live on lake drive.

_____

_____

4.   Diane lives in boston.

_____

_____

5.   Ed took a trip to los angeles.

_____

_____

6.   My brother works in texas.

_____

_____

Practice with Special Place Names

Remember, the names of streets, cities, states, and countries begin with a capital letter. The first letter in each part of the name is a capital letter.

DIRECTIONS → **Answer each question with a special place name. Begin each name with a capital letter.**

1. What is the name of the street where you live?

_____

_ _

_____

2. What is the name of the city or town where you live?

_____

_ _

_____

3. What is the name of the state where you live?

_____

_ _

_____

4. What is the name of the country where you live?

_____

_ _

_____

Writing Titles of Books

Begin the first word, last word, and all important words in a book title with a capital letter. Underline the title of a book.

Examples:

<u>The Silver Pony</u>
<u>Peas at Supper</u>
<u>Billy and Blaze</u>

DIRECTIONS → **Read each book title. Then, rewrite each title correctly. Use capital letters where they are needed. Underline each title that you write.**

1. red flags

_____

2. the black horse

_____

3. dad and me

_____

4. flowers for mom

_____

5. first grade day

_____

Period

Use a **period (.)** at the end of a telling sentence.
Example:
> I can swing.

Use a period at the end of the titles of people.
Examples:
> Mr.   Mrs.   Ms.   Dr.
>
> Mr. Hill went to see Dr. Green.

DIRECTIONS ▷ **Write each sentence correctly.**

1. The bears play a game

2. They throw a ball

3. Mrs Bear came home

4. Mr Frog came to visit

Question Mark

Use a **question mark (?)** at the end of an asking sentence.
Examples:

   Will it rain today?
   Where do the clouds go?

DIRECTIONS Write each asking sentence correctly.

1. Why is the sky blue

2. How do flowers grow

3. Where do the stars go

4. Why do the birds sing

5. When will the sun shine

Comma

Use a **comma** (,) between the day and the year in a date.
Examples:

    July 4, 1776   November 18, 2004

DIRECTIONS Read each sentence. Circle the date. Then, write the date correctly. Remember to use a capital letter to begin the name of the month.

1. I got a letter on may 23 2005.

_____

- -

_____

2. Jan had a party on january 1 2005.

_____

- -

_____

3. Kim was born on june 30 1997.

_____

- -

_____

4. Leo got a new puppy on october 31 2003.

_____

- -

_____

_____

- -

5. Today is _____.

Rhyming Words

Words that end with the same sounds are **rhyming words**. Here are some rhyming words.

Examples:

      car—star   boat—goat   top—drop

DIRECTIONS Read each sentence. Look at the word in dark print. Choose the word in ( ) that ends with the same sound. Write the rhyming word on the line.

1. It is lots of **fun**

      To play in the _____.
                (sand, sun)

2. I can run and **hide**

      And go down the _____.
               (slide, sled)

3. Our new gray **cat**

      Lay on a soft _____.
             (mat, mop)

4. The little black **bug**

      Went under the _____.
            (rag, rug)

5. A big green **frog**

      Sat on a _____.
         (log, lap)

Practice with Rhyming Words

Remember, words that end with the same sound are **rhyming words.**
Examples:

pin—win   bug—rug

DIRECTIONS → Draw a line between rhyming words.

1. pig   sock

2. door   flat

3. bat   big

4. clock   fan

5. man   floor

DIRECTIONS → Write a funny sentence using one of the rhyming pairs you made.

6. _____

_____

_____

_____

Rhymes

A **rhyme** is a short poem. The lines end with rhyming words.
Many rhymes are silly or funny.
Example:
    The cat took a rocket trip to the moon.
    It left in July and came back in June.

DIRECTIONS   Complete the rhymes. You may use the words in the box.

snow	me	night	sky

1. I wonder where the flowers go

_____

Every time it starts to _____.

2. Would you like to fly up high

_____

And ride a cloud across the _____?

3. I would like to ask a bee

_____

To make some honey just for _____.

4. Why does the sun's light

_____

Go away every _____?

Words That Mean the Same

Some words mean almost the same thing.
Example:
    hop—jump

◎ ◎

 **DIRECTIONS** **Change the word in dark print to a word that means almost the same thing. Use the words in the box.**

catch	road	big	home

1. The man ran from his **house**. _____

2. He skipped down the **street**. _____

3. The dog could not **get** him. _____

4. The dog was **large**. _____

Words That Mean the Same, page 2

Remember, some words mean almost the same thing.
Example:
   look—watch

DIRECTIONS **Read each pair of sentences. Look at the word in dark print in the first sentence. Circle a word in the second sentence that means almost the same thing. Write both words on the line.**

1. I hear a **sound**. The noise is my puppy.

_____

- -

_____

2. I **begin** to call his name. My puppy starts to bark.

_____

- -

_____

3. I **look** under my bed. I see him there.

_____

- -

_____

4. He is **glad** to see me. I am happy, too.

_____

- -

_____

5. My puppy is **little**. He is a small dog.

_____

- -

_____

More Words That Mean the Same, page 3

Some words mean almost the same thing.
Example:
    talk—chat

DIRECTIONS → Read the clues. Fill in the puzzle with words from the box.

| small | sad | silly | yell | skinny |

Down

1. This word means

the same as **thin**.

3. This word means

the same as **funny**.

4. This word means

the same as **unhappy**.

Across

2. This word means the

same as **shout**.

3. This word means the same as **tiny**.

Words That Mean the Opposite

Some words have opposite meanings.
Example:
　　happy—sad

> **DIRECTIONS** Read each sentence. Look at the word in dark print. Circle the word in ( ) that means the opposite.

1. Pete went **up** the stairs. (down, out)

2. He sat on his **soft** bed. (new, hard)

3. Soon it was **dark** outside. (light, cold)

4. He turned **on** the lamp. (red, off)

5. Pete looked **out** the window. (in, off)

6. He **closed** his eyes. (rubbed, opened)

7. Soon Pete was **asleep**. (hungry, awake)

Words That Mean the Opposite, page 2

Remember, some words have opposite meanings.
Examples:
up—down   hot—cold

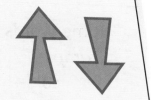

 **DIRECTIONS** Read each sentence. Look at the word in dark print. Choose a word from the box that means the opposite. Write the word on the line.

down	in	big	new	soft	off

1. I am **little**, and my sister is _____.

2. When I go **out**, she comes _____.

3. Her bike is **old**, but mine is _____.

4. First I get **on** my bike, then I get _____.

5. I go **up** the steps and _____ the slide.

6. I have a **hard** apple, and she has a _____ cookie.

More Words That Mean the Opposite, page 3

Some words have opposite meanings.
Example:

   cold—hot

DIRECTIONS **Read the clues. Fill in the puzzle with words from the box.**

wet	wrong	slow	young	tiny

Across

1. This is the opposite of **dry**.

2. This is the opposite of **fast**.

4. This is the opposite of **old**.

Down

1. This is the opposite of **right**.

3. This is the opposite of **huge**.

Words That Sound Alike

Some words sound alike, but they have different meanings.
Think about what you read carefully.
Examples:

    hear—here   there—their

DIRECTIONS Read each pair of sentences. Circle the words in each pair that sound alike.

1. I know what Jane said.
   She told her dog "no."

2. I yelled "hi" to Bill.
   He waved to me from a high window.

3. I had eight bugs.
   My frog ate seven of them.

4. Mom bakes cookies with flour.
   She draws a flower with pink icing.

5. I love to go to the sea.
   I like to see the boats.

6. My mother went to a sale.
   She got a sail for my boat.

7. I read a story yesterday.
   It was about a red dog.

8. I cannot hear you.
   Come over here.

Words That Sound Alike, page 2

Some words sound alike, but they have different meanings.
To and <u>two</u> sound alike. They mean different things.
Examples:

I went **to** my aunt's house.
She gave me **two** gifts.

> **DIRECTIONS** ▷ Complete each sentence. Circle the correct word in ( ).

1. I took a ball (to, two) Ben.

2. Now he has (to, two) balls.

3. Ben went (to, two) the game.

4. He ate (to, two) hot dogs.

5. He wants (to, two) play ball.

6. I have (to, two) hands.

7. I used them (to, two) clap.

8. My house has (to, two) doors.

Practice with <u>Their</u> and <u>There</u>

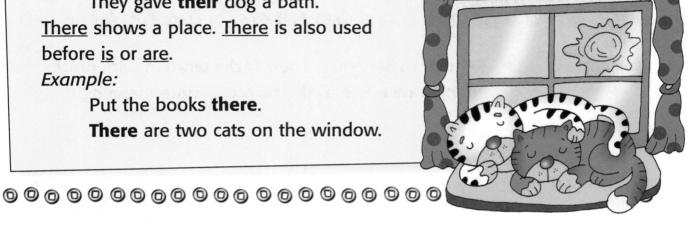

Remember, some words sound alike, but they have different meanings. <u>Their</u> and <u>there</u> sound alike. They mean different things. <u>Their</u> shows that something belongs to two or more people.
Example:
>   They gave **their** dog a bath.

<u>There</u> shows a place. <u>There</u> is also used before <u>is</u> or <u>are</u>.
Example:
>   Put the books **there**.
>   **There** are two cats on the window.

 **DIRECTIONS**   **Complete each sentence. Circle the correct word in ( ).**

1. The family got into (there, their) car.

2. The children hung up (there, their) coats.

3. Do you live (there, their)?

4. Mia and Dan played in (there, their) tree house.

5. (There, Their) are many kids in the park today.

Choosing the Right Meaning

Some words are spelled alike, but they have different meanings.
Examples:

roll—kind of bread   I had a **roll** for lunch.
roll—turn over and over   I like to **roll** down the hill.

 **DIRECTIONS**   Read each sentence. Look at the word in dark print.
Then, draw a line to the correct picture meaning.

1. Tony hit the ball with a **bat**.

2. The **bat** flies in the dark.   **a.**

3. Juan plays ball with a heavy **bat**.

4. How does a **bat** see at night?   **b.**

---

5. The **duck** made a loud quack.

6. We had to **duck** under the fence.   **a.**

7. We were asked to **duck**

   so they could see.   **b.**

8. The **duck** swam in the water.

Words That Show Order

Some words tell about **order**. Some order words are <u>first</u>, <u>next</u>, <u>then</u>, and <u>last</u>.
Example:

first   next   then   last

◎◎◎◎◎◎◎◎◎◎◎◎◎◎◎◎◎◎◎◎◎◎◎◎◎◎◎◎◎◎◎◎◎◎

DIRECTIONS ▷ **Complete the story. Use the words <u>First</u>, <u>Next</u>, <u>Then</u>, and <u>Last</u>.**

Jack the Bear had a loose tooth.

_____
_ _ _ _ _ _ _ _ _ _ _ _ _
_____ he wiggled his tooth.

_____
_ _ _ _ _ _ _ _ _ _ _ _ _
_____ it fell out.

_____
_ _ _ _ _ _ _ _ _ _ _ _ _
_____ he put his tooth under his pillow.

_____
_ _ _ _ _ _ _ _ _ _ _ _ _
_____ he found a toy under his pillow.

Practice with Words That Show Order

Remember, some words tell about order. Some order words are <u>first</u>, <u>next</u>, <u>then</u>, and <u>last</u>.

○ ○

DIRECTIONS ⟩ Look at each picture. Write a sentence for each order word to make a story.

1. First _____

2. Next _____

3. Then _____

4. Last _____

Compound Words

A **compound word** is made of two words. The two words are put together to make a new word.
Examples:

    song + bird = songbird
    bed + room = bedroom
    every + thing = everything

DIRECTIONS ➤ Complete each sentence. Use a compound word from the box.

sandbox	backyard	birdhouse

1. There are two trees in my _____.

2. There is a _____ in one tree.

3. I like to play in my _____.

DIRECTIONS ➤ Write a sentence. Use a compound word.

4. _____

_____

More Compound Words

Remember, a compound word is made of two words. The two words are put together to make a new word.

Example:

       star + fish = starfish

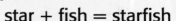

DIRECTIONS   Draw a line between two words that make a new compound word.

1. rain   shine

2. sea   bow

3. sail   boat

4. sun   shell

DIRECTIONS   Can you think of another compound word? Write it here.

5. _____

Writing Sentences with Naming Words

A sentence is a group of words. It tells a complete idea.
A sentence begins with a capital letter.
A naming word tells about a person, place, or thing.
Example:
The black **dog** barks.

DIRECTIONS ➤ Complete each sentence. Choose a naming word from the box. Write it on the line.

| flowers | garden | rain | seeds | store | sun |

1. Jo went to the _____.

2. She got some little brown _____.

3. Jo will plant the seeds in the _____.

4. The _____ will fall on the garden.

5. The _____ will warm the garden.

6. Pretty _____ will grow in the garden.

Writing Sentences with Action Words

A sentence tells a complete idea. A sentence begins with a capital letter.
An action word tells what something or someone does.
Example:
    Barry **drinks** some juice.

DIRECTIONS ▸ Complete each sentence. Choose an action word from the box. Write it on the line.

| bark | climbs | chase | eat | jump | run |

1. The two dogs _____ fast.

2. The dogs _____ up.

3. They _____ their food.

4. The dogs _____ the cat.

5. The dogs _____ loudly.

6. The cat _____ a tree.

Writing Sentences

A sentence tells a complete idea. A sentence begins with a capital letter. It has a naming part and a telling part.
Example:

Naming part	Telling part
The children	rode a bus to school.

 Look at the sentence parts in the box. Draw a line from a naming part to a telling part. Then, write the sentence on the line. Be sure to put a period at the end of the sentence.

Naming part	Telling part
1. The birds	digs
2. That frog	swims
3. The fish	hops
4. My dog	fly

1. _____

2. _____

3. _____

4. _____

Writing More Sentences

A sentence tells a complete idea. It begins with a
capital letter. A telling sentence ends with a period.
Example:

    I am reading.

DIRECTIONS ▷ **Write a telling sentence to answer each question.**

1. Are you a girl or a boy?

_____

- -

_____

2. Are you sitting or standing?

_____

- -

_____

3. Do you use a pen or a pencil?

_____

- -

_____

4. Do you walk or ride to school?

_____

- -

_____

5. Is it day or night now?

_____

- -

_____

6. Is it cold or hot today?

_____

- -

_____

Practice with Writing Sentences

Remember, a sentence tells a complete idea.
It begins with a capital letter. A telling sentence ends
with a period.
Example:

I like to dive.

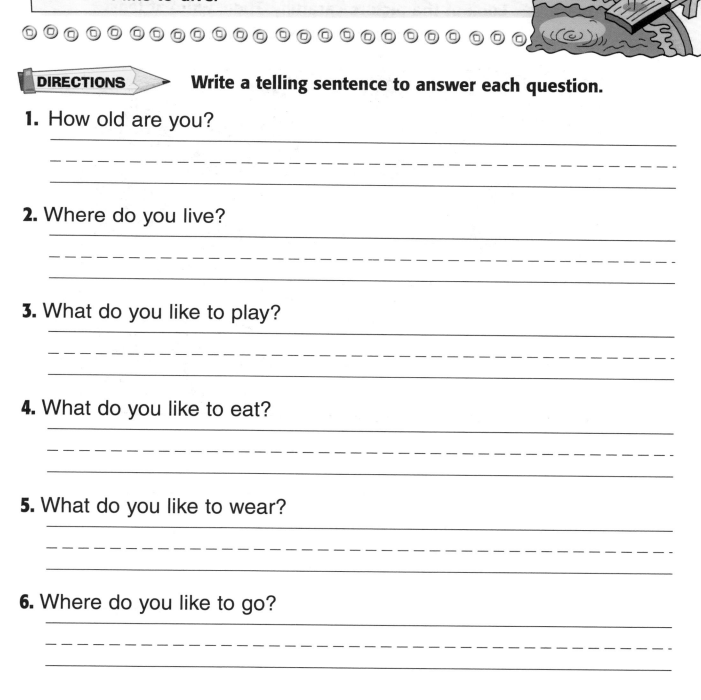

DIRECTIONS   **Write a telling sentence to answer each question.**

1. How old are you?

_____

_____

2. Where do you live?

_____

_____

3. What do you like to play?

_____

_____

4. What do you like to eat?

_____

_____

5. What do you like to wear?

_____

_____

6. Where do you like to go?

_____

_____

Writing Sentences about a Picture

A sentence tells a complete idea. It begins with a capital letter. It has a naming part and a telling part.

◎◎◎◎◎◎◎◎◎◎◎◎◎◎◎◎◎◎◎◎◎◎◎◎◎◎◎◎◎◎◎

DIRECTIONS → Look at the picture carefully. Then, write at least three sentences that tell about the picture.

_____

- -

_____

- -

_____

- -

_____

- -

_____

Paragraphs

A **paragraph** is a group of sentences. The sentences tell about one main idea. The first line of a paragraph is indented. This means the first word is moved in a little from the left margin.

The first sentence in a paragraph tells the main idea. The other sentences tell about the main idea.

Example:

Red Creek School is finished. The inside is nice and bright. The playground is very big. The school will open very soon. You will like the new school.

How to Write a Paragraph
1. Write a sentence that tells the main idea.
2. Indent the first line.
3. Write sentences that tell more about the main idea.

DIRECTIONS ▷ **Write sentences that tell about this main idea.**

I like school.

Writing a Story about You

A **story about you** is one kind of story you can write. In a story about you, you tell about something you did.
Example:

> I like to dive. I practice every day. At the pool I climb the ladder. Then, I walk to the end of the diving board. I put my arms up, and I dive. Splash! Into the water I go.

How to Write a Story About You
1. Think about things you have done.
2. Choose one thing to write about.
3. Begin your story.
4. Tell in order what you did.
5. Use words like I and me.

DIRECTIONS Answer the question.

What is the main idea of the example story? (Remember, the main idea is the first sentence of the paragraph.)

_____

— —

_____

Writing a Story about You, page 2

DIRECTIONS Think about something you have done. Write a story about you. Write your main idea in the first sentence. Indent the first sentence. Give your story a title. Draw a picture to go with your story.

Writing a Poem

A **poem** makes a picture with words. Some poems have rhyming
words. Rhyming words end with the same sound.
Example:

Home in the Sea

Dolphins and whales
So happy and free,
I wish I could go
To your home in the sea.

> **How to Write a Poem**
> 1. Try to paint a picture with words.
> 2. End some lines with rhyming words.
> 3. Give your poem a title.

DIRECTIONS ▸ **Complete the poem. Use rhyming words. Give the poem
a title.**

_____
- -
_____

I wish I could be

_____
- -
As tall as a _____ .

I wish I could fly

_____
- -
As high as the _____ .

Writing a Poem, page 2

Think about something you like. Write a poem about it. Use some rhyming words. Give your poem a title. Draw a picture to go with your poem.

Writing a Description

In a **description**, you tell about something. You use words that tell how the thing looks, sounds, tastes, smells, or feels.
Example:

The Fish Store

Our class went to a fish store. It was small and dark inside. There were many pretty fish. We watched a girl feed the fish. Then they swam fast!

How to Write a Description
1. Think about things you have seen.
2. Choose one to write about.
3. Write a sentence that tells what you are describing.
4. Write sentences that tell what the thing was like.
5. Use describing words. Give details about how the thing looked, sounded, tasted, smelled, or felt.
6. Give your description a title.

 **DIRECTIONS** ▶ **Complete the sentence.**

One describing word in the story is _____ .

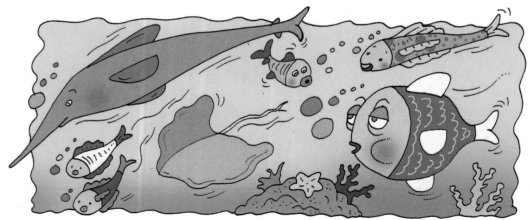

Writing a Description, page 2

Think about something you have seen. Write a description of it. Use describing words. Write your main idea in the first sentence. Indent the first sentence. Give your description a title. Draw a picture to go with your description.

Writing a Friendly Letter

You can write a **friendly letter** to someone you know. In it, you tell about yourself. A friendly letter has five parts. They are the heading, greeting, body, closing, and signature.

Example:

heading → July 27, 2005

greeting → Dear Sam,

body → I like my new house. At first, I was lonely. Then I met Jake. We played ball. Now he is my friend. And so are you!

closing → Your friend,

signature → Danny

How to Write a Friendly Letter
1. Choose a friend to write to.
2. Write about things you have done.
3. Use capital letters and commas correctly.
4. Use the five parts that are shown by the arrows.

DIRECTIONS — **Answer the question.**

Who wrote this letter? _____

Writing a Friendly Letter, page 2

DIRECTIONS Think about something you have done. Think of a friend to write to in a letter. Write a letter to your friend. Use capital letters and commas correctly. Be sure to use the five parts of a friendly letter.

_____
_ _ _ _ _ _ _ _ _ _ _ _ _ _ _ _
_____

_____
_ _ _ _ _ _ _ _ _ _ _ _ _ _ _ _
_____

_____
_ _
_____
_ _
_____
_ _
_____
_ _

_____
_ _ _ _ _ _ _ _ _ _ _ _ _ _ _ _
_____

_____
_ _ _ _ _ _ _ _ _ _ _ _ _ _ _ _
_____

Writing a How-to Paragraph

A **how-to paragraph** tells how to do or make something. The steps are told in order.

Example:

I can play hide-and-seek. You can play it, too. You will need places to hide. You also need some friends to play with. First, close your eyes. Then, count to ten while your friends hide. Last, go and find your friends.

How to Write a How-to Paragraph
1. Think about things you know how to do.
2. Choose one thing to write about.
3. Write how to do that thing.
4. Tell the things you will need to do it.
5. Tell the steps in the right order.
6. Use words like <u>first</u> and <u>last</u>.

 **DIRECTIONS**   **Answer the question.**

What does the example paragraph tell how to do?

_____

— —

_____

Writing a How-to Paragraph, page 2

DIRECTIONS Think about something you know how to do. Write a paragraph telling how to do it. Write what you will tell about in the first sentence. Indent the first sentence. Tell what is needed to do the thing. Use order words. Draw a picture to go with your how-to paragraph.

Writing a Book Report

A **book report** tells about a book you have read.
Example:

<u>Birthday Cookies</u>
by Ann Wilson

    <u>Birthday Cookies</u> is about Tom. He and his mother bake lots of cookies. Tom takes them to school for his birthday. My favorite part is when the other children eat all the cookies. I really liked this book.

How to Write a Book Report
1. Write the title of the book. Underline it.
2. Write the author's name.
3. Tell who or what the book is about.
4. Tell your favorite part.
5. Tell what you think about the book.

 **DIRECTIONS**   **Answer the question.**

What is the title of the book in the book report?

_____

- -

_____

Writing a Book Report, page 2

DIRECTIONS Think about a book you have read. Write a paragraph telling about the book. Tell the name of the book and who wrote it. Tell what happens in the book. Tell your favorite part. Tell if you liked the book. Indent the first sentence. Draw a picture to go with your book report.

ABC Order

The order of letters from <u>A</u> to <u>Z</u> is called **ABC order**.

a b c d e f g h i j k l m n
o p q r s t u v w x y z

ant

bear

cat

DIRECTIONS   Write the letters in ABC order.

1. a c b _____   _____   _____

2. f h g _____   _____   _____

3. c e d _____   _____   _____

4. p n o _____   _____   _____

5. i h j _____   _____   _____

6. z x y _____   _____   _____

ABC Order, page 2

Remember, the order of letters from <u>A</u> to <u>Z</u> is called ABC order. Words can be in ABC order, too. Use the first letter of a word to put it in ABC order.

Examples:

big	**c**at	**d**og
fish	**m**an	**s**un

DIRECTIONS Look at each group of words. Look at the letters in dark print. Put the words in ABC order. Write the words in ABC order on the lines.

1. a b c d e f

can   **b**ird   **d**ig

_____

_____

_____

2. e f g h i j

give   **h**elp   **f**ind

_____

_____

_____

3. m n o p q r

red   **o**ne   **n**ame

_____

_____

_____

4. s t u v w x

we   **s**he   **t**hey

_____

_____

_____

ABC Order, page 3

Remember, the order of letters from <u>A</u> to <u>Z</u> is called ABC order. Words can be in ABC order, too. Use the first letter of a word to put it in ABC order.

◎ ◎

DIRECTIONS → **First, number the words in ABC order. Then, write the words in order to make sentences. Be sure to put a period at the end of each sentence.**

1. _____ likes   _____ me   _____ He

_____

_____

2. _____ Dave   _____ playing   _____ is

_____

_____

3. _____ outside   _____ Anna   _____ goes

_____

_____

4. _____ Mouse   _____ Cat   _____ finds

_____

_____

Parts of a Book

The **title page** is in the front of a book. It tells the title of the book. It tells who wrote the book. And it tells what company published the book.

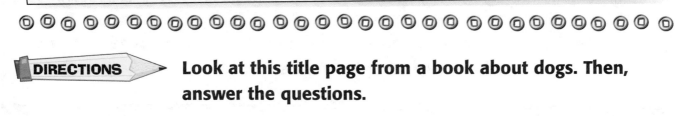

DIRECTIONS Look at this title page from a book about dogs. Then, answer the questions.

ALL ABOUT DOGS

by
Minnie Fleas

Barker Books
New York

1. What is the title of the book?

_____

_____

2. Who wrote the book?

_____

_____

3. What company published the book?

_____

_____

Parts of a Book, page 2

Some books have many stories or chapters. The **contents** of a book tells where each story or chapter begins.

 **DIRECTIONS** Look at the picture of the book. Write the page number where each chapter begins.

Contents

1. Food for Bears	_____	**2.** Where Bears Live	_____
3. What Bears Look Like	_____	**4.** Kinds of Bears	_____

Order of Events

The sentences in a story tell things in the order they happen.
Words such as <u>first</u>, <u>next</u>, <u>then</u>, and <u>last</u> help tell when things happen.
Example:

> Brett got ready for bed. **First**, she took a bath. **Next**, she brushed her teeth. **Then**, she put on her pajamas. **Last**, she read a story and got into bed.

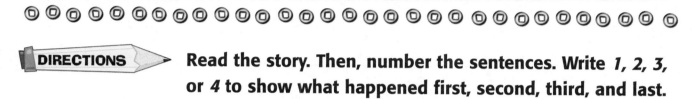

DIRECTIONS Read the story. Then, number the sentences. Write *1, 2, 3,* or *4* to show what happened first, second, third, and last.

Carla planted flowers. First, she got a shovel. Next, she dug some holes in the garden. Then, she put the flowers into the holes. Last, she put the shovel back in its place.

_____ First, she got a shovel.

_____ Then, she put the flowers into the holes.

_____ Last, she put the shovel back in its place.

_____ Next, she dug some holes in the garden.

Conclusions

A **conclusion** is a decision you make. You look at the facts. You think carefully. Then, you decide. You make a conclusion.
Example:

It has many teeth, but it cannot bite. What is it?
Answer: a comb.

 **DIRECTIONS** ⟩ **Read each animal riddle. Write the name of the animal.**

| bird | rabbit | monkey | whale |

1. This animal is very big.
It lives in the water, but
it is not a fish.
What is it?

_____

2. This animal can hop fast.
It has a small, fluffy tail.
It eats in my garden!
What is it?

_____

3. This animal can climb.
It has a long tail.
It lives in the tops of trees.
What is it?

_____

4. This animal sits on a branch.
It makes a nest.
It can fly up high.
What is it?

_____

Practice with Conclusions

Remember, to make a conclusion you look at the facts. You think carefully. Then, you decide.

 **DIRECTIONS** **Read each riddle. Write the name of the thing.**

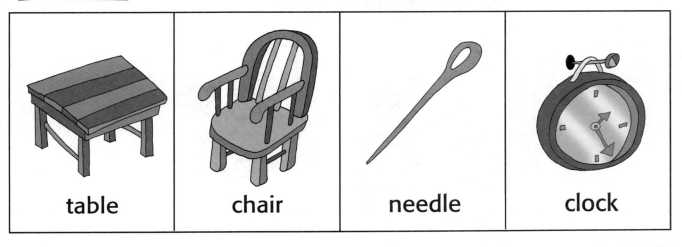

| table | chair | needle | clock |

1. You can eat on this thing. It has legs but cannot walk. What is it?

_____

_____

2. You can sew with this thing. It has an eye but cannot see. What is it?

_____

3. This thing tells time. It has hands but cannot clap. What is it?

_____

_____

4. You can sit in this thing. It has arms but cannot carry anything. What is it?

_____

_____

Classifying

Classify means to put things in groups. Think how things are alike. Then, you can put them in groups together.

▶ **DIRECTIONS** Look at the drawings. Think. How are the animals in each group alike? Write the word.

1. Animals that _____

2. Animals that _____

▶ **DIRECTIONS** Draw a picture of another animal for each group.

Comparing and Contrasting

Compare means to tell how things are alike. **Contrast** means to tell how things are different.

◎ ◎

DIRECTIONS — Look at the two pictures. Think. How are they different? How are they alike? Write one sentence telling how they are alike. Write one sentence telling how they are different.

_____

_____

_____

_____

_____

_____

_____

_____

More Comparing and Contrasting

Remember that compare means to tell how things are alike. Contrast means to tell how things are different.

DIRECTIONS Draw a picture of you and your best friend. Write one sentence about how you are alike. Write one sentence about how you are different.

Summarizing

Summarizing means to tell what happens in a story in your own words.

◎ ◎

DIRECTIONS ▷ **Read the story. Then, complete the story map.**

Matt's Birthday

Matt the Mouse was sad. Today was his birthday. He could not find any of his friends. He went for a walk in the garden. He looked at the plants. They were moving!

"Who is back there?" called Matt.

"Surprise!" shouted all his friends. "Happy birthday, Matt!"

"Thank you!" Matt smiled.

1. Who? _____

2. Where? _____

3. What happened first? _____

4. What happened next? _____

5. What happened at the end? _____

Fact or Fantasy?

Some stories tell **facts** about things. Facts are things that could really happen.
Some stories tell about things that could not happen. These stories are called **fantasy**.

 DIRECTIONS   **Read each sentence. Could it really happen? Circle <u>yes</u> if the sentence is a fact. Circle <u>no</u> if the sentence is not a fact.**

1. Sandy picks a flower.   yes   no
2. The flower starts to cry.   yes   no

3. A bee lands on a leaf.   yes   no
4. The leaf says, "You're heavy!"   yes   no

5. Sandy follows the bee.   yes   no
6. The bee smiles at Sandy.   yes   no

7. The bee reads a story.   yes   no
8. Sandy falls asleep.   yes   no

Fact or Fantasy?, page 2

Remember, some stories tell facts about things. Facts are things that could really happen.

Some stories tell about things that could not happen. These stories are called fantasy.

 **DIRECTIONS** **Read each sentence. Could it really happen? Circle <u>yes</u> if the sentence is a fact. Circle <u>no</u> if the sentence is not a fact.**

1. We go to the circus on Saturday.   yes   no
2. The horses greet us and shake our hands.   yes   no

3. My cat flies around the room.   yes   no
4. He purrs when I pet him.   yes   no

5. I like to eat peanut butter and jelly.   yes   no
6. Peanut butter and jelly likes to eat cheese.   yes   no

7. A butterfly flies into the classroom!   yes   no
8. It raises its hand to answer a question.   yes   no

Writing Skills

Unit 1: Words, Words, Words

HOW MUCH DO YOU KNOW?

Look at the words below. Circle the nouns. Draw a line under the verbs.

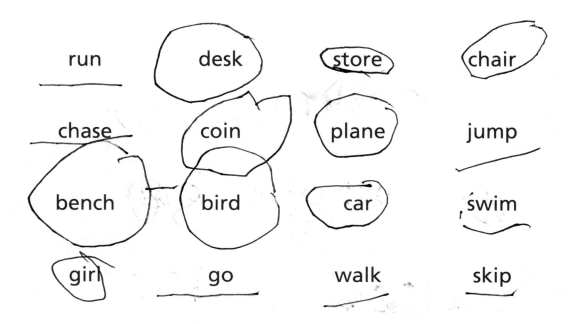

run

desk

store

chair

chase

coin

plane

jump

bench

bird

car

swim

girl

go

walk

skip

What Is a Noun?

A noun names a person, a place, or a thing.

Look at the Word Bank. Circle the nouns in the box. Then write them on the lines. Color the picture.

WORD BANK

jump

clown

balloons

float

boy

dog

walk

boat

man

clown   Dog

balloons   boat

boy   man

Picturing Nouns

Draw a picture of your classroom. On the lines below, write four nouns that are shown in your picture.

BOOK

TABLE

TOYS

CHAIR

Exact Nouns

Good writers use exact nouns to make their writing better.

Read these sentences:

The animal runs.

The dog runs.

Both sentences tell that something runs. The second sentence tells what kind of animal runs. <u>Dog</u> is a more exact noun than <u>animal</u>. When you use exact nouns, the reader will know what you really mean.

Read each sentence below. Think of a more exact noun to replace the underlined word. Then write the new word on the line.

Dan likes to play <u>sports</u>. _____TRACK_____

I love to eat <u>food</u>. _____ICE CREAM_____

My grandma bought me a new <u>toy</u>. _____AbUCUS_____

Mom cooks in the <u>room</u>. _____KITCHEN_____

What Is a Verb?

A verb is a word that shows something happening.

Look at each picture. Circle the verb above it that describes what happens in each picture. Then write it on the line.

swim   climb   pool

_____

_____

fall   run   shoes

_____

_____

sleep   book   read

_____

_____

hop   frog   legs

_____

_____

My Superhero

Think up a new superhero. Draw a picture of the superhero in the box below. Then fill in the blanks below with verbs that describe what your superhero can do.

[box for drawing]

My superhero can _____ , _____ ,

_____ , _____ ,

_____ , and _____ .

Exact Verbs

Good writers use exact verbs to make their writing better.

Read these sentences:

"Come back!" she said.
"Come back!" she shouted.

Both sentences tell what the woman said. See how the second sentence tells how she said it. The word <u>shouted</u> is a more exact verb. When you write, use exact verbs so that the reader knows what you really mean.

Read each of the verbs below. Choose a word from the Verb Bank that is a more exact verb. Write the words on the line.

say _____

look _____

go _____

drink _____

VERB BANK

yell

skip

sip

peek

Adjectives

An adjective is a word that tells about, or describes, a noun.

Look at each picture. Draw a line under the adjective that describes the things in the picture. Then write the correct word.

sunny   girl   water   _____

angry   new   ride   _____

cry   careful   messy   _____

wet   old   build   _____

All Mixed Up

The word pairs below do not make sense. Circle the adjectives. On the lines below, write the adjectives next to the correct nouns.

soft dinner   salty weather   delicious hair

curly pillow   green popcorn   sunny grass

_____   _____

-------------------------   -------------------------

_____ dinner   _____ weather

_____   _____

-------------------------   -------------------------

_____ hair   _____ pillow

_____

_____ popcorn

_____

_____ grass

Feeling Words

Look at the faces below. Beneath each picture, write two words that describe how the person is feeling. Use words from the Word Bank.

WORD BANK

sad	happy	shocked	upset
angry	mad	surprised	glad

_____ _____ _____ _____

_____ _____ _____ _____

_____ _____ _____ _____

Draw a picture to show how you are feeling. Next to the picture, write a word that describes how you are feeling.

_____

_____

Pronouns

A pronoun is a special word that can take the place of a noun.

Read these sentences:

<u>Maria</u> made a sandwich.
<u>She</u> made a sandwich.

The second sentence uses the word <u>she</u>. <u>She</u> is a pronoun. It takes the place of the word <u>Maria</u>.

These words are pronouns: <u>I</u>, <u>he</u>, <u>she</u>, <u>it</u>, <u>we</u>, <u>you</u>, <u>they</u>

Circle the pronoun in each of these sentences. Then write it on the line.

_____

Every morning, we ride the bus to school. _____

_____

It is very crowded. _____

_____

Peter asks, "Do you want to sit here?" _____

_____

Peter makes room for me. _____

Capital Letters for Names and Places

> The names of people and places begin with a capital letter.

Look at the facts from the book report below. Then write the report using correct capital letters.

<u>Grandma's House</u>

Author: nathan thompson

Main characters:
grandma rose and billy

Setting: denton, texas

Author: _____

Main characters: _____ and _____

Setting: _____ , _____

Titles for People

A title for a person begins with a capital letter
and usually ends with a period.

TITLES   Mr.   Mrs.   Miss   Ms.   Dr.

**Read each sentence. Circle the titles that are written incorrectly.
Then write the sentences correctly.**

1. mr Grayson is our bus driver.

_____

_____

2. I went to see dr Hubbard for a check-up.

_____

_____

3. My piano teacher is miss Marks.

_____

_____

4. mr and mrs Nelson live next door to us.

_____

_____

Days of the Week

The names of the days of the week begin with capital letters.

Find and circle the seven days of the week in the word search puzzle below. Look across and down. Then write your favorite day of the week on the line below.

```
k  f  h  m  v  b  n  W  p  c
s  S  u  n  d  a  y  e  i  F
d  c  e  d  f  x  o  d  d  r
p  d  a  c  S  u  g  n  a  i
M  o  n  d  a  y  j  e  y  d
i  g  r  u  t  d  i  s  u  a
r  f  T  h  u  r  s  d  a  y
h  a  u  w  r  v  t  a  y  m
b  y  e  n  d  d  c  y  l  j
c  o  s  y  a  a  o  k  c  t
x  m  d  f  y  y  d  a  y  s
n  s  a  b  u  m  e  t  s  b
w  s  y  x  s  k  p  r  l  k
```

Special Days

> The names of holidays and special days begin with capital letters.

Each holiday or special day needs capital letters. Even the word <u>day</u> should be capitalized when it is written after the name of the holiday.

Circle the holiday or special day in each sentence. Then write the words correctly in the blanks below.

Mom gave me a box of chocolates on valentine's day.

_____

_____

presidents' day is also in February.

_____

_____

I gave my mom a pretty dress for mother's day.

_____

_____

For memorial day, we had a picnic in the park.

_____

_____

Synonyms

Synonyms (say: sin-OH-nims) are words that mean the same thing.

Good writers use synonyms to make their writing more interesting. The words below are synonyms for the word <u>big</u>. Read the meaning of each word.

big	of great size
loud	easy to hear, loud in volume
tall	not short
old	having many years

Read each sentence. Choose a better word to write in place of the word <u>big</u>. Then write the sentence with the new word.

My brother is not <u>big</u> enough to go to school yet.

_____

_____

We do not use <u>big</u> voices in the library.

_____

_____

Antonyms

Antonyms (say: ant-OH-nims) are words that mean the opposite of each other.

The words <u>up</u> and <u>down</u> are antonymns.

The balloon goes <u>up</u>.

The balloon comes <u>down</u>.

In each group, draw a line to match the word to its opposite, or antonymn.

open	on
off	sit
out	in
stand	cry
laugh	close

Make a List

Think of a person, a place, or a thing. Then make a list of words that describe it, but don't tell what it is. Give the list to a friend and see if he or she can tell you what the object is.

These are words that describe the person, place, or thing I am thinking of:

_____

_____

_____

_____

_____

_____

_____

_____

Review

Circle the words that are adjectives. Underline the words that are pronouns.

pretty	she	soft
you	I	nice
angry	happy	he
it	thin	sleepy
old	kind	brown
loud	they	we

Write a word that is a synonym for each word.

cold   _____
_____

sleepy   _____
_____

nice   _____
_____

UNIT 2: What Is a Sentence?

HOW MUCH DO YOU KNOW?

In each pair, circle the group of words that is a sentence.

Alex does a cartwheel.

All over the playground

Singing at the top of her lungs

Mrs. Durand is my music teacher.

Look out!

Under the sofa

Write the following sentence correctly.

We had a lot of rain in april

_____

_____

_____

_____

Complete Sentences

> A sentence tells a complete thought or idea.

Read these sentences:

Matthew solved the puzzle.
Solved the puzzle

The first group of words is a sentence that tells a complete idea. It tells about something Matthew did. The second group of words does not tell who solved the puzzle. It is not a sentence.

Look at the pictures below. Draw a line to the sentence that tells about the picture.

Rufus sleeps on the sofa.

The flowers bloom.

Beth paints a picture.

Which One Is a Sentence?

Some groups of words are not sentences. Circle the sentence in each pair and write it on the line below.

Our class takes a field trip.   Our class

_____

_____

On a yellow school bus   We ride on a yellow school bus.

_____

_____

Takes us to the zoo   The bus takes us to the zoo.

_____

_____

We see all the animals.   All the animals

_____

_____

Statements

A statement is a sentence that tells something. A statement begins with a capital letter and ends with a period. (.)

This is a statement:
I like to play soccer.

Circle the statement in each pair. Then write it correctly on the line below.

Our team has a game today.   Our team game

_____

_____

Out to the field   We go to the field.

_____

_____

The game begins.   When will the game begin?

_____

_____

Eddie kicks the ball.   Kicks the ball hard

_____

_____

Find the Statements

There are five statements in the box below. Underline the sentences that are statements. Write the five statements on the lines.

Dad is in the garage.

We have four tickets.

Swimming in the lake

Bill has a pet goldfish.

Able to leap

I can read a book.

Do you like rabbits?

I had a silly dream.

Commands

This is a command: Use soft voices in the library.

Circle the sentences below that are commands.

There are many books in the library.

What is your favorite book?

Choose a book.

Mrs. Masted is the librarian.

Take your book to the front desk.

Read silently to yourself.

Do you know where to sit?

Do not shout.

Find an empty chair and be seated.

How many pages have you read?

Questions

A question is a sentence that asks something.
A question begins with a capital letter and ends
with a question mark. (?)

Circle the question in each pair. Then write it correctly on the
line below.

Do you know the answer?   Knowing the answer

_____

What is it?   You can figure it out.

_____

From the chalkboard   Can you write it on the board?

_____

Checking your work.   Did you check your work?

_____

Find the Question

There are five questions in the box below. Underline the sentences that are questions. Write the five questions on the lines.

Did you hear that?   A soft, fluffy pillow?

Is anyone home?   Mom asked me a question.

Listening carefully   How do you feel?

What did you have for lunch?   Are you coming with us?

_____

- -

_____

- -

_____

- -

_____

- -

_____

- -

_____

Exclamations

An exclamation is a sentence that shows strong feeling. An exclamation begins with a capital letter and ends with an exclamation point. (!)

This is an exclamation: What a great shot!

Read the sentences below. Underline the sentences that are exclamations.

Look out!

Wake up!

Is that a monster?

I will not eat that!

You can have a banana.

I hate peanut butter!

That is fantastic news!

When is your birthday?

Wait for me!

Let's go home.

Capital Letters and End Marks

A sentence begins with a capital letter.
It ends with a period, an exclamation point,
or a question mark.

Circle the sentences below that are written correctly.

my family goes to the circus.

Have you ever been to the circus?

We sit in the fourth row

Dad gets us some popcorn.

we watch the clowns juggle

That is amazing!

Six lions jump through some hoops.

Can you believe they can do that.

How Does the Sentence End?

Rewrite the sentences and add the correct capital letters and end marks.

let's go to the carnival

_____

_____

do you want to ride the roller coaster

_____

_____

i will buy some cotton candy

_____

_____

can we play a game

_____

_____

you won a prize

_____

_____

Fix the Sentence

Look at each sentence carefully. Rewrite the sentence with correct capital letters and end marks.

mom comes in

_____

_____

she has a box

_____

_____

it is for us

_____

_____

what is it

_____

_____

it is a new toy

_____

_____

Sentence Subjects

The subject of a sentence names who or what the sentence is about. It is the naming part of the sentence.

Read this sentence:
The birds chirp in the nest.

This sentence is about the birds. <u>Birds</u> is the subject of this sentence.

Read the sentences below. Answer the questions to help you find the subject, or naming part, in each sentence. Write the subject on the line below.

Autumn is finally here. What is finally here?

_____

_____

The leaves are falling. What is falling?

_____

_____

Children bundle up in warmer clothes. Who bundles up?

_____

_____

Searching for Subjects

Read each sentence. Underline the subject, or naming part.

The skateboard is fast.

My dog ripped my homework.

We swim in the pool.

Dad and I go for a walk.

Katherine brushes her teeth.

Subject Match-up

Complete each sentence with the correct subject, or naming part, from the Word Bank.

WORD BANK

Yellow baby car cake Winter radio

The ______________________ tastes delicious.

______________________ is my favorite color.

Your ______________________ is too loud!

The ______________________ is crying.

Our ______________________ is faster than his.

______________________ is my favorite season.

Sentence Predicates

> The predicate of a sentence tells what the subject does, has, or is. It is the telling part of the sentence.

Read this sentence:
Jamie likes to fly her kite.

The subject of this sentence is <u>Jamie</u>. The sentence tells us that Jamie likes to fly her kite. The predicate of this sentence is <u>likes to fly her kite</u>.

Read each sentence. Underline the predicate, or telling part.

Our teacher is nice.

My breakfast tastes delicious.

Grandma and I bake cookies.

Queenie takes a nap.

Choose a Predicate

Look at the box of predicates, or telling parts. Choose a predicate to go with the subject in each sentence. Write the predicate on the line to complete the sentence.

smells lovely.

lives in a blue house.

makes a lot of noise.

solved the puzzle.

is friendly.

is very short.

feels soft.

growled at me.

Our neighbor _____

The flower _____

His pet dog _____

Word Order

Words in a sentence must be in an order that makes sense.

Rearrange each group of words and write the sentence correctly.

park. We to go the

_____

- -

_____

sits Grandma a on bench.

_____

- -

_____

the in Two ducks pond. swim

_____

- -

_____

Carlos ducks. the feeds

_____

- -

_____

water. splash They the in

_____

- -

_____

Sentence Switch

The order of words can change the meaning of a sentence.

The two sentences below use the same words. See how the order of the words makes each sentence have a different meaning.

Lisa runs faster than Marcus.
Marcus runs faster than Lisa.

Rearrange the words to change the meaning of each sentence. Write the new sentence on the line below.

Mom called Grandma on the phone.

_____

_____

Erin is stronger than Peter.

_____

_____

The teacher borrowed a pencil from her student.

_____

_____

The dog chased the cat.

_____

_____

Combining Sentences

Read these sentences:
1. Mary likes fruit.
2. Mary likes vegetables.
3. Mary likes fruit and vegetables.

See how sentence 3 uses the word <u>and</u> to combine sentence 1 and sentence 2.

Read each pair of sentences.
Combine each pair into one sentence. Write it on the line below.

1. Rob can read.   Rob can write.

_____

_____

2. We ate pizza.   We ate hot dogs.

_____

_____

3. Chris plays basketball.   John plays basketball.

_____

_____

Complete the Sentences

Begin or finish each sentence. Use your imagination!
Remember to use correct capital letters and end marks.

_____

Emily likes to _____

_____

I wish I could _____

_____

_____ is the best movie I have

ever seen!

_____

I can't believe you _____

_____

_____ runs faster than my mom.

_____

The aliens told us to _____

Run-On Sentences

This is a run-on sentence:
It is hot outside do you want to go swimming?

The run-on sentence has too many ideas. It should be divided into two sentences like this:
It is hot outside. Do you want to go swimming?

Read each run-on sentence. Then divide it into two sentences and write them correctly on the lines below.

The movie was cool it had a lot of car chases.

_____

_____

_____

_____

_____

We ate popcorn it had a lot of butter on it.

_____

_____

_____

_____

_____

Review

Write each sentence correctly on the line.

sam likes to play on the playground

_____

- -

_____

do you want to go on the slide

_____

- -

_____

mom pushes the swing i like to go very high

_____

- -

_____

Read each sentence. Circle the subject. Draw a line under the predicate.

Emilio and Jana play tag.

The dog runs after them.

We like to play at the park.

UNIT 3: Sentence about a Picture

- -

HOW MUCH DO YOU KNOW?

Look at each picture. Circle the group of words next to the picture that is a complete sentence.

We bake cookies.
baking cookies

throws the ball to me
He throws the ball.

Finish the sentence with the more exact word below it.

_____

Keisha gives her ——————————— a bath.
(dog, animal)

Studying a Sentence

A sentence tells a complete thought.
It begins with a capital letter and ends with an end mark.

Look at each picture. Circle the group of words below the picture that is a complete sentence.

Dad rakes the leaves.
falling on the ground

six years old
Today is my birthday.

lives in a bowl
I have a pet fish.

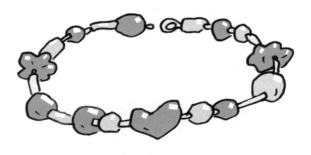

a pretty necklace
That is very pretty.

Sentence Matching

Look at each picture. Draw a line from the picture to the sentence that tells about the picture.

Jana hurt her knee.

The bug crawls on the leaf.

This tastes delicious!

Using Exact Words

Good writers use exact words to make their writing better.

Finish each sentence by choosing and writing the more exact word below it.

Tim gets a shiny, new _____ .

(bike, vehicle)

He _____ down the street.

(goes, rides)

He stops at the _____ .

(building, store)

Tim gives the clerk two _____ .

(quarters, coins)

Adding Adjectives

Adjectives are describing words that make sentences more interesting.

Read these sentences:

The rabbit hopped behind the bush.

The white rabbit hopped behind the prickly bush.

The second sentence is more interesting because it has the adjectives <u>white</u> and <u>prickly</u>. <u>White</u> describes what the rabbit looks like. <u>Prickly</u> describes what the bush feels like.

Read each sentence. Add adjectives, or describing words, to each sentence. Write the new sentence on the line. You can use the words in the Word Bank to help you.

WORD BANK

cherry	sunny	colorful	silly	delicious
fresh	tasty	sandy	funny	

Mom made a pie.

_____

_____

We watched the clown do tricks.

_____

_____

Proofreading Sentences

> **PROOFREADING HINTS**
> - Be sure your sentence begins with a capital letter.
> - Be sure your sentence ends with an end mark.

Read each sentence. Use the Proofreading Marks to correct the mistake in each sentence. Then write the sentence correctly. See the chart on page 648 to learn how to use the marks.

PROOFREADING MARKS	
⬭	spell correctly
⊙	add period
?	add question mark
≡	capitalize
ℒ	take out
¶	indent paragraph

most dogs are friendly animals.

_____

....

_____

They make good pets

_____

....

_____

Choose the Sentence

Look at each picture. Choose a sentence from the box that tells about it. Then write the sentence beneath the picture.

The soup is too hot.   In the woods   My shoes are new.

brand new shoes   Camping is fun.   alphabet soup

We wash our car.   soap and water   running faster

_____

- - - - - - - - - - - - - - - - - -

_____

_____

- - - - - - - - - - - - - - - - - -

_____

_____

- - - - - - - - - - - - - - - - - -

_____

_____

- - - - - - - - - - - - - - - - - -

_____

Tell about the Pictures

Look at the pictures. Write a sentence to tell about each picture.

_____

_____

_____

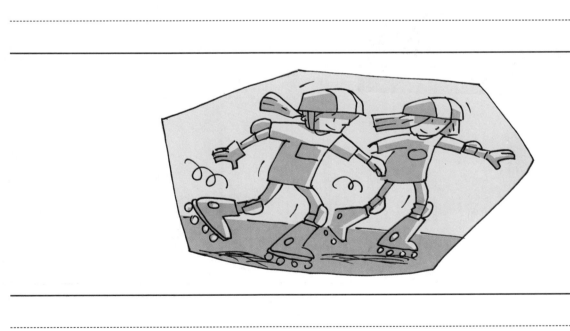

_____

_____

_____

Over the Rainbow

Finish the picture. Then write a sentence about the picture.

_____

- -

_____

_____

- -

_____

Up, Up, and Away

Finish the picture. Then write a sentence to tell about the picture.

_____

_____

_____

_____

Family Dinner

Draw food on the table to finish the picture. Then write a sentence to tell about the picture.

The Best Day Ever

Imagine that you could do anything you want today. Draw a picture to show what you would do. Write a sentence to tell about your picture.

Favorite Sport

Draw a picture that shows your favorite sport. Write a sentence to tell about your picture.

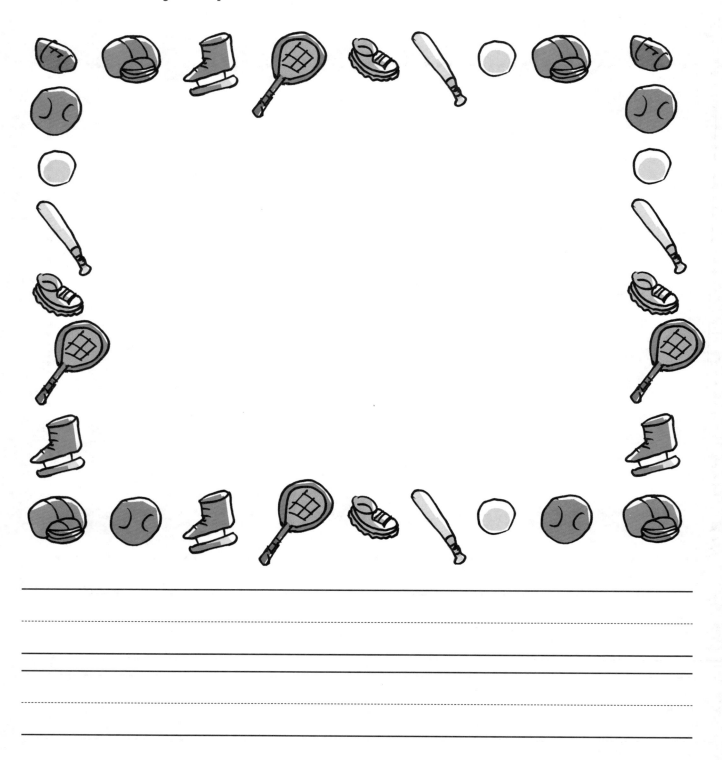

_____

- -

_____

- -

_____

Pet Monster

Imagine that you have a pet monster. Draw a picture of your monster. Write a sentence to tell about your picture.

Favorite Subject

Which subject do you like best in school? Draw a picture to show your favorite subject. Write a sentence to tell about your picture.

_____

- -

_____

_____

- -

_____

My Bedroom

Draw a picture of your bedroom. Write a sentence to tell about your picture.

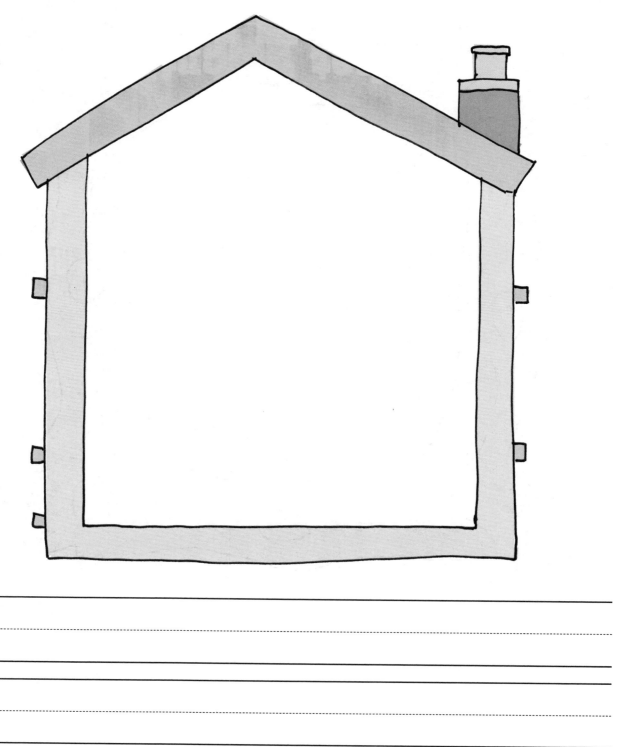

My Family

Draw a picture of your family. Write a sentence to tell about your picture.

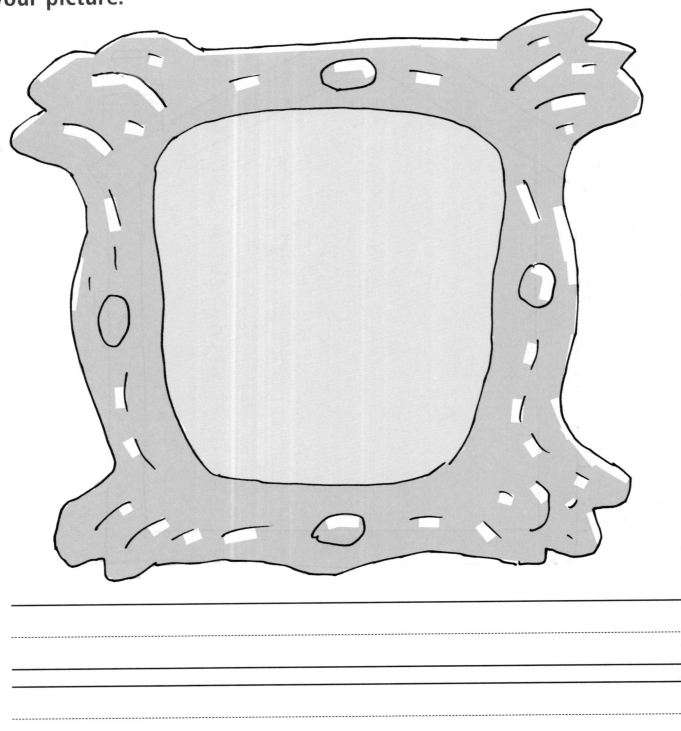

Review

Look at the picture. Circle the sentence that tells about the picture.

Holding up traffic

The workers fix the road.

Wearing hard hats

Write another sentence that tells about the picture.

_____

....

_____

UNIT 4: Writing and Completing Sentences

HOW MUCH DO YOU KNOW?

Think about things you like and things you do not like. Finish the sentences below. Be sure to end each sentence with an end mark.

My name is _____

I like _____

I do not like _____

Write a new sentence to tell something else about yourself. Remember to begin your sentence with a capital letter.

_____

_____

_____

Alphabet Sentence

Choose a letter of the alphabet. Draw a picture of something that begins with that letter. Then complete the sentence to tell about the picture.

_____ is for _____

(letter)

Colorful Sentences

Read the names of the color words below. Write a sentence to name something that comes in each color. The first one is done for you.

blue

The sky is blue.

yellow

_____

_____

green

_____

_____

brown

_____

_____

Having a Pet

Think about a pet you have or would like to have. Draw a picture of the pet. Then write complete sentences to answer the questions about your pet.

What kind of pet is it? _____

What is the name of your pet? _____

What does your pet eat? _____

Where does your pet sleep? _____

What does your pet like to do? _____

Sentences That Describe

Good writers use their five senses to make their sentences more interesting.

Draw a picture of your favorite food. Complete each sentence to describe the food.

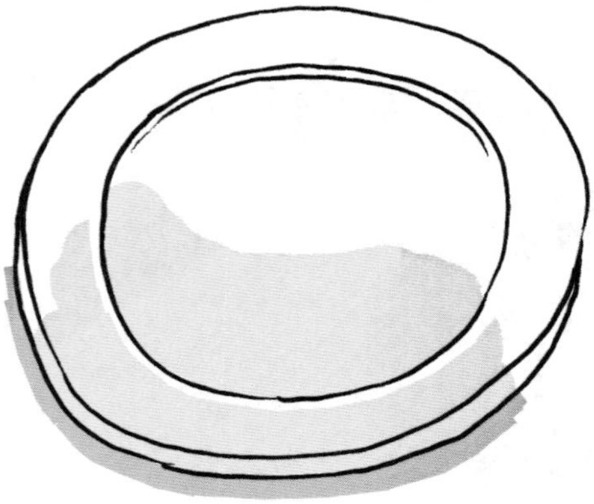

_____

My favorite food is _____

It looks _____

When I pick it up, it feels _____

It smells _____

When I eat it, it sounds like _____

It tastes _____

Make a Wish

Imagine that you could have three wishes. What would you wish for? Complete the three sentences below and draw a picture of your favorite wish.

First, I would wish _____

_____

Then, I would wish _____

_____

Last, I would wish _____

When I Grow Up...

Think about a job you would like to do when you grow up. Draw a picture of yourself doing the job. Complete the sentences below to tell about the job.

When I grow up, I would like to be a

I want to have this job because

The best part about this job would be

Joke of the Day

Read this riddle. Tell why it is funny.

Question: Why are all numbers afraid of seven?
Answer: Because seven eight nine!

The riddle is funny because

_____

_____

Do you know a funny joke or riddle? Write it on the lines below.

This is my joke!

_____

_____

_____

_____

_____

_____

What I Like about You

Think about one of your friends. Then complete the sentences to tell good things about your friend.

My friend's name is

_____

_____

My friend is great because

_____

_____

My friend also

_____

_____

The best thing about my friend is

_____

_____

Be sure to tell your friend the nice things you wrote about him or her!

Once upon a Time

Think about your favorite fairy tale. Write sentences to answer the questions below.

What is the title of the fairy tale?

_____

_____

Who are the main characters?

_____

_____

What is the problem in the story?

_____

_____

How is the problem solved?

_____

_____

In My Dream

> Good writers write about events in order.

Think about a dream you had. Write a sentence to tell what happened first, next, and last.

In my dream, first

_____

_____

_____

_____

Next,

_____

_____

_____

_____

Last,

_____

_____

_____

_____

_____

_____

What Do You Do Best?

Think about something you do well. Then write sentences to answer the questions below. Be sure to start each sentence with a capital letter and end it with an end mark.

What is something you can do well?

_____

_____

_____

How did you learn to do it well?

_____

_____

_____

How long have you done it?

_____

_____

_____

Who helped you learn to do it?

_____

_____

_____

comparisons

A comparison is a sentence that compares one thing to another. Good writers use comparisons to paint a better picture for the reader.

This is a comparison:
The kitten is as soft as a pillow.

Complete the comparisons below.

The librarian is as quiet as

_____

- -

_____

The runner is faster than

_____

- -

_____

The children on the playground are as wild as

_____

- -

_____

My grandma is sweeter than

_____

- -

_____

How Do You Feel?

Complete each sentence below to tell about a time when you felt a certain way. Remember to use an end mark at the end of each sentence.

I felt happy when

_____

_____

I felt scared when

_____

_____

I felt surprised when

_____

_____

I felt angry when

_____

_____

I felt embarrassed when

_____

_____

Weather Report

Draw a picture to show what the weather is like where you are today. Then write a sentence to describe the weather. Try to use as many adjectives, or describing words, as you can.

Far, Far Away

Think about a place you would like to travel. Complete the sentences below.

I would like to go to

_____

- -

_____

When I got there, first I would

_____

- -

_____

Then, I would

_____

- -

_____

I would see

_____

- -

_____

In an Emergency

Imagine that you had an emergency. Think about what you would do to get help. Write what you would do first, next, and last.

First, I would

_____

- -

_____

Next, I would

_____

- -

_____

Last, I would

_____

- -

_____

Safety First

Think about some rules for bike safety. Write three sentences to tell three things a person can do to stay safe on a bicycle.

RULES FOR BIKE SAFETY

1. _____

_____

2. _____

_____

3. _____

My Favorite Story

Think about a story you have read. Write a sentence to answer each question below. Be sure to begin each sentence with a capital letter and end with an end mark.

What is the title of the story?

_____

_____

Who are the main characters?

_____

_____

Where did the story take place?

_____

_____

What happened at the beginning of the story?

_____

_____

How did the story end?

_____

_____

A Million Dollars

Imagine that you won a million dollars. What would you do with the money? Think about what you would do first, next, and last. Then complete each sentence below.

If I won a million dollars, first I would

_____

_____

_____

Next, I would

_____

_____

_____

Last, I would

_____

_____

_____

My Favorite Season

Think about your favorite season. Then complete each sentence below.

My favorite season is

_____

_____

During this season, I wear

_____

_____

My favorite thing to do during this season is

_____

_____

Review

Read the questions below. Write a sentence to answer each question. Be sure to begin each sentence with a capital letter and end it with an end mark.

All About Me

What is your name?

_____

- -

_____

How old are you?

_____

- -

_____

What do you look like?

_____

- -

_____

What is the thing you like most about yourself?

_____

- -

_____

UNIT 5: Writing a Paragraph

HOW MUCH DO YOU KNOW?

Read the paragraph. Then answer the questions.

I love to visit the zoo. First, I go to the gorilla forest to watch gorillas play. Then, I go to see the giraffes. One eats leaves from a tall tree. Next, I visit the reptile house. Finally, I go to see the bird show.

What is the topic sentence?

_____

_____

_____

What happens last in the story?

_____

_____

_____

What Is the Topic?

A paragraph is a group of sentences that tells about one topic.

A paragraph has at least three sentences. The first sentence is indented. It begins a little to the right.

Good writers use details that tell only about the topic.

Read the story. Write the sentence that tells what the topic is. Underline the details that tell about the topic.

My room is a mess. There are clothes all over the floor. My bed is not made. My toys are scattered all over the room. It is so messy that I cannot walk across the room without hopping over piles of stuff.

What is the topic sentence?

_____

- -

_____

Reading a Personal Story

A personal story tells something you have done.
It can tell how you feel about something.
A story tells what happened in order.

Read the story.

I love summer vacation! The best part is the camping trip I take with my family each year. We drive for three hours to the lake. We stay in a tent and swim in the lake. Every morning, my dad cooks scrambled eggs for breakfast.

Write a sentence that tells what you like to do during summer vacation.

_____

_____

_____

_____

Proofreading a Personal Story

Read the story. Use the Proofreading Marks to correct six mistakes.

PROOFREADING MARKS	
⬭	spell correctly
⊙	add period
?	add question mark
≡	capitalize
℘	take out
¶	indent paragraph

one day, my brother and I went to an amusement park. First, we rode the carousel. Then, we raced to the go-karts. my brother almost crashed around around the last curve. Next, we waited in line for the roller coaster I was scared, but my brother told me it would be fun. He was rite. I had so much fun that we rode it again and again. i can't wait to go back to the amusement park!

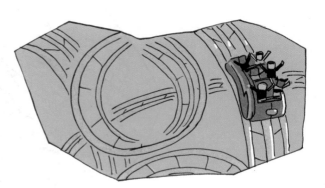

Saturday Afternoon

Think about what you did last Saturday afternoon. What happened first, next, and last? Write a paragraph about it.

_____

- -

_____

_____

- -

_____

_____

- -

_____

_____

- -

_____

When I Felt Sad

Write about a time when you were sad. What happened? Why did you feel sad? How did you feel better?

_____

- -

_____

_____

- -

_____

_____

- -

_____

_____

- -

_____

My Favorite Restaurant

Imagine that you are visiting your favorite restaurant. What do you do first, next, and last? Write a paragraph about your visit.

_____

- -

_____

_____

_____

- -

_____

_____

_____

- -

_____

_____

_____

- -

_____

Reading a Paragraph That Describes

A paragraph that describes tells what someone
or something is like.
The topic sentence names the topic.
The other sentences give details about the topic.

Read the paragraph. Then answer the questions below.

My cat looks so sweet when she is
sleeping. She makes a quiet purring
sound. Her little chest moves up and
down as she breathes. Her soft tail curls
around and brushes against her paw. Her eyes are closed tight.
She has a gentle smile on her face.

What is the topic of the paragraph?

_____

....

_____

What are two detail sentences in the paragraph that tell about
the topic?

_____

....

_____

....

_____

Proofreading a Paragraph That Describes

PROOFREADING MARKS

⬭	spell correctly
⊙	add period
?	add question mark
≡	capitalize
ℓ	take out
¶	indent paragraph

Read the paragraph. Use the Proofreading Marks to correct five mistakes.

What a wonderful day at the beach! The sun is shining down on the water. Lifeguards stand at the edge of the shore. children laugh and splash in the waves. A father bilds a sand castle with his son. I bury my toes deap in the warm sand and read a book

Delicious Dessert

Write a paragraph to describe your favorite dessert. Use adjectives to tell about the colors, the smells, and the flavors.

_____

_____

_____

_____

_____

_____

_____

_____

_____

_____

_____

_____

On the Playground

Imagine that you are playing on a playground. Write a paragraph to describe what you see, hear, feel, and smell.

_____

_____

_____

_____

_____

_____

_____

_____

_____

_____

_____

_____

_____

_____

Story Order

Good writers write sentences in an order that makes sense.

Read the sentences. Write a number (1, 2, 3, 4, and 5) next to each sentence to put them in the correct order.

_____ A noise woke her up.

_____ Amelia turned on a light at the bottom of the stairs.

_____ She got out of bed and went downstairs.

_____ Amelia was sound asleep.

_____ She saw that her cat had knocked over a plant.

Writing in Story Order

Read the sentences. Write the sentences in order so that the story makes sense. Remember to indent the first sentence of the paragraph.

Then, we grab our towels and goggles.

Today we get to go swimming.

Finally, we go to the pool to swim.

First, we put on our swimsuits.

_____

_____

_____

_____

_____

_____

_____

_____

_____

_____

_____

Write about the Planet X

Write a story about aliens on the imaginary planet called X.
Who lives on the planet? What do they do? What happens first,
second, and last?

Reading a Story

A story has a beginning, a middle, and an ending.
A story is often about solving a problem.
A story has a title.
It sometimes has more than one paragraph.

Read the story. Then answer the questions on the next page.

The Hiding Place

Julio loved playing hide-and-seek with the other children on his block. They were happy to let him play, but Julio was the youngest of the kids. No matter where he hid, Julio was always discovered by the older kids. They knew all the hiding places.

Today, Julio decided that he would have to find a hiding place that no one knew about. He searched and searched. Finally, he saw the tall bushes right next to Mr. Adam's house. Mr. Adam was not the friendliest neighbor, so Julio knew that the other kids would not want to hide or look near his house.

Quickly, Julio ran over to the bushes and sat behind them. He looked through the branches. One by one, the other kids ran and chased each other. At last, Julio was the only player left. When they finally called his name to come out, Julio stood up with a smile. He had finally won!

Reading a Story

Answer the questions about the story "The Hiding Place."

What is the title?

_____

_____

Who are the characters?

_____

_____

What is the problem?

_____

_____

How is the problem solved?

_____

_____

Adventure in the Woods

Answer the questions below to help you write a story about an adventure in the woods. Then write the story on the next page.

Who are the characters?

_____

- -

_____

Where does the story take place?

_____

- -

_____

What are the events in the story?

_____

- -

_____

What is the problem?

_____

- -

_____

How is the problem solved?

_____

- -

_____

Adventure in the Woods

Write a story about an adventure in the woods. Use the questions on page 626 to help you write.

_____

- -

_____

- -

_____

- -

_____

- -

_____

- -

_____

- -

_____

- -

_____

- -

_____

(Continue on your own paper.)

New Kid in School

Write a story about a student who is new to your school. Before you write, think about who the characters will be. Think about the beginning, middle, and end to your story.

_____

_____

_____

_____

_____

_____

_____

_____

_____

_____

_____

_____

_____

_____

_____

_____

_____

(Continue on your own paper.)

Studying Directions

Read the directions carefully. Then read what Steven did.

Mrs. Graham told her students to follow these directions:

1. Take out a piece of construction paper.

2. Fold the paper in half to make a card.

3. Use a marker to decorate the outside of the card.

4. Use a pencil to write a message on the inside of the card.

Steven took out a piece of construction paper. He folded the paper in half to make a card. He wrote a message on the inside of the card with his pencil.

Write the direction that Steven forgot to follow.

_____

_____

_____

_____

Extra Information

When writing directions, good writers tell only about the topic. They do not give extra information.

Read the directions for washing a dog. Circle the sentence that does not belong in the directions.

How to Wash Your Dog

1. Fill the bathtub or washtub with water.

2. Add soap to the water.

3. Help your dog get into the tub.

4. Dogs are the best kind of pet.

5. Wash the dog's fur, but be careful not to get soap in your dog's eyes.

6. Dry your dog off with a towel.

How to Get Dressed

Think about how you get dressed in the morning. What do you do first, second, and last? Write directions for how to get dressed below.

_____

1. _____

_____

2. _____

_____

3. _____

_____

4. _____

Writing Directions

HOW DO YOU DO THAT?

Think about something you know how to do. Write step-by-step directions below.

_____

HOW TO _____

_____

1. _____

_____

2. _____

_____

3. _____

_____

4. _____

Review

Read the paragraph. Write the sentences in an order that makes sense. Be sure to begin each sentence with a capital letter and end each sentence with an end mark.

After he got dressed, he ate breakfast. Then, he put on his clothes. Miguel had to get ready for school. Finally, he brushed his teeth. First, he got out of bed.

UNIT 6: Writing a Letter

HOW MUCH DO YOU KNOW?

Read the letter. Use red to circle the greeting. Use blue to circle the signature. Use green to circle the closing.

Then answer the question about the letter.

> March 3, 2005
>
> Dear Grandma,
>   I'm so glad that you came to visit last week. It was fun to show you my classroom. I'm also glad you got to meet my teacher, Mrs. Smith. I will miss having breakfast with you in the morning. I am looking forward to seeing you again this summer!
>
> Love,
> Yolanda

On what date was the letter written?

_____

_____

Parts of a Letter

A friendly letter has five parts. They are the heading, greeting, body, closing, and signature.

Look at the letter below and read the labels for each part. Then answer the questions below.

heading

greeting

December 14, 2005

Dear Mr. Evans,

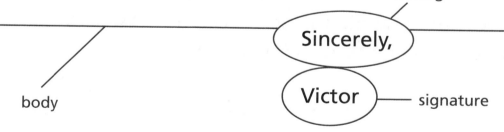

My class is collecting cans to recycle. We are going to use the money to buy some new jump ropes and balls for the playground. Do you have any empty cans you would like to donate? Thank you for your help.

closing

Sincerely,

Victor — signature

body

Who wrote the letter?

_____

_____

What is Victor's class collecting?

_____

_____

Label the Letter Parts

Read the letter. Circle each part of the letter. Use different colors.

Circle the heading with red.

Circle the closing with yellow.

Circle the greeting with blue.

Circle the signature with orange.

Circle the body with green.

June 2, 2005

Dear Mrs. Simms,

    Thank you for being my teacher this year. You helped me learn so much. I loved learning the songs you taught us. My favorite song was the one about the speckled frogs. I will miss you next year. Have a great summer vacation!

Your student,
Kelly

Addressing an Envelope

A letter is sent in an envelope. The center of the envelope has the address of the person who is receiving the letter. The top left corner has the address for the person who is sending the letter.

This is an envelope that Mark Smith sent to Juan Alvarez:

Mark Smith
923 Maple Drive
Evanston, Illinois 60201

Juan Alvarez
5423 Riggs Way
Houston, Texas 77077

Pretend you are addressing a letter to your teacher. Write the name of your teacher and the school address. Then write your own name and your home address in the top left corner.

Reading a Friendly Letter

Read the letter. Then answer the questions below.

July 8, 2005

Dear Mom and Dad,

Camp is a lot of fun. I am making lots of friends. Today, we went horseback riding. We followed a trail down to the lake. Then we got off the horses and went for a swim. After dinner, we sat by a campfire and sang songs. I will teach them to you when I get home! I hope you are doing well.

Your son,
Jamal

Who wrote the letter?

_____

_____

To whom did he write the letter?

_____

_____

What did he do after dinner?

_____

_____

Proofreading a Friendly Letter

PROOFREADING HINTS
- Be sure that the first sentence of the body is indented.
- Be sure that each sentence ends with an end mark.
- Check your spelling.

Read the letter. Use the Proofreading Marks to correct five mistakes.

September 12, 2005

Dear ashley,
I hope you like your new house.
I was very sad to see you move
away, but I know you will make
lots of friends at your new school.
My mom says that we can visit
soon I can't wait! I will bring your
favorite game. We can eat pizza
and stay up all night, just like we
used to do. I mis you very much.
Please write write back soon!

Your friend,
Vonda

PROOFREADING MARKS	
⬭	spell correctly
⊙	add period
?	add question mark
≡	capitalize
ꝑ	take out
¶	indent paragraph

Writing a Friendly Letter

Pretend that you are on a vacation. Write a friendly letter to a friend. Tell your friend where you are and what you are doing. Remember to include all five parts of a letter.

Reading a Thank-You Letter

Read the letter. Then answer the questions below.

January 30, 2005

Dear Officer Brown,

Thank you so much for coming to our class. It was really nice of you to talk to us about bike safety. We learned a lot. When I got home, I checked my helmet to make sure it was the right size. It was too small. My dad is going to get me a new helmet today after school. I will wear it every day. I will also remember to look both ways before I cross the street.

Sincerely,
Robert Chavez

To whom did Robert write the letter?

_____

_____

What did Officer Brown talk to Robert's class about?

_____

_____

Who is going to buy Robert a new helmet?

_____

_____

Proofreading a Thank-you Letter

PROOFREADING HINTS
- Be sure to use capital letters to begin names and months.
- Check your spelling.

Read the letter. Use the Proofreading Marks to correct six mistakes.

PROOFREADING MARKS

⬭	spell correctly
⊙	add period
?	add question mark
☰	capitalize
ℓ	take out
¶	indent paragraph

november 12, 2005

Dear Aunt Rebecca,

Thnak you so much for the pretty scarf it was such a nice birthday gift. Now that the weather is getting cooler here, I think I will wear it almost every day! each time I wear it, I will think of you and smile.

Love,

haley

Writing a Thank-You Letter

Imagine that a family relative, such as an uncle, gave you a nice birthday gift. Write a thank-you letter for the gift. Be sure to tell your relative what you like most about the gift. Remember to include all five parts of a letter.

Reading an Invitation

Read this invitation. Then answer the questions below.

March 12, 2005

Dear Sarah,

Please come to our school carnival. It will be held on March 26 from 9:00 a.m. until 4:00 p.m. at Rummel Creek Elementary School. There will be lots of rides and games. I hope you can come!

Your friend,
Omar

Who is invited?

_____

_____

What is the person invited to attend?

_____

_____

Writing an Invitation

Read the information below. Use the information to write an invitation to a friend.

What is it? A surprise party for Meghan

Date: February 2, 2006

Time: 4:00 p.m.

Place: Rollerworld Skating Rink

_____

_____

_____

_____

_____

_____

_____

_____

_____

_____

_____

_____

_____

_____

Make Your Own Invitation

Pretend you are having a party. Write an invitation to your friend. Remember to include the date, time, and place of the party.

Please come to my party!

Review

Read the letter. Then answer the questions.

March 14, 2005

Dear Mr. Smith,

    I'm sorry that I dented your car door. I was learning to ride my new bike and I did not stop fast enough. I accidentally hit the door with the front wheel of my bike. I am saving money every week, and I would like to pay to fix the dent. Please tell me how much it will cost.

Sincerely,

Jake

Who wrote the letter?

_____

_____

Why did this person write the letter?

_____

_____

_____

_____

Proofreading Marks

Use the following symbols to help make proofreading faster.

MARK	MEANING	EXAMPLE
◯	spell correctly	Today is a (specail) day. *special*
⊙	add period	It is Kevin's birthday⊙
?	add question mark	Do you celebrate birthdays at school?
≡	use capital letter	My teacher's name is Mrs. baker. ≡
✐	take out	She teaches us something new every ~~every~~ day.
¶	indent paragraph	¶ Yesterday, we learned how to sing a song about an octopus. First, she taught us the words. Then we sang it with a tune. Mrs. Baker even played her guitar as we sang.

Test Prep

WORD STUDY SKILLS

The text that appears in blue print is intended for an adult to read aloud.

Name the picture. Listen to the beginning sound. Read the words. Find the word with the same beginning sound.

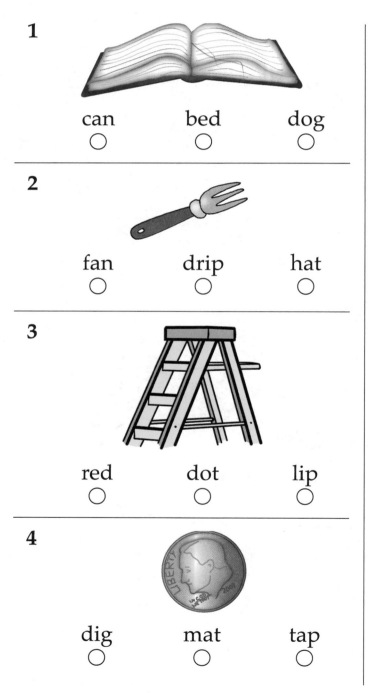

1

can ○   bed ○   dog ○

2

fan ○   drip ○   hat ○

3

red ○   dot ○   lip ○

4

dig ○   mat ○   tap ○

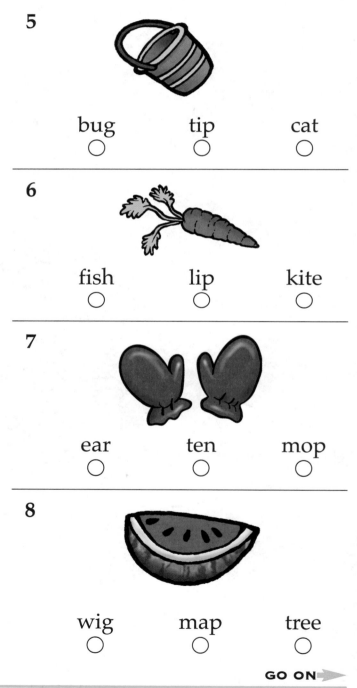

5

bug ○   tip ○   cat ○

6

fish ○   lip ○   kite ○

7

ear ○   ten ○   mop ○

8

wig ○   map ○   tree ○

GO ON ➡

Read the word that names the picture. Listen to the ending sound. Read the words below it. Find the word with the same ending sound.

1 car

cap	star	sit
○	○	○

5 grass

ten	kiss	bag
○	○	○

2 rain

man	far	cry
○	○	○

6 frog

rub	net	big
○	○	○

3 tree

top	cat	three
○	○	○

7 shirt

big	bat	bad
○	○	○

4 duck

kick	day	lamp
○	○	○

8 fish

note	time	wash
○	○	○

GO ON ➡

Look at the picture. Find the word that names the picture.

1

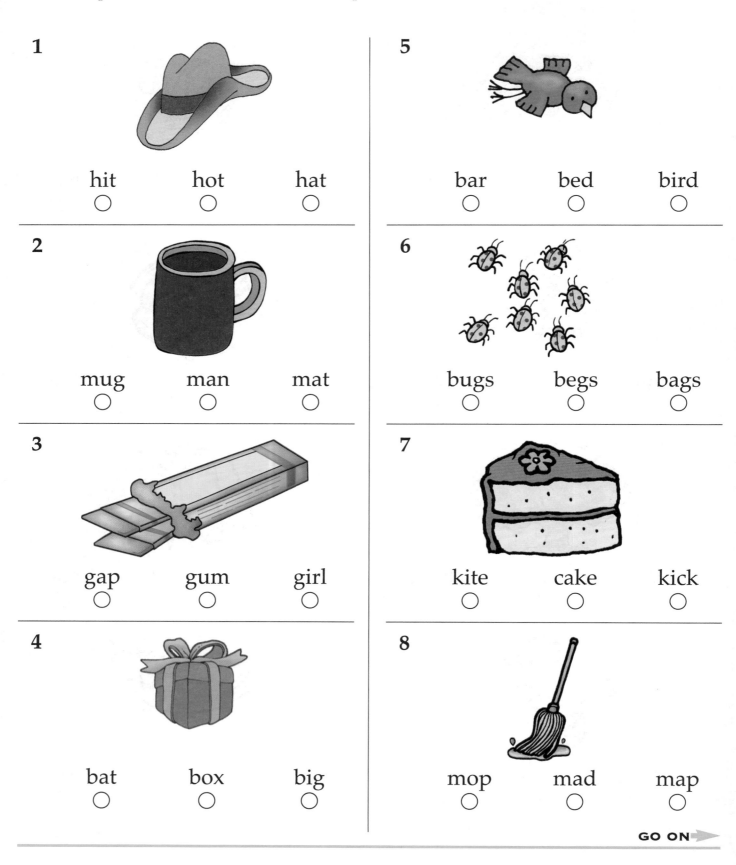

hit ○   hot ○   hat ○

5

bar ○   bed ○   bird ○

2

mug ○   man ○   mat ○

6

bugs ○   begs ○   bags ○

3

gap ○   gum ○   girl ○

7

kite ○   cake ○   kick ○

4

bat ○   box ○   big ○

8

mop ○   mad ○   map ○

GO ON ➡

Read the word. Find the word that rhymes.

1 bat

    bite   cat   cab
     ○   ○   ○

2 can

    pin   sit   tan
     ○   ○   ○

3 dress

    clap   yes   fish
     ○   ○   ○

4 ten

    men   tent   run
     ○   ○   ○

5 hot

    coat   hop   pot
     ○   ○   ○

6 rip

    lip   pig   pin
     ○   ○   ○

7 me

    game   time   tree
     ○   ○   ○

8 top

    two   hop   toy
     ○   ○   ○

9 look

    owl   log   cook
     ○   ○   ○

10 note

    boat   fan   nine
     ○   ○   ○

GO ON →

Name the picture. Listen to the beginning sound. Read the words. Find the word with the same beginning sound.

1

pup ○　　box ○　　dip ○

2

ant ○　　nail ○　　snow ○

3

book ○　　tape ○　　pop ○

4

tip ○　　sit ○　　nap ○

Read the word that names the picture. Listen to the ending sound. Read the words below it. Find the word with the same ending sound.

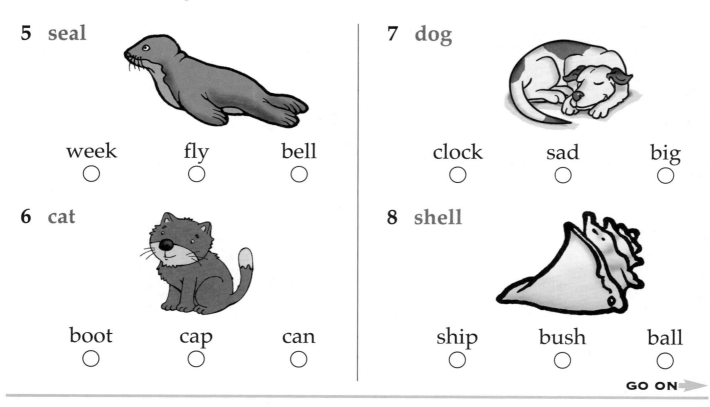

5 seal

week ○　　fly ○　　bell ○

6 cat

boot ○　　cap ○　　can ○

7 dog

clock ○　　sad ○　　big ○

8 shell

ship ○　　bush ○　　ball ○

GO ON →

654 TEST PREP

Look at the picture. Find the word that names the picture.

1

fun ○　　fan ○　　fin ○

2

jar ○　　bun ○　　bag ○

3

day ○　　draw ○　　door ○

4

grin ○　　gate ○　　gift ○

Read the word. Find the word that rhymes.

5 plays

miss ○　　days ○　　cross ○

6 fly

trip ○　　tree ○　　try ○

7 swim

ham ○　　him ○　　hum ○

8 plate

eat ○　　seat ○　　great ○

STOP

SIX READING SKILLS

SKILL 1: DETERMINING WORD MEANINGS

The text that appears in blue print is intended for an adult to read aloud.

Sometimes you can use word clues to find the meaning of a new word. Read along as I read these paragraphs. Try to find the meaning of the underlined word.

The new shoes did not fit. They were the <u>wrong</u> size.

1 In this paragraph, the word **wrong** means —

- ○ too big.
- ○ not right.
- ○ the same.

David won <u>first</u> prize in the spelling bee. He spelled every word right.

2 In this paragraph, the word <u>first</u> means —

- ○ the best.
- ○ in front.
- ○ before.

Sula cannot find her brother. She <u>peeked</u> into his room to see if he was there.

3 In this paragraph, the word **peeked** means —

- ○ called.
- ○ looked.
- ○ walked.

The teacher wanted her book back. She asked if I had <u>finished</u> reading it yet.

4 In this paragraph, the word <u>finished</u> means —

- ○ still.
- ○ liked.
- ○ done.

GO ON

The school bus came to a stop. There was a red light.

5 In this paragraph, the word stop means —

○ get on.
○ get off.
○ wait.

Ming turned the wheel. We watched it spin.

6 In this paragraph, the word spin means —

○ go around.
○ roll away.
○ go for a ride.

TEST TIP

Ask your child to explain the "clue" that led to each correct answer.

The teacher did not want us to run. She told us to walk slowly.

7 In this paragraph, the word slowly means —

○ at once.
○ not fast.
○ not slow.

Marta's job was to greet people. She stood at the door as they came into the room. She was smiling as she welcomed them.

8 In this paragraph, the word greet means —

○ to say hello.
○ to say good-bye.
○ to check.

STOP

The main idea is the meaning of the story. The main idea is often stated in the story. Read along as I read these stories. Then try to find the main idea.

Did you know that some birds can talk? Some parrots can talk. They say what they hear. Sometimes, they say things at the wrong time.

I have a parrot. It was a birthday present. My parrot says many things. One day, my mother was telling me to pick up my toys. The parrot said, "Be quiet!" Mom gave me a funny look. She told me to clean my room. "Be quiet!" said the parrot.

Mom got so angry that she told me to stay in my room for the rest of the day.

1 What is the main idea of this story?

○ Parrots make great gifts.

○ It is important to keep your room clean.

○ Parrots can say things at the wrong time.

Hint: Think about the whole story. Look at the first paragraph.

TEST TIP

To help your child find the main idea, ask, "What is the big idea in this story?" Read each answer choice aloud. Talk about whether each answer choice states the main idea.

TEST TIP

The Hints will help your child find the correct answer. Read them aloud if your child is having difficulty finding the answer.

GO ON ➡

Ricka says she wants to be an animal doctor. She loves all kinds of animals. She has three pets. She has two dogs and one cat.

Ricka takes care of all her pets. She makes sure that they eat well. She sees that they get plenty of rest and play. She brushes their fur. She does everything the animal doctor tells her to do.

I think that Ricka will be a good animal doctor one day.

2 What is the main idea of this story?

○ Ricka takes care of her three pets.

○ Ricka wants to be an animal doctor.

○ Ricka listens to the animal doctor.

Hint: What does the whole story talk about?

TEST TIP

After your child finds the correct answer, look back at the story. Ask your child to find the sentence that states the main idea. Your child should notice that this sentence is the first sentence in the story. Point out that many stories begin with the main idea. This strategy can help your child find the main ideas in test stories.

STOP

Facts and ideas are important. By finding them, you will know what the story is about. Read this story with me. Then answer the questions.

Tina and her family went to the beach last summer. One day, they went to see a lighthouse.

Mr. Beal, the man who worked at the lighthouse, told Tina all about it. The lighthouse is 90 years old. It is all white and it is 120 feet tall. It has a strong light. Sailors can see the light as far as 24 miles out at sea.

1 Tina and her family went to —

○ the city.

○ the beach.

○ the country.

Hint: Look at the first sentence.

2 Who is Mr. Beal?

○ a sailor

○ Tina's father

○ the man who works at the lighthouse

Hint: Read the second paragraph.

3 How tall is the lighthouse?

○ 90 feet

○ 120 feet

○ 24 feet

Hint: Look for the sentence that talks about how tall the lighthouse is.

TEST TIP

Help your child answer the questions by rereading sections from the story.

GO ON➡

It is helpful to put events in the order in which they happen. Read each story with me. Then answer the questions about what happened first, next, and last.

"What's the matter, Lucy?" asked her teacher.

"I lost my new gloves. I looked everywhere, but I can't find them."

When it was time to go home, Lucy put on her coat. She put her hands in her pockets. Then she started to smile. There in her pockets were her gloves, just where she had left them.

1 **Which of these happened first in the story?**

○ Lucy found her gloves.

○ Lucy lost her gloves.

○ Lucy looked for her gloves.

Hint: Look at the beginning of the story.

2 **When did Lucy put on her coat?**

○ when it was time to go home

○ when Lucy lost her gloves

○ when Lucy looked for her gloves

Hint: Look at the last paragraph.

3 **Which of these happened last in the story?**

○ Lucy put her hands in her pockets.

○ Lucy told the teacher she couldn't find her gloves.

○ Lucy found her gloves.

Hint: Look at the last paragraph.

TEST TIP

Emphasize signal words if you need to reread the story. Help your child recognize the meanings of words like *one day* and *then*.

GO ON ➡

Yuko and Rosa were playing outside. They saw a dog across the street. Just then Mr. Jackson came outside.

"Look at that poor little dog, Mr. Jackson. He looks hungry. What can we do to help him?" asked Yuko.

"I'll get him some food," said Mr. Jackson. He went inside and came back out with some food for the dog.

4 Which of these happened first in the story?

- ○ Mr. Jackson gave the dog some food.
- ○ Yuko and Rosa were playing outside.
- ○ The girls saw a dog.

Hint: Look at the beginning of the story.

5 When did Mr. Jackson get the dog some food?

- ○ when he saw the girls playing outside
- ○ when his sister asked him to
- ○ when the girls asked him for help

Hint: Look at the second paragraph.

6 Which of these happened last in the story?

- ○ The dog was given food.
- ○ Yuko and Rosa saw a dog.
- ○ Mr. Jackson came outside.

Hint: Look at the end of the story.

TEST TIP

After your child selects an answer, reread it and ask your child to explain why that answer is correct. Talking about answers can help your child find and correct mistakes.

STOP

Knowing what happened and why it happened helps you understand stories. Read these stories with me. Think about why things happen.

After Kenji was born, Grandma came to visit from Japan. She met my new brother Kenji for the first time. I think she likes him better than she likes me.

Everyone in my family likes Kenji because he is so cute. They talk about him all day. I like him, too, but I want my family to like me again. I came first. I am five years old. I have a lot to talk about. Kenji cannot talk. He just sleeps all day.

1 Why did Grandma come to visit?

○ She wanted to move from Japan.

○ She wanted to see the new baby.

○ She wanted to take a trip.

Hint: What happened that made Grandma come to visit?

2 Why does everyone like Kenji?

○ He's a cute little baby.

○ He is the first child.

○ He sleeps a lot.

Hint: What is it about Kenji that everyone likes?

TEST TIP

You might explain the words *cause* and *effect*. The reason why something happened is the *cause*. The thing that happens is the *effect*.

GO ON

Julia could not run very fast. She could not run as fast as the others. She wanted to do better. Every day she tried running faster and faster. Soon she was able to run so fast that she won a race. She was very happy.

3 **Why does Julia run every day?**

○ She is happy.

○ She likes to run.

○ She wants to run faster.

Hint: What makes Julia run every day?

4 **Why is Julia happy?**

○ She won a race.

○ It is her birthday.

○ She cannot run as fast as the others.

Hint: What made Julia happy at the end of the story?

STOP

Sometimes you can tell what might happen next. Read these stories with me. Think about what would make sense if the story kept going.

Tricia cannot decide how to spend her money. She got ten dollars for her birthday. She has had the money a month. She has not spent it yet. There are many things she wants to buy.

She wants to buy a book. She likes books with many pretty pictures. She likes books about animals.

She wants to buy a puzzle, too. She likes the ones with many pieces. She spreads the pieces all over the floor. It takes a long time to finish it.

1 What will happen next?

○ Tricia will buy some stuffed animals.

○ Tricia will ask for some more money.

○ Tricia will buy a book or a puzzle.

Hint: Think about what Tricia wants to buy with her money.

TEST TIP

Help your child choose the answer that makes sense. Explain that the details in the story are leading somewhere. Ask these questions:

• What did Tricia get for her birthday?

• What does she like?

GO ON ➤

Mia's aunt likes to collect things. She collects tiny glass animals. She has two dogs and three cats all made of glass. She has them on a shelf above her table. They are pretty to look at.

Mia's aunt also collects dolls. She has many dolls. Some of them wear fancy costumes. They come from many different countries.

Mia's aunt is coming to visit next week. Mia would like to buy her something.

2 What will Mia do tomorrow?

○ visit her aunt

○ go shopping for a gift

○ stay home from school

Hint: Read the last paragraph.

STOP

What a character says and thinks tells you what that person feels. Read these stories with me. Think about how the characters feel.

Patrick thinks his cat should have a collar. His cat likes to go outside. Sometimes the cat is gone for a long time. What if the cat cannot find his way home? Patrick decides to buy his cat a collar. Patrick's name and phone number will be on the collar. The cat's name will be on the collar, too.

Maine is a great place to visit. You can go swimming in the ocean. There are sandy beaches. There are many mountains too. You can go walking in the woods. You can climb up the mountains. When you get to the top you can see things far away. There are many fun things to do in Maine.

1 Why does Patrick want his cat to have a new collar?

- ○ The cat will be happier with one.
- ○ He is afraid his cat will get lost.
- ○ The collar he has now is very old.

Hint: Why is Patrick worried?

2 What do you know about the boy telling this story?

- ○ He likes to play baseball.
- ○ He is a good swimmer.
- ○ He likes to go to Maine.

Hint: Read the whole story. Look at the first and last sentences.

STOP

SOLVING RIDDLES

The text that appears in blue print is intended for an adult to read aloud.

Read these riddles with me. Find the picture that shows what the sentences tell.

1

I can be seen in the sky.
I can be seen at night.

○   ○   ○

2

I cannot fly.
I can sing.

○   ○   ○

3

It has wheels.
It is a toy.

○   ○   ○

4

It floats in the water.
You sit in it.

○   ○   ○

5

It gives light.
It is hot.

○   ○   ○

STOP

COMPLETING SENTENCES

Look at the picture. Then read these sentences with me. Find the word that best completes the sentence.

1 Cara and her mother are sitting on a

    lap   bed   chair
    ○   ○   ○

2 Cara's mother is reading her a

    letter   newspaper   book
    ○   ○   ○

3 Cara listens to her mother's

    song   voice   shout
    ○   ○   ○

4 Julio is making

    salad   soup   pancakes
    ○   ○   ○

5 He is wearing a cook's

    hat   sign   coat
    ○   ○   ○

6 Andy could not find his

    shoe   brother   pet
    ○   ○   ○

7 Andy looked under his

    bed   desk   pillow
    ○   ○   ○

8 There he found his

    rabbit   turtle   duck
    ○   ○   ○

STOP

Read these stories with me. Then answer the questions about the story.

Manny Helps Out

Manny likes to help his family. He is only four years old. He thinks he can do things his big brother can do. He wants to help his dad. His dad is painting the house. His dad gives Manny paint and a brush.

Manny gets paint all over his clothes. Dad says, "You will do better when you are five." Manny says, "I don't want to paint anymore. I want to have some fun." Dad laughs.

1 **Manny's brother is**
- ◯ older than Manny.
- ◯ younger than Manny.
- ◯ the same age as Manny.

2 **Why does Manny want to paint the house?**
- ◯ He is a good painter.
- ◯ He wants to help his dad.
- ◯ He does not like the color of the house.

3 **What happens to Manny's clothes?**
- ◯ He tears them.
- ◯ He washes them.
- ◯ He gets paint on them.

4 **What might happen next in the story?**
- ◯ Manny will paint more.
- ◯ Manny will go out to play.
- ◯ Manny will wash all of his clothes.

GO ON

Peppy

We have a new dog at our house. His name is Peppy. He is two years old. My sister and I like to play with Peppy. We throw a ball, and he brings it back. We take him for walks on our street. Peppy barks when he is hungry. I put food in his bowl. My sister gives him cool water. We take good care of Peppy.

5   How old is Peppy?

_____

- - - - - - - - - - - - - - - - - - -

_____

6   You can tell that the children
○   are unhappy with Peppy.
○   love Peppy.
○   are afraid of Peppy.

7   When does Peppy bark?
○   when he wants food
○   when he goes for a walk
○   when he is tired

8   This story tells about
○   two children and their new pet.
○   a man and his cat.
○   how to find a dog.

TEST

Read these riddles with me. Find the pictures that show what the sentences tell about.

1 I can smile.
I cannot walk.

○   ○   ○

2 It can fly.
It takes people places.

○   ○   ○

3 I can play games.
I wear clothes.

○   ○   ○

4 It is green.
It is an animal.

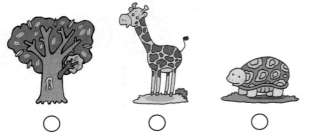

○   ○   ○

5 It is silver.
You can eat with it.

○   ○   ○

6 It is hot.
You plug it in.

○   ○   ○

7 It is clothing.
It is worn on the feet.

○   ○   ○

GO ON →

Look at each picture. Then read these sentences with me. Find the word that best completes the sentences.

8 Two actors are on a

stage ○   train ○   horse ○

9 The people watching will

sing ○   talk ○   clap ○

10 They will leave when the play is

over ○   beginning ○   written ○

11 Ted and Luis are putting up a

table ○   house ○   tent ○

12 Soon they will be

finished ○   arriving ○   rested ○

13 Sadako is wearing her mother's

coat ○   dress ○   gloves ○

14 She is having a lot of

trouble ○   visitors ○   fun ○

15 Sadako is

talking ○   crying ○   smiling ○

GO ON ➡

Rita's Find

One day Rita found a baby bird in the yard. There was no nest nearby. There was no mother bird.

Rita picked up the tiny bird. She kept it for three weeks. The bird grew strong.

Rita took the bird outside. It flew to a nearby tree. It began to sing. Rita knew that her bird would be fine.

16 **Where did Rita find the bird?**

_____

_____

_____

17 **Why did Rita take care of the bird?**

○ Its mother was gone.

○ She liked to sing.

○ Rita's teacher told her to keep it.

18 **Why did the bird fly to a nearby tree?**

○ It wanted to hide.

○ It saw its mother.

○ It was ready to take care of itself.

19 **You can tell that Rita is**

○ kind.

○ silly.

○ unhappy.

GO ON ➡

Elephants

Have you ever seen an elephant? The elephant has a very long nose. It is called a trunk. The elephant's trunk weighs about 300 pounds. Elephants can use their trunks to smell. Elephants use their trunks to hold things, too. They can hold up to 600 pounds. Elephants also use their trunks to reach food. Their trunks help them grab leaves high up in trees. They pull grasses from the ground. Elephants use their trunks in many ways.

20 **What is an elephant's nose called?**

   ○ a beak

   ○ a bill

   ○ a trunk

21 **How many pounds can elephants hold with their trunks?**

_____

_ _ _ _ _ _ _ _ _ _ _ _ _ _ _ _ _

_____

22 **This story tells some ways that elephants**

   ○ take baths.

   ○ use their trunks.

   ○ take care of their babies.

23 **For an elephant, the trunk is very**

   ○ important.

   ○ dusty.

   ○ light.

TEST TIP

Reread sentences from the story to help your child answer the questions.

STOP

MATH PROBLEM-SOLVING PLAN

OVERVIEW

THE PROBLEM-SOLVING PLAN

The text that appears in blue print is intended for an adult to read aloud.

Math problems are sometimes in words, like a story. Having a plan can help you decide how to find the answer. Here are the steps to do these math problems:

STEP 1:   WHAT IS THE QUESTION?
Read the problem. Can you see what you must find?
What is being asked?

STEP 2:   FIND THE FACTS
Find the facts:
A.   IMPORTANT FACTS are facts you need to do the problem.
B.   FACTS YOU DON'T NEED are facts not needed to do the problem.
C.   ARE MORE FACTS NEEDED? Do you need more facts to do the problem?

STEP 3:   GET A PLAN
Choose a way to do the problem.

STEP 4:   DO THE PROBLEM
Use your plan to do the problem.

STEP 5: DOES YOUR ANSWER MAKE SENSE?
Read the problem again.
Does your answer make sense?

GO ON→

Read the word problem with me. Then we'll work through each step together to find the answer to this math story.

Tania wants to buy a new fish tank. The one in the store can hold up to 15 fish. She has 6 goldfish and 5 guppies. Will this tank be large enough for all her fish?

STEP 1: WHAT IS THE QUESTION?

_____

- -

_____

STEP 2: FIND THE FACTS

_____

- -

_____

STEP 3: GET A PLAN

_____

- -

_____

STEP 4: DO THE PROBLEM

_____

- -

_____

STEP 5: DOES YOUR ANSWER MAKE SENSE?

_____

- -

_____

GO ON ▶

Read the word problem with me. Then we'll work through each step together to find the answer to this math story.

Kyle feeds the lions in the zoo. It takes him 5 minutes to prepare the food for each lion. He starts feeding the lions at 12:00 noon. At what time will he begin to feed the 3rd lion?

STEP 1:   WHAT IS THE QUESTION?

STEP 2:   FIND THE FACTS

STEP 3:   GET A PLAN

STEP 4:   DO THE PROBLEM

STEP 5:   DOES YOUR ANSWER MAKE SENSE?

STOP

MATH PROBLEM SOLVING

―UNDERSTANDING NUMERATION―

The text that appears in blue print is intended for an adult to read aloud.

1 Fill in the circle under the number ninety-four.

49   90   94   904
○   ○   ○   ○

2 Which number has 2 in the tens place?

427   472   4,072   247
○   ○   ○   ○

3 Which bird is third from the clouds?

○   ○   ○   ○

4 Look at the blocks. How many blocks are there altogether?

302   23   13   32
○   ○   ○   ○

5 Write the number that is 10 less than the number on the door.

21

STOP

1 Which pot has three out of its five flowers shaded?

○   ○   ○   ○

2 Which shape is divided into four equal parts?

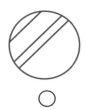 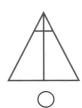 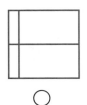 

○   ○   ○   ○

3 Which number sentence is equal to the number sentence in the box?

$$4 + 3 = 7$$

$3 + 7 = 10$	$7 - 2 = 5$	$4 - 3 = 1$	$7 - 3 = 4$
○	○	○	○

4 Which number goes in the box to make the number sentence correct?

$5 + 0 = \square$

10	5	0	1
○	○	○	○

STOP

1 Look for a pattern. Which number belongs in the empty box?

3	6	9		15

10   12   14   20

○   ○   ○   ○

2 Mrs. Inez numbered all the playground balls. This picture shows some of the balls in order. Fill in the circle under the ball that Mrs. Inez will mark number 29.

○   ○   ○   ○

3 Look for a pattern. Which picture shows the next two shapes in the pattern?

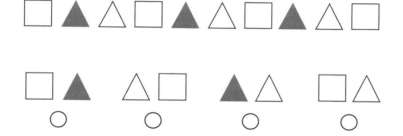

○   ○   ○   ○

4 Which card shows the next number in this pattern?

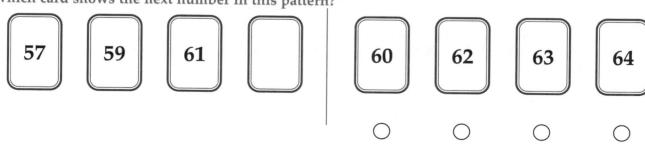

| 57 | 59 | 61 | | | 60 | 62 | 63 | 64 |

○   ○   ○   ○

STOP

1 Look at this graph. Which player won only five games?

Games Won	
Karen	IIII
Ling	IIII
Delia	IIII I
Steven	IIII III

Karen ○   Ling ○   Delia ○   Steven ○

---

2 Look at this chart. How many animal stories did Toby read?

Reading Chart		
Kind of Book	Jerry	Toby
Adventure	3	2
Animal	2	5
Poetry	1	1

_____

- -

_____

---

3 Ron plays a game with paper shapes. He puts one square, four triangles, six circles, and two diamonds into a box. Without looking, Ron picks one shape. Which shape is he most likely to pick?

○   ○   ○   ○

STOP

1 Look at the first shape. Which shape to the right is exactly the same shape?

○   ○   ○   ○

2 Which shape is a square divided into four triangles?

○   ○   ○   ○

3 Which shape has three sides?

○   ○   ○   ○

4 Which shape is the same shape as the first shape, but larger?

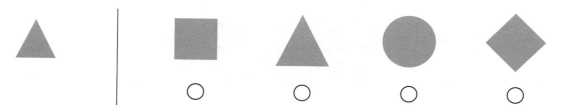

○   ○   ○   ○

STOP

1 Cathy measures her pencil with paper clips. About how many paper clips long is this pencil?

2	4	5	9
○	○	○	○

---

2 Which unit would you use to measure the weight of a crayon?

inches	tons	pounds	ounces
○	○	○	○

---

3 What time does the clock show?

6:30	7:30	8:30	9:30
○	○	○	○

---

4 Mr. Gallo's garden club meets on the third Saturday of each month. Look at the calendar. Write the date of the third Saturday of November.

November

Sun	Mon	Tues	Wed	Thur	Fri	Sat
			1	2	3	4
5	6	7	8	9	10	11
12	13	14	15	16	17	18
19	20	21	22	23	24	25
26	27	28	29	30		

STOP

1 I am thinking of a number that is more than 12 and less than 25. It has a 3 in it. Which of these numbers am I thinking of?

    30   23   17   3

    ○   ○   ○   ○

2 I am thinking of a number that is less that 38. You say its name when you count by fives. It has a 2 in it. Which of these numbers am I thinking of?

    20   27   35   40

    ○   ○   ○   ○

3 Ted sees nine ducks in the pond. Then four of the ducks swim to the other side of the pond. How many ducks are left? Fill in the circle under the number sentence that shows how to find the number of ducks that are left.

    ○   9 − 4 = ☐   ○   5 + 4 = ☐

    ○   ☐ − 4 = 5   ○   5 − 4 = ☐

STOP

The answer choice NH means that the answer is not here.

1 Rita saw 10 ducks swimming in the pond. She also saw 5 ducks standing near the pond. How many ducks did Rita see altogether?

10   **5**

4 ○   15 ○   18 ○   NH ○

2 Ira put 7 oranges in a bag. He put 12 oranges in another bag. How many oranges did Ira have altogether?

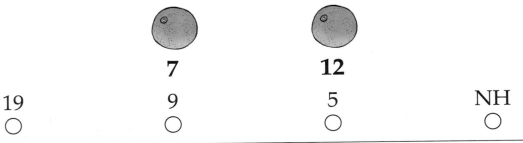

7   **12**

19 ○   9 ○   5 ○   NH ○

3 Mrs. Ling has 15 calculators on a shelf in her store. Then she sells 2 calculators. How many calculators does Mrs. Ling have left?

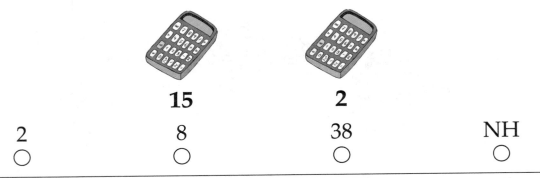

15   **2**

2 ○   8 ○   38 ○   NH ○

4 Tamiko has five plain shirts. She has three striped shirts. Write the number that tells how many shirts Tamiko has altogether.

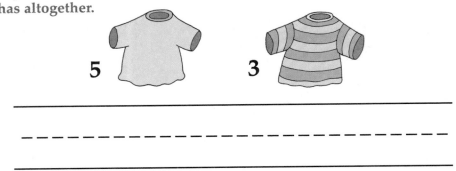

5   3

_____

- - - - - - - - - - - - - - - - -

_____

STOP

Find the answer to each addition or subtraction problem. Choose NH if the answer is not here.

1 $7 + 7 =$ ☐

| 0 | 12 | 14 | NH |
| ○ | ○ | ○ | ○ |

2 $6 + 4 =$ ☐

| 10 | 5 | 2 | NH |
| ○ | ○ | ○ | ○ |

3

$$\begin{array}{r} 3 \\ 8 \\ + 4 \\ \hline \end{array}$$

| 13 | 14 | 15 | NH |
| ○ | ○ | ○ | ○ |

4

$$\begin{array}{r} 65 \\ + 3 \\ \hline \end{array}$$

5

$$\begin{array}{r} 30 \\ + 27 \\ \hline \end{array}$$

| 17 | 37 | 57 | NH |
| ○ | ○ | ○ | ○ |

6 $8 - 5 =$ ☐

| 10 | 4 | 3 | NH |
| ○ | ○ | ○ | ○ |

7

$$\begin{array}{r} 14 \\ - 5 \\ \hline \end{array}$$

| 9 | 10 | 19 | NH |
| ○ | ○ | ○ | ○ |

8

$$\begin{array}{r} 43 \\ - 3 \\ \hline \end{array}$$

9

$$\begin{array}{r} 78 \\ - 21 \\ \hline \end{array}$$

| 99 | 69 | 57 | NH |
| ○ | ○ | ○ | ○ |

10

$$\begin{array}{r} 460 \\ - 30 \\ \hline \end{array}$$

| 430 | 400 | 490 | NH |
| ○ | ○ | ○ | ○ |

TEST TIP

Remind your child to look at the plus or minus sign to decide whether to add or subtract.

 STOP

1 Write the number that goes in the box to make the number sentence correct.

$$\square + 7 = 9$$

_____

- -

_____

2 Which numbers both have a three in the ones place?

34, 13   34, 31   43, 13   43, 31
  ○   ○   ○   ○

3 Which number is more than 49 and less than 72?

49 $\square$ 72   81   73   57   48
                        ○   ○   ○   ○

4 Which number means the same as 20 + 5?

$$20 + 5$$ 205   75   25   7
                    ○   ○   ○   ○

5 Leo uses leaves to measure a rake. About how many leaves long is the rake?

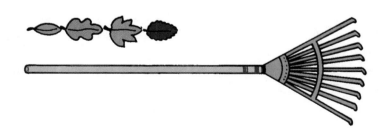

4   6   9   16
○   ○   ○   ○

GO ON

6 Which circle has one of its six parts shaded?

○　　　○　　　○　　　○

7 Which cake shows two of the three candles lit?

○　　　○　　　○　　　○

8 Which triangle is divided into equal halves?

○　　　○　　　○　　　○

9 Count by fives. Write the number that belongs in the box.

35	40	45		55

_____

– – – – – – – – – – – – – – – – – –

_____

10 There are 62 children inside the tent. The children pictured below are in line to go into the tent. Fill in the circle under the child who will be counted as number 64.

62　　　○　　　○　　　○　　　○

GO ON ➡

11 Which shape is exactly the same as the one at the beginning of the row?

○   ○   ○   ○

12 Look at the graph. Write the number that tells how many kittens were sold on Thursday.

Number of Kittens Sold

Monday	
Tuesday	
Wednesday	
Thursday	
Friday	

_____

- - - - - - - - - - - - - - - - - - - -

_____

13 Which shape is a square divided into two triangles?

○   ○   ○   ○

14 Lana puts marbles in a bag. She uses nine red marbles, three blue marbles, two orange marbles, and four yellow marbles. She picks one marble without looking. Which color is she most likely to choose?

red   blue   orange   yellow
○   ○   ○   ○

GO ON ➡

15 I am thinking of a number. It is more than 8 and less than 20. It has a 9 in it. Which of these numbers am I thinking of?

4   15   19   29
○   ○   ○   ○

---

16 Four frogs are sitting on a log. Two more frogs jump on the log. Fill in the circle under the number sentence that shows how to find the number of frogs that are now on the log.

○   4 + 2 = □   ○   4 − 2 = □
○   6 + 2 = □   ○   6 − □ = 2

---

17 Which shape has exactly four corners?

○   ○   ○   ○

---

18 Anton baked six square cookies and five round cookies. How many cookies did Anton bake?

   6   5

_____

- -

_____

GO ON➡

19 Misha counted 15 butterflies in the garden. Then he counted 4 more. How many butterflies did Misha count in all?

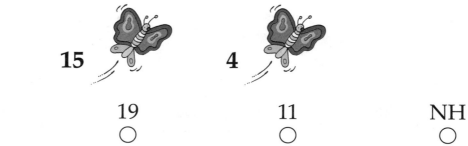

15   **4**

29   19   11   NH
○   ○   ○   ○

20 There are 15 trumpet players in the school band. There are 8 drummers. How many more trumpet players are there than drummers?

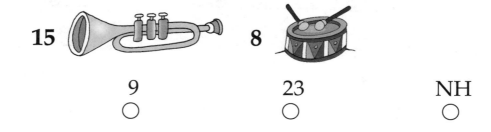

15   **8**

7   9   23   NH
○   ○   ○   ○

21 Claire is at the beach. She collects 26 shells. She puts 3 shells back because they are broken. How many shells does Claire have left?

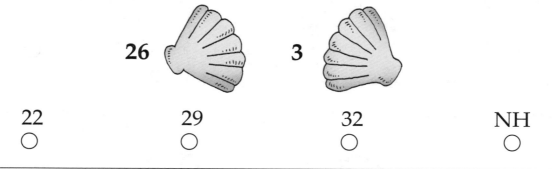

26   **3**

22   29   32   NH
○   ○   ○   ○

22 Mia took 24 balloons to school. She gave away 20 of the balloons. How many balloons did Mia have left?

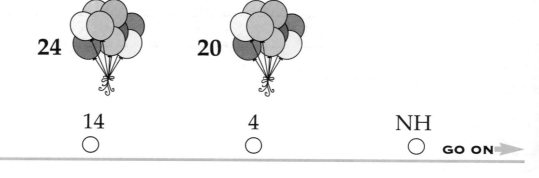

24   **20**

20   14   4   NH
○   ○   ○   ○   **GO ON** ➡

Find the answer to each addition or subtraction problem.

23

$$\begin{array}{r} 2 \\ 9 \\ + 3 \\ \hline \end{array}$$

24 ○   14 ○   12 ○   NH ○

24

$$\begin{array}{r} 66 \\ + 3 \\ \hline \end{array}$$

_____

- - - - - - - - - - - - - - - - - - -

_____

25

$$\begin{array}{r} 38 \\ + 40 \\ \hline \end{array}$$

48 ○   58 ○   68 ○   NH ○

26

$$\begin{array}{r} 72 \\ + 20 \\ \hline \end{array}$$

92 ○   52 ○   50 ○   NH ○

27 $5 - 5 = \square$

5 ○   1 ○   0 ○   NH ○

28

$$\begin{array}{r} 11 \\ - 3 \\ \hline \end{array}$$

6 ○   7 ○   8 ○   NH ○

29

$$\begin{array}{r} 58 \\ - 6 \\ \hline \end{array}$$

2 ○   22 ○   52 ○   NH ○

30

$$\begin{array}{r} 80 \\ - 20 \\ \hline \end{array}$$

_____

- - - - - - - - - - - - - - - - - - -

_____

31

$$\begin{array}{r} 549 \\ - 45 \\ \hline \end{array}$$

594 ○   584 ○   504 ○   NH ○

STOP

LISTENING

The text that appears in blue print is intended for an adult to read aloud.

Listen to these sentences as I read. Then find the word or words that best complete each sentence.

1. We don't want anything to *harm* our new puppy. To *harm* means to —
   help…heal…hurt.

2. If I *discover* some treasure, I will be rich. To *discover* something is to —
   hide it…find it…bury it.

3. Ava sat under a *clump* of trees. Another name for *clump* is —
   limp…bunch…shade.

4. Keesha *rescued* the baby bird from the cat. To *rescue* is to —
   save…wash…feed.

5. The color in my red shirt might *fade* in the wash. To *fade* is to —
   get lighter…get darker…get smaller.

6. Rodrigo gave Darla a birthday *gift*. Another name for *gift* is —
   box…present…cake.

7. We had to *pause* for a moment and rest. To *pause* is to —
   wait…sleep…hurry.

8. Kenji *aimed* the beanbag at the bucket. To *aim* is to —
   clap…mark…point.

9. Cheng fished in the *stream*. Another name for *stream* is —
   creek…sea…pond.

10. Dad *repaired* our toaster. To *repair* something is to —
    replace it…fix it…return it.

11. Her book is *below* the table. Another word for *below* is —
    over…above…under.

12. The sad story made us *weep*. To *weep* is to —
    yell…laugh…cry.

1
- ○ help
- ○ heal
- ○ hurt

7
- ○ wait
- ○ sleep
- ○ hurry

2
- ○ hide it
- ○ find it
- ○ bury it

8
- ○ clap
- ○ mark
- ○ point

3
- ○ limp
- ○ bunch
- ○ shade

9
- ○ creek
- ○ sea
- ○ pond

4
- ○ save
- ○ wash
- ○ feed

10
- ○ replace it
- ○ fix it
- ○ return it

5
- ○ get lighter
- ○ get darker
- ○ get smaller

11
- ○ over
- ○ above
- ○ under

6
- ○ box
- ○ present
- ○ cake

12
- ○ yell
- ○ laugh
- ○ cry

STOP

Listen to these stories as I read. Then find the picture that answers the question.

Every morning before school, Lila eats a good breakfast. After breakfast, she brushes her teeth. Next, she dresses and combs her hair. Then she is ready to walk to the bus stop.

1. What does Lila do after she eats breakfast?

Mr. Stone's class put on a talent show. Each student did something to help with the show. Marcia and Tom made the scenery. Sam played the trumpet. Jody did a tap dance. Marty and Kim sang a song.

2. What did Sam play in the talent show?

3. What is something another student might do in the talent show?

Mrs. Wallace owns her own bakery. She likes the smell of fresh baking.

4. Which picture shows something you could buy in Mrs. Wallace's store?

If I could, you know I would
Sail the ocean blue.
I'd have a big adventure,
And meet a pirate, too.

5. Which picture shows how the author of the poem could travel on the ocean?

I am sharp. My job is to cut hair. I can also cut flowers or paper.

6. What am I?

Ella made a Mother's Day card. She drew three roses in the middle. She drew a butterfly above the roses. Under the roses, she drew a bow. On top she wrote "To Mother."

7. Which card did Ella make?

Juan and Maria like to help their father. When the leaves have fallen from the trees, it is time for the family to start working.

8. Which picture shows how Juan and Maria help their father in the fall?

CHOOSING PICTURE ANSWERS

1

   ◯   ◯   ◯

2

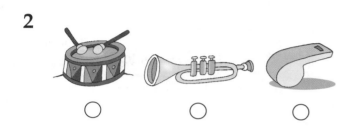

   ◯   ◯   ◯

3

   ◯   ◯   ◯

4

   ◯   ◯   ◯

5

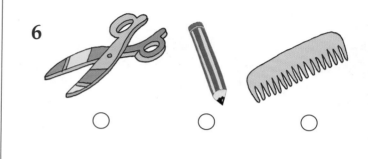

   ◯   ◯   ◯

6

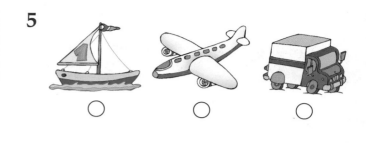

   ◯   ◯   ◯

7

   ◯   ◯   ◯

8

   ◯   ◯   ◯

STOP

Listen to these stories as I read. Then answer the questions.

Keiko just lost her tooth. She is happy it fell out. It had been loose for seven days. Now she can eat without feeling any pain.

1. When did Keiko lose her tooth?
   today…seven days ago…two weeks ago

2. How did Keiko feel about losing her tooth?
   glad…sad…mad

We saw a special parade at the zoo.
The animals lined up two by two!
The giraffes so tall,
The ferrets so small,
And the elephants, of course, were the
   biggest of all.

3. Why were the animals lined up?
   *It was raining….There was a parade….
   They were on their way to Africa.*

4. Which animals were tall?
   elephants…ferrets…giraffes

The word dinosaur means "terrible lizard." These creatures roamed Earth millions of years ago. Some were as small as chickens. Others were larger than elephants. We learn about dinosaurs from the things they left behind.

5. How small were some dinosaurs?
   *as small as bees…as small as teacups…
   as small as chickens*

6. How do we learn about dinosaurs?
   *from the things they left behind…from the people
   who were living then…from animals today*

- First, take the eggs, milk, and bread out of the refrigerator.
- Next, break the eggs into a bowl. Use a fork to mix them with the milk.
- Then put the bread in the bowl. Turn it over.
- Finally, cook the bread in a pan on the stove.
- When your French toast is ready, enjoy your breakfast!

7. What do these directions tell you how to make?
   biscuits…french toast…cereal

8. What should you do after you mix the milk and eggs in a bowl?
   *add the bread…put it on the stove…
   stir in some butter*

1 ○ today
○ seven days ago
○ two weeks ago

2 ○ glad
○ sad
○ mad

3 ○ It was raining.
○ There was a parade.
○ They were on their way to Africa.

4 ○ elephants
○ ferrets
○ giraffes

5 ○ as small as bees
○ as small as teacups
○ as small as chickens

6 ○ from the things they left behind
○ from the people who were living then
○ from animals today

7 ○ biscuits
○ French toast
○ cereal

8 ○ add the bread
○ put it on the stove
○ stir in some butter

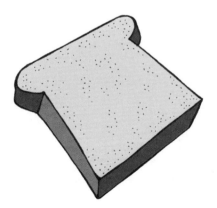

Listen to these sentences as I read. Then find the word or words that best complete each sentence.

1. My uncle lives in a *cabin* at the lake.
   A *cabin* is a —
   shed…boat…small house.

2. José has to *prepare* for his part in the play.
   To *prepare* is to —
   calm down…leave…get ready.

3. Zoe saw a *bug* on a leaf. Another name for
   bug is —
   insect…igloo…pet.

4. This instrument makes a sound when you *strike*
   it. To *strike* is to —
   hit…smooth…clean.

5. Our family took a *vacation* to the Grand
   Canyon. Another name for *vacation* is —
   illness…trip…excuse.

6. Su Ling missed the beginning of class because
   she was *tardy* this morning.
   To be *tardy* is to be —
   present…late…early.

7. I saw the movie the *day before today*. The *day
   before today* is called —
   tomorrow…tonight…yesterday.

8. My mom met a *pleasant* lady who gave us
   directions. *Pleasant* means —
   nice…rude…poor.

9. Katy found an *unusual* rock. If something is
   unusual, it is —
   not common…square…normal.

10. The knight was *brave* when he fought the
    dragon. *Brave* means —
    not afraid…not angry…not smart.

11. The weather forecaster said clouds might *appear*
    today. To *appear* is to —
    go away…be seen…get faster.

12. We walked through the *woods* and saw many
    animals and trees. Another word for *woods* is —
    ocean…desert…forest.

1
- ○ shed
- ○ boat
- ○ small house

2
- ○ calm down
- ○ leave
- ○ get ready

3
- ○ insect
- ○ igloo
- ○ pet

4
- ○ hit
- ○ smooth
- ○ clean

5
- ○ illness
- ○ trip
- ○ excuse

6
- ○ present
- ○ late
- ○ early

7
- ○ tomorrow
- ○ tonight
- ○ yesterday

8
- ○ nice
- ○ rude
- ○ poor

9
- ○ not common
- ○ square
- ○ normal

10
- ○ not afraid
- ○ not angry
- ○ not smart

11
- ○ go away
- ○ be seen
- ○ get faster

12
- ○ ocean
- ○ desert
- ○ forest

GO ON

Listen to these stories as I read. Then find the picture that answers the question.

Fatima helped her aunt make a quilt. Fatima cut four squares and three circles from the cloth.

13. Which picture shows how Fatima cut the cloth?

Miko turned on the water in the tub to take a bath. Then the telephone rang and Miko answered it. She talked to her friend for an hour and forgot about the water in the tub.

14. Which picture shows what probably happened next?

Amy is learning a new dance. Her teacher tells her to put her arms down at her sides and stand with her feet apart.

15. Which picture shows how Amy should stand?

Diego's grandmother gave him a box with a new pet in it. When Diego looked in the box, he saw long ears and a short, fluffy tail.

16. What pet did Diego receive?

Mr. Sakata told his class, "This week you will choose a book from the school library to read. The book must tell a story. Then you will write a report about your book."

17. What is the *first* thing each student must do?

Mr. Jordan made a delicious strawberry pie. First, he picked the berries. Then he mixed the dough for the crust. Finally, he rolled the dough flat.

18. What did Mr. Jordan do after he picked the berries?

No one had lived in the old house on Gulf Road for more than 10 years. It was very scary-looking. One night, Paul and his friend Steve visited the house. Just as they opened the front door, something small and furry brushed against their legs. The boys decided to explore the house some other day and they ran home.

19. Which picture shows the house on Gulf Road?

20. What probably brushed by the boys at the house?

Alex baked muffins for the bake sale. He measured and mixed the ingredients. Then he poured the batter into a pan and put the pan into the oven.

21. Which baking pan did Alex use?

13

○ ○ ○

14

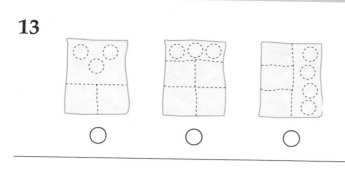

○ ○ ○

15

○ ○ ○

16

○ ○ ○

17

○ ○ ○

18

○ ○ ○

19

○ ○ ○

20

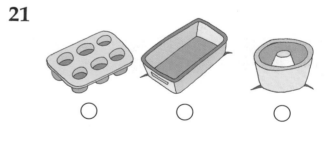

○ ○ ○

21

○ ○ ○

GO ON →

Listen to these stories as I read. Then answer the questions.

- First, take the kite out of the package.
- Second, insert the wooden pieces into the back of the kite.
- Next, attach the end of a ball of string to the center of the kite.
- Finally, make a kite's tail from pieces of cloth. Attach the tail to the kite.
- If you like, you can paint or decorate your kite.

22. You need to attach wooden pieces to the kite so that —
    the kite can fly…the kite won't blow away… you can decorate the kite.

23. To make the kite fly, you do not have to —
    attach some string…insert wooden pieces… paint the kite.

Rod helps out at his family's store every day. Before going to school, Rod sweeps the store. After school, Rod does his homework. Then he takes out the trash. When it is time to close the store, Rod makes sure all the lights are turned out.

24. Before school, Rod helps by —
    sweeping the store…taking out the trash… turning out all the lights.

25. Rod helps close the store by —
    doing his homework…taking out the trash…turning out all the lights.

There are many simple ways to save water. One is taking showers instead of baths. Showers use much less water and get you just as clean. You can also save water when you are washing your hands and brushing your teeth. Don't let the water run while you are soaping up your hands or brushing your teeth. Turn the water on just when you need it to rinse.

26. One thing that does not help save water is —
    taking a shower…catching rainwater…taking a bath.

27. When washing your hands, you should turn on the water only to —
    soap up your hands…rinse…take a bath.

"Oh, my goodness!" said Jake.
When he opened his backpack,
Out came a snake!

28. What came out of Jake's backpack?
    his frog…his snake…his homework

29. How did Jake feel when he saw it?
    surprised…tired…sad

Ms. Jackson's class did a science experiment. She divided the class into groups and gave each person a job. "In this group, Michiko will pass out the materials," Ms. Jackson said. "Jamal will be the recorder. Scott will be in charge of cleanup. Jenna will be the leader."

30. What was Ms. Jackson's class doing?
    practicing a play…running a race…doing a science experiment

31. Who will be the leader?
    Michiko…Jenna…Jamal

Mr. Diaz packed the gear for the camping trip. He packed the tent. He put food in a cooler. He packed lanterns, flashlights, and bug spray. At the campsite, the members of the family set up the tent. They cooked a meal over the fire. Only when it was time to go to bed did they discover that Mr. Diaz had forgotten to pack something.

32. What did Mr. Diaz probably forget to pack?
    sleeping bags…radio…flashlights

33. What is a good title for this story?
    "How to Go Camping"…"The Diaz Family's Problem"…"Fun with Flashlights"

22 ○ the kite can fly
○ the kite won't blow away
○ you can decorate the kite

23 ○ attach some string
○ insert wooden pieces
○ paint the kite

---

24 ○ sweeping the store
○ taking out the trash
○ turning out all the lights

25 ○ doing his homework
○ taking out the trash
○ turning out all the lights

---

26 ○ taking a shower
○ catching rainwater
○ taking a bath

27 ○ soap up your hands
○ rinse
○ take a bath

28 ○ his frog
○ his snake
○ his homework

29 ○ surprised
○ tired
○ sad

---

30 ○ practicing a play
○ running a race
○ doing a science experiment

31 ○ Michiko
○ Jenna
○ Jamal

---

32 ○ sleeping bags
○ radio
○ flashlights

33 ○ "How to Go Camping"
○ "The Diaz Family's Problem"
○ "Fun with Flashlights"

STOP

LANGUAGE

The text that appears in blue print is intended for an adult to read aloud.

Listen to the story. Then find the picture that answers the question.

It was Saturday and it was raining. Mei could not go out to play with her friends. After lunch, Mei told her mother, "I have nothing to do." Her mother asked, "Why don't you watch TV?" But Mei didn't want to watch TV. Then Mei's mother showed her a trunk filled with old clothes, purses, hats, and other things.

1. Which picture shows how Mei had fun on a rainy day?

Elena and Ricardo were helping their mother by setting the table. Elena placed the spoon and fork on either side of the plate. Ricardo crossed the spoon and fork and put them on the plate. Then the spoon cried, "That's not right!" and it jumped off the plate.

2. Which picture shows the part of the story that could not really happen?

My grandmother lives in the state of Maine.
When we go to visit her, we travel by ——.

3. Which picture shows something that will finish this rhyming poem?

Frankie's father gave him a box. When Frankie looked inside the box, he saw short ears and a wagging tail.

4. Which picture shows Frankie's new pet?

Mr. Henson was building a new birdhouse for his bird, Grover. First, he sawed the wood into pieces. Next, he nailed the pieces together. Finally, he painted Grover's new birdhouse.

5. What did Mr. Henson do first?

1

 ○

 ○

 ○

2

 ○

 ○

 ○

3

 ○

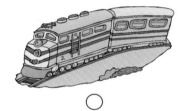 ○

 ○

4

 ○

 ○

 ○

5

 ○

 ○

 ○

STOP

Read with me as I read this report. Then answer the questions.

Ramona wrote this report titled Getting Around in the City.

> Many people drive cars.
> In large cities.
> Some people ride in taxis.
> Some people ride the bus.

1. Which sentence in Ramona's report is not a complete sentence?
   Many people drive cars....In large cities....Some people ride in taxis....

---

2. Choose the sentence that makes sense at the end of this paragraph.

> We live in the city.
> My father rides a bus to work.
> It is too far for him to walk.

Which sentence will Ramona write next?

A few people might walk to work....People work in a city....The city is noisy....

3. Look at the underlined words with the number 1 under them. Did Ramona use the right words? Should she write *We is living*, *We live*, or is the group of underlined words *correct the way it is*?

4. Look at the underlined words with the number 2 under them. Did Ramona use the right words? Should she write *My Father* (with both words capitalized), *my father* (with both words lowercased), or is the group of underlined words *correct the way it is*?

Getting Around in the City

Many people drive cars.
In large cities.
Some people ride in taxis.
Most people ride the bus.

1   ○   Many people drive cars.
     ○   In large cities.
     ○   Some people ride in taxis.

2   ○   A few people might walk to work.
     ○   People work in a city.
     ○   The city is noisy.

We lives in the city.
(1)
My father rides a bus to work.
(2)
It is too far for him to walk.

3   We is living   We live   Correct the way it is.
        ○   ○   ○

4   My Father   my father   Correct the way it is.
        ○   ○   ○

GO ON

Listen to this information about Larry's report. Then answer the questions.

Larry's teacher asked the class to write a story about their pets. Larry has a horse. He decided to write about the tricks his horse can do.

5. Why is Larry writing a story? Is it *to tell how to teach a horse tricks, to tell why he loves horses,* or *to tell a story about his pet?*

_____

6. Larry wanted to use these words in his story: *kiss, tricks,* and *hand.* Fill in the circle under the word that would be listed first in a dictionary.

Read with me as I read the first part of Larry's report, titled My Smart Horse.

> My horse can do many tricks.
> He lifts his leg to my hand shake.
> He gives me a kiss with his nose.
> My horse can also play hiding games.

7. Look at the underlined sentence. Did Larry write this sentence correctly? Should he write *He lifts his leg to hand shake my, He lifts his leg to shake my hand,* or is the sentence *correct the way it is?*

_____

8. Larry wants to describe what his horse looks like. Should he write *My horse is brown and white, I like to see my horse run,* or *My horse comes when he sees me?*

5
- ○ to tell how to teach a horse tricks
- ○ to tell why he loves horses
- ○ to tell a story about his pet

6

kiss	tricks	hand
○	○	○

My Smart Horse

My horse can do many tricks.
<u>He lifts his leg to my hand shake.</u>
He gives me a kiss with his nose.
My horse can also play hiding games.

7
- ○ He lifts his leg to hand shake my.
- ○ He lifts his leg to shake my hand.
- ○ Correct the way it is.

8
- ○ My horse is brown and white.
- ○ I like to see my horse run.
- ○ My horse comes when he sees me.

GO ON

ead with me as I read the next part of Larry's report.

> I gived my horse a treat after each trick.
> He likes carrots best.
> If I forget his treat, he shakes his head.

9. Look at the underlined word, *gived*, with the number 1 under it. Did Larry use the right word? Should he write *gave*, *give*, or is the word *correct the way it is*?

10. Look at the underlined word, *likes*, with the number 2 under it. Did Larry use the right word? Should he write *like*, *liked*, or is the word *correct the way it is*?

Now I will read to you about Vicki's class.

Vicki's class put together a report about how people travel from place to place. They put a table of contents at the front of the report. Read with me as I read the table of contents. Chapter 1 is called Over Tracks and begins on page 6. Chapter 2 is called Up in Air and begins on page 21. Chapter 3 is called On Land and begins on page 38. Chapter 4 is called By Water and begins on page 50.

11. Would an article about airplanes be in Chapter 1, 2, or 3?

12. Would you find information about ships on page 21, 38, or 50?

I <u>gived</u> my horse a treat after each trick.
     (1)

He <u>likes</u> carrots best.
       (2)

If I forget his treat, he shakes his head.

9 gave ○   give ○   Correct the way it is. ○

10 like ○   liked ○   Correct the way it is. ○

Table of Contents

11 1 ○   2 ○   3 ○

12 21 ○   38 ○   50 ○

STOP

Listen to these sentences. Three of the words will be listed. Find the word that is not spelled correctly.

1. I went along for the ride.

2. Did you see the cake I baked?

3. He was eating an apple.

4. Tony walked to the store by himself.

5. The two babies played quietly.

6. Alberto had a party at school today.

7. Please pass the milk.

8. I can cross the street now.

9. Those boys joined the baseball team.

10. The frog sat on the green grass.

11. It is Raul's turn to wash dishes.

12. Brian picked these flowers.

1. ○ wint
   ○ along
   ○ ride

2. ○ you
   ○ see
   ○ bakt

3. ○ wus
   ○ eating
   ○ apple

4. ○ walkt
   ○ store
   ○ himself

5. ○ two
   ○ babies
   ○ playd

6. ○ had
   ○ party
   ○ skool

7. ○ Pleaze
   ○ pass
   ○ milk

8. ○ can
   ○ cros
   ○ street

9. ○ boyes
   ○ joined
   ○ team

10. ○ frog
    ○ gren
    ○ grass

11. ○ turn
    ○ wash
    ○ dishs

12. ○ pickd
    ○ these
    ○ flowers

STOP

..n to these stories I read. Then answer the questions.

The house on Edmond Street has a pointed roof. The chimney is crooked.

1. Which picture shows the house on Edmond Street?

_____

Inez and Isabella are twins. Even though they look alike, they are very different. They like to do different things. They wear their hair the same way, but they always dress differently.

2. Which picture shows Inez and Isabella?

_____

Chris and his family went to the lake. They saw a family of bears swimming across the lake. Then the bears joined Chris and his family at the picnic table for lunch. Later, Chris offered to clean up the mess at the picnic table.

3. Which picture shows something that could not really happen?

_____

While we were walking by the lake,
We saw a black and yellow ——.

4. Which picture shows something that will finish this rhyming poem?

_____

Gloria was very busy on Saturday. She made her bed and then washed the dishes. When she was done, she went to her room to do her homework.

5. Which picture shows what Gloria did first?

1

○   ○   ○

2

○   ○   ○

3

○   ○   ○

4

  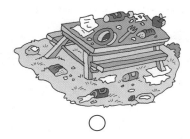

○   ○   ○

5

○   ○   ○

GO ON ➤

...n as I tell you about Pat's science project.

Pat is going to make a project for the science fair. She is going to tell how seeds move from place to place.

6. What should Pat do before writing her science report? Should she *list ways seeds move, plant some seeds,* or *glue seeds to paper*?

_____

7. What should Pat do to find more information about how seeds move? Should she *buy seeds from a store, find a library book about seeds,* or *go to a park*?

Read with me as I read the first part of Pat's report, titled Animals Move Seeds.

> Some animals move seeds.
> Birds pick up seeds to eat.
> They may dropping the seeds as they fly.
> I have a new dog.
> The seeds grow where they fall on the ground.

8. Look at the underlined word, *dropping*, in the first part of Pat's report. Did she use the right word? Should she write *drops, drop,* or is the word *correct the way it is*?

_____

9. Which sentence does not belong in this report? Is it *Some animals move seeds, Birds pick up seeds to eat,* or *I have a new dog*?

6
- ○ list ways seeds move
- ○ plant some seeds
- ○ glue seeds to paper

7
- ○ buy seeds from a store
- ○ find a library book about seeds
- ○ go to a park

Animals Move Seeds

Some animals move seeds.
Birds pick up seeds to eat.
They may <u>dropping</u> the seeds as they fly.
I have a new dog.
The seeds grow where they fall on the ground.

8
- ○ drops
- ○ drop
- ○ Correct the way it is.

9
- ○ Some animals move seeds.
- ○ Birds pick up seeds to eat.
- ○ I have a new dog.

GO ON

with me as I read the next part of Pat's report.

> Some seeds stick to the fur of animals.
> They dont fall off easily.
> The ends of the seeds are turned up.

10. Look at the underlined word, *dont*. Did Pat use the right word? Should she write *don't* (with the apostrophe between the *n* and the *t*), *do'nt* (with the apostrophe between the *o* and the *n*), or is the word *correct the way it is?*

_____

11. Pat wants to describe what the seeds look like. Should she write *The seed ends look sharp and look like a fishhook, The seed ends look sharp and like a fishhook,* or *The seed ends look like a sharp fishhook*

_____

12. Pat used these words in her report: *stick, seeds,* and *sharp*. Which word would be listed first in the dictionary?

Some seeds stick to the fur of animals.
They <u>dont</u> fall off easily.
The ends of the seeds are turned up.

10
○ don't
○ do'nt
○ Correct the way it is.

11
○ The seed ends look sharp and look like a fishhook.
○ The seed ends look sharp and like a fishhook.
○ The seed ends look like a sharp fishhook.

12
stick   seeds   sharp
○   ○   ○

GO ON➤

to these sentences. Three of the words will be listed. Find the word that is not spelled correctly.

13. The play was over at four o'clock.

_____

14. The pretty pink present is for Ida.

_____

15. Liz told a funny story.

_____

16. This is the end of the line.

_____

17. The boys splashed in the water.

_____

18. Max bought two brushes.

19. I didn't mean what I said.

_____

20. The pond is filled with fish.

_____

21. Your face has dirt on it.

_____

22. Put your toys away in your room.

_____

23. Mother parked close to the store.

_____

24. The snake lives under the rock.

13 ○ play
   ○ overe
   ○ four

14 ○ prety
   ○ pink
   ○ present

15 ○ told
   ○ funny
   ○ storie

16 ○ This
   ○ ende
   ○ line

17 ○ boys
   ○ splashd
   ○ water

18 ○ bought
   ○ two
   ○ brushs

19 ○ mean
   ○ what
   ○ sed

20 ○ pond
   ○ filld
   ○ fish

21 ○ fase
   ○ has
   ○ dirt

22 ○ put
   ○ toyes
   ○ room

23 ○ Mother
   ○ parkt
   ○ close

24 ○ livz
   ○ under
   ○ rock

STOP

The text that appears in blue print is intended for an adult to read aloud.

Listen to the word. Find the word that begins with the same sound.

1. *Soup*
   What word begins with the sound you hear at the beginning of the word *soup*?

2. *Doll*
   What word begins with the sound you hear at the beginning of the word *doll*?

3. *Bottle*
   What word begins with the sound you hear at the beginning of the word *bottle*?

4. *Happy*
   What word begins with the sound you hear at the beginning of the word *happy*?

5. *Toast*
   What word begins with the sound you hear at the beginning of the word *toast*?

6. *Friend*
   What word begins with the sound you hear at the beginning of the word *friend*?

7. *Wish*
   What word begins with the sound you hear at the beginning of the word *wish*?

8. *Kitten*
   What word begins with the sound you hear at the beginning of the word *kitten*?

9. *Purple*
   What word begins with the sound you hear at the beginning of the word *purple*?

10. *Ship*
    What word begins with the sound you hear at the beginning of the word *ship*?

11. *Rabbit*
    What word begins with the sound you hear at the beginning of the word *rabbit*?

12. *Grasshopper*
    What word begins with the sound you hear at the beginning of the word *grasshopper*?

1 sip ○   tip ○   plate ○

7 fit ○   mats ○   wet ○

2 gate ○   dig ○   puppy ○

8 cake ○   sat ○   take ○

3 tub ○   eat ○   bite ○

9 rip ○   ear ○   pen ○

4 hot ○   not ○   cot ○

10 shell ○   tell ○   well ○

5 most ○   sun ○   teeth ○

11 bear ○   air ○   run ○

6 pin ○   frog ○   barn ○

12 hill ○   green ○   four ○

GO ON ➡

to the word. Find the word that ends with the same sound.

13. *Bat*
    What word ends with the sound you hear at the end of the word *bat*?

14. *Rip*
    What word ends with the sound you hear at the end of the word *rip*?

15. *Toss*
    What word ends with the sound you hear at the end of the word *toss*?

16. *Mad*
    What word ends with the sound you hear at the end of the word *mad*?

17. *Wagon*
    What word ends with the sound you hear at the end of the word *wagon*?

18. *Trick*
    What word ends with the sound you hear at the end of the word *trick*?

19. *Shirt*
    What word ends with the sound you hear at the end of the word *shirt*?

20. *Fox*
    What word ends with the sound you hear at the end of the word *fox*?

21. *Last*
    What word ends with the sound you hear at the end of the word *last*?

22. *Butter*
    What word ends with the sound you hear at the end of the word *butter*?

23. *Swim*
    What word ends with the sound you hear at the end of the word *swim*?

24. *Wonderful*
    What word ends with the sound you hear at the end of the word *wonderful*?

| 13 | cut ○ | cup ○ | car ○ | 19 | hop ○ | hum ○ | hurt ○ |

| 14 | tub ○ | tan ○ | tap ○ | 20 | wax ○ | wig ○ | won ○ |

| 15 | mop ○ | mix ○ | mess ○ | 21 | ten ○ | test ○ | tree ○ |

| 16 | kick ○ | kid ○ | kitten ○ | 22 | family ○ | fast ○ | father ○ |

| 17 | head ○ | hot ○ | hen ○ | 23 | west ○ | name ○ | sweet ○ |

| 18 | duck ○ | trip ○ | rice ○ | 24 | belt ○ | bee ○ | bell ○ |

GO ON ➡

Read these directions aloud to your child.

Look at the picture. Find the word that names the picture.

25

ball   bell   bill
○   ○   ○

26

hands   ants   arts
○   ○   ○

27

bowl   boy   box
○   ○   ○

28

plane   plant   play
○   ○   ○

29

care   cake   cave
○   ○   ○

30

prince   pen   pond
○   ○   ○

31

cry   crayon   creep
○   ○   ○

32

sloppy   slide   sled
○   ○   ○

GO ON➡

Listen to the word. Find the word that rhymes.

33. *Feet*
What word rhymes with *feet*?

_____

34. *Play*
What word rhymes with *play*?

_____

35. *House*
What word rhymes with *house*?

_____

36. *Pie*
What word rhymes with *pie*?

_____

37. *Barn*
What word rhymes with *barn*?

_____

38. *Silly*
What word rhymes with *silly*?

39. *Moon*
What word rhymes with *moon*?

_____

40. *Brush*
What word rhymes with *brush*?

_____

41. *Night*
What word rhymes with *night*?

_____

42. *Park*
What word rhymes with *park*?

_____

43. *True*
What word rhymes with *true*?

_____

44. *Clocks*
What word rhymes with *clocks*?

| 33 | hoot ○ | hot ○ | heat ○ | 39 | nut ○ | noon ○ | new ○ |

33 hoot ○ hot ○ heat ○ **39** nut ○ noon ○ new ○

34 day ○ date ○ dark ○ **40** rash ○ rich ○ rush ○

35 mows ○ moon ○ mouse ○ **41** kite ○ kit ○ cat ○

36 fly ○ flower ○ fork ○ **42** shark ○ sheep ○ shoe ○

37 yarn ○ bear ○ here ○ **43** nap ○ now ○ new ○

38 sleepy ○ hilly ○ happy ○ **44** bows ○ balls ○ box ○

STOP

PRACTICE TEST 2: READING COMPREHENSION

PARENT PAGE

The text that appears in blue print is intended for an adult to read aloud.

Read these riddles with me. Find the picture that shows what the sentences tell about.

1. You can climb it.
   It is made of wood.

   _____

2. I have four legs.
   I cannot walk or run.

   _____

3. I have stripes.
   I can growl.

   _____

4. You can rock on it.
   It is a toy.

5. It is found in space.
   It can fly.

   _____

6. I am big.
   I have fur.

   _____

7. It has strings.
   It makes music.

   _____

8. It can float.
   It can swim.

1 You can climb it.
It is made of wood.

○   ○   ○

2 I have four legs.
I cannot walk or run.

○   ○   ○

3 I have stripes.
I can growl.

○   ○   ○

4 You can rock on it.
It is a toy.

○   ○   ○

5 It is found in space.
It can fly.

○   ○   ○

6 I am big.
I have fur.

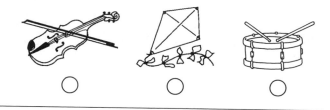

○   ○   ○

7 It has strings.
It makes music.

○   ○   ○

8 It can float.
It can swim.

○   ○   ○

GO ON ➡

Look at the picture. Then read these sentences with me. Find the word that best completes the sentence.

9. Gino is riding his big brother's —

10. Gino splashed water on Ms. Zamora's —

11. Aunt Abby is feeding her —

12. The baby is drinking from a —

13. The children are in a —

14. They listen to —

15. Eileen is holding a —

16. She caught a —

17. Eileen is —

9 Gino is riding his big brother's

tricycle   bicycle   wagon
○   ○   ○

10 Gino splashed water on Ms. Zamora's

dress   hat   car
○   ○   ○

11 Aunt Abby is feeding her

puppy   baby   self
○   ○   ○

12 The baby is drinking from a

cup   bottle   straw
○   ○   ○

13 The children are in a

classroom   store   mall
○   ○   ○

14 They listen to

a farmer   an artist   a teacher
○   ○   ○

15 Eileen is holding a

stick   fishing pole   broom
○   ○   ○

16 She caught a

cold   rabbit   fish
○   ○   ○

17 Eileen is

jumping   frowning   smiling
○   ○   ○

GO ON ➡

Read this story with me. Then answer the questions about the story.

Interesting Insects

Caterpillars and butterflies are interesting insects. They live in many places in the world. They live in cool places. They live in hot places.

Caterpillars are born in the early spring. They eat for many months. Then they become butterflies.

There are many kinds of butterflies. Some butterflies live only for a few weeks. Other butterflies live for several months. Some butterflies are brown and green. They can hide in the trees. Other butterflies have bright colors. All these butterflies help make a colorful world.

18. Where do caterpillars and butterflies live?

   only in hot places

   only in cold places

   in many places in the world

19. From this story you know that

   caterpillars eat very little.

   all butterflies live a long time.

   there are many different kinds of butterflies.

20. When do caterpillars become butterflies?

   in early spring

   after eating for many months

   after several years

21. Why can some butterflies hide in trees?

   Their colors are the same as the colors of a tree.

   They have very bright colors.

   They are very small.

Interesting Insects

Caterpillars and butterflies are interesting insects. They live in many places in the world. They live in cool places. They live in hot places.

Caterpillars are born in the early spring. They eat for many months. Then they become butterflies.

There are many kinds of butterflies. Some butterflies live only for a few weeks. Other butterflies live for several months. Some butterflies are brown and green. They can hide in the trees. Other butterflies have bright colors. All these butterflies help make a colorful world.

18 Where do caterpillars and butterflies live?

- ○ only in hot places
- ○ only in cold places
- ○ in many places in the world

19 From this story you know that

- ○ caterpillars eat very little.
- ○ all butterflies live a long time.
- ○ there are many different kinds of butterflies.

20 When do caterpillars become butterflies?

- ○ in early spring
- ○ after eating for many months
- ○ after several years

21 Why can some butterflies hide in trees?

- ○ Their colors are the same as the colors of a tree.
- ○ They have very bright colors.
- ○ They are very small.

GO ON ➡

Read this story with me. Then answer the questions about the story.

A Day of Fun

Kim went to the circus. She saw many things. There were three dancing bears. One of them wore a skirt. She also saw an elephant walk on its back legs.

Kim saw a tall clown in a little car. She laughed when the clown got stuck.

Kim looked up to watch people walking on wires. She sat very still. She was afraid they would fall. Kim wants to visit the circus again.

22. This story tells about

Kim's dog.

how to be a clown.

a trip to the circus.

23. On how many legs did the elephant walk?

Write your answer on the lines.

24. Why did Kim laugh?

She thought the clown was funny.

She thought the people on wires were funny.

She told a joke.

25. You can tell that Kim

didn't like the circus.

wants to go to the zoo.

enjoyed the circus.

A Day of Fun

Kim went to the circus. She saw many things. There were three dancing bears. One of them wore a skirt. She also saw an elephant walk on its back legs.

Kim saw a tall clown in a little car. She laughed when the clown got stuck.

Kim looked up to watch people walking on wires. She sat very still. She was afraid they would fall. Kim wants to visit the circus again.

22 This story tells about

  ○ Kim's dog.

  ○ how to be a clown.

  ○ a trip to the circus.

23 On how many legs did the elephant walk?

_____

- - - - - - - - - - - - - - - - -

_____

24 Why did Kim laugh?

  ○ She thought the clown was funny.

  ○ She thought the people on wires were funny.

  ○ She told a joke.

25 You can tell that Kim

  ○ didn't like the circus.

  ○ wants to go to the zoo.

  ○ enjoyed the circus.

STOP

PRACTICE TEST 3:
MATH PROBLEM SOLVING

PARENT PAGE

The text that appears in blue print is intended for an adult to read aloud.

1. Which picture can be folded on the dotted line so that the parts on each side of the line match exactly?

2. How many marbles are there altogether in this picture?

3. Which number shows *three hundred fifteen*?

4. Which box has the most hearts?

5. Which number tells how many blocks there are altogether?

6. Which bird is the fourth bird from the cage?

MATH PROBLEM SOLVING

1

 ○　 ○　 ○　 ○

2

32　　23　　21　　3
○　　○　　○　　○

3

315　　　350　　　3015　　　153
○　　　○　　　○　　　○

4

 ○　 ○　 ○

○

5

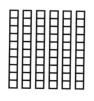

6　　106　　56　　66
○　　○　　○　　○

6

　 ○   ○ ○   ○

GO ON ➤

7. Which number means fifty plus eight?

8. Which number is 10 less than the number on the gift?

9. Which number sentence is in the same fact family as the number sentence in the box?

10. What number goes in the box to make this number sentence correct? Write the number on the lines.

11. Which of these numbers is more than 45 and less than 69?

12. Which two numbers have a seven in the ones place?

7

| 50 + 8 | 85 ◯ | 508 ◯ | 58 ◯ | 580 ◯ |

8

| 32 ◯ | 52 ◯ | 41 ◯ | 24 ◯ |

9

5 + 1 = 6

6 + 5 = 11 ◯   6 − 5 = 1 ◯   5 − 1 = 4 ◯   6 +1 = 7 ◯

10

8 + 0 = ☐

11

45 ☐ 69

| 81 ◯ | 38 ◯ | 73 ◯ | 52 ◯ |

12

71, 72 ◯   27, 17 ◯   71, 17 ◯   71, 67 ◯

GO ON ➡

13. Which numbers mean the same as *three plus four*?

_____

14. Which shape has one of its six parts shaded?

_____

15. Which square is divided into four equal parts?

_____

16. Which picture shows one of the three apples eaten?

_____

17. Look at the graph. How many boxes of flower seeds were sold?

13

$3 + 4$ | $4 - 3$ ○ $7 + 3$ ○ $7 - 4$ ○ $4 + 3$ ○

14

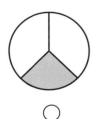 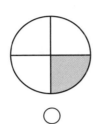 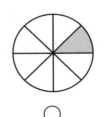 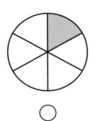

○   ○   ○   ○

15

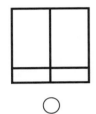 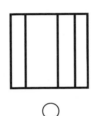 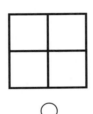 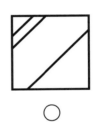

○   ○   ○   ○

16

○   ○   ○   ○

17

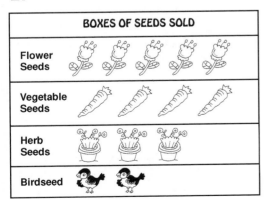

BOXES OF SEEDS SOLD

2 ○   3 ○   4 ○   5 ○

GO ON➤

18. Maria lives in apartment number 22. The doors are in order. Which door shows Maria's apartment?

19. Look at the tally chart. How many crayons does Monica have in her school box? Write the number on the lines.

20. Look for a pattern. Which piece of fruit comes next in this pattern?

21. Look at the figure on the left. Which figure on the right is exactly the same?

22. Which picture shows a triangle inside a square?

23. Yukio plays a game with paper shapes. She put eight diamonds, two squares, one triangle, and four circles into a box. If she picks a shape without looking, which shape will Yukio most likely pick?

18

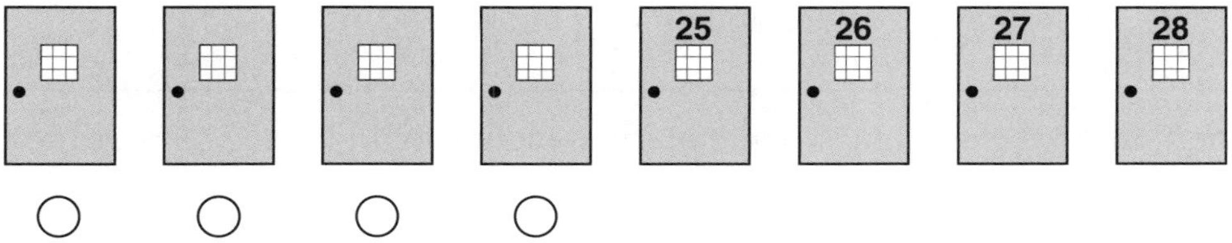

19

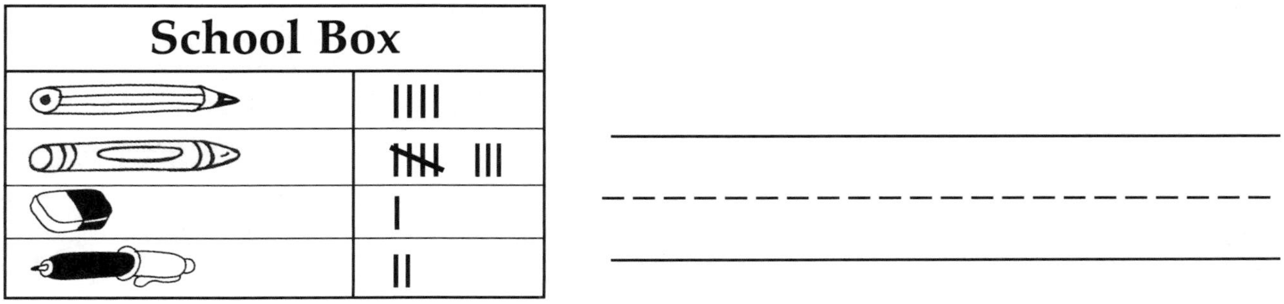

School Box	
✏️	IIII
🖍️	̶I̶I̶I̶I̶I̶ III
🧽	I
🖊️	II

20

21

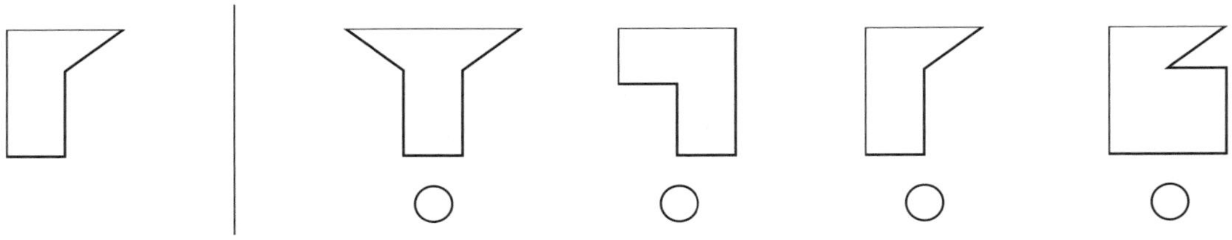

22

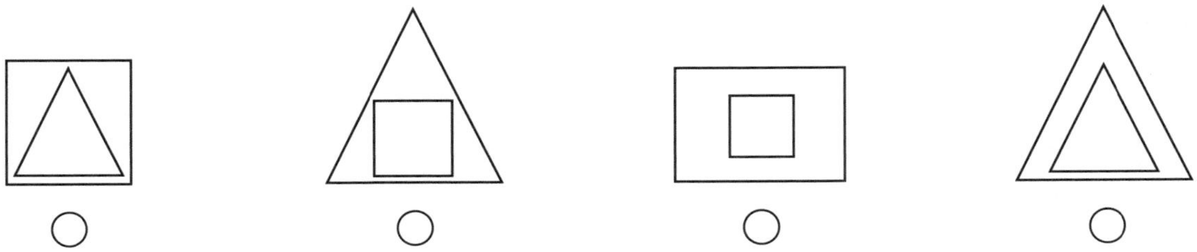

23

GO ON ➡

24. Which number tells about how many fish long the aquarium is?

_____

25. Jay is measuring flour to make cookies. What measurement should Jay use to measure the flour?

_____

26. Chandra has piano lessons every Saturday at the time shown on the clock. Which of the numbers tells the time when Chandra has piano lessons?

_____

27. I am thinking of a number that is between 41 and 60. It has a 5 in it. Which of these numbers am I thinking of?

_____

28. I am thinking of a number that is less than 22. You say its name when you count by twos. It has an 8 in it. Which of these numbers am I thinking of?

24

9	2	4	6
○	○	○	○

25

miles	inches	cups	gallons
○	○	○	○

26

9:30	3:30	4:30	4:00
○	○	○	○

27

15	42	54	65
○	○	○	○

28

28	18	14	11
○	○	○	○

STOP

The text that appears in blue print is intended for an adult to read aloud.

The answer choice NH means that the answer is not here.

1. Jason collects leaves. Yesterday he went hiking through the woods near the lake. He found five oak leaves. Then he found eight maple leaves. How many leaves did he find altogether?

2. Write the number that goes in the box to make the number sentence true. Add nine plus two.

3. Ellen likes rag dolls. She has seven rag dolls. For her birthday, she received three more rag dolls. How many rag dolls does Ellen have altogether?

4. The pet store is having a fish sale. There are 20 fish in one tank. There are 15 fish in another tank. How many fish are there in all?

1

5    8

14    ○
13    ○
12    ○
NH   ○

2

$$9 + 2 = \square$$

_____

- -

_____

3

7    3

4   10   13   NH
○   ○   ○   ○

4

20    15

5   25   35   NH
○   ○   ○   ○

GO ON ➡

5. Rita checked out 7 books from the library. She returned 4 of the books the next Saturday. How many library books does she still have?

6. Chi-Hun went to the airport. He saw 16 airplanes. He saw 6 helicopters. How many more airplanes than helicopters did he see?

7. There are 37 balls in the gym. Coach Ellis uses 4 balls for a game. How many balls are left?

8. Ms. Todd bought a package of 50 dinosaur stickers. She gave away 30 of the stickers to students in her class. How many dinosaur stickers does she have left?

5

7   4

_____

- - - - - - - - - - - - - - - - - -

_____

6

16   6

22   10   8   NH
○   ○   ○   ○

7

37   4

41   3   33   NH
○   ○   ○   ○

8

50   30

20   40   80   NH
○   ○   ○   ○

GO ON →

9 $4 + 3 = \square$

1	6	8	NH
○	○	○	○

10
$$\begin{array}{r} 5 \\ + 5 \\ \hline \end{array}$$

_____

- - - - - - - - - - - - - - - - - - - -

_____

11
$$\begin{array}{r} 9 \\ + 6 \\ \hline \end{array}$$

16	15	3	NH
○	○	○	○

12
$$\begin{array}{r} 4 \\ 2 \\ + 3 \\ \hline \end{array}$$

8	7	6	NH
○	○	○	○

13
$$\begin{array}{r} 53 \\ + 2 \\ \hline \end{array}$$

55	59	61	NH
○	○	○	○

14
$$\begin{array}{r} 83 \\ + 6 \\ \hline \end{array}$$

99	89	77	NH
○	○	○	○

15
$$\begin{array}{r} 62 \\ + 10 \\ \hline \end{array}$$

82	80	72	NH
○	○	○	○

16
$$\begin{array}{r} 27 \\ + 21 \\ \hline \end{array}$$

48	46	6	NH
○	○	○	○

17
$$\begin{array}{r} 9 \\ 4 \\ + 5 \\ \hline \end{array}$$

16	17	18	NH
○	○	○	○

18
$$\begin{array}{r} 66 \\ + 22 \\ \hline \end{array}$$

_____

- - - - - - - - - - - - - - - - - - - -

_____

GO ON ➡

19 $8 - 7 = \square$

0   1   15   NH
○   ○   ○   ○

20 $13 - 6 = \square$

7   8   28   NH
○   ○   ○   ○

21
$$\begin{array}{r} 14 \\ -\ 7 \\ \hline \end{array}$$

7   8   21   NH
○   ○   ○   ○

22
$$\begin{array}{r} 45 \\ -\ 4 \\ \hline \end{array}$$

_____

- -

_____

23
$$\begin{array}{r} 98 \\ -\ 3 \\ \hline \end{array}$$

96   94   65   NH
○   ○   ○   ○

24
$$\begin{array}{r} 62 \\ -\ 51 \\ \hline \end{array}$$

113   13   11   NH
○   ○   ○   ○

25
$$\begin{array}{r} 70 \\ -\ 20 \\ \hline \end{array}$$

_____

- -

_____

26 $25 - 6 = \square$

31   19   18   NH
○   ○   ○   ○

27
$$\begin{array}{r} 17 \\ -\ 8 \\ \hline \end{array}$$

25   19   9   NH
○   ○   ○   ○

28
$$\begin{array}{r} 328 \\ -\ 18 \\ \hline \end{array}$$

300   310   318   NH
○   ○   ○   ○

STOP

TEST PREP **755**

PARENT PAGE

The text that appears in blue print is intended for an adult to read aloud.

Listen to these sentences as I read. Then find the word or words that best complete each sentence.

1. The part of your body that you use to think is your —

   forehead…brain…heart.

2. My dog's tricks might amaze you. To *amaze* is to —

   surprise…upset…scare.

3. When Grandpa rescued a baby, he was called a hero. A *hero* is someone who does something —

   brave…easy…quickly.

4. After drinking a bowl of milk, the kitten was content. Another word for *content* is —

   happy…worried…funny.

5. It is Fred's turn to raise the flag. To *raise* is to —

   bring down…lift…fold.

6. Lee's sister has a cold, but Lee is not ill. Another word for *ill* is —

   lazy…sick…absent.

7. We sat at the back of the bus. Another name for the *back* is the —

   front…rear…middle.

8. Uncle Jeff will manage the new store. To *manage* is to —

   take care of…leave…talk about.

9. He made a sketch of the town. A *sketch* is a —

   song…book…drawing.

10. This is where we switch trains. To *switch* is to —

    change…tear…count.

11. The clown told a foolish joke. Another word for *foolish* is —

    excited…angry…silly.

12. Santos is waiting for us where two streets meet. A place where two streets meet is called —

    an avenue…a corner…a road.

13. Tia had to run quickly to get her books. To *run quickly* is to —

    dash…wander…slide.

1 ○ forehead
   ○ brain
   ○ heart

2 ○ surprise
   ○ upset
   ○ scare

3 ○ brave
   ○ easy
   ○ quickly

4 ○ happy
   ○ worried
   ○ funny

5 ○ bring down
   ○ lift
   ○ fold

6 ○ lazy
   ○ sick
   ○ absent

7 ○ front
   ○ rear
   ○ middle

8 ○ take care of
   ○ leave
   ○ talk about

9 ○ song
   ○ book
   ○ drawing

10 ○ change
   ○ tear
   ○ count

11 ○ excited
   ○ angry
   ○ silly

12 ○ an avenue
   ○ a corner
   ○ a road

13 ○ dash
   ○ wander
   ○ slide

GO ON ➤

Listen to these sentences as I read. Then find the picture that answers the question.

Some animals have fur. Some animals have feathers.

14. Which of these animals does not have fur or feathers?

When Juan got home from school, he played with his dog, Scooter. They played until almost dark, when Juan's mother told him that it was time to come in and give Scooter his dinner.

15. Which picture shows how Juan gave Scooter his dinner?

Ryan's mother came home from the hospital with his baby sister, Christine. Ryan carried the suitcase into the house. Then Ryan helped wash the baby. Then Ryan's mother told him that he could feed Christine. He sat in the rocking chair and gave Christine her bottle.

16. What did Ryan do first?

17. Which picture shows how Ryan fed the baby?

Anita and her family went camping. They decided to swim in the lake before lunch. They put their lunch basket on the picnic table. Anita and her family did not know that a mother bear and her cubs were nearby.

18. Which picture shows what Anita and her family found when they returned to the picnic table?

Olivia and her mother went shopping. Olivia found a rack of hats and tried some on. Her mother laughed when Olivia tried on a hat that was so big it covered her eyes. When Olivia and her mother got home, it looked as if it might rain. "Please get my purse, Olivia, and take it into the house," said her mother. "And please make sure that rain can't get into the car."

19. Which picture shows what Olivia looked like when her mother laughed?

Animals have different things that they use to protect themselves. Some, like deer and goats, have horns. Others have sharp teeth.

20. Which picture shows something else animals might use to protect themselves?

Every weekend in the fall, Andrew has three jobs he has to do before he can play. First, he waters his mother's plants. Next, he washes the dishes. Then he helps his dad by raking the leaves in the yard. Now Andrew can go out and play.

21. What is the first thing Andrew does?

Today is Gina's seventh birthday. Her aunt gave her a pair of dancing shoes. Her uncle made her a dollhouse. Her stepfather also gave her a wonderful present—a fluffy white poodle named Snowball.

22. What did Gina's aunt give her for her birthday?

Listen to these stories as I read. Then answer the questions.

Patrick and his mother had just stepped out of their car when a heavy rain began to pour down. "Stand under the awning," Patrick's mother said. "I have to get something from the car so we won't get wet."

23. Patrick's mother went to the car to get —
    a flag…an umbrella…a sandwich.

Everyone enjoys the Plum Creek Library. In the mornings, retired people meet there to discuss books they have read. During the afternoons, young children check out books, listen to stories, and see puppet plays. In the evenings, students come there to study and do research.

24. Retired people meet at the library to —
    discuss books…play softball…put on puppet plays.

25. Students use the library to do research and —
    sleep…cook…study.

The Warners live in Chicago. They are going on a trip. First, they will drive to the airport. Then they will fly in a plane to Seattle. From there they will sail on a boat to Alaska. In Alaska, they will take a train to see different parts of the state.

26. The Warners are going on a trip to —
    California…Hawaii…Alaska.

27. The first thing they will do is —
    sail on a boat…ride in a car…fly in a plane.

Rolanda loves to visit her grandparents in Mexico. She goes there with her parents every summer. She sees all her aunts and uncles and cousins. When Rolanda and her family arrive, there is a big celebration. Then over the next few weeks, the family goes to parks, museums, and restaurants. Rolanda's favorite part is listening to her grandparents tell stories about the family. When it is time to go home, Rolanda is sad. But she knows that she'll be going back next year.

28. There is a big celebration because Rolanda and her family —
    come to visit…are leaving…have a birthday.

29. A good name for this story would be —
    "Rolanda and Her Aunts"…"Celebrations in Mexico"…"Rolanda's Trips to Mexico"

Jerome told Larry that Jerome's turtle could beat Larry's dog in a race. Larry didn't believe him, so they decided to see what would happen. The dog ran very fast, and the turtle crawled very slowly. But just before the dog reached the finish line, he saw another dog and ran off to play with it. The turtle kept crawling until he reached the finish line.

30. The dog didn't finish the race because he —
    became tired…stumbled and fell…ran off to play.

Wesley and Beth were building a snow friend. First, they made three balls of snow. Then they stacked up the snowballs. They found two sticks for arms. They made a face with a carrot nose and raisin eyes and mouth. They put a cowboy hat on top of their snow friend's head. "I guess we can call it a snow cowpoke," said Beth.

31. Beth and Wesley are playing in the —
    sand…snow…dirt.

32. Wesley and Beth called their snow friend a cowpoke because of its —
    hat…nose…arms.

33. After building their snow friend, Beth and Wesley probably felt —
    afraid…proud…angry.

Robin's aunt and uncle took her to a theme park. The first thing Robin wanted to do was see the princess's castle. Then they rode on several rides. Robin's favorite ride went underwater. Cartoon characters waved at them as they walked around the park. The first day ended with a big parade and fireworks. As they walked to their hotel, Robin thanked her aunt and uncle for the wonderful gift.

34. The wonderful gift Robin's aunt and uncle gave her was a —
    trip to the theme park…gold bracelet…new sweater.

35. The first thing Robin wanted to see was the —
    cartoon characters…underwater ride… princess's castle.

36. The cartoon characters in the park —
    took Robin on a ride…waved at Robin… showed Robin a castle.

23 ○ a flag
   ○ an umbrella
   ○ a sandwich

24 ○ discuss books
   ○ play softball
   ○ put on puppet plays

25 ○ sleep
   ○ cook
   ○ study

26 ○ California
   ○ Hawaii
   ○ Alaska

27 ○ sail on a boat
   ○ ride in a car
   ○ fly in a plane

28 ○ come to visit
   ○ are leaving
   ○ have a birthday

29 ○ "Rolanda and Her Aunts"
   ○ "Celebrations in Mexico"
   ○ "Rolanda's Trips to Mexico"

30 ○ became tired
   ○ stumbled and fell
   ○ ran off to play

31 ○ sand
   ○ snow
   ○ dirt

32 ○ hat
   ○ nose
   ○ arms

33 ○ afraid
   ○ proud
   ○ angry

34 ○ trip to the theme park
   ○ gold bracelet
   ○ new sweater

35 ○ cartoon characters
   ○ underwater ride
   ○ princess's castle

36 ○ took Robin on a ride
   ○ waved at Robin
   ○ showed Robin a castle

STOP

PARENT PAGE

The text that appears in blue print is intended for an adult to read aloud.

Listen to these stories as I read. Then answer the questions.

Forest Lane is an old country road. There is a covered bridge on Forest Lane that is only wide enough for one car to drive across at a time.

1. Which picture shows Forest Lane?

_____

Every morning before school, Lita eats a good breakfast. After breakfast, she always brushes her teeth. Next, she dresses and combs her hair. Then she is ready to walk to the school bus stop.

2. What is the first thing Lita does in the morning?

_____

Rudy the goldfish lives in a fishbowl. Once Rudy lived in a sparkling stream in the woods. There he liked to hang in the trees near the stream.

3. Which picture shows something that could not really happen?

_____

Sam and Rolando were walking in the woods one night. As they passed under a tree, Rolando felt something sticky on his face. He wiped his face to get it off.

4. What did Rolando feel on his face?

_____

We looked all around for Richard's toy bear.
We finally found it behind a —.

5. Which picture shows something that will finish this rhyming poem?

1

    ◯   ◯   ◯

2

    ◯   ◯   ◯

3

    ◯   ◯   ◯

4

    ◯   ◯   ◯

5

    ◯   ◯   ◯

GO ON ➡

Listen as I tell you about Matt's pool party.

Matt is having a pool party at his house. He is sending invitations to his friends.

6. Matt used these words in his invitation: *when…wish…water.*
   Which of these words would come first in a dictionary?

7. What information will Matt *not* put in his invitation?

   the time the party begins

   the size of the pool

   his house number and street name

Read with me as I read Matt's invitation.

> Dear Sam,
> I am having a pool party.
> It will be this Friday, August 19.
> Come to my house at 359 Pine Road.
> We will much fun have.

8. Look at the words with the number 1 under them. Did Matt use the right words? Should he write

   friday, august 19 (with *August* lowercased), *friday, August 19* (with *August* capitalized), or is it *correct the way it is*?

9. Look at the sentence with the number 2 under it. Did Matt use the right words? Should he write

   We will have much fun, We will have fun much, or is it *correct the way it is*?

6

when ○
wish ○
water ○

7

○ the time the party begins
○ the size of the pool
○ his house number and street name

Dear Sam,

I am having a pool party.
It will be this <u>Friday, August 19.</u>
                 (1)
Come to my house at 359 Pine Road.
<u>We will much fun have.</u>
(2)

8

friday, august 19 ○
friday, August 19 ○
Correct the way it is. ○

9

○ We will have much fun.
○ We will have fun much.
○ Correct the way it is.

GO ON →

Listen to these sentences. Three of the words will be listed. Find the word that is not spelled correctly.

10. Mr. Jones read two stories to the class.

_____

11. The teacher called your name.

_____

12. Please give her a turn.

_____

13. Rosa was careful not to wake her father.

_____

14. My friend is riding his bike.

_____

15. Please pick up your toys before you leave.

16. Maria fell and bumped her nose.

_____

17. The girl made three wishes.

_____

18. Did you win first prize?

_____

19. The children played in the sun.

_____

20. There are not many days until my birthday.

_____

21. We packed our bags for the trip.

10   ○   read
     ○   two
     ○   storys
	16 ○ fell
	     ○ bumped
	     ○ noze

11   ○   teacher
     ○   calld
     ○   name
	17 ○ girl
	     ○ three
	     ○ wishs

12   ○   give
     ○   hir
     ○   turn
	18 ○ win
	     ○ first
	     ○ prise

13   ○   carful
     ○   wake
     ○   father
	19 ○ children
	     ○ playd
	     ○ sun

14   ○   frend
     ○   riding
     ○   bike
	20 ○ many
	     ○ dayes
	     ○ until

15   ○   pick
     ○   toyes
     ○   leave
	21 ○ packt
	     ○ bags
	     ○ trip

STOP

What is STEM?

Have you heard of STEM? The word STEM has 4 letters. Each letter stands for a subject:

Science: learning about the world around us

Technology: inventions, tools, and ideas that make life easier

Engineering: figuring out how to build new things

Math: numbers

All these subjects work together. People use all four at once to solve problems.

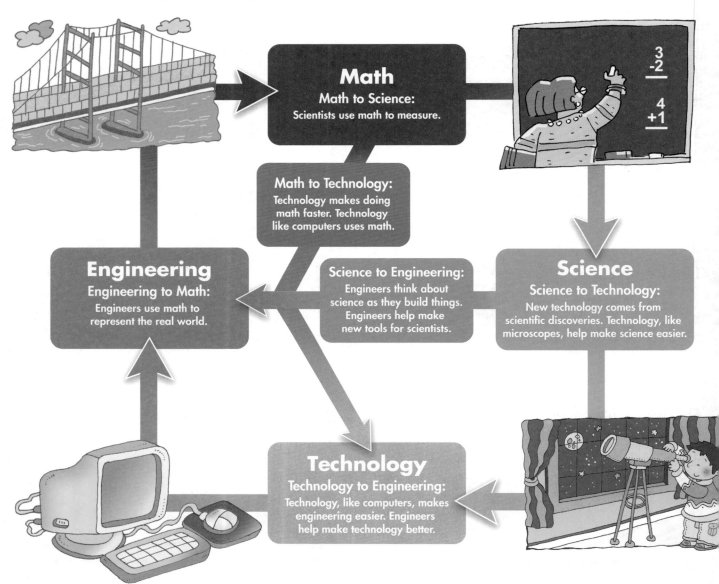

Math
Math to Science:
Scientists use math to measure.

Math to Technology:
Technology makes doing math faster. Technology like computers uses math.

Engineering
Engineering to Math:
Engineers use math to represent the real world.

Science to Engineering:
Engineers think about science as they build things. Engineers help make new tools for scientists.

Science
Science to Technology:
New technology comes from scientific discoveries. Technology, like microscopes, help make science easier.

Technology
Technology to Engineering:
Technology, like computers, makes engineering easier. Engineers help make technology better.

The Parts of STEM

The subjects that make up STEM are **S**cience, **T**echnology, **E**ngineering, and **M**ath:

Science means studying the world around us. Scientists look at things and write down what they see. They also do experiments to test how things work. They try to figure out how and why things happen in nature.

Scientists follow certain steps. They make guesses about things, test their guesses, and then correct them when they are wrong.

There are many types of science:

- **Life science** studies living things, like plants or animals.

- **Earth science** studies rocks, oceans, weather, and space.

- **Chemistry** studies chemicals and materials.

- **Physical science** studies motion, forces, and actions.

Technology is tools, machines, and ideas that make our lives better.

"Technology" may make you think of computers and phones, but technology is also older inventions like cars and radios. It is even simple things like pens and pencils.

Technology can also be materials, like waterproof clothes. It can be ideas, like computer programming. Technology can also do work for us, like a washing machine. It can keep us safe, like a bicycle helmet. It can also help us play, like phones and the internet.

Engineering is how people plan and build things. Say an engineer is planning a building. They think about all its parts, like the walls, floors, pipes, wires, windows, and doors. They figure out what each part should be made of. They think about how big each part should be and how they should all fit together.

Engineers think about how people use objects, like phones and car seats. Then they try to make them better and easier to use.

There are many kinds of engineers. They each build different things:

- **Computer engineers** build apps, programs, games, and gadgets.

- **Civil engineers** build roads, bridges, buildings, bike paths, and cities.

- **Transportation engineers** build cars, trains, airplanes, and ships.

- **Mechanical engineers** build the machines that make other things.

- **Chemical engineers** build new chemicals and materials.

- **Bioengineers** work with plants and animals to grow better food.

Design is what makes two cars, or two chairs, look different from each other? Designers decide out how things should look. They use art and engineering to make things beautiful.

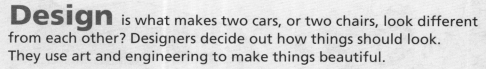

Designers make clothes, cars, phones, furniture, apps, books, bridges, and many other things you see every day.

Mathematics is a part of STEM you know about already. Math is working with numbers. It also uses shapes or **geometry**. Numbers can also show information, like answers to a survey. Math helps you measure. It can help you know how much of something you will need. It helps you compare groups or things. Math is part of every other STEM subject.

Scientists use math to measure things. Engineers use math to see how parts with different shapes and sizes, fit together. Technology uses math in computers.

Why is STEM important?

STEM plays a big role in our world. It will play an even bigger role in the future. You probably use STEM, and things that come from STEM, every day.

Where is STEM in my life?

Engineering: makes homes safe and warm

Science: tells which foods are healthy

Technology: keeps food fresh

Technology: saves work by doing things by machine

Engineering / Design: makes things pretty

Science: grows more and better food

Math: measures nutrients

Math / Engineering: makes the parts of your home fit together

What jobs use STEM?

- Doctors and nurses
- Medical scientists
- Scientists
- Farmers
- Animal caretakers
- Building designers
- Road, bridge, and city designers
- Sports trainers and equipment manufacturers
- Power, water, and internet workers
- Computer programmers
- Game designers
- Inventors
- Environmental workers
- Miners and quarry workers

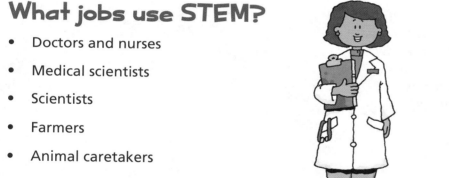

STEM Problem-solving

STEM problem-solving is a step-by-step process that helps you come up with and test ideas to solve real-world problems. You repeat the steps over and over to create the best solution.

1. **Describe the problem.** Be specific. Say what you want to make, improve, or change.

2. **Imagine ideas.** Write down as many ideas as you can. Don't be afraid to be goofy, or weird, or even impossible!

3. **Pick the best idea.** Which idea is most likely to solve the problem?

4. **Build the idea.** Choose the materials and tools you will use, and how to put them together.

5. **Test the idea.** Perform a realistic test that recreates the problem. Do the test more than once, so you can make sure the test worked the way it should have. Record the results.

6. **Decide if it worked.** Did your idea work? Great! Did it not work? That's also great! Figure out what went wrong. Do you need to use different materials? Is it the wrong size or shape? Or do you need to try one of your other ideas?

   6a - Can you make your idea even better! To improve your solution, start again at step 4.

   6b - If your idea is not successful, what did you learn and how can you make it work next time? If you need a new idea, start again at step 3.

Limitations

All problem-solvers must work with limitations. Limitations might include a time deadline, a specific type of materials, or a small space. Thinking about your limitations is an important part of STEM problem solving.

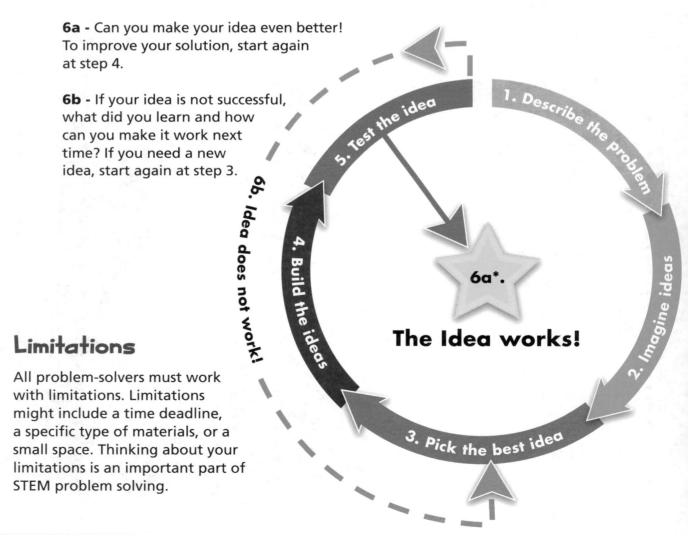

Questions for Review

1. The E in STEM stands for_____.

2. The study of rocks, soil, weather, and space is _____.

3. What is technology? (Circle the correct answer.)

   a. computers and phones

   b. cars or radios

   c. computer programming

   d. all of the above

4. What would a civil engineer help build? (Circle the correct answer.)

   a. an airplane

   b. a waterproof fabric

   c. a bike path

   d. a new food crop

5. Math that studies shapes is called _____.

6. In STEM problem-solving, why should you test things more than once?

   _____

   _____

   _____

   _____

   _____

Answers:
1. engineering
2. earth science (geology)
3. d. all of the above
4. c. a bike path
5. geometry
6. In STEM problem solving, you should test an idea more than once to make sure that there were no errors in the test. For example, when you test how far a paper airplane flies, you want to test the airplane, and not how hard you threw it. Testing it multiple times ensures that the test is fair. (Answers may vary.)

STEM projects

The next few pages describe some STEM projects you can do yourself. Each project uses science, technology, engineering, and math.

There may be no "right" or "wrong" answer. Use STEM problem-solving to come up with your own ideas. Test them to see how well they work.

STEM project tips:

- to come up with ideas, set a timer for 2 minutes. Write down everything you can think of until the timer goes off.

- be realistic when you choose an idea. Think about the materials and time you have.

- test your idea more than once. That way, you know the test worked.

- keep track of everything you do. Measure things with a ruler or tape measure. Take notes, pictures, or even videos.

- get an adult to help you with things that are sharp, hot, or heavy. Have an adult help if you need to use the internet.

- do not be afraid to fail. You learn something new every time a test goes wrong.

 Always partner with an adult before beginning a project

Paper Tower

Engineers have to work with the materials they have. If you wanted to make a tower, what would you use? You would use blocks, or bricks, or something strong to hold the tower.

Could you use paper? How can you make paper strong and tall enough to build a tower?

- ☐ notebook or printer paper
- ☐ scissors
- ☐ tape or glue
- ☐ string or twine

1. Think about how to make paper into a shape that can hold itself up.

2. Experiment with folding or rolling the paper. What makes it stiff and strong? Use tape to hold the shape in place.

3. Build a tower with the paper. What shape should you use to put the paper together?

4. Can you build the tower even taller?

5. What shape of paper is the strongest? What shape of tower is the strongest?

_____

_____

_____

_____

_____

_____

_____

_____

_____

_____

Make a "Lava Lamp"

A "lava lamp" makes beautiful colors and shapes in a liquid. You can make a homemade lava lamp.

- ❏ a clear glass or plastic jar, glass, or vase
- ❏ water
- ❏ cooking oil
- ❏ food coloring
- ❏ fizzy antacid tablet
- ❏ flaslight (optional)

1. Fill the container a little less than half full of water.

2. Fill most of the rest of the container with oil. What happens? Stir the mixture. What happens?

3. Next, you will add several drops of food coloring. What do you think will happen? Write down your guess.

4. Add 3 to 4 drops of food coloring. What happened? Did it match your guess?

5. Finally, you will drop in the antacid tablet, which will fizz and foam. What do you think will happen? Write down your guess.

6. Drop the antacid tablet into the mixture. What happened? Did it match your guess?

7. Watch your lamp move! To make it really shine, turn off the lights or bring it into a dark room. Shine the flashlight on the container.

_____

_____

_____

_____

_____

_____

Answer Key

P. 9
2. yes
3. yes
4. yes
5. no
6. yes
7. yes

P. 10
house: birdhouse, cabin, house
food: cherries, ice cream, sandwich
people: people making cookies, girl
in rain coat, grandma

P. 12
1. construction worker
2. jack-in-the-box
3. dad
4. spider
5. mom
6. children and dad
7. mom and dad
8. house

P. 13 (top)
Row 1: Dan, Will
Row 2: Mom, Dad
Row 3: Nan
Row 4: children
Row 5: Jill
(bottom)
1. cannot walk
2. is in a house
3. can eat
4. is new

P. 15 (top)
2. The Raccoon's Home
(bottom)
1. Food for People
2. The Raccoons Get Food

P. 16
1. no
2. yes
3. yes
4. yes
5. no
6. yes
7. no

P. 18
1. bee/beehive
2. raccoon/tree
3. bird/nest
4. baby/house
5. bear/cave

P. 19
1. flowers
2. something
3. home
4. food
5. good
6. it
7. eat

P. 20
1. bear
2. bee
3. hills
4. make a new house
5. bugs and flowers

P. 21
Story 1:
2. What Animals Eat
Story 2:
3. Something for Mom
Picture 1:
2. Bees take something from flowers.
3. Bees work here.
Picture 2:
1. Dan gets something new.
3. Dan sees something new here.

P. 23
1. squirrel
2. bird
3. raccoon
4. children
5. people

P. 24
1. yes
2. no
3. no
4. yes
5. yes
6. yes
7. no
8. yes
9. no
10. yes

P. 26
2. b
3. b
4. c
5. a

P. 27
1. d
2. c
3. a
4. no picture
5. b

P. 29
1. Picture b
2. Picture a
3. Picture a
4. Picture b
5. Picture b

P. 30
1. ant
2. bird
3. corn
4. duck
5. bee
6. people
7. ant

P. 32
2. b
3. b
4. a
5. a
6. b

P. 33
1. bugs
2. fish
3. hill
4. play
5. swim

P. 34 (top)
1. duck
2. frog
3. flower
4. fish
5. raccoon
6. grass
(bottom)
3. The Animals Have Fun

P. 35 (top)
1. The Fox Will Not Eat a Frog
(bottom)
1. fun
2. corn
3. swim
4. you
5. bugs

P. 37 (top)
c. get food
b. "I will not eat a chipmunk."
(bottom)
1. ground
2. run
3. lives

P. 38
1. on the ground
2. happy people
3. two rocks
4. a frog by a flower
5. on the grass
6. is a bird

P. 40 (top)
2. A Snake in the House
(middle)
1. fast
2. door
3. rocks
(bottom)
Correct Order: 3, 1, 2

P. 41
2. c
3. a
4. a
5. c

P. 43 (top)
1. c
2. b
(bottom)
1. on a squirrel
2. on a raccoon
3. under a flower
4. on the hill
5. in a spider's home
6. on the corn

P. 44
1. chipmunk
2. fish
3. kids playing
4. ladder

P. 45 (top)
2. b
3. a
4. b
(bottom)
1. The Happy People

P. 46 (top)
1. mud
2. a snake
3. away
4. a door
5. bugs
6. a hill
(bottom)
1. a
2. b

P. 47 (top)
1. happy
2. fast
3. want
(bottom)
Correct Order 3, 2, 1

P. 49
2. a
3. b
4. c
5. b
6. c

P. 50 (top)
2. new
3. hop
4. back
5. finger
6. paws
(bottom)
2. paw
3. back
4. pouch
5. tail
6. front

P. 51
2. It
3. She
4. It
5. He
6. They
7. It

P. 53
2. b
3. a
4. c
5. c

P. 54 (top)
1. new
2. food
3. swim
4. pond
5. fun
6. walk
(bottom)
1. Ducks swim.
2. The duck walks with Mother Duck.
3. A duck is eating.

P. 55 (top)
2. It
3. They
4. She
5. He
(bottom)
Correct order: 2, 3, 1

P. 56
1. c
2. b

P. 57
3. c
4. a
5. b
6. c
7. b
8. b

P. 58 (top)
2. morning
3. robin
4. Mrs.
5. oak
6. blue
7. Mr.
8. nest
(bottom)
1. The oak tree is big.
2. Three eggs are in the nest.
3. The robin finds some grass.

P. 59 (top)
1. them
2. They
3. him
4. it
5. Her
(bottom)
Correct order: 3, 2, 1

P. 60
1. a

P. 61
2. c
3. a
4. c
5. b
6. a
7. c

P. 62 (top)
2. forgot
3. lettuce
4. milk
5. money
6. children
7. afternoon
8. corner
(bottom)
2. house
3. walk
4. girl
5. black

P. 63 (top)
1. It
2. them
3. They
4. He
5. him
(bottom)
Correct order: 2, 1, 3

P. 64 (top)
1. four
2. zero
3. zero
4. four
5. four
6. zero
7. zero
8. four
(bottom)
1. He
2. They
3. them

P. 65 (top)
1. pouch
2. food
3. afternoon
4. again
5. park
6. night
7. front
(bottom)
1. c
2. b
3. b

P. 66 (top)
1. hop
2. grass, mud
3. tub
4. forgot
5. back
6. money
7. grass
(bottom)
Correct order: 2, 3, 1

P. 67
1. d
2. c
3. b
4. e
5. a

P. 68
1. c

P. 69
2. b
3. a
4. b
5. b
6. a
7. b

P. 70 (top)
1. seven
2. bottom
3. Sunday
4. evening
5. eight
6. shelf
7. every
8. toys
9. middle
(bottom)
Color and place objects on shelves as directed.

P. 71 (top)
1. top
2. top
3. play
4. play
5. care
6. care
(bottom)
1. Bill
2. Bev
3. Bob
4. Bob
5. Bev
6. Bev

P. 72
1. c

P. 73
2. c
3. b
4. a
5. a
6. a
7. c

P. 74 (top)
1. c
2. no
3. no
4. yes
5. no
6. yes
7. no
8. yes
9. yes
(bottom)
1. bug
2. fox

P. 75 (top)
2. out
3. down
4. off
5. stop
6. little
7. bad
(bottom)
1. 4
2. Rabbit's House
3. no

P. 76
1. b

P. 77
2. a
3. c
4. c
5. c
6. a
7. b

P. 78 (top)
8. b
9. c
10. c
(bottom)
1. hopped
2. tiger
3. green
4. left
5. tall
6. hunt
7. quick

P. 79 (top)
4, 5, 6, 8, 9
(bottom)
1. a
2. c
3. a

P. 80
1. May
2. Jeff
3. Rita
4. Ted

P. 81
1. c
2. a
3. a
4. c
5. b
6. c

P. 82 (top)
7. a
8. c
9. b
(bottom)
1. hurry
2. shoe
3. school
4. second
5. watched
6. started
7. Monday
8. ready
9. last
10. playground
11. race

P. 83 (top)
1. start
2. winner
3. runners
4. run
(bottom)
1. 8
Color the flags in this order: blue, green, red, red, red, red, brown, yellow.
Circle the brown flag.

P. 84
1. a

p. 85
2. b
3. c
4. b
5. c
6. c
7. b

p. 86 (top)
1. less
2. mittens
3. lost
4. snow
5. white
6. Thursday
7. money
(bottom)
1. c
2. b

p. 87 (top)
2. Monday
3. Tuesday
4. Wednesday
5. Thursday
6. Friday
(bottom)
1. b
2. c
3. b

p. 88
1. d
2. g
3. b
4. a
5. c

p. 89 (top)
Colors: yellow, white, green
Numbers: eight, seven, nine
Animals: tiger, worm, duck
(bottom)
1. less
2. hunt
3. second
4. left
5. evening
6. last
7. quick
8. every

p. 90
1. hill
2. snow
3. water
4. fish
5. worm
6. tiger

p. 91 (top)
Put an X on the middle book, color
the top book green, color the
bottom book orange, make a brown
hole in the bottom of the shoe, and
color the shoe yellow.
(middle)
1. left
2. left
3. last
4. last
(bottom)
1. Put an x on 3.
2. Underline *The Ice Melts*
3. 6

p. 93
1. c
2. c
3. b
4. b
5. c
6. a

p. 94 (top)
1. spring
2. window
3. never
4. found
5. purple
6. plant
7. surprise
(bottom)
1. up
2. came
3. drop
4. there
5. never

p. 95 (top)
1. .
2. ?
3. ?
4. .
5. .
6. ?
(bottom)
1. Every flower they planted was red.
2. Little green plants came up
before the flowers.
3. They did not know the purple
flower was there.

p. 96
1. c

p. 97
2. c
3. a
4. b
5. c
6. b
7. b
8. c

p. 98 (top)
1. c
2. d
3. a or e
4. no match
5. a or e
6. b
(bottom)
1. They had one girl and two boys.
2. He came out of the school at noon.
3. They lost the book one more time.

p. 99 (top)
1. three
2. Mr.
3. lost
4. let's
5. lunch
6. button
(bottom)
Where: 2, 3, 6, 7
When: 1, 4, 5, 8

p. 101
1. b
2. a
3. b
4. b
5. c
6. a

p. 102 (top)
1. pup
2. mother
3. rock
4. gone
5. baby
6. barked
7. swim
8. smell
(bottom)
1. ?
2. ?
3. .
4. ?
5. .
6. ?
7. ?
8. ?

p. 103
2. c
3. a
4. a
5. b
6. c
7. c
8. b
9. c
10. a

p. 104
1. a

p. 105
2. a
3. c
4. c
5. b
6. c
7. b

p. 106 (top)
1. jar
2. front
3. legs
4. tails
5. shorter
6. jelly
(bottom)
Put a ✓ on 2, 5, 8.
Mark X on 1, 3, 4, 6, 7.

p. 107
1. b
2. c
3. b
4. b

p. 109
1. b
2. a
3. a
4. c
5. c
6. b

p. 110 (top)
1. near
2. grab
3. nothing
4. pond
5. foxes
6. wish
7. until
8. wings
9. land
(bottom)
1. ?
2. .
3. .
4. ?
5. ?
6. .
7. ?
8. ?
9. ?

p. 111 (top)
1. b
2. b
(bottom)
1. c
2. b
3. a

p. 113
1. b
2. a
3. b
4. c
5. b

p. 114 (top)
1. reach
2. tiny
3. mouth
4. grab
5. crawl
6. lifted
7. watch
8. neck
9. drink
(bottom)
1. meat
2. meat
3. plants
4. plants

p. 115 (top)
1. b
2. b
3. b
(bottom)
Put a ✓ by 2, 4, 5, 8.
Mark X by 1, 3, 6, 7.

p. 117
1. b
2. c
3. b
4. a
5. a

p. 118 (top)
6. a
7. c
8. b
(bottom)
2. suit
3. ice
4. skinny
5. voice
6. feathers
7. several
8. stomach

p. 119 (top)
Correct order: 2, 3, 1
(bottom)
2. voice
3. suit
4. each
5. warm
6. bills

p. 121
1. a
2. c

p. 122 (top)
3. c
4. b
5. c
(bottom)
1. followed
2. flippers
3. waved
4. parents

p. 123 (top)
1. X
2. X
3. ✓
4. X
5. ✓
6. ✓
(middle)
Make sure the lines were drawn to the correct parts of the penguin.
(bottom)
1. flippers
2. same
3. flash
4. gills

p. 124 (top)
Animals: 2, 4, 8, 11
Places: 1, 3, 9, 12
Numbers: 5, 6, 7, 10
(bottom)
1. lift
2. reach
3. shorter
4. helper
5. until
6. barked
7. tadpole

p. 125 (top)
Circle the fox's nose.
Check the seal's nose.
(middle)
1. yes
2. no
3. yes
4. no
5. yes
6. yes
7. no
8. yes
9. yes
10. no
(bottom)
1. ?
2. ?
3. ?
4. .
5. ?
6. .
7. .

p. 126
1. Color six flowers purple and one flower red.
2. Draw hands to 5 o'clock.
3. Add four green buttons to the coat.
4. Color the little foxes brown and the Mother Fox red.
(bottom)
When: 3, 4, 5, 7, 9
Where: 1, 2, 6, 8, 10

p. 127 (top)
1. b
2. a
3. a
(bottom)
1. care
2. never
3. surprise

SPELLING SKILLS

p. 132
The letter **m** should be written for these problems: 1, 3, 4, 6, 7, 8, 9, 10, and 11.

p. 133
The letter **d** should be written for these problems: 1, 2, 4, 5, 6, 7, 9, 10, and 12.

p. 134
The letter **f** should be written for these problems: 1, 2, 4, 5, 6, 7, 10, 11, and 12.

p. 135
The letter **g** should be written for these problems: 1, 2, 3, 6, 7, 8, 9, 10, and 12.

p. 136
The letter **b** should be written for these problems: 1, 3, 4, 5, 6, 8, 9, 11, and 12.

p. 137
The letter **t** should be written for these problems: 1, 2, 4, 5, 7, 8, 9, 10, and 12.

p. 138
The letter **s** should be written for these problems: 1, 3, 4, 5, 6, 8, 10, 11, and 12.

p. 139
The letter **w** should be written for these problems: 1, 4, 5, 7, 10, and 11.

p. 140
The letter **k** should be written for these problems: 1, 2, 4, 5, 7, 8, 9, 10, and 11.

p. 141
The letter **j** should be written for these problems: 1, 3, 6, 8, 9, and 11.

p. 142
The letter **p** should be written for these problems: 1, 2, 4, 5, 7, 8, 10, 11, and 12.

p. 143
The letter **n** should be written for these problems: 1, 2, 3, 6, 7, 8, 9, 10, and 11.

p. 144
The letter **c** should be written for these problems: 1, 3, 4, 5, 6, 8, 10, 11, and 12.

p. 145
The letter **h** should be written for these problems: 1, 2, 4, 5, 7, 8, 9, 10, and 11.

p. 146
The letter **l** should be written for these problems: 1, 2, 3, 5, 6, 8, 9, 11, and 12.

p. 147
The letter **r** should be written for these problems: 1, 2, 4, 6, 7, 8, 9, 11, and 12.

p. 148
The letter **v** should be written for these problems: 1, 2, 4, 5, 6, and 11.

p. 149
The letter **y** should be written for these problems: 1, 3, 5, 7, 10, and 12.

p. 150
The letter **z** should be written for these problems: 1, 2, 5, 8, 9, and 11.

p. 151
The letters **qu** should be written for these problems: 1, 3, 5, 6.
The letter **x** should be written for these problems: 8, 9, 10.

p. 152
1. m
2. f
3. b
4. k
5. s
6. d
7. m
8. g
9. j
10. t
11. d
12. w

p. 153
1. r
2. h
3. c
4. g
5. d
6. x
7. v
8. t
9. s
10. p
11. y
12. n
13. qu
14. z
15. w
16. m

p. 154
The letter **a** should be written for these problems: 1, 3, 4, 5, 7, 8, 9, 11, and 12.

p. 155
The letter **a** should be written for these problems and the pictures should be colored: 1, 2, 4, 6, 8, and 9.

p. 156

Say the word that names the first picture.
Circle the pictures whose names rhyme with the word.

p. 157
1. fan
2. van
3. pan
4. man
5. can
6. tan
7. bat
8. cat
9. hat
10. mat
11. rat

P. 158
The letter **e** should be written for these problems: 1, 2, 4, 6, 7, 8, 9, 10, and 11.

P. 159
The letter **e** should be written for these problems and the pictures should be colored: 1, 2, 5, 6, 7, and 9.

P. 160

P. 161
1. bell
2. sell
3. shell
4. well
5. smell
6. hen
7. men
8. ten

P. 162
The letter **i** should be written for these problems: 1, 2, 3, 5, 7, 8, 10, 11, and 12.

P. 163
The letter **i** should be written for these problems and the pictures should be colored: 1, 3, 4, 5, 8, and 9.

P. 164
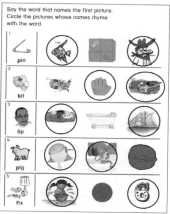

P. 165
1. hit
2. kit
3. sit
4. dig
5. pig
6. wig
7. big

P. 166
The letter **o** should be written for these problems: 1, 2, 3, 5, 6, 8, 9, 11, and 12.

P. 167
The letter **o** should be written for these problems and the pictures should be colored: 1, 2, 5, 6, 7, and 9.

P. 168

P. 169
1. hop
2. mop
3. pop
4. knot
5. dot
6. hot
7. pot

P. 170
The letter **u** should be written for these problems: 1, 2, 4, 6, 7, 8, 9, 11, and 12.

P. 171
The letter **u** should be written for these problems and the pictures should be colored: 1, 2, 4, 6, 7, and 9.

P. 172
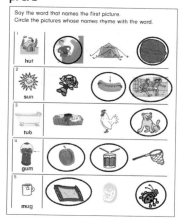

P. 173
1. mug
2. hug
3. jug
4. bug
5. tug
6. rug
7. cut
8. hut
9. nut

P. 174
1. u; nut
2. i; bib
3. o; rod
4. e; web
5. a; map
6. e; vest
7. i; zip
8. u; duck
9. u; bug

P. 175
1. man
2. pop
3. pin
4. men
5. mop
6. fan
7. fin
8. pan
9. hen
10. nut
11. hop
12. cut

P. 176
For each problem, the word is written on the writing line and in the boxes.

P. 177
1. am
2. can
3. at
4. ran
5. fast
6. last

P. 178
Randy Rabbit **ran** on a path. The path was **at** the park. Randy ran well. He ran **fast**. That was **last** week. Now he will run again. "I **am** ready," Randy says. "I **can** do it."

P. 179
1. at
2. can
3. am
4. Lad is fast.
5. We ran to Dad.
6. I was the last one.

P. 180
For each problem, the word is written on the writing line and in the boxes.

P. 181
1. van
2. that
3. hand
4. sat
5. have
6. has

P. 182
Nan **sat** with her dad. They sat in their **van**. Nan had a book in her **hand**. She got it from the library in her town. The library **has** many good books to read. Nan likes **that** library. Do you **have** a library where you live?

P. 183
1. van
2. has
3. that
4. We have a van.
5. I sat in back.
6. Mom held my hand.

P. 184
For each problem, the word is written on the writing line and in the boxes.

P. 185
1. wet
2. red
3. ten
4. end
5. seven
6. tell

P. 186
Rex washes his socks. Some are **red**. Some are white. The socks are dripping **wet**. Rex puts them on the line. He has five pairs. There are **ten** socks on the line. Three socks on the **end** fall. Now only **seven** socks are on the line. Who will **tell** Rex?

P. 187
1. ten
2. seven
3. end
Answers to problems 4 to 7 will vary.

P. 188
For each problem, the word is written on the writing line and in the boxes.

P. 189
1. pet
2. when
3. best
4. went
5. get
6. help

A puppy is a good **pet**. Would you like to **get** a puppy? You can **help** take care of it. You can feed your puppy **when** it is hungry. You can play with it. You will wonder where the time **went**. Do you think a puppy is the **best** pet?

P. 191
1. pet
2. when
3. best
Sentences written for the writing activity will vary. The sentence should include a spelling word.

P. 192
For each problem, the word is written on the writing line and in the boxes.

P. 193
1. sick
2. with
3. is
4. in
5. quit
6. it

P. 194
Sometimes people get **sick**. Then they must stay **in** bed. It **is** not much fun. You can make a picture for a sick friend. Get some paper. Draw on **it**. Paint on it **with** bright colors. Don't **quit** until it looks great. Give it to your friend. Say, "Get well quick!"

P. 195
1. sick
2. is
3. in
4. it
5. quit
6. sick
7. with

P. 196
1. am
2. fast
3. can
4. have
5. has
6. that

P. 197
1. get
2. help
3. when
4. with
5. sick
6. in

P. 198
For each problem, the word is written on the writing line and in the boxes.

P. 199
1. six
2. if
3. sit
4. big
5. did
6. this

P. 200
I have **six** little kittens. My kittens will not always be little. Soon they will be **big**. The kittens **sit** on me. They go to sleep in my lap. They wake up **if** I move. Then **this** is what they do. They cry, "Mew! Mew!" They **did** it just now!

P. 201
1. big
2. did
3. this
4. am; big; can
5. has; if; six
6. ran; sit; this

P. 202
For each problem, the word is written on the writing line and in the boxes.

P. 203
1. hop
2. stop
3. on
4. hot
5. not
6. top

P. 204
Bonnie likes to **hop**. She hops and hops. Bonnie hops **on** the path. She hops on the grass. She does **not** fall. Then she hops to the **top** of the hill. When will Bonnie **stop**? She will have to stop when she gets too **hot**!

P. 205
1. on
2. not
3. stop
4. Is Mopsy at the top?
5. Is Mopsy hot?
6. Will he hop down?

P. 206
For each problem, the word is written on the writing line and in the boxes.

P. 207
1. sock
2. mop
3. job
4. fox
5. lock
6. box

P. 208
Bob the ox had a **job** to do. He had to **mop**. A **fox** came in. He had a **box**. The fox took out a brush. "Put this on your **sock**," he said.
Bob did it. Then he put a brush on his other sock. He started to mop. "This is fast!" Bob said. "Soon I can **lock** up and go have fun!"

P. 209
1. job
2. box
3. mop
Sentences written for the writing activity will vary. The sentence should include a spelling word.

P. 210
For each problem, the word is written on the writing line and in the boxes.

P. 211
1. us
2. run
3. jump
4. duck
5. fun
6. much

P. 212
A baby **duck** is called a duckling. A duckling cannot **run** fast. A duckling can have **fun**. It can **jump** into the water. It can swim, too. The mother duck quacks if a duckling swims too far away. She is saying, "You have gone **much** too far. Come back to **us**!"

P. 213
1. us
2. fun
3. much
Sentences written for the writing activity will vary. The sentence should include a spelling word.

P. 214
For each problem, the word is written on the writing line and in the boxes.

P. 215
1. bus
2. must
3. cut
4. just
5. but
6. up

P. 216
Do you know what to do on a **bus**? You **must** sit down when the bus is moving. You cannot stand **up**. You can play a game. You can sing a song, too. You can draw, **but** do not use scissors. You might **cut** yourself. You can read, or you can **just** sit and rest.

P. 217
1. just
2. bus
3. must
4. The cut is on my hand.
5. My house is up the street.
6. We are going home now.

P. 218
1. i; did
2. i; this
3. i; big
4. stop
5. on
6. not

P. 219

Label the Picture
The words in the box go in this picture.
Write each word on the correct line.

job box sock

job
box
sock

P. 220
For each problem, the word is written on the writing line and in the boxes.

P. 221
1. make
2. game
3. name
4. same
5. take
6. made

P. 222
What is your **name**? Play a **game** with your name. To begin, **take** the first letter of your name, such as P. Think of words that begin with the **same** letter. Next, **make** a sentence with the words. Then, add more words to the sentence you **made**.

P. 223
1. take
2. name
3. game
Sentences written for the writing activity will vary. The sentence should include a spelling word.

P. 224
For each problem, the word is written on the writing line and in the boxes.

P. 225
1. pay
2. day
3. stay
4. may
5. play
6. say

P. 226
Some work places have a special **day**. Children **may** go to work with an adult. They can **stay** all day. They learn about jobs. They have fun, but it is not a time to **play**. The children **say** they learn a lot. They see how adults work for their **pay**.

p. 227
1. stay
2. play
3. say
4. We may play with Jay all day.
5. He will pay Kay today.

p. 228
For each problem, the word is written on the writing line and in the boxes.

p. 229
1. we
2. eat
3. he
4. me
5. be
6. she

p. 230
My family sleeps a lot in winter. We need food before **we** sleep. We **eat** a lot! Today Mom showed **me** how to catch fish. Then **she** showed my brother. I know **he** likes fish. Soon we will find a cave. A cave is a good place to **be** in winter.

p. 231
1. be
2. we
3. he
4. My sister went with me.
5. She likes to be with me.
6. We went to eat pizza.

p. 232
For each problem, the word is written on the writing line and in the boxes.

p. 233
1. tree
2. street
3. feet
4. see
5. keep
6. three

p. 234
Dee's dad took her on a hike with **three** of her friends. They all live on the same **street**. "Please **keep** walking on the trail," Dad said. Something went splash! "What is on the other side of that **tree**?" Dad asked.
"I **see** a creek!" Lee said. "Some kids are in the water. May we get our **feet** wet, too?"

p. 235
1. tree
2. keep
3. feet
Answers to questions 4 to 6 will vary.

p. 236
For each problem, the word is written on the writing line and in the boxes.

p. 237
1. hide
2. mine
3. time
4. ride
5. five
6. nine

p. 238
A bike contest can test how well you **ride**. Don't run and **hide**. Set up nine big **cones**. Ride around them one at a **time**. Ride slowly for four or **five** minutes. Now you are ready for the contest. You might get to say, "The prize is **mine**!"

p. 239
1. ride
2. time
3. five
Sentences written for the writing activity will vary. Each sentence should include a spelling word.

p. 240
1. made
2. take
3. game
4. play
5. say
6. day

p. 241
1. eat
2. she
3. we
4. see
5. three
6. keep

p. 242
For each problem, the word is written on the writing line and in the boxes.

p. 243
1. cry
2. fly
3. why
4. my
5. try
6. by

p. 244
I made a kite. I made **my** kite from a bag. I wanted it to **fly** up high. People stood **by** me. They asked **why** I used a bag. I wanted to **try** it. That's why. The bag did not fly very high, but I did not **cry**. I just made another kite.

p. 245
1. my
2. fly
3. by
Sentences written for the writing activity will vary. Each sentence should include a spelling word.

p. 246
For each problem, the word is written on the writing line and in the boxes.

p. 247
1. so
2. told
3. over
4. go
5. cold
6. old

p. 248
JoJo wanted to **go** to a special place. She wanted to go **over** the rainbow. JoJo packed an **old** bag. She got her coat in case it was **cold**. JoJo **told** Gran about her plan. Gran wanted to go, too, **so** they went together. Good luck, JoJo and Gran!

p. 249
1. over
2. so
3. go
4. We were in an old store.
5. Mom was by the milk.
6. I told Mom I was cold.

p. 250
For each problem, the word is written on the writing line and in the boxes.

p. 251
1. road
2. hope
3. coat
4. nose
5. home
6. note

p. 252
One day Mole wanted to take a walk. Dad was not at **home**. Mole write Dad a **note**. Then she walked down the **road**. She walked a long way. A cold wind came. Mole's **nose** was blue. She wanted her warm **coat**. "I **hope** I am not lost!" she said. Then Mole saw her house. She smiled and went inside.

p. 253
1. coat
2. hope
3. home
4. home; note; road
5. go; nose; told

p. 254
For each problem, the word is written on the writing line and in the boxes.

p. 255
1. moon
2. school
3. room
4. soon
5. zoo
6. food

p. 256
Would you like to camp at a **zoo**? At one zoo, you can sleep in a **room** with beds. You can sleep under the **moon** and stars, too. You can give **food** to the animals. Your class from **school** might want to go zoo camping. Find out about zoo camping **soon**!

p. 257
1. school
2. zoo
3. food
Sentences written for the writing activity will vary. Each sentence should include a spelling word.

p. 258
For each problem, the word is written on the writing line and in the boxes.

p. 259
1. do
2. too
3. you
4. who
5. two
6. shoe

p. 260
Look at your **two** feet. Is there a **shoe** on each foot? Shoes keep your feet safe. Shoes should not be **too** big or too small.
No one knows **who** made the first shoes. Early people made them from animal skins. Now **you** can buy shoes in a store. What kind of shoes do you like to wear?

p. 261
1. do
2. two
3. you
4. Who are those two girls?
5. That shoe is too big.
6. Did they go to the store?

p. 262
1. try
2. why
3. my
4. over
5. go
6. told

p. 263
1. coat
2. hope
3. road

MATH SKILLS

p. 270

0	1	2	3	4	5
0	1	2	3	4	5

p. 271

3	2
0	1
5	4

p. 272

1	2	3	4	5
6	7	8	9	10

p. 273

5	6
2	7
9	1
4	10

p. 274

8　6
1　3
10　5
4　9
2　0

p. 275
1 lettuce, 2 grapes bunches,
3 watermelons, 4 carrots, 5 lemons,
6 red apples, 7 strawberries,
8 oranges, 9 green apples, and
10 bananas.

p. 276
after writing the numbers students
should draw circles to show one
more
4　5
2　3
9　10
7　8

p. 277
5　4
9　8
2　1
6　5

p. 278

0	1	2		5	6	7
7	8	9		2	3	4
3	4	5		1	2	3
6	7	8		8	9	10

p. 279
1　2　3
4　5　6
7　8　9

p. 280
1　2　3　4
3　4　5　6
5　6　7　8
2　3　4　5
7　8　9　10

p. 281
1 2 3 4 5
1 2 3 4 5 6 7
1 2 3 4 5 6 7 8 9
1 2 3 4
1 2 3 4 5 6 7 8 9 10

p. 282
2　4　6　8　10
2　4　6　8　10
2　4　6　8　10

p. 283
2　4　6　8　10
2　4　6　8　10
2　4　6　8　10

p. 284
1 2 3 4 5 6 7 8
2 4 2 4 2 4 2 4
1 2 1 2 1 2 1 2
7 8 7 8 7 8 7 8
1 3 5 1 3 5 1 3

p. 285
red circle
blue square
blue rounded square
yellow triangle

p. 286

1	2	3	4	5	6	7
0	1	2	3	4	5	6
4	5	6	7	8	9	10

7	8	9		0	1	2
4	5	6		8	9	10

1	2	3		6	7	8
0	1	2		3	4	5

2　4　6　8　10

p. 287
5 bananas, 2 potatoes, 4 lemons,
0 apples, 1 container of milk,
2 loaves of bread

blue square

p. 288
3; 5; 4; 2; 6

p. 289
5; 4; 6; 4

p. 292
1 + 3 = 4; 3 + 3 = 6; 4 + 1 = 5;
2 + 4 = 6; 2 + 1 = 3

p. 293
2 + 3 = 5; 1 + 5 = 6; 4 + 0 = 4;
2 + 1 = 3; 2 + 4 = 6

p. 294
3 + 2 = 5　　　1 + 1 = 2
6 + 0 = 6　　　5 + 1 = 6
2 + 5 = 7　　　4 + 3 = 7

p. 295
2 + 4 = 6　　　3 + 1 = 4
1 + 1 = 2　　　4 + 2 = 6
5 + 0 = 5　　　2 + 1 = 3

p. 296
8, 10, 9, 7, 10

p. 297
5 + 2 = 7; 3 + 6 = 9; 4 + 1 = 5;
6 + 4 = 10; 5 + 3 = 8

p. 299
4 + 6 = 10; 7 + 3 = 10;
1 + 9 = 10; 2 + 8 = 10;
5 + 5 = 10

p. 300
1 + 0 = 1　　　0 + 2 = 2
0 + 3 = 3　　　4 + 0 = 4
5 + 0 = 5　　　0 + 6 = 6
7 + 0 = 7　　　0 + 8 = 8
9 + 0 = 9　　　10 + 0 = 10

p. 301
1 + 1 = 2; 2 + 2 = 4; 3 + 3 = 6;
4 + 4 = 8; 5 + 5 = 10

p. 302
10　6
2　5
9　8
10　5
7　10

9　8　7
7　4

p. 303
5 + 3 = 8
6 + 2 = 8
4 + 0 = 4
3 + 7 = 10

p. 304
5, 4, 3, 2, 1, 0

p. 305
6, 5, 4, 3, 2, 1, 0

p. 306
6, 5, 4, 3, 2, 1, 0

p. 307
3 − 0 = 3
5 − 0 = 5
9 − 0 = 9
4 − 0 = 4
10 − 0 = 10
2 − 0 = 2
7 − 0 = 7

p. 308
4, 5, 3, 0, 1

p. 309
1, 3, 0, 6, 4

p. 310
7, 6, 5, 4, 3, 2, 1, 0

p. 311
8, 7, 6, 5, 4, 3, 2, 1, 0

p. 312
9　8
3　4
5　0
1　6

p. 313
4, 1, 3, 6, 0, 7, 2

p. 314
1 + 2 = 3　　　3 + 1 = 4
2 + 1 = 3　　　1 + 3 = 4
3 − 2 = 1　　　4 − 3 = 1
3 − 1 = 2　　　4 − 1 = 3

4 + 1 = 5　　　3 + 2 = 5
1 + 4 = 5　　　2 + 3 = 5
5 − 4 = 1　　　5 − 3 = 2
5 − 1 = 4　　　5 − 2 = 3

p. 315
4 + 2 = 6　　　5 + 2 = 7
2 + 4 = 6　　　2 + 5 = 7
6 − 4 = 2　　　7 − 5 = 2
6 − 2 = 4　　　7 − 2 = 5

4 + 3 = 7　　　5 + 3 = 8
3 + 4 = 7　　　3 + 5 = 8
7 − 4 = 3　　　8 − 5 = 3
7 − 3 = 4　　　8 − 3 = 5

p. 316
3　3
3　8
2　1

1　4　5
5　7　4

5 + 3 = 8　　　6 + 4 = 10
3 + 5 = 8　　　4 + 6 = 10
8 − 5 = 3　　　10 − 6 = 4
8 − 3 = 5　　　10 − 4 = 6

p. 317
1st row: 6 + 2 = 8; 2 + 6 = 8;
8 − 6 = 2; 8 − 2 = 6
2nd row: 5 + 4 = 9; 4 + 5 = 9;
9 − 5 = 4; 9 − 4 = 5
3rd row: 3 + 2 = 5; 2 + 3 = 5;
5 − 2 = 3; 5 − 3 = 2
4th row: 7 + 3 = 10; 3 + 7 = 10;
10 − 7 = 3; 10 − 3 = 7

p. 318
10　11
12　13
14　15
16　17
18　19

p. 319
10 + 4 = 14　　　10 + 0 = 10
10 + 9 = 19　　　10 + 3 = 13
10 + 5 = 15　　　10 + 7 = 17
10 + 1 = 11　　　10 + 8 = 18

p. 320
10　20
30　40
50　60
70　80
90　100

p. 321
60　30
10　90
100　20
50　80
70　40

p. 322

Tens	Ones	
1	6	= 16
1	9	= 19
2	0	= 20
1	2	= 12
1	3	= 13
1	7	= 17
1	5	= 15
1	4	= 14

p. 323

Tens	Ones	
2	3	= 23
2	7	= 27
3	0	= 30
2	5	= 25
2	1	= 21
2	8	= 28
2	4	= 24
2	2	= 22

p. 324

Tens	Ones	
3	2	= 32
3	8	= 38
3	6	= 36
3	4	= 34
3	9	= 39
4	0	= 40
3	1	= 31
3	3	= 33
3	7	= 37
3	5	= 35

784 ANSWER KEY

p. 325

Tens	Ones	
4	8	= 48
4	5	= 45
4	1	= 41
4	9	= 49
4	4	= 44
4	2	= 42
5	0	= 50
4	7	= 47
4	3	= 43
4	6	= 46

p. 326

Tens	Ones
1	3
2	8
3	5
4	7
5	4

p. 327

Tens	Ones
1	9
2	2
3	6
4	7
2	8

p. 328

Guess	Check
30 or 40	32
40 or 50	46
20 or 30	29

p. 329

Guess	Check
40 or 50	45
20 or 30	27
30 or 40	33

p. 330

Tens	Ones	
7	3	= 73
5	6	= 56
9	2	= 92
7	1	= 71
8	5	= 85
10	0	= 100
8	4	= 84
6	9	= 69
5	3	= 53
9	9	= 99

p. 331

Tens	Ones	
5	2	= 52
7	8	= 78
5	8	= 58
7	7	= 77
8	9	= 89
8	1	= 81
9	4	= 94
6	5	= 65

p. 332

42	43	44	45
86	87	88	89
19	20	21	22
35	36	37	38
70	71	72	73

p. 333

63	64	65	28	29	30
16	17	18	81	82	83
37	38	39	70	71	72
46	47	48	94	95	96
68	69	70	55	56	57

p. 334

<	>
>	>
<	>
<	>

p. 335

=	<
>	<
<	=
>	>

p. 336

about 20	about 10
about 10	about 40

p. 337

12	about 10
18	about 20
63	about 60
84	about 80
39	about 40
97	about 100

p. 338

10 + 3 = 13	10 + 5 = 15
80 + 10 = 90	50 + 10 = 60
40	70

Tens	Ones	
3	6	= 36
6	0	= 60
8	2	= 82
9	5	= 95

<	<
=	>

91 92 93 94 95 96 97 98 99 100

p. 339

Guess	Check
30 or 40	27
40 or 50	43
about 20	17

p. 340
4¢, 9¢, 8¢, 18¢

p. 342
6¢, 9¢, 10¢, 18¢, 15¢

p. 343
9¢ matches the third set of coins.
12¢ matches the second set of coins.
6¢ matches the first set of coins.
17¢ matches the last set of coins.
10¢ matches the fourth set of coins.

p. 344
11¢, 14¢, 20¢, 22¢, 30¢

p. 345
40¢ matches the second set of coins.
17¢ matches the first set of coins.
10¢ matches the third set of coins.
25¢ matches the last set of coins.
21¢ matches the fourth set of coins.

p. 346
16¢, 15¢, 19¢, 20¢, 22¢

p. 347
46¢ matches the second set of coins.
35¢ matches the third set of coins.
23¢ matches the fourth set of coins.
36¢ matches the first set of coins.
31¢ matches the last set of coins.

p. 348
1 nickel matches 5 pennies.
1 dime and 1 penny match
6 pennies and 1 nickel.
1 dime matches 2 nickels.
1 nickel and 1 penny match
6 pennies.
2 dimes match 4 nickels.
1 dime and 5 pennies match
1 dime and 1 nickel.

p. 349

6¢	13¢
13¢	6¢
22¢	17¢
17¢	22¢
7¢	7¢

p. 350
Possible answers are given.
13¢: Circle 1 dime and 3 pennies.
14¢: Circle 1 dime and 4 pennies.
20¢: Circle 2 dimes.
35¢: Circle 3 dimes and 1 nickel.

p. 351
Possible answers are given.
30¢: Circle 3 dimes.
31¢: Circle 3 dimes and 1 penny.
6¢: Circle 1 nickel and 1 penny.
22¢: Circle 2 dimes and 2 pennies.
40¢: Circle 4 dimes.

p. 352
Possible answers are given.
2 dimes, 1 nickel
1 nickel, 1 penny
1 nickel
1 nickel, 1 penny
2 dimes, 1 nickel, 1 penny

p. 353
Possible answers are given.
2 pennies
1 nickel, 1 penny
2 dimes
1 dime, 1 nickel
1 dime, 1 penny

p. 354
7¢, 18¢, 14¢, 26¢

11¢	17¢
17¢	11¢

p. 355
Possible answers are given.
Students should draw the coins
needed.
3 dimes
1 dime, 2 pennies
1 penny
2 pennies

p. 356

p. 357

5; 12	7; 12
11; 12	2; 12
6; 12	9; 12
12; 12	1; 12

p. 358

11:00; 11	4:00; 4	9:00; 9
3:00; 3	8:00; 8	5:00; 5
7:00; 7	12:00; 12	1:00; 1

p. 359

7:00	11:00
1:00	8:00
3:00	10:00
5:00	9:00

p. 360
Students should draw the hands on
the clocks to show each time.

3:00	5:00
1:00	7:00
2:00	9:00
12:00	10:00

p. 361
Students should draw the hands on
the clocks to show each time.
5:00, 10:00, 1:00, 11:00

p. 362
2; 3; 6
10; 11; 6
8; 9; 6
4; 5; 6
12; 1; 6

p. 363
1; 2; 6
6; 7; 6
11; 12; 6
3; 4; 6
9; 10; 6

p. 364

7:30	11:30
12:30	8:30
3:30	10:30
4:30	9:30

p. 365
5:30 matches the second clock.
6:30 matches the third clock.
12:30 matches the last clock.
9:30 matches the first clock.

p. 366

3:00	11:30
2:30	9:00
4:30	11:00
1:00	5:30

p. 367

4:30	10:00
3:00	7:30
8:00	12:30

p. 368

1:00; 1	7:00; 7	9:00; 9
10:00; 10	4:00; 4	2:00; 2
12:30	2:30	8:30

p. 369
11:00
4:30
1:00
10:00
8:30

p. 370
cube, prism, pyramid, sphere, cone, cylinder

p. 371
prism—flower box
sphere—globe
cube—cardboard box
cone—traffic cone
pyramid—Egyptian pyramid
cylinder—can

p. 372
triangle, circle, square, rectangle, triangle

p. 373

rectangle	triangle	square
circle	square	triangle
circle	rectangle	circle

p. 376

4	4
3	3
4	4
0	0
3	3
4	4

p. 377

yes	yes	no
yes	yes	no
yes	yes	no
no	no	yes
no	yes	yes
no	yes	yes

p. 378
4, 6, 3

p. 379
5, 4, 6

p. 380
4 in., 5 in., 1 in., 2 in.

p. 381
6 in., 3 in., 4 in., 5 in.

p. 382
10 cm, 13 cm, 4 cm, 6 cm

p. 383
15 cm, 7 cm, 10 cm, 15 cm

p. 384
Guesses may vary.
4 in., 2 in., 5 in., 3 in.

p. 385
Guesses may vary.
10 cm, 5 cm, 13 cm, 8 cm

p. 386
spheres, cones, cylinders
12 cm   4 in.

p. 387
Guesses may vary.
3 in., 6 in., 2 in.

LANGUAGE ARTS

p. 390
1. boy, 2. girl, 3. dog, 4. cat

p. 391
1. man, 2. baby, 3. school, 4. store, 5. car, 6. fish

p. 392
1. doctor, 2. farmer, 3. worker, 4. cook

p. 393
Answers may vary. 1. fish, 2. frog, 3. fox, 4. bird, 5. dog, 6. cat

p. 394
1. lake, 2. house, 3. park, 4. farm

p. 395
1. cup, 2. crayons, 3. apple, 4. bed, 5. hat, 6. box

p. 396

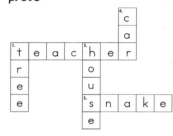

p. 397
1. Chris, 2. Lina, 3. Lee Chin, 4. Main Street, 5. "All About Worms"

p. 398
1. Sam, 2. Mr. Sosa, 3. Parker School, 4. Bakers Road

p. 399
1.–5. Answers will vary, but all names should begin with a capital letter.

p. 400
1. birds, 2. bug, 3. girls, 4. dog, 5. frogs

p. 401
1. trees, 2. flowers, 3. seeds, 4. nests

p. 402
1. I, 2. me, 3. I, 4. I, 5. me

p. 403
1. I, 2. me, 3. I, 4. me, 5. I

p. 404
1. We are here., 2. They are not here., 3. We will play ball., 4. They found a kitten.

p. 405
1. They are brothers., 2. We are sisters., 3. They are in second grade., 4. We are in first grade.

p. 406
1. She likes to write., 2. He likes to read., 3. It is on the table., 4. She saw the bird.

p. 407
1. He, 2. It, 3. She, 4. It, 5. She, 6. He

p. 408
1. eats, 2 waves, 3. talks, 4. sing, 5. ride

p. 409
1. The fish swims in the lake., 2. The rabbit hops up and down., 3. The snake crawls on the ground., 4. The birds fly in the sky.

p. 410
Action words and sentences will vary.

p. 411
Answers may vary. Possible responses are given. 1. jump, jumps, 2. roll, rolls, 3. bark, barks

p. 412
1. shines, 2. grow, 3. hops, 4. need, 5. gets

p. 413
Today is the first day of school. Madison <u>eats</u> pancakes. She <u>puts</u> on her dress and shoes. She and her sister <u>walk</u> to school. Madison <u>finds</u> her classroom. The teacher <u>welcomes</u> the students. The children <u>smile</u> at their new teacher. Madison <u>thinks</u> it will be a good year.

p. 414
1. Two little ducks played in the water., 2. The mother duck looked at them., 3. Two little ducks jumped out of the water., 4. They all walked away.

p. 415
1. fished, 2. watched, 3. listen, 4. painted, 5. cook

p. 416
1. is, 2. is, 3. are, 4. are, 5. are, 6. is

p. 417
Luke <u>is</u> very smart. We <u>are</u> best friends. We <u>are</u> in first grade. Mr. Jackson <u>is</u> our teacher. We <u>are</u> learning about birds. Luke <u>is</u> making a birdhouse.

p. 418
1. was, 2. were, 3. were, 4. was, 5. was, 6. was

p. 419
Tyler and Haley <u>were</u> moving to a new house. Mom and Dad <u>were</u> filling the truck. Haley <u>is</u> putting her toys in a box. Tyler <u>was</u> cleaning his room. The children <u>were</u> ready to see their new home. They <u>were</u> also sad to leave their old house.

p. 420
1. ran, 2. run, 3. saw, 4. came, 5. come, 6–7. Sentences will vary.

p. 421
1. came, 2. see, 3. run, 4. ran, 5. saw, 6. come

p. 422
1. went, 2. went, 3. go, 4. went, 5. go, 6. go

p. 423
1. went, 2. go, 3. went, 4. go, 5. go, 6. went

p. 424
1. don't, 2. won't, 3. can't, 4. isn't, 5. haven't, 6. shouldn't

p. 425
1. shouldn't, 2. haven't, 3. isn't, 4. can't, 5. won't, 6. don't

p. 426
1. in, 2. on, 3. under, 4. up, 5. out

p. 427
1. on, 2. up, 3. under, 4. in

p. 428
1. green, 2. loud, 3. wet, 4. two, 5. blue, 6. funny

p. 429
1. sleepy, 2. sick, 3. hungry, 4. glad, 5. angry

p. 430
1. big, 2. small, 3. tall, 4. round, 5. Sentences will vary.

p. 431
Answers may vary. 1. green, 2. pink, 3. yellow, 4. blue, 5. white, 6. red

p. 432
1. one, 2. four, 3. two, 4. five, 5. seven

p. 433
1. sour, 2. fresh, 3. salty, 4. smoky, 5. Sentences will vary.

p. 434
1. soft, 2. quiet, 3. hot, 4. cold, 5. noisy

p. 435
1. cloudy, 2. snowy, 3. sunny, 4. rainy, 5. windy

p. 436
1.–6 Describing words will vary.

p. 437
1.–5. Answers will vary.

p. 438
1. smaller, 2. bigger, 3. biggest, 4. taller

p. 439
1.–4. Check to see that the correct picture is circled.

p. 440
1. a, 2. a, 3. an, 4. an, 5. a, 6. a, 7. an, 8. an

p. 441
a column: radio, bear, fish, lamp, queen
an column: uncle, airplane, ape, inch, ocean

p. 442
1. I see a lion., 2. Jan throws the ball., 3. I hear a bird., 4. My cat can jump., 5. The dog barks.

p. 443
1. yes, 2. no, 3. no, 4. yes, 5. yes, 6. no, 7. no, 8. yes

p. 444
1. A frog, 2. A cat, 3. A dog, 4. chew bones, 5. eat worms, 6. walks to school

p. 445
1. The fisherman gets a fish., 2. The dancer spins on stage., 3. The artist draws a picture., 4. The doctor helps the sick girl.

p. 446
1. Rick, 2. His mother, 3. The bear, 4. The monkey, 5. The tiger, 6. The turtle.

p. 447
Answers may vary. 1. My sister, 2. Amy, 3. The wind, 4. The blue kite, 5. The red kite.

p. 448
1. found a puppy, 2. ate some food, 3. played with Anna, 4. named the puppy Skip, 5. threw the ball, 6. ran after the ball

p. 449
Answers may vary. 1. are fun to grow, 2. will show you, 3. plant seeds, 4. waters the seeds, 5. gives them light

p. 450
1.–8. Answers will vary. Be sure that a naming part is given.

p. 451
1.–8. Answers will vary. Be sure that a telling part is given.

p. 452
1. Jim swims fast., 2. Jane can not swim., 3. Mike likes art., 4. Eva walks to town., 5. Kim sees a bird., 6. The birds sing to me.

p. 453
1. I have a pig., 2. He and I play., 3. He has a cold nose., 4. My pig is my friend., 5. We have fun.

p. 454
1.–3. Sentences will vary.

p. 455
1. What is your name?, 2. Where do you live?, 3. When is your birthday?, 4. Do you have a pet?, 5. Who is your best friend?

p. 456
Answers may vary. 1. When, 2. Who, 3. What, 4. Where, 5. Who, 6. What

p. 457
1. tell, 2. ask, 3. tell, 4. ask, 5. ask, 6. tell, 7. ask

p. 458
Answers will vary. Possible responses are given. 1. cold, 2. crunchy, 3. three, 4. brown, 5. black, 6. white, soft

p. 459
1. Turtle and Fox hid., 2. Jon and Teri played ball., 3. Brett and Max ate lunch., 4. Cat and Frog played with Duck.

p. 460
Answers may vary slightly. 1. Chet reads and writes., 2. The ducks swim and quack., 3. I found a coin and a comb., 4. We will eat some cake and ice cream.

p. 461
1. The sun is hot., 2. We will go home., 3. You can come with us., 4. I will get some water., 5. Do you have a cup?, 6. Where is the door?

p. 462
1.–4. Answers will vary. Be sure each sentence begins with "I can."

p. 463
1. Pat Long, 2. Eva Ramos, 3. Uncle Thomas, 4. Will Smith, 5. Ling Chung, 6. Mori Adams

p. 464
1.–5. Answers will vary, but all names should begin with a capital letter.

p. 465
1.–6. Names given to animals will vary. Be sure each written answer begins with a capital letter.

p. 466
1. Monday, 2. Friday, 3. Sunday, 4. Wednesday, 5. Tuesday, Thursday, 6. Sunday, Saturday

p. 467
1. January, 2. February, 3. March, 4. April, 5. May, 6. June, 7. July, 8. August, 9. September, 10. October, 11. November, 12. December

p. 468
1.–5. Answers will vary, but all month names should begin with a capital letter.

p. 469
1. Valentine's Day, 2. Arbor Day, 3. Independence Day, 4. Thanksgiving Day, 5. Halloween

p. 470
1. jane street; Billy lives on Jane Street., 2. river road; My uncle lives on River Road., 3. lake drive; I live on Lake Drive., 4. boston; Diane lives in Boston., 5. los angeles; Ed took a trip to Los Angeles., 6. texas; My brother works in Texas.

p. 471
1.–4. Answers will vary, but all place names should begin with a capital letter.

p. 472
1. Red Flags, 2. The Black Horse, 3. Dad and Me, 4. Flowers for Mom, 5. First Grade Day

p. 473
1. The bears play a game., 2. They throw a ball., 3. Mrs. Bear came home., 4. Mr. Frog came to visit.

p. 474
1. Why is the sky blue?, 2. How do flowers grow?, 3. Where do the stars go?, 4. Why do the birds sing?, 5. When will the sun shine?

p. 475
1. may 23 2005; May 23, 2005, 2. january 1 2005; January 1, 2005, 3. june 30 1997; June 30, 1997, 4. october 31 2003; October 31, 2003, 5. Answers will vary.

p. 476
1. sun, 2. slide, 3. mat, 4. rug, 5. log

p. 477
1. pig/big, 2. door/floor, 3. bat/flat, 4. clock/sock, 5. man/fan, 6. Sentences will vary.

p. 478
Answers may vary. 1. snow, 2. sky, 3. me, 4. night

p. 479
1. home, 2. road, 3. catch, 4. big

p. 480
1. sound, noise; 2. begin, starts; 3. look, see; 4. glad, happy; 5. little, small

p. 481

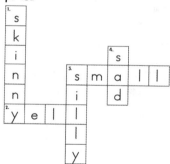

p. 482
1. down, 2. hard, 3. light, 4. off, 5. in, 6. opened, 7. awake

p. 483
1. big, 2. in, 3. new, 4. off, 5. down, 6. soft

p. 484

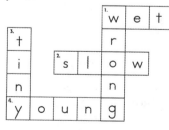

p. 485
1. know, no; 2. hi, high; 3. eight, ate; 4. flour, flower; 5. sea, see; 6. sale, sail; 7. read, red; 8. hear, here

p. 486
1. to, 2. two, 3. to, 4. two, 5. to, 6. two, 7. to, 8. two

p. 487
1. their, 2. their, 3. there, 4. their, 5. There

p. 488
1. a, 2. b, 3. a, 4. b, 5. a, 6. b, 7. b, 8. a

p. 489
First, Next, Then, Last

p. 490
1.–4. Answers will vary.

p. 491
Answers may vary. 1. backyard, 2. birdhouse, 3. sandbox, 4. Sentences will vary.

p. 492
1. rainbow, 2. seashell, 3. sailboat, 4. sunshine, 5. Words will vary.

p. 493
Answers may vary. 1. store, 2. seeds, 3. garden, 4. rain, 5. sun, 6. flowers

p. 494
Answers may vary. 1. run, 2. jump, 3. eat, 4. chase, 5. bark, 6. climbs

p. 495
Answers may vary. 1. The birds fly., 2. That frog hops., 3. The fish swims., 4. My dog digs.

p. 496
1.–6. Answers will vary. Be sure each written response answers the question.

p. 497
1.–6. Answers will vary but all sentences should tell a complete thought, begin with a capital letter, and end with a period.

p. 498
Answers will vary.

p. 499
Answers will vary.

p. 500
Main Idea: The writer likes to dive.

p. 501
Answers will vary.

p. 502
Answers may vary. Possible answers: 1. tree, 2. sky

p. 503
Answers will vary.

p. 504
Answers will vary. Possible responses: small, dark, pretty, fast

p. 505
Answers will vary.

p. 506
Danny

P. 507
Answers will vary.

P. 508
play hide-and-seek

P. 509
Answers will vary.

P. 510
Birthday Cookies

P. 511
Answers will vary.

P. 512
1. a b c, 2. f g h, 3. c d e, 4. n o p,
5. h i j, 6. x y z

P. 513
1. bird, can, dig; 2. find, give, help;
3. name, one, red; 4. she, they, we

P. 514
1. 2, 3, 1; He likes me., 2. 1, 3, 2;
Dave is playing., 3. 3, 1, 2; Anna
goes outside., 4. 3, 1, 2; Cat finds
Mouse.

P. 515
1. All About Dogs, 2. Minnie Fleas,
3. Barker Books

P. 516
1. 8, 2. 12, 3. 4, 4. 14

P. 517
1, 3, 4, 2

P. 518
1. whale, 2. rabbit, 3. monkey,
4. bird

P. 519
1. table, 2. needle, 3. clock, 4. chair

P. 520
1. swim, 2. fly

P. 521
Answers will vary. Possible
responses: Alike: They are both tall.,
Different: They are made of
different things.

P. 522
Answers will vary.

P. 523
1. Matt the Mouse; 2. in the
garden; 3. Matt was sad because he
couldn't find his friends on his
birthday.; 4. He saw the plants
move.; 5. His friends had a surprise
birthday party for him.

P. 524
1. yes, 2. no, 3. yes, 4. no, 5. yes,
6. no, 7. no, 8. yes

P. 525
1. yes, 2. no, 3. no, 4. yes, 5. yes,
6. no, 7. yes, 8. no

WRITING SKILLS

P. 528
Circle: desk, store, chair, coin,
plane, bench, bird, car, girl.
Underline: run, chase, jump, swim,
go, walk, skip

P. 529
Circle and write: clown, balloons,
boy, dog, boat, and man

P. 530
any four nouns that can be found in
a classroom

P. 531
Answers will vary, but should be
exact nouns.

P. 532
swim
run
read
hop

P. 533
Answers will vary, but should be
action verbs.

P. 534
yell
peek
skip
sip

P. 535
sunny
new
messy
wet

P. 536
delicious dinner
sunny weather
curly hair
soft pillow
salty popcorn
green grass

P. 537
shocked, surprised
happy, glad
angry, mad
sad, upset

P. 538
we
it
you
Me

P. 539
Nathan Thompson
Grandma Rose and Billy
Denton, Texas

P. 540
Mr. Grayson is our bus driver.
I went to see Dr. Hubbard for a
check-up.
My piano teacher is Miss Marks.
Mr. and Mrs. Nelson live next door
to us.

P. 541

Possible answers:
Sunday
Monday
Tuesday
Wednesday
Thursday
Friday
Saturday

P. 542
Valentine's Day
President's Day
Mother's Day
Memorial Day

P. 543
My brother is not old enough to go
to school yet.
We do not use loud voices in the
library.

P. 544
open, close
off, on
out, in
stand, sit
laugh, cry

P. 546
Circle: pretty, soft, nice, angry,
happy, thin, sleepy, old, kind,
brown, loud.
Underline: she, you, I, he, it, they,
we.
Answers to synonyms will vary.

P. 547
Alex does a cartwheel.
Mrs. Durand is my music teacher.
Look out!
We had a lot of rain in April.

P. 548
Picture 1: The flowers bloom.
Picture 2: Rufus sleeps on the sofa.
Picture 3: Beth paints a picture.

P. 549
Our class takes a field trip.
We ride on a yellow school bus.
The bus take us to the zoo.
We see all the animals.

P. 550
Our team has a game today.
We go to the field.
The game begins.
Eddie kicks the ball.

P. 551
Underline and write: Dad is in the
garage.
We have four tickets. I can read a
book.
Bill has a pet goldfish.
I had a silly dream.

P. 552
Circle: Choose a book. Take your
book to the front desk. Read silently
to yourself. Do not shout. Find an
empty chair and be seated.

P. 553
Do you know the answer?
What is it?
Can you write it on the board?
Did you check your work?

P. 554
Underline and write: Did you hear
that? Is anyone home? How do you
feel? What did you have for lunch?
Are you coming with us?

P. 555
Underline: Look out! Wake up! I
will not eat that! I hate peanut
butter! That is fantastic news! Wait
for me!

P. 556
Circle: Have you ever been to the
circus?
Dad gets us some popcorn.
That is amazing!
Six lions jump through some hoops.

P. 557
Let's go to the carnival.
Do you want to ride the roller
coaster?
I will buy some cotton candy.
Can we play a game?
You won a prize!

P. 558
Mom comes in.
She has a box.
It is for us.
What is it?
It is a new toy.

P. 559
Autumn
The leaves
Children

P. 560
The skateboard
My dog
We
Dad and I
Katherine

P. 561
cake
Yellow
radio
baby
car
Winter

p. 562
is nice
tastes delicious
bake cookies
takes a nap

p. 564
We go to the park.
Grandma sits on a bench.
Two ducks swim in the pond.
Carlos feeds the ducks.
They splash in the water.

p. 565
Grandma called Mom on the phone.
Peter is stronger than Erin.
The student borrowed a pencil from her teacher.
The cat chased the dog.

p. 566
Rob can read and write.
We ate pizza and hot dogs.
Chris and John play basketball.

p. 568
The movie was cool. It had a lot of car chases.
We ate popcorn. It had a lot of butter on it.

p. 569
Sam likes to play on the playground.
Do you want to go on the slide?
Mom pushes the swing.
I like to go very high.
Circled: Emilio and Jana
Underlined: play tag
Circled: The dog
Underlined: runs after them
Circled: We
Underlined: like to play at the park

p. 570
We bake cookies.
He throws the ball.
Keisha gives her dog a bath.

p. 571
Dad rakes the leaves.
Today is my birthday.
I have a pet fish.
That is very pretty.

p. 572
Picture 1: This tastes delicious!
Picture 2: Jana hurt her knee.
Picture 3: The bug crawls on the leaf.

p. 573
bike
rides
store
quarters

p. 575
most dogs are friendly animals.

They make good pets ⊙

p. 576
This soup is too hot.
We wash our car.
My shoes are new.
Camping is fun.

p. 587
Circle: The workers fix the road.

p. 605
Answers will vary, but might include: Wear a helmet. Look both ways before crossing a street. Stay on the sidewalk. Use hand signals.

p. 608
Answers will vary, but should include descriptions appropriate to the season.

p. 610
I love to visit the zoo.
The writer goes to see the bird show.

p. 611
Topic: My room is a mess.
Underlining may vary, but your child may have underlined clothes all over the floor, bed is not made, toys are scattered, cannot walk, piles of stuff.

p. 613
one day, my brother and I went

to an amusement park. First, we rode

the carousel. Then, we raced to the

go-karts. my brother almost crashed

around ~~around~~ the last curve. Next,

we waited in line for the roller

coaster ⊙ I was scared, but my brother

told me it would be fun. He was

right
~~rite.~~ I had so much fun that we rode

it again and again. i can't wait to go

back to the amusement park!

p. 617
My cat looks so sweet when she is sleeping.
Answers will vary but may include any of the last five sentences of the paragraph.

p. 618
¶ What a wonderful day at the beach!

The sun is shining down on the

water. Lifeguards stand at the edge

of the shore. children laugh and

builds
splash in the waves. A father ~~bilds~~ a

sand castle with his son. I bury my

deep
toes ~~deap~~ in the warm sand and read

a book ⊙

p. 621
2, 4, 3, 1, 5

p. 622
Today we get to go swimming. First, we put on our swimsuits. Then, we grab our towels and goggles. Finally, we go to the pool to swim.

p. 625
The Hiding Place
Julio and other children
Julio did not have a good hiding place.
Julio hid behind the tall bushes beside Mr. Adam's house.

p. 629
The direction Steven did not follow is: Use a marker to decorate the outside of the card.

p. 630
Circle: 4. Dogs are the best kind of pet.

p. 633
Miguel had to get ready for school. First, he got out of bed. Then, he put on his clothes. After he got dressed, he ate breakfast. Finally, he brushed his teeth.

p. 634
Dear Grandma should be circled in red. Yolanda should be circled in blue. Love should be circled in green.
March 3, 2005

p. 635
Victor
cans

p. 636
June 2, 2005 should be circled in red. Dear Mrs. Simms should be circled in blue. Thank you for being my teacher this year. You helped me so much. I loved learning the songs you taught us. My favorite song was the one about the speckled frogs. I will miss you next year. Have a great summer vacation! should be circled in green. Your student should be circled in yellow. Kelly should be circled in orange.

p. 638
Jamal wrote the letter.
He wrote it to his mom and dad.
They sat by a campfire and sang songs.

p. 639

September 12, 2005

Dear ashley,
≡

¶ I hope you like your new house. I

was very sad to see you move away,

but I know you will make lots of

friends at your new school. My

mom says we can visit soon ⊙ I can't

wait! I will bring your favorite

game. We can eat pizza and stay up

all night, just like we used to do. I
miss
⟨mis⟩ you very much. Please write

~~write~~ back soon!

Your friend,

Vonda

p. 641
Officer Brown
bike safety
Robert's dad

p. 642

november 12, 2005
≡

Dear Aunt Rebecca,
Thank
⟨Thnak⟩ you so much for the pretty

scarf ⊙ it was such a nice birthday

gift. Now that the weather is getting

cooler here, I think I will wear it

almost every day! each time I wear

it, I will think of you and smile.

Love,

haley
≡

p. 644
Sarah
A school carnival

p. 645
Invitation will vary but should include event, date, time, and place.

p. 647
Jake wrote the letter.
He wanted to tell Mr. Smith he is sorry for denting his car door.

Letter answers are provided for each question. When the first choice is correct the answer is A. When the second choice is correct, the answer is B. When the third or fourth choices are correct, the answers are C or D, respectively.

p. 650
1. B
2. A
3. C
4. A
5. A
6. C
7. C
8. A

p. 651
1. B
2. A
3. C
4. A
5. B
6. C
7. B
8. C

p. 652
1. C
2. A
3. B
4. B
5. C
6. A
7. B
8. A

p. 653
1. B
2. C
3. B
4. A
5. C
6. A
7. C
8. B
9. C
10. A

p. 654
1. A
2. C
3. A
4. C
5. C
6. A
7. C
8. C

p. 655
1. B
2. A
3. C
4. C
5. B
6. C
7. B
8. C

p. 665-657
1. B
2. A
3. B
4. C
5. C
6. A
7. B
8. A

p. 658-659
1. C
2. B

p. 660
1. B
2. C
3. B

p. 661-662
1. B
2. A
3. C
4. B
5. C
6. A

p. 663-664
1. B
2. A
3. C
4. A

p. 665-666
1. C
2. B

p. 667
1. B
2. C

p. 668
1. B
2. C
3. B
4. C
5. A

p. 669
1. C
2. C
3. B
4. B
5. A
6. C
7. A
8. B

p. 670-671
1. A
2. B
3. C
4. B
5. two
6. B
7. A
8. A

p. 672-675
1. A
2. C
3. B
4. C
5. B
6. B
7. B
8. A
9. C
10. A
11. C
12. A
13. B
14. C
15. C
16. in the yard
17. A
18. C
19. A
20. C
21. 600
22. B
23. A

p. 677
Step 1. Will Tania's fish fit in the new tank?
Step 2. The tank holds 15 fish. There are 6 goldfish and 5 guppies.
Step 3. Add to see how many fish Tania has.
Step 4. 6 + 5 = 11. There are 11 fish. The tank can hold more than 11 fish, so it is large enough.
Step 5. Yes, because 11 is smaller than 15.

p. 678
Step 1. When will he begin to feed the third lion?
Step 2. He starts feeding at noon. It takes 5 minutes to feed each lion.
Step 3. You can make a list of feeding times.
Step 4. First lion: 12:00 to 12:05. Second lion: 12:05 to 12:10. Third lion: 12:10 to 12:15. He begins to feed the third lion at 12:10.
Step 5. Yes, because the third lion begins eat after 10 minutes.

p. 679
1. C
2. A
3. B
4. D
5. 11

p. 680
1. A
2. D
3. D
4. B

p. 681
1. B
2. B
3. C
4. C

p. 682
1. B
2. 5
3. C

p. 683
1. A
2. D
3. C
4. B

p. 684
1. C
2. D
3. D
4. November 18

p. 685
1. B
2. A
3. A

p. 686
1. B
2. A
3. D
4. 8

p. 687
1. C
2. A
3. C
4. 68
5. C
6. C
7. A
8. 40
9. C
10. A

p. 688-693
1. 2
2. C
3. C
4. C
5. C
6. D
7. B
8. A
9. 50
10. B
11. C
12. 3
13. B
14. A
15. C
16. A
17. B
18. 11
19. B
20. A
21. D
22. C
23. B
24. 69
25. D
26. A
27. C
28. C
29. C
30. 60
31. C

p. 695
1. C
2. B
3. B
4. A
5. A
6. B
7. A
8. C
9. A
10. B
11. C
12. C

p. 697
1. C
2. B
3. A
4. C
5. A
6. A
7. B
8. A

p. 699
1. A
2. A
3. B
4. C
5. C
6. A
7. B
8. A

p. 701-705
1. C
2. C
3. A
4. A
5. B
6. B
7. C
8. A
9. A
10. A
11. B
12. C
13. B
14. C
15. B
16. A
17. A
18. C
19. A
20. A
21. A
22. A
23. C
24. A
25. C
26. C
27. B
28. B
29. A
30. C
31. B
32. A
33. B

p. 707
1. C
2. C
3. B
4. B
5. A

p. 709-713
1. B
2. A
3. B
4. C
5. C
6. C
7. B
8. A
9. B
10. C
11. B
12. C

p. 715
1. A
2. C
3. A
4. A
5. C
6. C
7. A
8. B
9. A
10. B
11. C
12. A

p. 717-723
1. B
2. C
3. B
4. C
5. A
6. A
7. B
8. B
9. C
10. A
11. C
12. B
13. B
14. A
15. C
16. B
17. B
18. C
19. C
20. B
21. A
22. B
23. B
24. A

p. 725-731
1. A
2. B
3. C
4. A
5. C
6. B
7. C
8. A
9. C
10. A
11. C
12. B
13. A
14. C
15. C
16. B
17. C
18. A
19. C
20. A

21. B
22. C
23. B
24. C
25. A
26. B
27. A
28. A
29. C
30. C
31. A
32. B
33. C
34. A
35. C
36. A
37. A
38. B
39. B
40. C
41. A
42. A
43. C
44. C

p. 733-739
1. B
2. A
3. B
4. C
5. C
6. B
7. A
8. B
9. B
10. A
11. B
12. B
13. A
14. C
15. B
16. C
17. C
18. C
19. C
20. B
21. A
22. C
23. two
24. A
25. C

p. 741-749
1. C
2. B
3. A
4. B
5. D
6. B
7. C
8. A
9. B
10. 8
11. D
12. B
13. D
14. D
15. C
16. A
17. D
18. B
19. 8
20. C
21. C
22. A

23. A
24. D
25. C
26. B
27. C
28. B

p. 751-755
1. B
2. 11
3. B
4. C
5. 3
6. B
7. C
8. A
9. D
10. 10
11. B
12. D
13. A
14. B
15. C
16. A
17. C
18. 88
19. B
20. A
21. A
22. 41
23. D
24. C
25. 50
26. B
27. C
28. B

p. 757-761
1. B
2. A
3. A
4. A
5. B
6. B
7. B
8. A
9. C
10. A
11. C
12. B
13. A
14. C
15. B
16. B
17. C
18. B
19. A
20. B
21. C
22. A
23. B
24. A
25. C
26. C
27. B
28. A
29. C
30. C
31. B
32. A
33. B
34. A
35. C
36. B

p. 763–767

1. A
2. A
3. C
4. A
5. C
6. C
7. B
8. C
9. A
10. C
11. B
12. B
13. A
14. A
15. B
16. C
17. C
18. C
19. B
20. B
21. A